A Commentary on the Plays of *Sophocles*

James C. Hogan

Southern Illinois University Press

Carbondale and Edwardsville

Edited by Sally Master
Designed by Edward King
Production supervised by Hillside Studio

Library of Congress Cataloging-in-Publication Data
Hogan, James C.
    A commentary on the plays of Sophocles / James C. Hogan.
    p.   cm.
    Includes bibliographical references and indexes.
    1. Sophocles—Criticism and interpretation   I. Title.
PA4417.H64   1991
882'.01—dc20   90-36643
ISBN 0-8093-1664-1   CIP
ISBN 0-8093-1665-X (pbk.)

For Aurelia

Contents

Acknowledgments

I wish to thank friends and colleagues who have helped me in the preparation of this commentary. Janet Bean and Rosalind Macken typed the manuscript and provided invaluable assistance with the computer programs. Don Vrabel of Allegheny's Pelletier Library was constantly prompt and helpful in securing interlibrary loans. Several friends have read parts of the manuscript and offered useful notes. I wish to thank John Hanners, Dan Hooley, Gordon Kirkwood, Jim McGlew, David Schenker, Bill Scott, and Brit Smith for their suggestions and encouragement. I am particularly grateful to my friend and colleague of twenty years, Sam Edwards, for his good company. Allen Fitchen came to my aid at a crucial moment. I dedicate this book to my wife Aurelia, who is due far more.

A Commentary
on the Plays of
Sophocles

The Theater of Sophocles

SOPHOCLES' first victory in the dramatic competitions at the festival of Dionysus came in 468 B.C. He would have been between twenty-five and thirty. For the next sixty years and more he wrote and directed over a hundred plays, seven of which survive. His last, the *Oedipus at Colonus*, was produced posthumously in 401 B.C., five years after his death. Until midcentury, like most playwrights, he also acted in his plays. Aristotle (*Poetics*, chap. 4) credits him with adding the third actor and with the introduction of painted scenery, innovations already assimilated by the time of the *Oresteia* (458 B.C.). If we may believe the tradition, Sophocles was actively involved in the political and religious life of fifth-century Athens, perhaps serving as a state treasurer, general, and, in the crisis following the Sicilian disaster, select committeeman. A priest, he was particularly associated with the reception into Athens of a cult for Asclepius. Although ancient biographical learning is seldom completely trustworthy, Sophocles' popularity and civic-mindedness seem more secure than most such traditions.

Sophocles' career began when Aeschylus was still writing and directing for the theater, and for the last fifty years of his life he competed with Euripides, who died in 406, less than a year before Sophocles himself. Born a little before the first Persian invasion, Sophocles lived to see the rise of the Athenian empire and only missed by a scant two years witnessing the final defeat of his city in the Peloponnesian War (431–404 B.C.). He was the friend of Herodotus and Pericles, watched the building of the Parthenon, attended the plays of Aristophanes, and was a contemporary of the Sophists and Socrates. At least four of the extant plays (*Oedipus the King, Electra, Philoctetes, Oedipus at Colonus*) were produced after 430, and none seems much earlier than 450. Despite their production during the most active intellectual and artistic period of classical Athens, the plays do not reveal an obvious topical, historical engagement with the controversies of his day. Which is not to say that, for example, political issues are absent from Sophoclean theater, but rather that Sophocles preferred to frame dramatic conflict in contexts somewhat removed from the immediate issues of a war or election. The *Antigone* is a thoroughly political play, but our ability to date it to about 442 does not derive from any internal evidence.

Our earliest manuscript containing the surviving plays dates from the tenth century A.D. While these plays seem to have come to us relatively free of the kind of corruption handwritten manuscripts inevitably suffer, they are not perfect facsimiles of Sophocles' holograph. Consequently, the reader will find in this commentary discussions of words, phrases, lines and passages variously labeled "spurious," "corrupt," "interpolated," and the like. The causes for textual corruption are varied. Sophocles wrote for a specific production, not for a printed edition. Since few plays of any of the dramatists were given a second production in Athens during the fifth century, the need for a reliable text was not immediate. No doubt copies of the plays circulated privately, and there must have been productions in other cities of the Greek world, but the playwright had no copyright and no control over the text or subsequent uses of his text. Professional copyists of later times made mistakes in transcription, and we can be sure that informal copies made by actors for their own use were even more subject to the vicissitudes of time. Some changes in the text were introduced accidentally, others were the result of particular requirements of new performances. For example, it has been argued that the conclusion of the *Oedipus the King* has been modified from Sophocles' original version to make the *Oedipus at Colonus* follow it more consistently (perhaps twenty-five years separated the first appearances of these two plays, which were not part of a Theban trilogy). Apart from changes made by actors, there were defects occasioned even by those whose intentions were to reproduce a sound text. Ancient scholarship in the post-Aristotelian period sought to secure historically accurate texts. Inevitably scholars disagreed. Their notes and emendations, known as *scholia*, appeared in the margins of ancient manuscripts, and now and then a copyist inadvertently introduced into the new copy a marginal gloss, variant reading, or erroneous correction. Some of these errors are easily spotted, but fourteen hundred years of transcription "codified" others, so that modern scholarship can only make educated speculations about the nature and extent of the corruption. Fortunately, the Sophoclean text is fairly sound, and there is no reason to believe that we have lost from any of the extant plays even a single page.

Several criteria enable scholars to spot textual corruption. Perhaps the most important stems from the fact that these are verse dramas. The spoken passages are in iambic trimeters (three units of the form × ‑ ˅ ‑ , where ‑ is a long syllable, ˅ a short syllable, and × is common, i.e., either long or short); less frequently we find meters such as the hexameter (base unit ‑ ˅˅ ‑ ˅˅), trochaic tetrameter (base unit ‑ ˅ ‑ ×), and anapests (base unit ⌣⌣ - ⌣⌣ - ; used in recitative). While the lyrics of choral song and monody display a great variety of meter and rhythm, they are never free verse. Variations and substitutions within a given metrical system follow fairly strict rules. Given the fact that all Greek meters are based on quantity (long and short syllables, not word accent), it is usually not difficult to identify an irregularity. In the lyric passages, where the stanzas marked in our translations by strophe and antistrophe are metrically responsive, we have a local, internal check on meter. Of course, merely suspecting, or even knowing, that something is amiss does not guarantee successful emendation, but the modern reader can at least be advised to use caution in interpretation. Other criteria of textual integrity include grammatical and syntactical propriety and regard for norms in style, diction, and metaphor. In all of these categories the scholar must exercise great care, if only because our knowledge of Sophoclean usage, not to mention classical Greek of the fifth century, is severely limited by the small number of surviving texts. It is always well to remember that we have no more than six percent of his actual work, and probably not that. In describing textual problems I have attempted to restrict myself to those significant for interpretation, as well as to give a fair hearing to the most likely solutions.

As for Sophocles' theater, during the second half of the fifth century it did not change much in its essential physical arrangements (the stone theater of Lycurgus was not built until the fourth century). The orchestra, surrounded by the semicircular auditorium, remained the center of theatrical productions. Strangely enough, in a great age for building, which saw not only the Parthenon but even in the immediate precinct two new buildings (a temple of Dionysus and a long hall parallel to the orchestra's terrace wall), the Athenians never raised a permanent scenic building. Throughout the century they used a temporary wooden structure, for which grooves and postholes in the renovated terrace wall are our evidence. Its foundation, some nine by twenty-six feet, is generally thought to have supported a stage, elevated three or four feet above the level of the orchestra. The main door of this scenic building led to the long hall behind it; this door was the primary, and perhaps the only, exit from the stage. Entrances on either side of the orchestra (the *parodoi;* singular *parodos*) continued to provide access for the audience as well as for the players. The Greeks must have found some advantage in these temporary arrangements. In a four day festival, with at least four plays a day, and five when a comedy followed in the evening, different scenic backdrops would have been wanted by the competing playwrights. The *choregoi* (producers) sometimes spent lavishly on costume and scenic design; significant redesign and staging would have been feasible at night, before the next day's tetralogy. The Greeks liked display, liked to paint their temples and statuary, and movable panels, decorated for each play, may have been a common theatrical device. Although the extant Sophoclean plays offer nothing so sensational as the finale of Euripides' *Orestes* or the destruction of the palace in the *Bacchae,* some scenes, such as Ajax among the slain animals, the supplication beginning *Oedipus the King,* and the arrival of the dying Heracles, show that Sophocles knew how to achieve striking effects of spectacle and staging. Oedipus, Jocasta, Athena, and Heracles (in the exodos of the *Philoctetes*) could have been sumptuously gowned.

Nor did changes in style and theme from the plays of Aeschylus alter essentially the role of the chorus or the central place of song and dance in Greek tragedy. By most standards Sophoclean plays are more realistic than those of Aeschylus. But even if we find, with Aristotle, that the Sophoclean chorus is more "in character" than its Euripidean counterpart, the plays remained operatic, with a good deal more song and dance than we notice when discussing themes and characterization. Like Aristotle, we read more plays than we see; for the Greeks theater was spectacle. Later plays like the *Electra* and *Philoctetes* demonstrate a supple integration of choral lyric, monody, and lyric dialogue, but neither Sophocles nor Euripides ever abandoned the independent stasimon, which by its very nature must somewhat retard speech and action. In sum, there was much more of the opera, ballet, and oratorio in Greek tragedy than our criticism implies.

We should not forget the festive context. The day preceding the first set of plays was given over to processions that took the statue of Dionysus Eleuthereus from his temple below the orchestra to another temple in the Academy, whence he was returned with pomp and circumstance, accompanied by a torchlit parade, with priests and young men attendant upon the newly arrived god. Next morning a religious procession brought the sacrificial offerings to the precinct of Dionysus. Priests of the god had seats of honor in the theater. Among others in this magnificent holiday gathering were the choregoi who sponsored as a civic responsibility the performances of tragedy and the dithyrambic choruses. The festival was a competition, and the victorious choregoi gave parties and made sacrifice for their success and often raised public monuments to commemorate them. Every set of tragedies was followed by a satyr play (a farcical burlesque) and, during one period at least, a comedy in the evening. Just as Dionysus himself embodies both the ecstatic freedom of wine and life with the sacrificial offering of blood (in myth human victims torn limb from limb), so the festival combined the serious and the profane, the saturnalian revel with the death of and lament for the hero.

In scenic organization, the Aeschylean structure remains essentially unchanged: a prologue is followed by the choral entry (the parodos); subsequent scenes are divided by choral songs (the *stasima;* singular *stasimon*). In two plays, however, Aeschylus forgoes the prologue, and in only one (*Agamemnon*) are there more than five scenes (counting the prologue as the first scene). Two of the prologues are monologues. Such observations, however, ignore much of the fluidity of Aeschylean drama. Lyric dialogue, such as those in the *Agamemnon* between, first, Cassandra and the chorus, then between Clytemnestra and the chorus, extend the formal and expressive range of Greek tragedy far beyond the simple formula of prologue, parodos, scene, stasimon, scene, etc. Still, these terms do point to a certain kind of formal structure and may be useful if we do not neglect to keep a fresh eye on each new play. In his seven surviving plays Sophocles lengthens somewhat the prologue, always introduces at least two characters, and has at least six scenes (seven in the *Women of Trachis* and the *Oedipus at Colonus*). The proportion of dialogue to speeches and lyric is significantly increased, and dialogue and stichomythia (single lines spoken alternatively) become much more important for dramatic movement. Good examples of this more dramatically fluent and integrated style will be found in the recognition scenes in *Oedipus the King* (1110–85) and *Electra* (1098–1384). Earlier plays (*Ajax, Women of Trachis, Antigone*) offer more monologue and extended speech, but in the later plays solo arias, duets, and lyric dialogue between character and chorus are more frequent and varied. Electra, for example, sings her first lines and then, after the chorus's entrance, joins with it in a lyric dialogue. Thus there is more incident in Sophocles than in Aeschylus, more interaction of characters, and a freer utilization of lyric dialogue between chorus and actors.

We have almost no firsthand information about staging in the fifth century. The stage directions in these translations derive from the history of textual interpretation that goes back to Alexandrian times, roughly two hundred years after the first performances, and from the translators' understanding of the staging as it is suggested by the surviving text. I have frequently suggested alternative staging, in part because this has been extensively discussed in recent scholarship, in part because I hope to draw the reader's attention to the often problematic nature of our understanding. While we have some vase paintings depicting masks, costumes, and scenes, few of these sources were intended to report on actual productions and staging. Masks seem to have been fairly naturalistic, but of course they were larger than life and only occasionally changed during a performance. Hence their design gave the character a single visual persona. The actor's response to good and bad news had to be conveyed by voice and gesture.

In the large, open-air theater, there was necessarily less place for the nuance of inflection than we find in our own theaters. Not infrequently we hear one character commenting on the appearance or manner of another, especially at a new entrance. Such cues to the audience are one of our primary sources for interpreting tone and manner. Another clue to staging is the meter. All speeches are in verse, almost always iambic trimeter, and that is also true for most of the one- to four-line comments regularly attributed to the chorus but actually spoken by the leader of the chorus, the *coryphaeus*. When the meter changes to anapests, we have a recitative chant. When lyric meters occur, we have choral song or individual monody. These lyric meters vary a great deal in their rhythm and dynamics, and in many cases their combination with certain types of scene, for example lament or physical suffering, offers us an index to their expressive values.

For these and other reasons there is much to argue about in the matter of staging Greek tragedy. Very often our views come down to more or less explicit assumptions about categories such as realism and illusion. In the notes on staging I have tried to represent fairly the most reasonable modern views, but this selection is naturally colored by my doubts that we should think of Greek tragedy as a theater that attempted to create the illusion of life or a naturalistic setting. Without a curtain, in the open air, almost if not quite in the round, with a chorus constantly present and regularly singing and dancing, the Greek theatrical experience was more a ritual enactment than a slice of life. It was more concerned with the intensification and heightening of experience than with its representation. By our standards it was an artificial drama, observant of conventions not only in style and form but in its stories and topics as well. Long accustomed to such artifice and increasingly delighted with the power of rhetoric, the fifth-century Greeks found its means as well as its matter credible and convincing. We have only to read Plato and Aristotle on tragedy to know how moving contemporary audiences felt it to be.

A little over seventy years separates the production of our first extant Greek tragedy, Aeschylus' *Persians,* from the last, *Oedipus at Colonus.* Much changed over those years. The Athenian empire came into being and was destroyed. What we call the Sophistic movement brought a profound intellectual revolution to the Greek world. Yet in this brief introduction it may be more useful to comment on certain continuities in the Greek theater, rather than elaborating differences. Throughout the fifth century the tragedians drew on a common body of traditional stories which we know as the Greek myths. The heroes and heroines of myth and their adventures were known to every child. Their troubles and suffering had for centuries been the substance of poetry and education.

They had always grappled with those divine powers the Greeks called gods. In that sense every hero's life was a religious experience, and Greek drama is through and through religious.

Readers familiar with Greek mythology are likely to know one version of any story. The Greeks of Sophocles' time knew many versions, some of which seem to us radically different. Although the stories treat gods and heroes long established in cult and worship, the poets who told these stories were free to elaborate new incidents and to depict the characters according to their own imaginative conceptions. Thus, while the audiences knew the stories of Attic drama, they also knew in some cases several versions, and they expected new variations on old themes. To take an example from Sophocles, neither Homer nor Aeschylus had sent Oedipus, after he discovered his murder of Laius and marriage to Jocasta, into exile. Sophocles' *Oedipus the King,* however, seems to demand exile, even though the actual events of the last scene leave the issue somewhat in doubt. Later, in the *Oedipus at Colonus,* the king has been in exile for a number of years. For the Greek, then, the interplay between the familiar version(s) and the new staging was an obvious source of dramatic tension, which the dramatists seldom failed to exploit. One reason for extensive notes on these plays clearly derives from our need to understand as best we can this mythic context.

These stories more often than not involve strife within families, and the family is the fundamental social unit. Among the surviving plays only the *Philoctetes* does not depict the effects of a family subjected to violent internal division. Since the families feature kings and princes, the social and political consequences of trouble within the family send vibrations through society. Sometimes, as in the *Ajax* and *Women of Trachis,* the family suffers because the hero is drawn into conflicts outside of it; elsewhere, as in the Theban plays and the *Electra,* division of purpose and internal violence tear the family apart. While the family as represented by Homer can hardly have been the same social unit as that of fifth-century Athens, the continuities were strong, and the increasing importance of the city (polis) imposed new demands and obligations that were often in conflict with loyalty to family and clan. Sophocles' *Antigone* dramatizes such a conflict. Oedipus' commitment to saving his city becomes the occasion for the discovery of his own personal fate. The Homeric Ajax had become a civic hero before Sophocles' play was staged, and that ambiguous mixture of the archaic and contemporary enriches the play's texture: Ajax' wife and friends press their personal claims; the army would treat him as a criminal; the audience knows that somehow the play must "save" this man who had in honor given his name to one of the ten tribes of the city. From the fifth-century Athenian perspective, Ajax is a political anachronism, the all too familiar example of the individual who puts personal vendetta beyond any regard for the rule of law. Such individualism was always, as we see in Homer's Achilles, in conflict with the values attached both to family and the state. When civic values are absent or in abeyance, as they seem to be in the *Electra,* we seem left with a hero and heroine who have lost an essential human mooring.

Myths set tasks for men, or present enemies to be confounded, or evil to be avoided. Ajax and Philoctetes belong to the Trojan expedition and thus join in the greatest task of Greek myth. Although their problems in our plays are largely personal, they take their meaning from the context of the Trojan war and the purpose of its Greek leaders. As for the hero's enemy, in the traditional story it is typically a dragon, and the Sphinx of the Oedipus legend is a refinement on the primitive chthonic monster. In most myths, however, the primary enemy is either a divinity or someone in the hero's own family. Ajax is such a victim: he has defied Athena's power, and she will destroy him. More mysteriously, Oedipus seems shadowed by an unexplained interest of Apollo (in some versions, though not in our plays, Laius' rape of Chrysippus accounts for the curse on the house); Neoptolemus assigns Philoctetes' suffering to a violation of the shrine of Chryse. When man confronts god, the issue is never in doubt. When the enemy is a member of the hero's own family, as in the case of Orestes and Antigone, the dramatic issue will at least seem more problematic, but very often the gods also intervene in these conflicts to make their will known. The third category, avoidance of an evil, is familiar from the myths of Perseus, Telephus, Oedipus, and others. An oracle pronounces that a son, usually as yet unborn, will kill his father or some other near kin. In trying to escape that fate, the child eventually kills the person by accident, or at least in ignorance of his identity. Since oracles are from a god, we want to know something more of them.

The Greek gods are anthropomorphic, human in appearance and very like men in their designs and feelings. Athena is just as sensitive to insult as Ajax himself. The deities of the underworld have their rites and privileges; when Creon defies them, he stands in great risk. The gods have their favorites, like Odysseus and Heracles. Their patronage may result from kinship (Heracles is the son of Zeus) or likemindedness (the affinity of Odysseus and Athena) or rest on social and moral considerations (in the case of Apollo and Orestes). In relation to mortals, their primary concern is respect. Man worships divinity by observing rites and ritual and by taking care not to violate, by word or deed, the particular interest of the divinity. In Greek polytheism these interests are divided among powers ranging from the Olympian father Zeus to Hades in the underworld. Between are the children of the high gods and a variety of minor divinities and daimons whose prerogatives may be very local and specialized (e.g., the Furies are spirits of vengeance). Each and every one has a special concern for its own station and power. They are primarily defined by their power: they are always stronger than men, and to violate or defy their offices or persons brings violent retaliation. As the Greeks say, the gods are jealous of their power; man must avoid transgressing it. Thus, while some divinities are associated with moral and social functions, and in some contexts Ares is simply War, Aphrodite Love, Greek religion does not present deity as concerned with the moral or spiritual improvement of man. Man must respect and fear divine power; he is not expected to love the gods. To illustrate with small matters, both Creon (*OK* 644–49) and Lichas (*Tr* 399–401) take oaths, and Zeus is the god who oversees the sanctity of oaths. Creon swears truly and is taken seriously; Lichas forswears himself, though the truth is soon forced from him. Some of my students have connected the false oath with Lichas' terrible death, seeing in it the indirect wrath of Zeus. Such an interpretation confuses the listener's respect for the invocation of deity with Zeus's concern for this social and legal institution. In this case, that is, Lichas has no intention of defying divine power, nor does he infringe upon it greatly by abusing Deianira. The oath has solemn value because the god may take an interest, not because he must or necessarily will. If Zeus were not a person, if he could be *identified* with moral propriety, then Lichas would be in trouble. In another context forswearing might indeed offend Zeus, but that context would be one in which man meant to defy the god. This example may seem trivial, but the question why the gods do not save Antigone is not, and it illustrates the same point. Ismene refuses to help in the burial of Polyneices; there is no indication that she incurs divine wrath for that refusal. Antigone invokes divine law as sanctioning the burial, and events prove that the gods do punish those who deny proper burial. Yet the gods do not demand right conduct of her with respect to men, only in regard to themselves. Consequently, Creon is punished, but Antigone is not saved. Fulfilling the divine law does not protect Antigone; violating it does endanger Creon.

One man, Heracles, transcended the limits of his mortality and became a god. Man is subject to death; the gods are not. Man is limited in power and knowledge; the gods are not. Man is the victim of chance; the gods are not. An apparent exception to these boundaries may be seen in the case of the demigods of cult, mortal men who after death are worshipped at their graves, receive sacrifice, and are thought to exert their influence locally, from the grave. Oedipus, Ajax, and Orestes all had such cults. But the limits imposed by the place are real, and these heroes do not achieve the freedom and universality of the Olympians. Nonetheless, as in the case of many local daimons, their presence in the world makes it a more complicated, spiritually rich place. Tragedy, more than the bare bones of myth, explores the spiritual limits that define mortal and immortal.

By the end of the fifth century, Greek tragedy is full of indications that the intellectual critique of the Sophists was influencing the spiritual life of all Athens. But we must not, out of intellectual convenience, ignore the divine as a concrete, felt presence. Aeschylus is supreme for representing on the stage this aspect of the Greek sensibility. It is truly hard not to believe, with Clytemnestra, that "the old stark avenger" (*Agamemnon* 1501) has struck down her man. The fatalism of Eteocles, in Aeschylus' *Seven against Thebes,* is not merely resignation but the total, personal sense that the daimonic curse's will must be done. With Sophocles we are on more tricky ground because it is clear that, especially in the later plays, some greater distance between the divine and the human has gradually and ambiguously emerged. For an example, let us consider Oedipus. It is unfortunate that we do not have Aeschylus' treatment of Laius and Oedipus, but it is a fair bet that he gave more particular reasons for their suffering than we find in *Oedipus the King.* There was available the tale of Laius' rape of Chrysippus, son of Pelops, a sexual crime that was also a violation of Pelops' hospitality. For Aeschylus crime begets crime, and the gods drive man on to pay the penalty of lust and violence. Implicated in his father's futile efforts to escape retribution, Oedipus would have gone down with him. In a sense this is the case in Sophocles' play, with the great difference that we are never told of any crime of Laius. Jocasta simply reports that Apollo's oracle had once told Laius that he would die at the hands of his own son (*OK* 711–14b). No reason, no punishment, no crime, is mentioned. Sophoclean distance is immediately evident in the god's purely predictive stance. Like all such victims in myth, Laius attempts to avoid "fate": he exposes the child, thinking to have it killed. By chance it is saved; by chance it grows up to find occasion to consult the oracle on its own behalf. "You will kill your father and sleep with your mother." Thus the oracle to Oedipus, who, like his father, attempts to avoid this evil lot. The god knows; he does not condemn, he does not give reasons, but when Oedipus is happily married to his mother and deep in sin, a plague comes on Thebes. Not a plague sent by Apollo, not one necessarily sent by any god, just a plague caused, as the oracle on request announces, by a polluted murderer. Apollo knows; Thebes and its king must solve the problem. Finally, when the murderer is exposed, the new regent (Creon) feels obliged to consult the oracle once again, this time to discover what is to be done in the extraordinary circumstances of a self-cursed king, polluter of his kingdom and bed.

Myths became paradigms of heroic striving. Man wins a little happiness, which soon wanes. As the chorus sings,

Oedipus, you are my pattern of this.
(*OK* 1193)

Viewed retrospectively, these examples of success and suffering have the aspect of fated as well as fatal patterns. Although Aristotle says little or nothing about fate and the gods, modern readers are intrigued, and perhaps a little puzzled, by Greek attitudes toward human destiny. At times our texts seem to say that man's lot is his own doing; at other times the gods seem to determine the human condition; elsewhere we find talk of an impersonal, objective destiny that affects not only man but the gods as well. Our English versions translate a variety of Greek words for fate/destiny in a variety of ways. Perhaps the safest course through this tangle is to chart the range of meanings and thus to try to gain some general feeling for the Greek perception. One fundamental sense of fate is "lot" or "portion." It may be purely quantitative (a long or short life). It may be qualitative (misery or happiness). When Hyllus speaks of Heracles' "usual good luck" (*Tr* 88), he seems to refer to a happy knack (lot) for getting out of trouble. When the chorus sings of Philoctetes as second only to Ixion

. . . of all mankind
whose destiny was more his enemy when he met it
(*Phil* 681–82)

they think only of the miserable life he has fallen heir to. Thus fate can be simply the observed good or bad fortune of anyone's existence. The meaning lot/portion goes over to "function" and what is due. So when Hyllus is reluctant to consent to his demands, Heracles says

I see the man will not give me my due (*moira*)
(*Tr* 1238)

Oedipus (*OC* 278) speaks of the *moira* of the Eumenides, of what is their prerogative and office. More personally, bad luck was particularly associated with the belief in a *daimôn* that shadowed man from birth. So Deianira calls "out loud to her fate (*daimôn*) and to her house" (*Tr* 910–11), and Heracles in his suffering cries "Oh! Oh! my fate (*daimôn*)!" (*Tr* 1025). This is familiar language in tragedy, but how far it reflects common Greek belief is harder to say. Man sees what is unexpected and outside his own control. He attributes the often violent effect on his fortunes to some personal agency. That does not mean that human agency is totally controlled by gods or daimons, only that they may explain the otherwise inexplicable. Deianira knows full well that she has made a mistake in trusting the centaur's advice. No *daimôn* made her do it. Choice is clear in the exchange between Ismene and Antigone:

Ismene
> Oh my poor sister. How I fear for you!

Antigone
> For me, don't borrow trouble. Clear your fate.

> (*Ant* 82–83)

Antigone's response means "set your own house in order: you have chosen your way, I mine." Sophoclean tragedy constantly dramatizes such decisions. From the Greek point of view there is no contradiction between the belief in personal freedom and the recognition that external, often divine, agencies may destroy our best laid plans. Antigone will later complain that she is to die "before my course (*moira*) is run" (*Ant* 896), i.e., before she has completed the natural portion of life she might have expected. Her own decision and action have cut across her destiny.

When fate is tied to the will of the gods or oracular pronouncement, we are most tempted to discover some more comprehensive supernatural plan. Jocasta reports that Apollo's oracle told Laius

> that it was fate (*moira*) that he should die a victim
> at the hands of his own son, a son to be born
> of Laius and me.

> (*OK* 714–16)

She doubts that the prophecy was fulfilled. Laius, in attempting to kill the baby Oedipus, tried to avoid his fate. Oedipus himself fled from Corinth and his supposed parents when he heard that he would kill his father. Neither Laius nor Oedipus is fatalistic; both attempt to forestall fate, as both fail. In our plays oracles and prophecies always come true. One may say that they are self-fulfilling (Oedipus and Laius are moved by the oracles to do the very things that bring about their prophecies); one may say that they reflect the will of the gods. But there is a difference between knowing/predicting and causing. God's knowledge transcends man's. Man seeks to know the future from divine prophecy, but like Jocasta, he knows that the servants of Phoebus err (*OK* 707–13), and again, like Heracles, he will put the best face on ambiguous reports (*Tr* 1166–73). Even though divine purpose and knowledge are inscrutable, the intellectual Greek finds purpose and meaning after the fact. Such discovery does not annul his own responsibility any more than it makes certain the nature of divine purpose.

There is
nothing here which is not Zeus.
(*Tr* 1277–78)

This last sentence of the *Women of Trachis* states a belief, not a fact.

This brief survey will have indicated only a few of the dramatic values to be found in Greek myth. More than old stories, the myths flexibly admitted new problems with new interpretations. Social structures are latent in them and were elaborated in various directions so that, for example, the response of democratic institutions to tyrannical behavior became a topic in the mid-fifth century. Both Sophocles and Euripides greatly extended the psychological dimension of these stories. All of the plays are in some way political, but for the most part the problems have moved beyond Homer's ken. The Homeric Ajax has become a civic hero before Sophocles' play is staged, and that historical fact gives the hero's lot a special poignancy for the Athenian spectators. Myth tends to emphasize individualism; in tragedy man is a political animal, a citizen of a particular social organization that makes demands, expects his loyalty, and asserts paramount claims on his values. If individualism was a fact of life and literature, the preeminent demands of the polis were no less real. Creon is our paradigm for these civic values, applied, as it turns out, narrowly and perversely. Theseus may be their most benevolent advocate, but the decline of Oedipus is precipitated by his wholehearted commitment to saving his city. Although Greek drama was heavily in debt to myth and the heroic Homer, it is never far from vital contemporary issues, and that mix accounts for much of its enduring vitality.

A Note on the Commentary

$THIS$ commentary is based on the translations published by the University of Chicago Press and edited by David Grene and Richmond Lattimore. It follows the same scheme as my *Aeschylus*, to which the reader will often find reference. The notes, beginning with the *Oedipus the King*, follow the text of the translation line by line. The numeration in the margins refers to the lines of the Greek text; not infrequently the English versions use more lines than the Greek, and I have once again used the adscripts a, b, c, etc., to designate these extra lines. Less frequently the English version has fewer lines. For the reader consulting critical essays, however, the difference between the standard reference to the Greek text and the corresponding passage in these versions will seldom be more than two or three lines.

My first priority has been to offer information that will enlarge the reader's understanding of Sophocles' text, his dramaturgy, style, and the cultural context in which the plays were first produced. In some matters, for example the identification of allusion to myth, there may be relatively little disagreement among scholars. On more problematic issues such as textual corruption, difference of opinion is inevitable. Whatever the nature of the emendation, the reader should understand that the disagreement over the proper text is usually far from an arbitrary preference for one interpretation over another, but in fact represents the effort of the scholarly tradition to discover our best approximation to the fifth-century Greek text. Translators are compelled to make choices constantly and, for the most part, to leave their reasons unnoted. In reporting critical opinion on such matters I have attempted to give the reader a larger understanding of our version and some of the more promising alternative readings. In a commentary of this type such information is naturally limited, but I hope that my selection has been judicious; the reader will always find a fuller discussion of textual problems in the English commentaries of Jebb, Kamerbeek, and others cited in my notes.

In matters of dramaturgy, our translations offer brief staging directions in italics. These notes are interpretative, like my own, and not derived from the manuscript tradition. We have no firsthand information of Sophocles' own staging practice; all staging is inferred from the texts and from collateral information provided by archeology, vase painting, and the like. On the controversial issues, I have referred the reader to more comprehensive treatments in English.

Compared with Aeschylus, Sophoclean drama is more subtle, problematic, and ambiguous in ethical and psychological matters. A commentator may feel obliged to eludicate certain issues more fully than Aeschylus requires. I have yielded to the temptation to explain purpose and character, but on the more controversial points I have given the reader an account of, or reference to, other interpretations. Translations are themselves, of course, interpretations. "Love," "sin," and "crime" are loaded words in English, pointing the reader in directions not authored by "friendship," "error," and "suffering." Where I have differed from the translators in my preferences, I have tried to make clear the grounds for choice.

The plays are discussed in the order presented in the Chicago translations. If the reader prefers to read the plays in their chronological sequence, he should, in my judgment, read the *Ajax* (*Aj*), *Women of Trachis* (*Tr*), *Antigone* (*Ant*), *Oedipus the King* (*OK*), *Electra* (*El*), *Philoctetes* (*Phil*), and *Oedipus at Colonus* (*OC*). While topics and problems are generally taken up as they appear, the reader should note the indexes. Some technical terms are pervasive in criticism and useful in their way; definitions will be found from the subject index.

Translation is an art rather than a science. It is a very rare occurrence when a word in one language precisely duplicates denotation and connotation of a word in another language. Context is all important, and translators quite sensibly vary their diction in English to reflect contextual nuance. In an effort to give the reader a surer grasp of Greek meanings and patterns, I have transliterated Greek words more often in this commentary than in the *Aeschylus*. Thus the common adjective/substantive *kakos* (the *-os* suffix is regularly masculine in gender; *-ê* transliterates the feminine suffix eta; *-on* the neuter singular, *-a* the neuter plural) appears as "traitor," "liar," "sin," and "evil," among others, in *Oedipus the King*. For such words it is useful to track the more significant occurrences, and the simplest method is to transliterate with cross-referencing. As in my *Aeschylus*, when the reader finds a boldface **ally** (*OK* 135) and references, it should be assumed that the Greek word or a cognate appears in the other passages. The equal sign (=) is used similarly and often introduces an alternative translation. My intention in such notes is not to correct the translation but to provide amplification and clarification, often in a more prosaic version than is suitable for the text. "Interpretative" usually denotes a word or phrase not explicitly represented in the Greek; every English version is naturally interpretative in some sense, but I have reserved this comment for the more significant glosses. Notes on style are another difficulty. Being an inflected language, Greek is more supple in its word order than is English. The Greek text, particularly in the early plays, is more mannered in its style, more given, for example, to antitheses, and these effects, pleasing to the Greek ear and mind, are neither so easy in English nor so acceptable to the modern sensibility. In commenting on the original I have wanted more to supplement the reader's understanding than to suggest a better version.

In transliterating the Greek alphabet I have distinguished the omega from the omicron and the eta from the epsilon by the use of the macron for the long vowels (thus $\hat{o}$ = omega; o = omicron; $\hat{e}$ = eta; e = epsilon). Upsilon has been transliterated with y in most cases, with u occasionally. The reader will notice different spellings of the same word. In a few cases, such as that of Clytaemestra (also spelled Clytemnestra), this difference originates in Greek usage. Most of them, however, are due to two different systems of spelling Greek proper names. While the Greek system transliterates names directly from the Greek (thus Athene, Oidipous, Kronos), the Latin system first gives Latin values to the Greek letters and then brings them into English (so Athena, Oedipus, Cronus). There are only a few differences among these translations, and the index of proper names will help to clarify some variations in spelling.

It is the nature of a commentary to draw heavily on preceding scholarship. My debt is particularly large, but nonetheless I have tried not to burden the reader too much with extensive citation and acknowledgement. Citations without reference are to commentaries on the plays (see bibliography). Most of the commentaries cited are in English, and although they annotate the Greek text, the interested reader will often find their notes accessible. When quoting the views of European scholars, I have translated the original German and French. In citing other Greek authors, I have preferred standard or readily available translations to editions lacking an English version. Thus the Loeb editions are cited for the facing translations, even though in most cases the Greek text has been superseded. The bibliographical references are generally to studies available to the English reader and the bibliography itself is, with a few exceptions, limited to studies actually cited in my notes.

Oedipus the King

The Theban Plays

LAIUS, king of Thebes, is warned by an oracle not to have children. When he gets a child by his wife Jocasta, he sends him away to be exposed on Mt. Cithaeron. He expects, of course, that the child will be destroyed by wild animals, but the herdsman in charge gives the child to a shepherd tending the flocks of the king of Corinth. The child's feet are so bound that one is swollen from the wound; his name Oedipus, "Swellfoot," comes from this incident. He is reared the only son of the rulers of Corinth. As a young man he is taunted by a drunk for being a bastard. Resolving to have certain knowledge of his birth, Oedipus goes to Delphi where he asks the oracle who his true parents are. To this the god responds that he will kill his father and marry his mother. Neither putting a second question nor the first question a second time, he hurries away, taking a road away from Corinth and toward Thebes. On this journey he meets at a crossroads Laius on his way to Delphi. Father and son dispute passage in the road; Laius strikes Oedipus; the son pays him back by killing him and others of his party on the spot. So he has killed his father. Then he travels to Thebes, at that time persecuted by the Sphinx, a terrible monster sent by Hera. This Sphinx has the habit of eating her victims, but first she sets them a riddle. Oedipus is able to answer the riddle, and in chagrin the beast destroys herself. The city is saved, in thanks for which the queen Jocasta is given as wife to the conquering hero, her son. So he has married his mother.

This story was well known to Sophocles' Athenian audience. In the literary tradition, however, the fate of Oedipus after this marriage was handled variously. How much time passed before he discovered his crimes, how he reacted to the discovery, whether he remained in Thebes or went into exile, what his relations were to his children, all these questions were treated in at least some texts in a manner different from that of Sophocles. For example, in the *Odyssey* we read,

> He killed his father
> and married her [Jocasta], but the gods soon made it all
> known to mortals.
>
> (*Odyssey* 11.273–74)

The reading "soon" has been disputed, but what cannot be disputed is that Homer goes on to tell how Oedipus continued to rule over Thebes after the death of Jocasta (or Epicaste, as she is known in the *Odyssey*). So we read of the tomb of Oedipus at Thebes (*Iliad* 23. 679). In his trilogy, of which the last play, *Seven against Thebes*, survives, Aeschylus keeps the ruined king in his city where he continues the curse of the Labdacids by condemning his sons to mutual slaughter. It seems likely that more than one reason for the quarrel between his sons Polyneices and Eteocles may have been offered. *Seven* 927ff. suggests their fratricidal struggle resulted from the curse of their incestuous begetting, while *Seven* 785ff. alludes to a curse Oedipus pronounced on the sons because of their "cruel tendance of him."

Turning from uncertainties and problems to Sophocles, we may say he had a good deal of freedom to develop the particulars of the Theban plays as he wished and that he made significant changes and additions. In the first place, in the *Oedipus the King* Oedipus' curse on himself and probable exile are hardly demanded by the tradition, nor need Sophocles have postponed the discovery so long as he did. Since in earlier versions Oedipus did not go into exile, it is clear that Creon, both in the *OK* and the *OC*, is, if not a new character, one whose importance as a dramatic figure is greatly increased by the motif of exile. In the *Antigone*, Creon's regency elevates him to the status of a worthy antagonist, but more important for this play is the question of burial, which, so far as we know, Sophocles added whole-cloth to the tradition. If we recall that for Homer Oedipus is buried at Thebes, we can hardly doubt that such a liberal tradition would have tolerated the burial of Polyneices as well (we cannot use the argument of the last scene of Aeschylus' *Seven* as evidence on this question because many scholars believe it was added to that play sometime after the first production of the *Antigone*). Apparently, Sophocles added both the prohibition of burial and Antigone's violation of the prohibition. Thus in a matrix of traditional myth the central crisis turns on the dramatist's innovation.

In the *Oedipus at Colonus*, Sophocles unites the tradition of Oedipus' exile, which is left ambiguously uncertain at the end of the *Oedipus the King*, with the legend of the father's curse on his sons. Whereas the old versions and Aeschylus kept Oedipus at home after the discovery, thus making his curse on Eteocles and Polyneices a domestic matter, in the *Colonus* the curse is postponed for many years, until Oedipus, old, exiled, and about to die, confronts the suppliant son and roundly condemns the brothers' failure to care for him. This bitter finale is preceded by a reprise for Creon, who comes to Colonus to bring the now valuable Oedipus home, by hook or by crook. Perhaps this last play creaks a bit from the load of dramatic incident, but the character of the old king and the varied and violent action guarantee its success in the theater.

What particularly fascinates us about Oedipus in the *Colonus* is his attitude toward his crimes. In the *Oedipus the King* the discovery brings violent guilt: he would kill Jocasta if she were not quicker, and his self-blinding is followed by a demand that he be cast from the city, self-cursed and loathsome to himself, his countrymen and his family. Thus in the earlier play the full force of polluting murder and incest is acknowledged as both personal and social. The child of Fortune has proven to be both blessing and curse to himself and his city. The murder of king and father cancels the triumph over the Sphinx. Sophocles obviously knew his Aeschylus very well, and he could have had Oedipus undergo those formal rites of absolution and expiation that purify Orestes and other similar victims in Greek myth. But Sophocles wanted a more personal—and more problematic—story. On three occasions in the *Colonus,* Oedipus defends his innocence, and yet both he and the chorus of Athenians remain profoundly sensitive to the pollution that still clings. Oedipus rationalizes the murder: it was an accident; he did not know the man; he was provoked. A court of law would be sympathetic. Still, the stain remains: he recoils from embracing Theseus, afraid of harming his generous host (*OC* 1130–39). His rationalized and intuitive sense of his own innocence cannot deny the social and religious opprobrium. What is dramatized is more than a personal odyssey; it is as much the edge of cultural change, where irrevocable sin meets rational introspection and personal accountability. The fundamental mystery of his fate so carefully charted in the *Oedipus the King* will be, for some, resolved by the final heroization, and Theseus' ready hospitality may seem to vouch for a socially acceptable purification. Yet he has not convinced himself. No confession of sin, no rationalization of circumstance, no years in the desert, have washed away the sense of guilt and shame. Perhaps his terrible and vindictive curse on his sons confirms, at least psychologically, the necessity of his personal alienation. We may think of Lear. Unlike Lear, Oedipus never achieves peace, is never fully reconciled, and must die alone amid thunder and lightning, closer to the daimons of the earth than to humanity.

Scene: None of the extant plays requires more than a single door. The altar is needed for Jocasta's prayer and sacrifice (919a–21). No other sets are necessary. Several references to "children" present an obvious metonymy for Oedipus' relation to his people (cf. the messenger's "son" at 1030–31); see also on 15–19. If this play begins with a tableau, it would be unique among the surviving plays. A slow procession to the door of the palace would have been efficient for Sophocles and will effectively highlight the suppliants' distress.

1 Besides **children** the first line contains a word (*trophê*) that plays on the ideas of nurture and descent (see on "ingrained" and "cherish" at 99–99a). **Cadmus** is the founder of Thebes (see on *OC* 1534a).

2–5 This is a scene of supplication: they sit on the steps before the palace to petition the king (cf. 20–21, 41). Suppliants normally carry olive branches wrapped with strips of wool. **Crowns** is probably transferred from the wreathed branch to the person carrying it (cf. 20). The **incense** is for sacrifice (cf. 913). The **hymns** are called paeans, which are normally songs for victory; here and at 186 they are apparently songs to the god of healing (Paean, also spelled Paeon; he is the physician of the gods whose name is also an epithet for Apollo the healer).

8 Great means "famous" (as at 1207). Such a boast is characteristic of the Greek hero; cf. Odysseus' introduction of himself to the Phaeacians:

I am Odysseus son of Laertes, known before all men
for the study of crafty designs, and my fame goes up to heaven.
                                                        (*Odyssey* 9.19–20)

Cf. the priest's praise at 35–40 and Antigone's aspiration at *Ant* 502.

10–13 Oedipus does not ask this question in ignorance of the plague (see 58–61). The question signifies his sympathy and readiness to help. In one of the many inversions in this play the king who feels pity for the suppliants becomes an object of pity (1296, 1474) and a suppliant (1447 in "beseech"); he lives to suffer because he was saved by a herdsman who pitied the exposed child (1179a). In the final scene his own children are present. Aristotle argued that tragedy effects "through pity and fear what we call the catharsis [purgation] of such emotions" (*Poetics,* chap. 6).

14 My (end-line in the Greek) perhaps recognizes that Oedipus, though king and "father," is nonetheless a foreigner. So **altar** is more literally "your altars" (the common plural for singular); cf. at 219a–24 his self-conscious admission that he is a foreigner.

15–19 The received Greek text explicitly recognizes three age groups among the suppliants: children **who cannot yet fly far** (a metaphor from fledglings); old men, among whom the priest numbers himself; young men of marriageable age (**these children . . . among the young**). Various attempts to emend away this last group seem unwarranted.

20–23 Double stands for "two." Aeschylus (*Seven against Thebes* 489) and others know a temple of Athena (= **Pallas**) Onca; the second has not been identified. **Ismenus** (also a local river) had a cult and was worshipped as a son of Apollo; his sanctuary was southeast of the city.

Oracles by fire are had either from the remains of sacrificial offerings or from the flames themselves.

24–24b The imagery of the ship of state is traditional (cf. *Ant* 162–63). Oedipus is the pilot of the ship (104, 691, 923), which may soon be emptied by the plague (56–57). For the priest **bloody** may merely signify the death caused by the pestilence, but the word also means "murderous" and thus points to the cause of the pestilence, namely the murder of the preceding helmsman Laius by the present pilot. This secondary metaphorical significance is anticipated by **prow**, which is literally "head"; as Kamerbeek notes, "head" shifts the image from a sinking ship to a drowning man. See further on 420.

If we look at the *Oedipus the King* as anthropologists, we shall wonder why the plague, whether it be retribution for murder or for incest, or both, comes so late on Thebes, years after the death of Laius (561–62), when Oedipus and Jocasta have grown children. Primitive belief anticipates a more rapid response to the violation of these taboos, and so do we, once we consider the "problem." For example, in the account in the *Odyssey* we read,

> He killed his father
> and married her, but the gods *soon* made it all known to mortals.
>
> (11.273–74)

Yet despite prompt divine action, in Homer's version Oedipus continues his rule in Thebes after full disclosure. In this, as in the negligent inquiry into Laius' death (129–30), Sophocles sacrifices some probability by the standards of realism for the dramatic gain to be had from the fall of a king happy and secure in throne and family.

25–30 The pestilence affects plants and animals as well as women in childbirth, and if we take **a God that carries fire** more or less literally, it would seem to be some sort of fever. The priest may use this phrase of Ares (cf. 191). That an entire city should pay for the crime and pollution of a single inhabitant can be paralleled in other Greek myths: e.g., Sophocles' lost *Alcmeon* may have told how the exiled Alcmeon's presence caused a pestilence in Psophis, where he had sought purification for killing his mother Eriphyle; Orestes, having killed his mother, incurs similar personal defilement and must flee into exile and seek absolution. **Black Death** is Hades, lord of the underworld, also called Ploutos ("Rich"), a name the priest alludes to in **grows rich**.

31–36 Not . . . as of a God = "not because we judged you equal to the gods." Counting, equating, and measuring are metaphors for rationality, but the priest uses them to avoid blasphemy. Here **have to do with more than man** (= "dealings with the gods") and **tribute which we paid**

add commercial metaphors by which the priest sees Oedipus as the savior who has freed the city from the Sphinx's taxation and set its accounts straight. This arithmetical language may be underscored by translating line 53 "be equal (to your former self) in bringing good fortune" and line 61 "I am equally as sick as you suppliants."

One of the primary questions posed by the play is how Oedipus stands with the gods. Because he was able to rid the city of the Sphinx, itself a sign of divine malice, the priest and people assume Oedipus has a special standing with divinity: **with more than man** means "with the gods." It is characteristic Greek thinking to attribute both human success and failure to a god, even when no particular deity can be named. To have divine help is a sign of favor (39–39a) as well as reason for praise; one of the larger ironies of the play is that this famed and favored ruler is revealed as most hateful in the eyes of the gods (see 816 and 1360).

37 Hesiod describes the **Sphinx** as the daughter of Chimaera (or on some interpretations Echidna) and Orthos (*Theogony* 326–27). The former is part lion, part snake, part goat, the latter a monstrous dog. She often appears in Greek art, most commonly represented as a winged lion with the head of a woman (see Apollodorus 3.5.8). Since the name suggests "binding" and like the Sirens she is dangerous because of her song (cf. 391), it would seem that at least one early version thought of her as paralyzing her victims, whereas Apollodorus and others report she eats those who fail to answer the riddle. The **tribute** is the victim demanded by the monster; cf. the victims annually devoted to the Minotaur in the legend of Theseus. Other references to the Sphinx at 130, 391, 508, and 1201.

43 The **wise word from some God** alludes to consulting an oracle (see 70–71 and 151).

51 **Raise up our city:** the same phrase ends line 46, and the root idea, something like the English "set it straight," also occurs in "saved our lives" (39b) and in **set . . . on high** (50; = "put us on our feet"); cf. 419b, 528; *Ant* 167.

52 **Luck** (*tychê*), as in English, may mean either good or bad fortune; this is a major motif in the play, summed up in Oedipus' proclamation of himself as "a child of Fortune" (see the note to 1080–86). Cf. Creon's "good fortune" (89); at 103 this word is translated "fate."

58–61 His first line repeats **known** ("you come desiring something known and not unknown to me"); cf. the repeated **sick.**

67 **Ways wandering in thought** points metaphorically both to the imagery of hunting (see on 108–13) and to Oedipus' chance meeting with his father at the "threeways" (see 801). He thinks of intellectual roaming but the language also suggests "wandering in illusion."

69 Creon is the son of **Menoeceus**, who was the son of Pentheus. The genealogy from Cadmus is as follows:

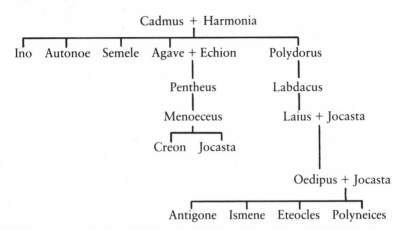

Creon, then, is both cousin (fourth generation) and brother-in-law to Oedipus. It is likely that Cadmus and Harmonia had only female descent in the original version and that Polydorus was invented to give legitimacy to the Labdacid dynasty.

71 The **Pythian temple** is Apollo's shrine at Delphi; it is named for the dragon (Pytho or Python) that Apollo killed there when he claimed the site for his own. As at 603–4, the punning here on **learn** (72) (*puthoith'*) and **Pythian** (*Puthika*) might be translated "deal with Delphi."

73 One shift in dramatic focus moves from the city to the man. **Save this city** (35, 48, 51) provides the initial impulse for their supplication and the king's reaction, or action, since in sending Creon he has anticipated their need and request. Gradually, however, the question of who murdered Laius takes over, and then the question of what part, if any, Oedipus had in the murder. Though we are allowed to "forget" the city, Oedipus discovers the source of pollution and thus, presumably, saves Thebes.

76–79 The irony is that he will prove a **villain** (*kakos*) by doing what the god commands; it is "liar" in his confession at 1421–22. For *kakos* see the note to 522–23. **Commands** also means "makes clear," at which moment Creon appears, so that the priest rightly sees a good omen (**gracious words**) in the happy responsion of word and deed. **Your servants** interprets the pronoun ("these men"), who may be some of the suppliants.

78–132 Translations often do not reflect the formal structure of the Greek dialogue. The pattern of the dialogue: Priest and Oedipus: 2 : 2 : 2 : 3; then Creon enters (86): 2 : 2 : 2 : 2; then Creon has four lines (95–

99b) announcing the matter of the oracle, after which Oedipus has three single line responses (99c, 103, 105), while each of Creon's utterances is two lines long. From 106 to 132 each man has exactly two lines in turn.

80–82 The Greek for **face** also means "eye" and "expression" (a similar phrase at 1483 is translated "bright eyes"). Like all the actors, the actor playing Creon wears a mask; for the spectators to know that he is beaming with good news, Oedipus must describe his aspect. Apart from this stage convention, blindness and sight pair with ignorance and knowledge to describe a fundamental metaphor for Oedipus' life. He is a man learning to see (cf. Creon's question at 528), who blinds himself when he has come face to face with the facts (cf. 1372 and 1385). **Bring us to safety** = "come with saving luck" (*tychê:* see on 52); cf. the priest's prayer at 149–50. At this point the dramatic questions are Who will save the city? and How will it be saved? The priest looks to Oedipus, who looks to Apollo and later to Teiresias (304b). The blind prophet, however, refuses the role of savior, and when Oedipus perseveres in his personal effort to save the city, he discovers that he has been preserved for this role by the shepherd of Corinth (1030) and the Theban herdsman (1180); in this salvation he sees the hand of fate (1457–59).

84–85 Laurel is sacred to Apollo and so appropriate to an emissary from his shrine.

93–94a In general the Attic tragedians make their kings more democratic than one might expect absolute rulers to be, but we may also appreciate Oedipus' willingness to do business in public as indicating a frank, open nature. The irony in **heart** is that it means "self" and "life" (*psychê*).

95–99d The Delphic oracle responded to both public and private inquiry, and two types of inquiry and response are found in this play. The oracle to Laius (see 711–14b) simply predicts his death at the hands of a still unborn son. He is free to believe or disbelieve, and his reaction indicates both attitudes: he credits the oracle's power enough that he is willing to expose his only male child (the implication of the exposure is, of course, that he can take measures to avoid the consequences of the birth and the prediction of Apollo). The present embassy illustrates a second type of utterance in which a state asks the god what it should do in such and such circumstances, or what will happen if such and such comes about. In these cases the god may offer a prediction, often couched in riddling terms, or he may, as here, command more or less specific actions. When the Thebans ask what they should do about the pestilence, Apollo responds that, since a murderer pollutes the land, they must drive out the murderer. This oracle is solicited by Oedipus. While there is much talk in the play about the veracity of oracles, there is no necessary connection between the prediction to Laius and the present command to Thebes, i.e., there is no evidence, save the natural but logically false inference, that a common source entails a common plan, that the two oracles belong to a distinct and single scheme of the god.

Apollo (**King Phoebus**) has announced that the plague is the result of a pollution (*miasma:* see also 313, 353, and 1012), which is a physical taint (833) or stain that the city can **drive out** (Jebb compares *Libation Bearers* 966–68: "after the stain is driven entire from the hearth by ceremonies that wash clean and cast out the furies"). Hence **purification** is a cleansing, often a ritual washing away of the infection; so Orestes says "My blot [*miasma*] of matricide is being washed away" (*Eumenides* 281); cf. 1227. The pestilence, then, comes from an impure presence, in this case Oedipus the murderer, and can be cured by banishing (100) the person who carries the impurity (see 823 and 1382 for this language). Nowhere in the play is repentance an issue, either for the god, for whom it is meaningless, or for Oedipus, for whom it is futile. That is, the god cares not for the guilt but for the fact.

Ingrained and **cherish** are from the same stem (*treph-*) and allusively imply something (someone) reared or nurtured, i.e., the native son who is the pollution. For a time the question of his rearing remains covert: see 324b ("reared"), 356 ("cherish"), 374a (note) and 1396 ("nurse").

100–102 **Expiation** suggests a freeing or paying out of one murder by another. Oedipus will refer several times to driving out the murderer (137, 229a, 243).

103 On **fate** see the note to 52. **Pronounces** = "denounces" or "lays information against." For Oedipus as the advocate who takes the god's information to court see 244a–45.

104 Besides the nautical metaphor in **piloted**, the verb also means "correcting," "setting something straight," and "conducting a public examination of accounts."

105 As in English, "I see" may mean "I know." Apart from the irony that Oedipus has seen Laius, various senses of these words such as "understand," "witness," and "have sight" permeate the play. For some examples see 284–87, 294b, 303, and 371.

106 Creon does not quote verbatim the words of the god (the colon is misleading), and so the plural (**murderers**) may be his and not Apollo's (if we ask why Creon uses the plural, we may look to the witness's report which Creon cites at 123–24a).

108 Commenting on irrational elements in plots, Aristotle (*Poetics,* chap. 24) observes, "Best that there should not be anything irrational in them at all, but if there is, let it be outside the story told, as, in *Oedipus Tyrannus,* Oedipus's not knowing how Laius died." Presumably Aristotle thinks that what is irrational and omitted from the plot is a dramatic treatment of events at Thebes immediately following the death of Laius and accession of Oedipus, when the new king might naturally have been expected to inquire after his predecessor's fate. Because Sophocles wants to compress action into a brief, climactic plot, numerous events and otherwise irrational factors, as, for example, Oedipus' "pierced ankles" (718), which in real life a wife would have noticed and inquired about, may be detected by the fastidious rationalist.

108–13 Trace means "track" and is a common metaphor from hunting (cf. 220–22, 475–79, 542, 544a). Again, the Greek does not make it clear that Creon quotes the oracle. Is found = "may be caught" (or "captured," as at 544a) so that if the god's words are quoted he has anticipated Oedipus' metaphor from tracking! See 577, where "proved" = "caught/taken."

114–14b Oedipus proceeds by division (at home; in the countryside; in another country). This logic is followed by close questioning, inference, and language that emphasizes seeing, knowing, and learning.

122 Hope is a traditional motif: see 158, 835, and the passages cited at *El* 810.

123 This man (the herdsman who enters at 1110) lied about the number of robbers because when he returned to Thebes he recognized Oedipus, who had already taken the wife of Laius (757–63); or he lied, as the scholiast thinks, because, having fled when he saw Laius dead, he wanted to cover his own cowardice by increasing the number of assailants. Once again the traditional version of the story presents problems that the play does not ask us to solve. Voltaire, sensitive to the improbability of the new king not inquiring after the death of Laius, shortens the interval since Oedipus' accession to two years and further accounts for the lack of an inquiry by making Oedipus considerate of Jocasta's grief (*Oedipus* 1.196–203). See the note to 758–63.

124b–25 Oedipus regularly refers to the murderer in the singular (139a, 225, 236, 250, 265) either because he is confident someone has suborned the murderers or because Greek idiom permits the singular to be used generically for the plural. The poetic motive, however, is obviously to heighten the irony of unconscious personal reference. His suspicions of treason and mercenary motives typify the Greek tyrant and are not peculiar to him (cf. 380–90, 532–38, *Ant* 290–303, *OC* 1028–31).

130 The full riddle does not seem to be known to us until well after Sophocles' time. Edmunds (p. 12) translates its "fullest form": "There walks on land a creature of two feet, of four feet, and of three; it has one voice, but sole among animals that grow on land or in the sea, it can

change its nature; nay, when it walks propped on most feet, then is the speed of its limbs less than it has ever been before." Oedipus' **hinder you** translates a compound from "foot" ("in your way," or "under foot"); "feet" is crucial to the riddle; Creon speaks of immediate troubles as being **at our feet;** and Oedipus means "Swellfoot" (see the note to 1036). More feet at 318, 479a, 866, 878.

133 Bring this to light (the *phan-* stem): This verb and its cognates signify "showing," "proving," "making evident or manifest," and "making clear." Sophocles has used this stem extensively: it echoes "mysterious" (131; we can catch the play with "I shall make clear the unclear"); showing forth the truth is linked to "luck," "god's help," and "falling" (145–46); the god has shown the way ("proclaimed" at 244a); Teiresias could reveal all but won't (329–29a) until he is provoked ("proven" at 458); Oedipus thinks Creon *manifestly* (534) the murderer; even when the evidence starts to be *plain* (754a) we know that Oedipus will *prove* (852) more than the murderer of Laius; and so he becomes determined *to bring* his birth *to light* (1059). At last all comes clear in the light (1183–85; cf. 1229–30), *proved* by the god (1382). See Reinhardt's chapter on illusion and reality.

135 The *Ajax* is about a man who is *theomachos,* i.e., one who "opposes a god," while the *OK* is about a man who is an **ally** of the god (cf. "champion" at 244b, 264, and 274). Oedipus' stand is one of traditional piety (see the note to OC 1375–76), with which self-interest is compatible.

136 Champion = "revenger" and echoes Creon's "punish" (107). Oedipus uses the same word again at 140 (in "dispatch").

138 Friend's: keeping the Greek plural (friends') adds a certain poignancy, since it would include father, mother, and children, all of whom may be styled *philoi.* Oedipus continues (cf. 124b–25) to suspect a political conspiracy; hence **my own interest.**

142–44 He dismisses the suppliants and at the same time announces that the chorus will represent the people of Thebes (**the assembly**).

145–46 Another version: "For either we shall be shown fortunate with (the help of) the god, or we shall be shown (to be) fallen." See on 133.

151 Most commentators prefer the view that the suppliants depart, and the chorus, which comes in answer to Oedipus' call for an assembly (143), now enters. Thus the parodos has an internal motivation and brings a new, distinct group to the orchestra. They are old men, the elders of the city.

151–215 As Ax has shown, the parodos is, formally, a prayer and is consequently best understood in terms of its liturgical form and content. Like many other prayers, it has three parts: invocation (first antistrophe, 156–67), argument or motivation (the second strophic pair, 168–89), and the specific requests (third strophic pair, 190–215). These three sections are preceded by the first strophe that links the parodos to the prologue. These four parts may be summarized as (1) What is the meaning of Apollo's oracle? (2) May Athene, Artemis, and Apollo come to protect us; (3) Our afflictions are beyond reckoning; (4) May Zeus and his children come to drive off the pestilent Ares. In style, the formal and liturgical elements bring an ornate, baroque expression, with the glitter of gold and traditional poetic epithets remote from a personal tone.

151–58 The strophe begins in the Greek with a vocative ("O sweet-spoken word of God") and returns to the same form (**immortal voice**) in closing. Cf. the repeated **golden. God** is Zeus, father of Apollo (see the note to *OC* 792–93). The oracle is **sweet spoken** because the speakers hope it will prove to be sweet or pleasing (a good example of the proleptic adjective). **Voice** = "word" (43). **O Delian Healer:** Apollo was born on the island of Delos and is here called Paean (**Healer;** see note to 2–5) as a god of healing. **Doom** is, more precisely, "debt," and **bring to pass** probably means "require us to pay." The debt may be new or old, i.e., may have come back in the **revolving years.** That Apollo requires the city to pay an old debt does not entail his responsibility for it, i.e., Apollo did not make the city harbor the criminal. In the next stanza Apollo's aid in defending the city is invoked, while in the fifth stanza (190–200) Ares is blamed for pestilence. Clearly, then, for the chorus, the Delphic god has not caused the present blight. The **voice** of the oracle is the **child of hope** because it comes from Apollo, who is their hope, or because it is begotten by their hope.

159–67 Language and phrasing give a strong Homeric cast to these lyrics. For example, **deathless** (= **immortal** in 157), **daughter of Zeus** for Athene, **Earth Upholder** (in Homer regularly of Poseidon; here it probably means "protector of the land"), "rich in gold" (151), "glorious" (152) "revolving years" (156), "golden," (158), and **Far Shooter** (the archer god can strike his victim from afar) are all common in the *Iliad* and *Odyssey*. **In the throne which men call Fame:** Frazer (*Pausanias,* vol. 2, p. 124) says that "the goddess of Good Fame, who was commonly identified with Artemis, had an image and an altar in the marketplace of every town in Boeotia and Locris." **Averters of Fate** is modeled on a Homeric compound; here **Fate** means "death." **Come to us now, if ever before:** requests are commonly based on past services, established patronage, and assumed reciprocity. Diomedes prays to Athene (= Atrytone):

'Hear me now, Atrytone, daughter of Zeus of the aegis:
if ever before in kindliness you stood by my father
through the terror of fighting, be my friend *now also*, Athene;
(*Iliad* 5.115–17)

Cf. the prayer at *Ant* 1145 that Bacchus "be manifest" (a similar request is found at 214 below, where "combat" may also be translated "approach").

168–77 This and the following stanza enumerate the ills besieging the city. In the Greek, the first clause of this strophe has a transitional "for" which explains why they call on the gods. **Ship's timbers are rotten** is more specific than the Greek: "all the host is sick." The culprit is Ares (see 190–91), so the chorus sings that there is **no spear of thought** for defense, meaning that thought has not found a weapon against the enemy. **One with another:** or "one on another," the idea being that the spirits of the dead dart toward the underworld like birds in startled flight. **The Western God** is Hades, whose house may be reached by a voyage to the edge of the world. Homer compares the souls of the dead suitors to the flight of bats:

And as when bats in the depth of an awful cave flitter
and gibber, when one of them has fallen out of his place in
the chain that the bats have formed by holding one on another.
(*Odyssey* 24.6–8)

The image of the darting birds is fused with that of **fire unmastered** (**quicker** may modify both **one** and **birds**).

178–89 **Spreading contagion of death:** it is often argued that the plague that devastated Athens in the early years of the Peloponnesian War offered a vivid historical context for Sophocles' description. Perhaps the strongest argument in this direction is the odd association of Ares, in fact a preeminent protector of Thebes, with the plague. This link would make more sense to the Athenian struck at once by war (Ares) and the pestilence. Thucydides' description (2.49) emphasizes the terrible fevers attending this disease, which was perhaps a form of typhus. **Hymn . . . rings out** translates a synaesthesia like that at 474a (more literally, "the hymn shines clear"). Although we might expect Artemis to be invoked to save women and children perishing at childbirth, the **golden Daughter of Zeus** is probably Athena (cf. 159). Kamerbeek suggests that **deliverance** is personified.

190–200 The preceding invocation leads naturally to a prayer (**grant that**). In the translation the continuing narrative form of lines 190–91 somewhat blurs the division between stanzas. The **War God** is Ares (the first word of the Greek strophe); **savage** (= "raging") is a Homeric epithet for fire and complements **burns**. The imagery passes from battle to racing and then to the mythical antipodes of west and east: the **great palace of Amphitrite** is probably the Atlantic Ocean and the **Thracian sea** is the Black Sea. Amphitrite is the consort of Poseidon. Ares is asked, in elevated language, to go drown himself. **Whatsoever . . . revisits** translates lines both intrinsically uncertain for sense and difficult to link, on any reading, to the context. Perhaps Ares is the subject, with the sense: "For he does his work, and whatever the night leaves the day takes." But the sententious abstraction of the Greek is vague. Zeus the god of **lightning** (cf. *Tr* 1086–88) is asked to blast Ares. Cf. the prayer to Bacchus at 214–14a.

201–15 The first words of the stanza are **Lycean King** (= Apollo); here Sophocles thinks of Lycean as derived from "light," but see the note to *El* 6 for another etymology. The reference to the **Lycean hills**, a district in Asia Minor, as the haunt of his sister Artemis offers yet another association of this adjective, one whose relevance is hard to see. Other elements in the stanza continue the ornate, generic diction: two compounds from golden (**golden corded** and **turban of gold**); **gleaming** = "that carries fire" (200); **wine flushed** (**wind** is a misprint; cf. "wine-dark" at *OC* 674a); the god as eponymous divinity (**who gave his name to this country**; cf. *OC* 65). The **torches of Artemis** would more naturally be associated by the Greek audience with festivals, in which the goddess is often identified with Hecate and the moon, than with weapons for repelling Ares. **Scours** means "darts around" (a verb proper to the movement of fire is transferred to the goddess). Dionysus (**the Bacchic God**) is often represented on vases as dressed in oriental finery. With **gave his name** cf. *Tr* 511. **Evian** comes from the shout "euoi" (see *Tr* 219) cried by the Bacchic revel. This company is usually female and called **Maenad** from the *madness* inspired by the god; since their rout often takes place at night, they carry **torches**. **Combat** means "approach." Already in the *Iliad*, Ares is **unhonoured among the gods**, "the most hateful of all the gods" (spoken by Zeus at 5.890).

216–18 Oedipus' first words are very abrupt ("you ask [for help], and what you ask for . . .") and may imply he has heard all or part of the song. On the other hand, Sophocles often practices a kind of dramatic economy that permits a new entry with full or partial knowledge of preceding events (thus Teiresias knows the proclamation [350–53]; cf. Creon's informed entry at 513, where, however, the speaker explains how he knows). **Strength** = "deliverance" (189). **Fight the plague** contains an odd ambiguity since, as Jebb notes, "the commoner use of the word . . . would mean to *humour* the disease" (Jebb's italics). Even if we can understand "Who helps the disease remedies it" (so Schneidewin), the primary meaning of the word translated **fight** is "to serve as a rower on a ship" (a radical metaphor equates plague and helmsman). To follow the plague's direction would be, in this case, to find its cause and banish it (the political helmsman, Oedipus himself).

219–75 In a number of ways this speech refers to the procedures of Attic law, some of which significantly differ from our own practice in cases of homicide. In the first place, a formal charge could be laid against a person or persons unknown. The verb at 103 ("pronounces") indicates that, initially, Apollo is cast in the role of one who denounces a criminal. Then Oedipus, self-conscious of his foreign origin (219a–20), assumes this responsibility, specifically noting that he has become a citizen (and is thus entitled to prosecute; a slave, foreign resident, or noncitizen might legally bring a charge of homicide, but only a citizen could formally prosecute the case). Secondly, Attic law proceeded in two stages. The first, corresponding roughly to our grand jury, was an inquiry into the nature and legitimacy of the charge. The second corresponded to our trial. Lines 219–45 abbreviate the first stage: the accuser identifies himself, lays the charge of murder (in Athens the accuser would make this public charge in the marketplace), demands that those who have knowledge of the crime should come forward with evidence (225–29), and offers pardon and immunity to anyone who assists the prosecution (229–32). Finally, he forbids the murderer access to home, public place, and religious ritual (236–44: these restrictions are more motivated by religious scruple than by legal procedure). In the third place, we should note the function of the oath in Attic law: both accuser and accused are obliged to swear, the one that his charge is valid, the other that he is innocent. The validity of the oath is based on the swearer's willingness to involve himself in the curse, should he be guilty or be wrongly bringing a charge. Failure to take such an oath is evidence against the party (i.e., there is no constitutional right to refuse to take an oath or offer evidence on the grounds of self-incrimination). See the curse and oath of Oedipus at 246–51. A fourth and vital distinction between our law and Athenian practice explains the inclusion and emphasis of lines 259–68, a passage that on first view seems to us crudely ironic. While anyone may bring a charge, it was the family, usually the nearest male relative, that was required by law to prosecute a case for homicide (Athens did not have a district attorney). The Athenians viewed this legal action as an act of vengeance on behalf of the dead man; hence it was natural to require the dead man's kin to take to law what in more primitive times they would have taken in personal retribution. Thus Oedipus has legal reasons for asserting his citizenship (219a–24) and surrogate kinship (259–64); he is led, then, by an anachronistic legal fiction to the logically dubious but ironically true claim that he acts "as for my father" (264). While it may have been the case that citizens other than kin were permitted to prosecute for homicide (see MacDowell, *Athenian Homicide Law*, pp. 12–19), the Greek audience normally expected some affirmation of kinship and may have found the proceedings illegal without it.

As it runs in the manuscripts, the Greek text and our translation confuse to some extent the two stages of indictment and prosecution (in actual practice these two proceedings would be distinct in time and venue). Various transpositions to bring the text into a more exact parallelism with the actual course of legal procedure have been proposed, the most thoroughgoing of which has been accepted into the text by Dawe. He transposes 244b–51 to follow 268: the presence in our text at 244a of a pronoun meaning "being such a person" and modifying Oedipus gives these lines an apt reference to the argument of 259–68; secondly, Dawe places 269–72 after 244a, so these lines become a curse on those who fail to help him apprehend the murderer. The chief advantage of this double transposition, apart from clarifying two pronoun references, which are no trouble in the English version, is that the curse on the murderer at 244b–51 does not now run on confusedly after the public denunciation, and, better still, it finds a climactic position in the accusatory section, immediately after he has urged his own personal right to pursue the homicide. The more we dwell on the Athenian distinction between the two types of proceeding and their unmistakable influence on the whole speech, the more this transposition, perhaps less complicated as a scribal error than my explanation would allow, recommends itself. See Dawe, *Studies* 1, pp. 221–26, Knox, *Oedipus at Thebes*, pp. 80–98, and Greiffenhagen. For a survey "Law and Drama," see Garner, chap. 4.

219a Stranger also means "foreigner."

220–22 The emphasis in this conditional statement falls on **alone**: since he is a stranger to the deed and story, alone, without the help of the Thebans, he can not be expected to find the trail of the crime. Now, however, he can invoke the aid of the city. The sentence does not imply that he has a **clue**.

223–24 After all was finished: i.e., with the murder committed and the traces of it faint.

226 Adding the father's name is the formal, and legal, way of identifying a person. Cf. the still more formal genealogy at 266–68.

228 Blame has a technical ring; so "charge." Cf. 529 ("accused").

229a Because of the manner and length of Athenian trials, exile (**leave this land unharmed**) was an option for the murderer; see the note to 236.

230–32 The preceding section has assumed that the murderer may be a Theban and that he may be denounced by another Theban or be persuaded to denounce himself. Now Oedipus takes up the possibility that the murderer may be a foreigner, and by a natural syntactical ambiguity the Greek may mean "if someone (a foreigner or a native) denounces another person (a foreigner)" so that both subject and object may refer, ironically, to Oedipus himself.

236–44 That man refers to the murderer (not to any concealer). From the perspective of Attic law, lines 236–44 represent the customary exclusion of an accused murderer from civic and religious activities which his presence would pollute (244); but Oedipus is also the king and as such cries exile, the traditional punishment for homicide. The accused is denied intercourse with man (**greeting**) and god (**sacrifice**). **Water for his hands** refers to ritual cleansing before taking part in sacrifice. Cf. the punishment threatened for Orestes at *Libation Bearers* 290–96.

246–51 The legitimacy of the accusation is vouched for by the **curse** that will fall on his own house, should the king violate his own interdiction. The **hearth** is the center of daily family worship; to share the hearth is to belong within the sacral bond of the family. See *El* 881.

254–55 For the God = "for Apollo." **By the God forsaken** (*atheos*) occurs again in "without God's blessing" (660–61) and in "godless" (1360); the phrase has the general sense of "without the help of the gods." As usual, the capitalized God should not be taken for premature monotheism. **God's ordinance** means "impelled by god(s)" and alludes to the oracle; at 992 this word is rendered "from the Gods"; cf. *Ant* 279.

257 A good man is a nobleman.

260 That once was his translates an adjective that at 459b is "a fellow sower"; it usually means "sown from the same stock" and appears in poetry as an elegant variant for "brother" or "sister" (as at *Tr* 211). Here we expect the meaning "a bed and wife shared (sown) by both men," and that is apparently Oedipus' meaning, but the audience must hear a more sinister overtone. For elaborations on the metaphor from sowing see 1210, 1257, and 1498. Knox (*Oedipus at Thebes*, p. 115) and Goldhill (*Reading Greek Tragedy*, p. 207) discuss this metaphor.

261–63 Unfortunate and **fortune** repeat *tychê* (see note to 52). The metaphor **leaped upon his head** depicts a daimon destroying a man, as again at 1301.

266–68 For the genealogy see the note to 69.

269–72 The curse of sterility is traditional and aims to transfer the general pestilence to a single guilty party. **Plough** is particularly ironic in light of later imagery; for its metaphorical values see 1211–12.

274 For the personification of **Justice** (*dikê*) cf. 886 and OC 1382.

284–86 The seer **Teiresias** is intimately associated with Thebes and its legends; he first appears in Greek literature in the *Odyssey* where, to hear his predictions, Odysseus takes a detour to the underworld (11.90–151). He was blinded either (1) for revealing the secrets of the gods, or (2) because he saw Athena naked, or (3) because he offended Hera when he pronounced that women enjoy sex nine times as much as men (these are the reasons given by Apollodorus, 3.6.7; all involve some perception or understanding that violates the boundaries between mortals and immortals). In the *Antigone* he enters late with crucial advice, which Creon only reluctantly accepts (see *Ant* 985–1096); see also Euripides, *Phoenician Women* 865–95 for his pronouncement on the fate of Oedipus. Teiresias studies the manners of birds for his immediate knowledge (see 399a and *Ant* 1000–1012), but in the present case he has apparently known for some time the secret of Oedipus. His source of knowledge is vaguely represented as coming from Apollo (see 376–77 and 410–11). The intimacy of Apollo's knowledge and Teiresias' is stressed in the Greek by the juxtaposition of **Lord . . . Lord** and **Teiresias . . . Apollo**, who "see the same."

288–89b For the second time (cf. 68–71) Oedipus has anticipated a proper course of action. Here, too, he is impatient (cf. 73–75). **Creon's word** will motivate Oedipus' suspicion that the seer and brother-in-law conspire against him (see 378 and 380–89a). **Two messengers** means messengers on two occasions, a foreshadowing of the seer's reluctance (316–19).

290–96 The preceding lines lead us to expect Teiresias immediately. Since these six lines merely repeat the story of Laius' murder already reported by Creon, adding that the power of the curse should frighten any man, we must look for a new dramatic reason for their inclusion. In the following scene Teiresias will accuse Oedipus of the murder (353, 362), a charge the king takes as nothing more than slander (354, 363). Oedipus is able to reject Teiresias' plain accusation as baseless in part because of the plural (**wayfarers**), in part because he has a clue (the **faint story**) in which he has, as yet, no reason to implicate himself.

297–99 **His prosecutor** denotes the one "who will put him to the proof." Although it is not a technical term of law, the Greek is natural to any context of interrogation. The coryphaeus (the leader of the chorus speaks these lines, not the chorus as a group) is thinking of the killer, who is much nearer for questioning than he knows. **Truth is native** reflects the same metaphor noted at *OC* 1113.

300–15 The speech is formal and deferential, with not a touch of the arrogant scorn Oedipus will later exhibit for Teiresias' powers (390–99a). Oedipus is sincere, and when Teiresias refuses to share his knowledge, sincerity turns into the anger of a king treated contemptuously.

301–2 Things not to be spoken are probably those "divine secrets" so often attributed to seers like Teiresias and Melampus; here there is also unconscious foreshadowing of unspeakable murder and incest. **Earth-creeping** things translates a single, unique compound. Note the pairs, polarities, and antitheses.

304a-b Champion contains a latent allusion to "Apollo defender" (*Tr* 208), whose statue was often found in front of Greek houses. **Rescue** translates a noun paired with **champion** and means "savior."

310–14 With **way of prophecy** compare "path of prophecy" (*Agamemnon* 1154). **Save . . . save . . . redeem** translate the same word (triple anaphora), but when its object becomes **pollution,** a second meaning drawing on a legal and commercial metaphor makes the sense "redeem the debt incurred on the land by the presence of the dead man."

316–19 Wisdom translates the verb (*phronein*) that Oedipus uses at 303 ("know"); it is repeated in its participial form in **wise** and again in 326 and 329; cf. 330 and the note to 404–4a. "Knowing" and "understanding" are more proper to the Greek than "wisdom," which may smack of the antique crackerbarrel. **Had forgotten it:** since Teiresias will refuse, until he is provoked, to reveal what he knows, the poet wishes to explain why he came at all. Cf. *Phoenician Women* 891–95.

320–21 Destinies is possible, but the Greek more vaguely omits any specific noun as object: "you bear yours, and I'll bear mine." This scene begins with good will on both sides: Oedipus genuinely wants Teiresias' help, while the prophet has not come to hurt Oedipus.

323–24b The Greek translated by **rob** has commercial overtones (cf. "profit" in 317) and in the context of his obligation to the city may suggest "fraud"; the tone, however, is not yet angry, and the king may think that he is humoring the seer's vanity.

324c–25 For **mark** (*kairos*) see on 631. In the Greek the second clause may imply that he now turns to leave: "(I am going) since I fear my words, too, will miss the mark" (we understand the "I am going" from 320); or Oedipus interrupts (**For God's sake**) before he can finish the sentence.

326–28 Kneel is particularly strong (= "reverence" at OC 1653) and has offended some who cannot think Oedipus humbles himself before Teiresias.

329c–31 In the legal context Teiresias, although summoned prior to Oedipus' proclamation, appears as the first witness in the investigation of Laius' death. Like the coryphaeus (276–79), he is expected either to produce evidence or to take an oath that he cannot offer relevant testimony. Instead he tells the prosecutor to give up the case, a response that naturally inspires Oedipus to impugn his loyalty as a citizen. As we see later (351), Teiresias is represented as familiar with the proclamation, a bit of dramatic legerdemain that enhances the judicial aspect of this inquiry. Insofar as we perceive Oedipus as pursuing a proper criminal investigation, and that role still animates the next scene with Creon (513 ff.), he will seem justified in his anger. With perfect personal and legal decorum he has appealed to the seer, who without reason, so it seems, refuses to help. At this point, he is indignant on behalf of the city and not yet from a sense of personal affront (cf. 345–49b).

335–37 The man who resists humane appeal is as stubborn as the sea and as hard as **stone.** So Patroclus condemns Achilles:

> it was the grey sea that bore you
> and the towering rocks, so sheer the heart in you is turned from
> us.

> *(Iliad* 16.34–35)

In a typical tragic periphrasis Oedipus says "You would provoke the nature of a stone." **Provoke** translates the first of five Greek words that play on the same stem *(orgê):* "temper" (338, meaning "disposition") and "angry" (346) serve in the English; cf. 364, 405, 524, and 806 for the same word describing his hot temper. Cf. *OC* 854–55 for the same trait. His temper and self-confidence are often called his flaws (see, e.g., Kitto, *Greek Tragedy,* pp. 143–44; cf. Jones, p. 211), but Sophocles does not moralize his temper in such a way that we can equate his suffering with punishment for rash action. For his anger as a motif from the epic tradition see the note on *Seven against Thebes,* 782–91.

338–39 Eustathius (in his commentary on *Iliad* 9.342) noticed an ambiguity in **your own that lives within you:** the Greek does not repeat **temper** and may also be understood to mean "your (wife) that lives with you." This is the sort of secondary ambiguity that most auditors may not have noticed.

341 Hide, i.e., "cover them with silence" and so "guard them in silence."

348 On **complotter** see the note to 1077–78.

350–53 On **pollution** see on 95–99d. Oedipus, angry and confident of his own innocence, takes the truth as an insult (for "pollution" = "filth" as a term of abuse see *Tr* 987 and *Ant* 746 ["poisoned"]; this usage is common in Aristophanes). More literally, Teiresias says "you are the unholy polluter": "polluter" *(miastôr)* is used by Aeschylus *(Eumenides* 177) and Sophocles *(El* 605) of the avenger of murder; cf. *Medea* 1371.

357 Who has taught you truth?: **truth** is not expressed in the Greek, so that Oedipus seems, ambiguously, to continue his indignant questioning (354–55) *and* to respond to the seer. **Profession** *(technê:* see on *Phil* 79b–85) is "skill" at 389a; cf. 390–97.

359 How far Oedipus is from the track is illustrated by **Speak what?**, as if he had unconsciously uttered a chance word that had clued Teiresias to the truth.

363 Calumnies = "pains," so "calamities," a more exact word than he knows.

366–68 You love best will mean to Oedipus "those dearest to you," while **live with** will simply mean "associate with"; cf. Oedipus' own euphemistic use of the same verb at 1185. Carrière (p. 7) suggests that these lines, for Oedipus, refer to the supposed scandal of his having become a member of his victim's family. It would, of course, be the height of shame to marry the wife of the man you had murdered, as we see from Oedipus' reaction at 821–22.

370–71 Blind in mind and ears: the Greek abuse begins with a violent zeugma ("yoking"): "blind in ears. . . ." For blindness cf. 303, 389, 413, 419a–b, 454a, 528.

374a–75 Another version: "you are nourished by one night"; see the note on the *treph-* stem at 95–99d.

376–78 With most editors this translation accepts Brunck's emendation of these lines. Knox (*Oedipus at Thebes,* pp. 7–8), protesting the ascription of Oedipus' fate to Apollo, translates the manuscript reading: "It is not destiny that I should fall at your hands, since Apollo is enough, and it is his affair." For this interpretation to fit the context, we must translate 374a–75 "Your life is one long night so that neither I nor any man who sees the light would ever hurt you." This is possible from the Greek, but the sentiment then becomes less contemptuous and more demeaning to the king. Knox has taken this line of interpretation because, on the general view, Teiresias seems to assign Oedipus' fate to Apollo, i.e., to an external agency that we may as well call fate. But we need not take Teiresias so literally (he may mean no more than this: now that the plague is upon us and Apollo's oracle has demanded the killer be sought out, it is inevitable that you will be found out), nor, if we do take him literally, do we need believe that he is exactly accurate in making Apollo the cause of Oedipus' fate. Despite the **fate** (*moira*), the Greek is a good deal less precise about this than, say, Orestes is when he claims Apollo must bear equal responsibility with him for the death of Clytemnestra (see *Eumenides* 465–69 and 579–79a). On Oedipus and Fate see E. R. Dodds, "On Misunderstanding the *Oedipus Rex.*"

378 The typical Greek ruler fears plots and conspiracies; Oedipus naturally implicates his brother-in-law, who recommended Teiresias' advice (289). The suspicion has the dramatic function of motivating Creon's return (513).

380–82 Oedipus apostrophizes those qualities which, he assumes, have attracted the envy of Creon. **Skill** (*technê* is "profession" at 357) anticipates another attack on Teiresias (see 389a). Most commentaries reject the construction **for the contrivance of** in favor of "in a much-envied life." **Great store of jealousy fill your treasury chests** may also be interpreted thus: "how great is the store of jealousy you (i.e., wealth, rule, skill) guard, if . . ." The metaphor treats the envied attributes as if they were hoarding (or nurturing) envy (*phthonos*). Wealth, rule (tyranny), and the life of the gods incite envy (see Archilochus frag. 22; Anacreon frag. 8; and Simonides frag. 71). Sophocles varies the traditional set by substituting skill for divine bliss and by a personification of wealth, rule, and skill so that they may be said, virtually, to court malicious envy. See also Creon's variation on this commonplace at 584–600.

385 The translation has dropped two lines (383–84 in the Greek text): "how great is the envy stored up, if, for the sake of this rule, which the city handed to me, a gift unsought, the trusted Creon, (my) old friend, thus secretly attacks me." The tone is scornful: cf. "the noble Brutus" and "the worthy Creon" (*Ant* 31).

387–90 With this abuse of Teiresias cf. Pentheus' abuse of the same seer at *Bacchae* 255–60, where "gain" is also the motive for betrayal. See the greedy soothsayer in Aristophanes' *Birds* 959–91.

391–92 **The dark singer, the sphinx** = "the Rhapsode . . . dog." Cf. 37 for "singer." Jebb suggests she is called "dog" because she is the watchful agent of Hera (Aeschylus, in his *Sphinx*, had previously called her a dog); her ancestry is also canine (see the note to 37).

398 Here too (see note to 385) the article (in the Greek) enhances both irony and truth: "the know-nothing Oedipus."

403 **To drive me out** translates "to drive out one polluted."

404–4a This is a Sophoclean variation on "learning through suffering": see on *Agamemnon* 176–78. **Treason** is interpretative: "you would learn a lesson from your intention."

404b–7 A typical speech by the coryphaeus tries to placate both parties; here, as often, the mediation is ignored; cf. *Ant* 724–26. He comments on the tone (**anger**) rather than the substance of Teiresias' charges (cf. 489–95).

408–9 The request, or demand, to speak in rebuttal is a familiar feature of agonistic scenes: cf. Creon at 544b–c and Electra at *El* 555–56. This is not really a defense, however, so much as a tirade.

412 **Enroll myself . . . patron** contains a double meaning: (1) I am not a resident alien (*metoikos*) who requires the protection of Creon or any other citizen; (2) I take Apollo as my patron (cf. 882).

414a-b **Where you are in sin** = "where you are in calamity" (368). The difference in translation reflects the vague ambiguity of *kakos* (see on 522–23), which is translated "evils" at 424b. The same language is translated "Your situation's desperate; can't you see?" at *Aj* 388. All Oedipus can see is the insulting and infuriating fustian of a devious and suspect seer.

418–19 Curse and Fury (see on *OC* 40–43) are often equated (see *Eumenides* 417), and the latter are hounds (*El* 1389) that **drive** down on their victims ("bronze-shod" *El* 491; "with long strides" *Aj* 837) and leap on their heads (*Eumenides* 370–76). Hence **deadly footed** is usually taken as a generic epithet, without allusive reference to the foot of Oedipus (*Oidipous: deinopous*). In this context, however, the generic assumes peculiar secondary connotations ("a foot that inspires terror/fear" is the more natural meaning of this striking compound that occurs only here). Cf. 467–68 where a common poetic idiom for running cannot escape similar allusive reference (cf. 479a). **Double striking** (another compound adjective) refers first to curse of mother and father ("your" father in the Greek) and secondly to the lash or scourge that a *daimôn* lays on its victim (see, e.g., *Prometheus Bound* 683–84, *Agamemnon* 642).

420–24a The fusion of image (**harbour, Cithaeron . . . in echo**) and metaphor (**steered to a haven**) with its paradox (**haven no haven; after a lucky voyage**) is not calculated for clarity, though the concise allusiveness has extensive resonance for the audience; see the nautical metaphor at 24–26, the harbor ("haven") at 1208, the apostrophe to Cithaeron at 1392. Our translation has made the passage less elliptical and terse: **the secret of** is interpretative, and the subject of **steered** is Oedipus ("to which you steered"). This metaphor links the ship of state (24–26, 923) to the womb as harbor (1208).

424b–25 Another rendering of the manuscript reading indicates the obscurity of his cryptic threat: "evils [*kaka*] that will make you equal to yourself and to your children." Wilamowitz has emended the passage to keep the second person: "in respect of which evils you make yourself and your children equal." Cf. 1509 and the note to 32.

426 Creon has not yet spoken. Read "Creon" for **Creon's.**

430 Finding this speech all insult and nonsense, Oedipus dismisses Teiresias, who prepares to leave and is starting off as he speaks 435–36. Then, hearing a more direct reference to his parents, the king bids him **Stop!** (437).

435–40 Five of the six lines (except 439) contain a form of the verb *phuô*, which means "to be (by nature)," as in 435 and 440 and, in transitive forms, "breed" and "beget" (436, 437, 438). Jebb's **will show your birth** lessens the riddle: "This day will give you birth and will destroy you." Sophoclean tragedy brings action to its crisis in a single day; for the motif's articulation see *Aj* 756–58, *Tr* 739–40 (note), and *Phil* 83; cf.

Alcestis 147, *Helen* 1470, *Orestes* 49. Aristotle notes (*Poetics*, chap. 5) "tragedy endeavors as far as possible to keep within one revolution of the sun, or to exceed this limit but little," but that limit is for him, as for Sophocles, more a function of the unity of the action than any regard for the unit of time as such.

As Dawe points out, inasmuch as elsewhere in the play Oedipus is confident that his parents are Polybus and Merope of Corinth (774–75), he ought not now to be troubled, or even curious, at Teiresias' **parents**; at the expense of some consistency Sophocles makes him jump at this reference, just as he once was stung by a drunk's aspersion of bastardy (779a–82).

442 Luck was emended to "skill" (*technê*, as translated at 389a) by Bentley and is now accepted by Dawe. Oedipus has mocked Teiresias' skill ("profession" at 359a; cf. 564), and if the emendation is correct, Teiresias would be turning the sarcasm against the king. The scholiast's note ("you understood the riddle") could certainly be a gloss on "skill." If Teiresias mocks him with "luck," it is an anticipation of several passages on this motif, which culminate with 1077–86, where *tychê* is "Fortune." See the note at 52. Skill is more integral to this scene.

447 Oedipus should begin his exit now and should be offstage no later than 457. If he remains through 461, as most modern critics and commentators would have, we must face the fact that he does not understand, or can somehow ignore, the prophecy that Teiresias now offers. Lines 458–59c correspond too plainly and exactly to the prophecy of Apollo reported by Oedipus himself at 792–94a, where he makes no connection between Teiresias' prediction and the oracle's terrifying answer (even then it is only the murder that seems to him a possibility). If, furthermore, we are to view Oedipus as leaving this scene only after 461, defeated by the overwhelming authority of the seer's unambiguous message, then we must explain why this "loser" (Bain, *Actors and Audience*, p. 74) is able to return so aggressively in the next scene and why he can ignore so long this "defeat." But the subsequent scenes show no trace of a defeated Oedipus, no indication of doubt induced by this passage. And an offstage psychological recovery after a scene of great psychological subtlety is more difficult to explain than an exit beginning at 447 that lacks a certain textual marker or than the more subjective complaint that to leave Teiresias alone, addressing an absent king, is "grotesque" (Ibid., p. 74) and leaves Teiresias looking the "old fool" (Friis Johansen, "Sophocles," p. 231). Whether or not Teiresias hears Oedipus depart (as Knox argues), his prophecy triumphantly fulfills all the audience's expectations: the ironies earlier in the play depend upon their knowledge of the story and content of the oracle, even though the play has not yet introduced this content; now they see Oedipus disdainfully exit at the very moment that Teiresias realizes the claims made for him by the chorus (284–87) and acknowledged by Oedipus (300–315). His truth (299, 356, 369b) is victorious, or will be, as the audience now knows with certainty, but Oedipus, angered and baffled by his earlier enigmas, as yet knows nothing of this victory. For a full exposition of this argument see Knox, "Sophocles, *Oedipus Tyrannos* 446"; Bain, *Actors and Audiences,* pp. 73–75; Taplin, *Greek Tragedy in Action,* pp. 43–44. For another speech to a departing character see the note *Ant* 324–31.

An untranslated phrase ("I am going," 448) announces Teiresias' intention. **I have said** = "when I have said" (anticipating the following prophecy). Because of the masks, references to the way a character looks are seldom purely descriptive; because Teiresias is blind, how Oedipus looks (**countenance**) is a matter of inference.

452 Stranger: cf. Oedipus at 219a–20. **In name** = "in report," i.e., as is commonly thought; the antithesis is one of word (appearance) and deed (fact): cf. 72, 885.

459b For **a fellow sower** see on 260.

460–61 Teiresias returns to the second person. **Reckon that out** may seem empty if Oedipus is not on stage, and Knox (see on 447) suggests that he hears the king departing and throws this final taunt at him as the door closes; he offers *El* 1322–23 and *Ion* 515–16 as evidence that the stage doors made an audible sound. The last word is the same as that ending 404a (*phronein:* "have no understanding in prophecy").

462–512 Two pairs of stanzas, formed from different rhymthic bases, comprise the first stasimon. In the first pair the lyric meditates on the fugitive condemned by Apollo's oracle; in the second pair the quarrel between Oedipus and Teiresias is assessed, with the chorus unable to accept the prophet's charges. Thus the dramatic issue is approached obliquely, as the paramount issue of Teiresias' truth is postponed to the second half of the lyric. Cf. *Medea* 824–65, where the first two stanzas praise Athens. Then the second pair, turning to the dramatic issue, asks how that city can accept the murderess Medea.

462–73 Lyrics often begin with questions: *OK* 151, *Aj* 1186, *El* 1058 (though not in this translation), *Agamemnon* 681, 975. **Rock:** Delphi, the site of Apollo's oracle, is two thousand feet above sea level and below the peaks of Parnassus (474). **Doer of deeds:** this line, like "lonely, and lonely" (479a), translates the same word repeated immediately in a different grammatical case (*arrêt' arrêtôn*); see the note to *Tr* 193–99. **With a stronger foot than Pegasus:** the famous winged horse is not mentioned; more literally, "stronger than storm-swift horses." "Storm-swift" belongs to the poetic tradition, as in Simonides' "Hail, daughters of storm-footed horse" (of mules!). Apollo, **the child of Zeus,** has borrowed his father's weapons. With **leaps** cf. 1301, 1312. **Fates** are the Keres, death spirits (see on *Agamemnon* 206), often identified with the Furies.

474–82 With **voice** cf. the same word at 157. The "bull in the forest" was apparently proverbial for a difficult catch. The participle translated **lonely** would normally mean "to be without/to lack," and suggests a widower. The **navel of the earth** (*omphalos*) was a round stone displayed at Delphi; see the note to *Eumenides* 39ff. The fugitive tries to flee the prophecies that fly (**flutter**) about like spirits of curses and vengeance (see the end of first strophe).

483–95 They have understood Teiresias' charge, but seeing no grounds for it (**quarrel**), they will not attack Oedipus. After **foreboding** add the explanatory "neither seeing (clearly) in the present nor into the future," which has been omitted. **Labdacus:** see on 69; **Polybus** is the king of Corinth and supposed father of Oedipus (774b). They want a motive and evidence. In **bring as proof** we have the common metaphor from a touchstone, and this word and idea are repeated below at 510 (in "test"): the translation has preferred the legal connotations (the word is used of "inquiry by torture," such as the shepherd undergoes at 1154c). **Attacking:** the military metaphor is continued in the words translated **take vengeance for:** "an ally assisting the line of Labdacus because of the undiscovered death." **Undiscovered** = "unknown" (476); the word connotes obscurity and mystery.

496–512 All is interpretative; the sentiment is pious but Greek myths are not about all-knowing gods. The antithesis between divine and human knowledge is common, as is the notion that while the divinity may be infallible, his agent, whether an auger like Teiresias or the manager of an oracle, may garble the divine message. For skepticism in this play see 707–25, 846–57 and 964–73. **May pass another:** this may contain a metaphor from racing and possibly continues a metaphor from contests in the preceding sentence: "but among men there is no true judgment to tell whether the prophet or I shall carry off the prize." **Wisdom** (*sophia*) occurs twice in the Greek; cf. 510. **Right beyond doubt:** "a word (report) proved straight." **Sphinx** translates "the winged girl."

If we accept the view (see Hester's discussion, "Very Much the Safest Plan") that the chorus represents an "ideal spectator" that directs our thought and attention as Sophocles intended, then obviously we should not think the previous scene has displayed a protagonist of only average intellect or one who has wrongly and abusively dismissed patently good information. The chorus wants hard evidence before it believes Teiresias' charges; meantime it will stick by the proven intelligence of the king. Yet the chorus is clearly not "ideal" in the sense that it knows and understands the deeper levels of word and action, nor does it foresee the truth that will appear; we understand from its perception the plausibility of Oedipus' response, but we also know, for all that, the fundamental truth of Teiresias' prophecy.

513 In this scene the ground shifts a little from the murderer of Laius to the alleged plot of Creon and Teiresias. Creon has already heard the accusation and enters protesting his innocence. Oedipus has not forgotten Laius (534a), but in accusing the two of conspiracy he has opened a new proceeding ("highway robbery of my crown" 535) which becomes at least as much the issue for this scene as the murder of Laius. From a legal point of view, the charge of conspiracy, which attacks the state as well as its ruler, is distinct from a charge of murder, but dramatically one charge is laid on top of the other. Thus Oedipus' investigation is deflected still more from Laius toward his own standing, but for the time being that standing is defined as political (the king is threatened by a plot) and not yet as personal.

514 **Deadly** is strong for *deinos*, which, like our "terrible" (cf. 1298), degenerated to a cliché of tragic diction; see the note to 545 and Guthrie, *History of Greek Philosophy*, vol. 3, p. 32.

522–23 **Traitor** (*kakos*) translates another maid of all work; see on 76–79, 1271–74a, and 1396–98. "Base" is too old-fashioned in English, but that is the idea. The same word appears in "guilty" at 548, in "a criminal" (552, from the Greek adverb), and in "false" at 582. See the note to 545. This word appears to be roughly twice as frequent in Sophocles as in Aeschylus.

524–24a There is no **sudden gust** here, only a tactful **anger**.

530–31 The chorus will not be drawn into the action: cf. *Ant* 211–20, 471–72, and even *Tr* 588–89. Sophoclean choruses are usually sympathetic with the protagonist, but pragmatism and caution are also common attributes.

533 For the motif **daring** see the note to *Tr* 582–84.

545 Oedipus' antithesis is actually between "clever" (*deinos;* for this sense see *OC* 860) Creon and **slow** (*kakos:* see on 522–23) Oedipus; with ironic understatement he belittles his wit.

549–51 **Obstinacy** = "stubbornness" at *Ant* 1027. See the note to *Prometheus Bound* 447 and Knox, *Heroic Temper*, pp. 19–21.

555 Jebb translates the word for **mumbler** as "reverend seer"; it appears from similar expressions in Euripides (*Hippolytus* 490: "high moralizing") that pompous solemnity is the target.

560 Oedipus is not stuttering: "has vanished and gone by mortal violence." Kamerbeek compares *Aj* 1033. The sentence is weighty, emphatic, periphrastic.

562–63 Profession: as at 357. Creon responds that he was similarly *sophos* ("wise" at 568; cf. 503 and 510).

568 Say this then, i.e., "make these (charges) against me." It is not clear how much of the interview between Teiresias and Oedipus Creon is assumed to know, but 525–26 and 573–75 imply some particulars.

574–77 Kamerbeek seems right to find a certain evasiveness in Creon's answer; even though we know he is innocent, Oedipus does not. **Proved:** see on 108–13.

578 At 583–615 Creon reasons that the charges brought against him are implausible. In these last seven verses of dialogue his interrogation lays the ground for that analysis. To judge from Creon's argument, Oedipus has hardly ruled as a paranoid autocrat.

583–615 Oedipus has charged that wealth, power, and skill have incited envy (380–82); Creon responds that he already has the benefits of power without its responsibilities, without its burdens and insecurity. Arguments from probability were of special interest to the rhetoricians and speech writers of the second half of the fifth century, who left their mark on drama. Hippolytus' defense of himself against the charges of his father, Theseus, (*Hippolytus* 1002–35) offers a number of parallels to the present speech: both men argue that the crime is out of character; both argue that second place in the kingdom is superior to the uneasy nature of power; both take the oath that they are innocent (see below 644–46). Other arguments from probability will be found at *Hecuba* 1199–1232 and *Iphigenia in Tauris* 677–86. The topic "the burden of rule" was also a commonplace: see Herodotus 5.106 ("I have all I want, so what motive could there be for treachery? Is not what is yours, mine? And have I not the honour of sharing all your counsels?"), Euripides, *Ion* 621–32, *Iphigenia in Aulis* 446–50.

589 What kings do is the exercise of power.

590 Fear is the reading of all manuscripts, but we should perhaps accept, with Dawe, Blaydes' emendation "envy" (*phthonos* for *phobos*), which is much more germane to this context. On the topic of the tyrant's envy see Herodotus 3.80. Oedipus himself has already noticed how envy leads to conspiracy (380–89a; note to 380–82).

592 Against the grain means unwillingly, according to the dictates of office rather than those of character.

593 Since there is little evidence in the play that we should view Oedipus as a despot in our sense of the word, **despotic rule** (*tyrannis*) should not be taken to imply abusive power.

596 Every man's my pleasure: the Greek phrase seems to mean "I am at ease with everyone."

600 This sententious line is not so clear in the Greek as in the English version; Blaydes excised the line, and it seems a likely interpolation from a marginal gloss that has itself displaced some more particular referent for **treason** and **plot** (so Dawe).

611–15 Moralizing on the nature of friendship pervades Greek tragedy; for the mutability of friendship see *Aj* 675–82, Euripides, *Heracles* 55–59, and especially *OC* 611–24, where the test of time is elaborated. See 1213.

616–17 Not safe echoes "with certainty" (614). Since the word has the root meaning "not stumbling" (whence the common sense "safe/ secure"), we may be tempted to see an allusive reference to the maimed feet of Oedipus (so Gould). **Fall,** then, anticipates "not stumbling."

623 Perhaps the missing lines are 625 and 627:

Oedipus: No, certainly; kill you, not banish you. 623
Creon: When you will show the quality of your grudge
      (envy). 624
Oedipus: 625
Creon: You talk like a man who will neither yield nor trust.
Oedipus: . . . .
Creon: I do not think that you've your wits about you.

Both men have used arguments from envy (624). Creon's version, i.e., the tyrant's suspicious malice, is more recently before us. Yielding is usually difficult for the protagonist, not for the secondary character (see 651 and 673).

626–29 The four lines in the Greek are in *antilabe* (a line divided between two or more speakers). Interrupted sentence, abuse, and exclamation reflect their anger.

629b I must be ruler: the verb is passive and is better taken simply to mean "there must be obedience," i.e., "obey." Creon's response is also impersonal: "not when one rules badly." Of course they are talking about themselves, about Oedipus and Creon as ruler and subject, but the stylistic tendency to abstraction, and so to a touch of the sententious, is fully Sophoclean. Also, there is enough ego in Oedipus without overshading it into mindless vanity. Insofar as he perceives Creon as a conspirator against himself, he is also a conspirator against the state. That Oedipus is wrong to suspect plots does not mean he has no reason to suspect them.

629d O, city, city: if this exclamation is parodied at *Acharnians* 27, which seems a thin reed, then our play can be dated before 425 B.C.

634 Jocasta is known to Homer as Epicaste (*Odyssey* 11.271–80, where her suicide by hanging is reported). She will also have been known to the audience from the epic poems about Thebes and from Aeschylus' trilogy (see the preface to *Seven against Thebes*).

643 Tricks (*technê*) was earlier "skill" and "profession" (see on 357 and 442); he intends to link Creon and Teiresias.

644–46 His exclamation is in effect an oath of innocence, as Jocasta recognizes (648). Primitive legal proceedings as well as Attic law accepted the oath of the accused as evidence of innocence (cf. Hippolytus' oath at *Hippolytus* 1025–31).

649–96 This section of lyric verse is called a *kommos* in most texts, though that word is sometimes reserved for lyric lament (see the note to *Libation Bearers* 306–475). A sung strophe (649–67) is answered responsively by an antistrophe (679–96), with nine lines of iambic trimeter intervening (669–77). A second kommos occurs at 1313–68.

653 Spare him, i.e., have regard for the sanctity of his oath. For the idea (*aidôs*) see on OC 1268.

656–57 Before all men's eyes seems to be a misreading (*enargê* for *enagê?*). Chantraine and Masson (p. 89) interpret: "this kinsman who has placed himself under the power of divine punishment; do not insult this man by accusing him on a mere suspicion." If Creon foreswears himself, he runs the risk of divine retribution.

658–59 His thinking is natural if not strictly logical: if Creon and Teiresias are not guilty of conspiracy, as you would have me believe, then I must answer to Teiresias' charges (362) and suffer my own curse (**death or banishment;** cf. 669–70) on the culprit.

660 Invoking the **Sun** is common in oaths (see the exclamation at 1184 and the note to 1425–28). For **without God's blessing** see on 254. The exile is beyond the pale of god and man, and this is the condition invoked in the oath.

672–75 Since Oedipus' last word is **hate** and Creon's first word is a cognate adjective (here **sulk**), we may catch the linking wordplay with "him I shall hate." "Hateful you'll clearly be, though you yield." **Out of temper:** the Greek has been interpreted to mean (1) that he has passed through his anger but still remains dangerous, and (2) that he has advanced far into anger. Prefer the first meaning and note that Creon only sees him yielding from the threatening language and gesture of anger, not from its substance. Cf. the comment at *Ant* 471–72.

686 Straight of judgment means "well disposed," "with good intentions."

691–95 Steered = "carried with a fair wind." **Crazed** mixes the metaphor and has medical overtones (the same verb is "bewildered and distraught" at *Phil* 174). **God grant that:** interpretative, but the line is corrupt; some sort of tempered wish ("may you, if possible . . .") seems right.

701 **Them** is the chorus, who, though they protest their confidence in Oedipus, are far from condemning Creon (681, 685).

704a Dawe notices the dramatic importance of Jocasta's question, which seemingly takes the charge seriously so that the direction of the inquiry may move toward oracles.

707–25 For Oedipus' own skepticism about prophecy see 387–90. Like Jocasta, Orestes makes a distinction between divine knowledge and human agency,

> Apollo's oracles
> are strong, though human prophecy is best ignored.
>   (Euripides *Electra* 399–400)

Euripides makes Teiresias grumble bitterly about his trade and the fact that people only like what they want to hear (*Phoenician Women* 954–59). Despite the implicit choral censure (see 863–71), Jocasta is not to be held terribly impious for these views. Her example, the supposedly unfulfilled oracle to Laius (713–15), is intended to discredit, a fortiori, the mortal seer Teiresias. What she accomplishes, however, is to remind him of the time he met Laius.

708 **Learn,** as Jebb translates, "for thy comfort": Jocasta makes a special point of reassuring Oedipus.

712–14a Apollo's **servants** are the priests who tend the oracle and interpret the utterances of the possessed priestess through whom he speaks. Both Aeschylus (*Seven against Thebes,* 742–50) and Euripides (*Phoenician Women,* 17–20) make the oracle an interdiction forbidding Laius a child on pain of his own death. This version is probably derived from the epic *Thebais.* Sophocles, however, omits any condition of celibacy: the oracle simply notifies Laius of his **fate** (*moira*).

716 **Where three roads meet** catches his ear (her exact phrasing is repeated by Oedipus at 730 but is there translated "at the crossroads"). The traveler and antiquarian Pausanias visited this spot: "Further along the road you come to the SPLIT as they call it; on this road Oedipus murdered his father . . . the memorial of Laios and his servant is on the midmost of three roads, under a mound of uncut stones" (10.5.2).

717–20 Exposure of infants is one of the stock motifs in the stories of ancient heroes (e.g., Moses, Romulus and Remus, Cyrus, and, in Greek myth, Perseus and Telephus). "There can be little doubt that the exposure of surplus children was practised throughout antiquity" (Lacey, *The Family in Classical Greece,* p. 164) and just as little doubt that no family, much less a royal one, would expose its first and only male heir unless extraordinary circumstances compelled it. **Pierced his ankles:** they were pinned and tied together to lessen still further the chances of survival. See on 1034. This vile work was entrusted to the hands of others to avoid the guilt of killing one's own kin and, no doubt, from more personal scruples. The **pathless hillside** belongs to Mt. Cithaeron (1026).

720–24 Failed and **false** should not be taken to indicate any blasphemy on Jocasta's part. We may also translate, "Apollo did not bring it about that the son should be the murderer of his father, nor that Laius should die by his child's hand, the terrible thing that he feared."

724b–25 Here too **and false** is only implicit. **Discovers** suggests a metaphor from hunting or tracking (cf. "search" at 566). She means that if the gods want to reveal a truth, they can easily do so (without prophets). As Archilochus says:

Among the gods Zeus is a faultless seer
and himself holds the end.

(frag. 84)

She would dismiss oracles as fallible, but the audience will grasp a connection between the plague and the god's command to search out the murderer. **Shows** (*phan-*) is the last word while "I'll show" (710) begins her example.

726–28 I could run mad translates a noun phrase coordinated with **a wandering of the soul:** if we maintain the parallelism, it may be "and a swinging of the mind." The personification (these abstractions "hold" him) suggests distraction and agitation, and she responds by noticing his anxiety (= **trouble**).

734 Daulia is a town in Phocis, east of Delphi and north of the crossroads. See the note to 716.

744 O God translates the conventional "woe is me" (see on *Phil* 426–28).

753–55 See Oedipus' narrative at 803. A cry of grief (*aiai*) precedes **plain** (*phan-*). He immediately fears the worst.

756 This is the **servant** mentioned by Creon (118) who reported that robbers (123–24a) attacked the party.

758–63 Creon's account (118–24a) does not say that the survivor **saw you king,** and if the story were historical and factual, it would have been improbable that Oedipus had already attained the throne prior to the slave's return. As Sheppard observes, the inconsistency is unimportant; Jocasta "now realizes that the man may have had good reason for his request." We hear "fear in her voice" as she speaks 761; and subsequently "she pretends that she has seen nothing sinister." Yet there is nothing explicit in the text to mark this fear, and the questions that follow (766, 769a–70; cf. 837) seem more innocent than dissimulating.

767–70 O dear Jocasta, as at 726 and "Jocasta" at 800, translates a single word meaning "wife." The same word is untranslated in line 755. **Oedipus** = "lord" (untranslated at 746). In short, the Greek words are more generic and formal; see on 771. **That I have spoken far too much:** he refers to the curse on the murderer, which is irrevocable (cf. 815–22); as yet he has no idea, of course, that Laius was his father, much less that Jocasta is his mother.

771 Jocasta knows his origin in Corinth, but Oedipus has never told his wife the secret fear that inspired his flight. Hence this speech, while largely a narrative of past events until line 813, reveals both to her and the audience circumstances of a·personal nature, and Dawe rightly notes a more intimate tone in these first lines (see also 800) than one often finds in Greek tragedy.

774a Fortune (*tychê:* see on 52 and 1080–86) = "chance" at 777.

774b–75 Polybus was probably the name of Oedipus' foster-father according to the tradition; Merope's name is less certain. **Dorian** denotes one of the three branches of the Greeks and is particularly associated with those in the Peloponnesus.

776 He was **greatest of the citizens** because he was heir apparent (940).

783 For Euripides' version see *Phoenician Women* 28–35.

789–90 Oedipus asked Apollo "who are my parents?" He is **unhonoured** because he is denied the respect that an answer to his request would signify. **Foretold** (the *phan-* stem) = "makes clear" (*Tr* 849a), a customary word for oracular pronouncements.

792 Incest is not an uncommon motif in Greek stories. Sophocles wrote a tragedy *Thyestes* that may have led to a recognition between Thyestes and Aegisthus, his son by his daughter Pelopeia.

793–94 Campbell notices a slight syntactical ambiguity that also makes it possible to take the sentence to mean "to show an accursed breed which men could not endure to see" ("to see" is in our version **to daylight**). The ambiguity plays on whether Oedipus or "men" will see these children and obliquely anticipates his blinding (he will not see his children when their true nature is finally revealed).

794b Although the oracle is absolute and predictive, not conditional, Oedipus flees, hoping, and thus thinking it possible, that he may yet escape his fate. With similar ambivalence toward fate Laius has attempted to kill the son destined to kill him.

795 Measure from the stars may have already been a proverb for keeping a certain place as distant as possible from oneself. Cf. "I plot my course under the stars" (Aeschylus, *Suppliant Maidens* 383). As Jebb notes, the language is natural to a sailor who has no bearings but the stars. Incredibly enough, Euripides has Oedipus return to Corinth after receiving the oracle (*Phoenician Women* 44–44a).

806 In his several pleas in the *Oedipus at Colonus*, which was written perhaps twenty years or more after *Oedipus the King*, the old Oedipus argues more strongly the involuntary and ignorant nature of his crime (see on 265–74) than self-defense (*OC* 271). That he was attacked by force and so acted in self-defense would have, if proven, secured his acquittal in an Athenian court. His temper (**angry:** see on 335–37 and *OC* 592) is emphasized in both plays.

809a The **goad** was used for driving the team. The driver (= **coachman**) had apparently gotten out of the wagon, leaving his goad for the old man to use as a weapon.

810 **In full** (*isos*) is another example of Oedipus the accountant (see on 32); cf. 842–45.

813–14 **Any tie of kinship** allusively avoids identifying Laius as the stranger (= **this man**), while his indirection resonates, for the audience, with questions of his own status (219–20) and kinship with Laius (259–64).

816 **Hated by the gods** = "has a more hostile *daimôn*"; he returns to this idea at 829. The compound adjective translated by this phrase, although it occurs only here, is based on a common type: cf. "unlucky" ("with an evil *daimôn*") at *Hippolytus* 1362.

817–20 He is thinking of his own public explusion of the killer (236–43). With **cursed myself** cf. 250–51.

821–23 The irony of **pollute the bed** derives from his ignorance of his incestuous pollution. **Evil** (*kakos*): see 522–23. **Unclean** is truer and stronger than he knows, for as yet it is only the fear of his own curse and the fact that Laius was king before him that is in view; elsewhere in tragedy it is used of murder in the family.

828 **Rightly judge** picks up the motif of "setting it straight" (*orthos:* note at 419a–b): "would not someone set the story straight when he judged. . . ."

830–33 **Holy** means "pure," the contrary of "unclean" (823). For **God on high** read "gods." He has already seen that day, but he will not see it out. **Out of men's sight** was "vanished" at 560 (the *phan-* stem). **Taint** is "stain" at *OC* 1133; see also *OK* 1384.

840 **Guilt** translates a Greek word (*pathos*) more neutral than its English renderings: the basic notion is "what is experienced or suffered" (so "suffering" at *Ant* 1315 and "sorrows" at *OK* 1330), and it usually denotes misfortune: so it is euphemistic at 732 ("where he was murdered") and fairly weak, given the scene, at *OK* 1298 ("a terrible sight"). Here,

as Jebb notes, it is a euphemism ("trouble"; "calamity" may be too strong) to cover his fear that he murderd Laius.

842–46 Robbers: in fact Creon used the plural at 107 in speaking of the oracle and again at 123 ("robbers") in reporting the rumor; Oedipus refers to Jocasta's "robbers" (715). Sophocles has woven this thread into the plot casually so that we are not likely, till now, to notice the significance of the count; Oedipus himself has used both singular and plural (e.g., 124b and 309), while preferring the singular. **The same as many:** = "equal to many," with an equivocal sense like the English "add up to" and "be the same as." **Guilt** (cf. 840) is here "work" or "business" (*ergon* was "deed" at 348); he shrinks from naming it. **Inclines** touches on a common metaphor from weighing in scales; at 961 the messenger says "a small weight will put old bodies asleep."

847 The entire passage is in iambic trimeters, despite the English prose. **How he told** is, more literally, "how it appeared" (the *phan*-stem); her insistence on appearances implies, for the first time, some anxiety. For **prove** see on 458. **Squares** (*ortho*- stem) suggests "he will never prove rightly that the murder of Laius falls in line with the prophecy." Even if, as she nervously doubts, the slave recants, the prophecy touching him is impugned by the fact that the prophecy concerning Laius was incorrect. The play, then, from this angle is about setting these stories straight and squaring up the accounts. **Loxias** (Apollo) is a cult epithet, common in poetry, and perhaps means "riddler," i.e., "he who speaks indirectly."

863–910 This celebrated lyric, the second stasimon, is also one of the most controversial and problematic choral songs in Sophocles. Modern criticism has divided over whether it refers to Oedipus or to Jocasta or to Oedipus and Jocasta or to someone or something outside the drama (Pericles and Athens have been offered in this last category but will not be given a hearing in these notes). Does the stasimon look back to reflect on recent events onstage, or is it more an anticipation of later developments? Does the chorus still support the king, or has it begun to condemn him? On another plane, is this the voice of a definable character in the play or the voice of Sophocles himself, or do we find here an example of A. W. Schlegel's "ideal spectator"? The reader will see how criticism has found so many responses. The problem is not so much ambiguity in word or phrase as a generality of reference, the assimilation of several conventional topics, and a tone more meditative than personal. At the same time, theme and metaphor constantly echo earlier language in this play so that the auditor is encouraged to transfer metaphor from its immediate environment to the characters of the play. To take but one example, while the first strophe (863–71) praises "laws that live on high," the personifying metaphors ("begotten," "father," "nature," "brought to birth") urge our attention to questions touching on the birth of Oedipus and the relation of Laius to his child (and the former topic has so far only been adumbrated, even if every spectator must know the direction the action will now take). Such language is quite natural to Greek choral lyric, but here, linked to "high-footed" and "forgetfulness," it takes on a peculiar local suggestiveness (e.g., how does Oedipus stand with this immutable law?) that develops a thematic counterpoint to the primary theme of the stanza. In its immediate dramatic context the ode is placed between Jocasta's skepticism about the Apolline oracle and her sacrifice and prayer to the same god (911–23). Some critics seem to me inclined to exaggerate the "blasphemy" of the former speech, yet there can be little doubt that the second pair of stanzas (883–910), and especially the last, bear more and more on the topics of right conduct toward the gods and the veracity of oracles. Perhaps these ties give more forward thrust than reflective summation to the lyric's dramatic value. For example, it is hard to describe Oedipus as a "tyrant" (872), if we judge only his actions to this point, and still harder to call him "hybristic" (see on "insolence," line 872), so it may seem the lyric raises, rather than answers, questions about the king's behavior. Since he has left the stage dejected (cf. 914–18) and evidently still determined to search out the murderer, even though he fears he may have cursed himself, the lyric offers an ominous, and to some extent unfounded, anticipation of events to come.

863–71 In trying to reassure Oedipus, Jocasta has slurred Apollo's oracle. Apparently taken aback by this impiety, the chorus prays that it may ever be **pious** (= "lead a life of holy purity"; see on 830–33). **Destiny** (*moira*) is personified, as are the laws, which are usually taken to be the same as the "unwritten laws" of Antigone's eloquent defense (*Ant* 450–70; on this topic see chapter 2 of Ehrenberg's *Sophocles and Pericles*). **That live on high** translates a compound adjective of a type much favored by the Greek poets: Homer's "Zeus who sits on high" (*Iliad* 4.166), Hesiod's "high-minded Zeus" (*Theogony* 529), and Pindar's "high-throned Nereids" (*Nemean* 4.65) are typical. The present compound appears only here in extant Greek and may have been coined by Sophocles; it is, more literally, "high-footed," i.e., "that walk on high"; cf. "feet" at 878. Dawe, rejecting any thematic connection between the two, observes that "The foot metaphor is so common in tragedy that at *Phil* 1260 Sophocles can even write 'perhaps you may keep your foot clear of tears.' " Despite the idiomatic frequency of feet in Greek poetry, I cannot think that Sophocles has planted so many feet casually; see the note to 418–19. **Olympus** is the mountain, the home of the gods, then, as here, the height of the heavens; cf. *OC* 1654 (note). Periphrastic phrases like

the "nature (i.e., physique) of Laius" (740), as well as more easily translated usage (cf. 674), ring variations on the relevant dramatic sense of
nature as "origin" and "birth"; cf. 1080–86. The contrast between **mortal**
and immortal is the most fundamental Greek distinction between the
human and the divine. **Forgetfulness** is personified by Hesiod (*Theogony*
227) and is traditionally associated with Sleep, the brother of Death (*Iliad*
14.231; *Odyssey* 13.80). The Greek is *Lêthê,* which has come into English
as a place and river in the underworld. **God** (871) seems here to mean "a
divine element." Sheppard cites Heraclitus (frag. 253 Kirk and Raven):
"For all the laws of men are nourished by one law, the divine law; for it
has as much power as it wishes and is sufficient for all and is still left
over."

872–82 **Insolence** is *hybris,* which is frequently linked, either as
parent or child, with **surfeit** (see the notes to *Agamemnon* 751ff. and
763–71). What has either idea to do with Oedipus? or anyone else in
the play? Some commentators point to Oedipus' treatment of Creon as
hybristic, which is too far removed from this lyric for much dramatic
coherence; others point to the arrogant manner of the king and suggest
the chorus fears for what he may become; yet he has just departed,
threatened and dejected. In any case *hybris* is not so often, even in the
fifth century, applied to a state of mind but is usually the violent and
abusive treatment of another person. Again, **tyrant** (*tyrannos*) is the regular word in Greek tragedy for "king"; its pejorative sense here hardly fits
its use elsewhere in the play ("king" or "rule"): 514, 542, 589, 593
("despotic rule" in the translation is not required), 1094a ("our king" in
a lyric is clearly sympathetic). Finally, if we are to take this sentiment of
Oedipus—and what other *tyrannos* would the audience think of?—we
would expect "tyranny breeds insolence" (Blaydes), not the converse.
Cf. Solon's "For tyranny is the mother of injustice" (frag. 8) but also
Eumenides 533–34: "for the very child of impiety is violence (*hybris*)."
Our chorus, having prayed for a pure life sanctified by divine law, turns
in the antistrophe to the contrasting life of *hybris.* Such a contrast is more
natural and logical to the Greek, for whom religion is primarily a matter
of dealing successfully with divine power. Purity (first strophe) is a life
blameless in the sight of god (man has not violated any rules imposed by
divinity); *hybris* is wanton violence in word or deed (see 883–93 for a
variation) and as such arrogates power in an unnatural degree to a mortal.
The gods, always jealous of their power, are quick to strike the man who
acts like a god, i.e., who acts as he will, without regard for limits, divine
or human. Greek moral piety is thus derived from a cosmology that makes
power the central category and that has given supreme, but not absolute,
power to a very human set of divinities. To make a difficult choice, I

would prefer our translation's version over Blaydes' emendation. Since it is dramatically impossible that the chorus should accuse the king of *hybris* (throughout the play the chorus is sympathetic: see 1216–23, when the worst has been revealed), we must suppose that while these lines suggest an oblique or unconscious reference to Oedipus, the lyric does not accuse the king but rather reveals the chorus's anxiety that oracles may indeed prove vain, that god is not in them, and that all piety is meaningless. The first strophe affirms their own trust and piety (where will Thebes be if Jocasta's doubts are extended to Apollo's most recent pronouncement?), but the facts (Laius apparently did not die at his son's hand; they do not want to believe Oedipus is fated for incest and parricide) breed doubt which is now expressed in conventional skepticism about human prosperity leading to ruin. After the usual manner, *hybris* is personified and in a mixture of metaphors likened to someone so **glutted** by overindulgence that seasonable and profitable action are impractical; in a frenzy he rushes to a height. Though the passage does not actually describe a fall (**down**), it is implicit in **climbs to the roof-top** and in **sheer**. Cf. the similar metaphor at *Libation Bearers* 933–34: "Since Orestes reached the top of much blood, this we choose, that the eye of the house shall not utterly fall in ruin" (my trans.). **Ruin that must be** is "necessity" (*anagkê*), apparently a shorthand for "compelling fortune" (*Aj* 486), a restraint that denies man choice and leaves him precariously teetering (**there its feet are no service**). This mad, infatuated and self-destructive activity is then (at 880) contrasted with "good wrestling" (= **eager ambition**) that serves the state: even if **feet** alludes to the king, yet his past service has won a fall against the Sphinx, and he is still its best hope to purge the present pollution. **Protector** = "defender" (Apollo: see *Tr* 209). Note the praise of god corresponding to that ending the first strophe (871).

883–96 The *hybris* theme continues in **haughtiness** (cf. *Ant* 123–33), which is defined by "fearless of Justice" (= **gives no heed to Justice**) and "not reverencing the shrines of the gods." **Doom** is *moira* ("destiny" in 863). **Ill-starred pride of heart** introduces another traditional word for the wantonness characteristic of forgetful *hybris* (see on *Prometheus Bound* 437). **If he reaps gains**: note the parallelism with the first clause of this stanza, which is repeated in a third conditional clause at 895 (**When such deeds** = "if such deeds"); it is difficult to attach this motif to Oedipus, but **untouchable things** has been taken as an allusion to Teiresias' charges of incest (?). **Itch** translates another topical word for whatever is rash or vain (see on *Tr* 587); in 875 an untranslated adverbial form of this stem ("rashly") modifies "glutted." **Shafts of the God** is an emendation that refers to the punishment by arrows (of lightning bolts, as at *Ant* 131). Otherwise the corrupt text may refer to "shafts that pierce the heart";

but the text remains uncertain. As dramatis personae they have no reason to dance, i.e., they refer to the present song and dance in the context of the tragic festival honoring Dionysus. This last clause seems a possible, and unexpectedly sudden, break of the dramatic illusion: the story enacted by the play, with its discredited oracles, would on this view question the reasons for staging the story. Jocasta's skepticism and Apollo's apparent failure to predict accurately raise more general doubts about the value of religious observance. Though **honour the Gods** is the translation's free interpretation, it seems the obvious sense. Possibly, however, we should compare *El* 1069 and find no more than a natural reference to dance as a function of any religious celebration.

897–910 Still anxious, the chorus sees no reason to consult oracles if these are not verified. They appeal to Zeus to make his power and word manifest. Their piety has driven them, though they hardly seem aware of this, to pray for the fulfillment of prophecies that threaten Oedipus. For the **navel of the earth** (= Delphi) see 480. **Abae** in Phocis had an oracle of Apollo; **Olympia** in Elis had an oracle of Zeus. They speak only of the **oracles concerning Laius**, which Jocasta has doubted, but they have also heard of oracles to Oedipus. **For all men's hands to point at** = "manifest." **Sovereign lord** and **all-mastering** must be seen in the god's actions, for otherwise he is wrongly named god, wrongly invoked. Men will have no reason to perform religious service if Zeus is not capable of honoring his son Apollo. **Men regard them not** = "some [unspecified plural subject] are removing the fading oracles of Laius" (Dawe). The oracles Oedipus has reported concerning himself are ignored. **Clear** = "manifest" (the *phan-* stem).

911–23 After her disdain for oracles at 850–57, this appeal to Apollo the healer may strike us as contradictory. While the choral reaction clearly marks their repugnance at this dangerous impiety, most Greeks would have shared some skepticism about prophecy, if only because they realized that the human agency delivering them was liable to error and venality. The messenger toward the end of the *Antigone,* in different circumstances, can observe that "No prophecy can deal with men's affairs" (*Ant* 1160). Jocasta is more concerned for her husband than for oracles, which have cost her a child by Laius and are by all evidence invalid. Her sincerity distinguishes Jocasta, and the present tone of this speech, from the dramatically symmetrical scene at *El* 635 ff., where Clytemnestra has come out of the house to offer sacrifice to Apollo. Clytemnestra is purely self-interested, openly hostile to her son and daughter. In both scenes, however, the prayer for help is immediately answered by the appearance of a messenger who seemingly brings good news for the person offering the prayer; in both cases the good news is specious.

915–16 The Greek habit was to use both history and myth as paradigm, and **what will be from what was** was the way of history, philosophy, and poetry (see, e.g., Herodotus 2.33.2; Solon admonished man "to interpret the unseen from the seen"). Beneath her generalized concern (**a man; the speaker**) lies, apparently, a reference to the improbability of truth in Apollo's oracles, but of course she can have no argument against Oedipus' anxiety that he may have killed the old king. We should not be tempted to reconstruct an offstage conversation.

919a–21 **Lycaean:** an ambiguity in **escape free of the curse** (also = clear/conspicuous resolution") implies an etymology from "light"; cf. 205 and see *Agamemnon* 1257. **Who are nearest** refers to the (common) presence of cult statues outside houses. No sooner has she prayed for **escape** (also "resolution") than a man appears who will prove not only the stain of murder but also of parricide and incest.

925–26 Rhyme and punning on the name of Oedipus mark three successive end-lines in the Greek: *mathoim' hopou* (**Might I learn where**): *estin Oidipou* (is . . . **of Oedipus**): *ei katisth' hopou* (**if you know where**). Sophocles knows the etymology that makes Oedipus mean "Swellfoot" (see 1036), but the present passage puns on "learn" and "know" (*oida*). In the mouth of the messenger the punning is playful, "his first homely enquiry seemingly making sport of the similar sound in Greek of Oedipus' name and the word for 'where' " (Seale, p. 237).

Aristotle's comment (*Poetics,* chap. 11), though mistaken about the particulars, points to the essential dramatic irony of the scene: "Reversal (peripety) is, as aforesaid, a change from one state of affairs to its exact opposite, and this, too, as I say, should be in conformance with probability or necessity. For example, in *Oedipus,* the messenger comes to cheer Oedipus by relieving him of fear with regard to his mother, but by revealing his true identity, does just the opposite of this." Of course the messenger comes to tell of Polybus' death and Oedipus' imminent election as king (*tyrannos*) of Corinth, not to relieve him of fear with regard to his mother. But Aristotle's point is not affected since the messenger's intention is one thing, the effect just the opposite. Aristotle goes on in the same chapter to discuss recognition ("a change from ignorance to knowledge") and to prescribe as the best form "that which is accompanied by a reversal, as in the example from the *Oedipus.*"

943 **Oedipus' father** is a conjecture; the messenger is not, in any case, in a hurry to correct their misapprehension about Oedipus' parentage, as we see from 955–60. The manuscripts repeat Polybus' name, some adding "old"; our reading is likely but not certain.

945–48 Her address to the servant is the first evidence of the servant's presence. It seems probable that the queen is always attended by servants.

Excited, relieved, apparently vindicated, she does not hesitate to add **of the gods** (cf. 951–52); contrast the more cautious attitude of the messenger at *Ant* 1160, with its variation on the motif of chance. **Where are you now?**: a triumphant exclamation rather than a true question. **In the course of nature** (*tychê*): we can better bring out the motif of chance/fortune with "by some chance," though the course of nature is the case (960–63).

950 The apparent intimacy of **Dearest Jocasta** translates a common periphrasis, literally "dearest head of (my) wife Jocasta" (also at 1235); cf. the note to *Tr* 38–39.

959 Gone down to death is very like our "dead and gone."

960 As at 34a, a commercial metaphor goes untranslated: "in the business of treachery or sickness?"

962 Poor old man (*tlêmôn*) is conventional tragic commiseration: in the lyric at 1195 it is "luckless," at 1300 "poor wretch"; the coryphaeus says the same of Oedipus at 1286 and Oedipus uses it of himself at 1332 (both untranslated).

964 Ha! Ha!: this cry more often represents grief or sympathy (as at 1303 and 1307) than triumph. Perhaps here the tone is wonder and surprise (Blaydes).

966 He mentions **birds screaming** because Teiresias usually gets his views from the birds (395–96).

969a–71 Dawe considers **died of longing for me** "a strained attempt at humor," while Kamerbeek points to *Odyssey* 11.202, where Odysseus' mother says,

> but, shining Odysseus, it was my longing for you, your cleverness
> and your gentle ways, that took the sweet spirit of life from me.
> (*Odyssey* 11.202–3)

Like Dawe, the translator seems to think the tone "triumphant," but that must be tempered by relief, as we see from **misled by my fear** (974), as well as his continuing fear of his mother's bed (976).

977 For **chance** (*tychê*) as **all in all** see *Ant* 1155 ("luck"), *Aj* 486 ("fortune"). Chance is frequently contrasted with planning (e.g., Thucydides 1.144, Herodotus 8.87), but since the Greeks speak of the "luck that comes from the gods" (Pindar *Olympian* 8.67) and coordinate luck and destiny (Archilochus frag. 8), we should probably not find terrible blasphemy here, although the irony is very heavy. Cf. 1080–82. Bowra (p. 208) cites Democritus (frag. 119): "Men have made an image of Luck as an excuse for their own lack of wisdom." But Jocasta is not making excuses, nor does she defy the gods, as Bowra has it, even if she is close to the wind. Certainly the more pious in the audience would find her skepticism dangerous.

979 She violates an injunction of Heraclitus (frag. 47): "we should not judge lightly concerning the greatest matters."

980–82 The Greek follows on less logically than the translation (as well as oracles is missing in the Greek), but this is apparently the sense. Cf. the dream of the aspiring tyrant Hippias (Herodotus 6.107.): "The previous night Hippias had dreamed that he was sleeping with his mother, and he supposed that the dream meant that he would return to Athens, recover his power, and die peacefully at home in old age." Plato (*Republic* 571c) also refers to incest with one's mother as a desire roused during sleep. Dreams were a common source for divination, and a chorus in Euripides tells us that Earth

> bred a band of dreams
> Which in the night should be oracular
> To men, foretelling truth.
> (*Iphigenia in Tauris* 1261–65)

985 The **must** is emphasized; his caution contrasts with the skepticism one might expect from his attitude at 964–72.

987 **Light of comfort** is literally "eye," which is widely used metaphorically for a person much prized and for anything hopeful. The best parallel seems to be *Libation Bearers* 934, which is none too good, since there the "eye" is a person (Orestes), here, literally, "funeral rites" (= death).

998–99 **Great happiness** offers a compound of the *tychê* stem, so also "successfully/fortunately." **Face** is literally "eyes"; cf. 1385.

1002 Note the repeated use of the same word for **fear** (974, 980, 988, 989, 991, 1013; a synonym appears in 986 and 1000). For **Why should I not free** prefer "And why did I not free. . ." (he thinks his news has freed Oedipus from fear).

1004–8 The messenger repeats the first phrase of Oedipus' line ("Well, surely . . .") with a note of familiar bantering. **Thanks:** he expects a gratuity for his trouble (see on *Tr* 191). **Son** = "child" (the plural is "children" at 58), a familiarity indicating the fellow's easy confidence (cf. 1014).

1011 **Right** translates a word that has been "clear" and "clearly": 106 (of the oracle), 390 (Oedipus doubts the clarity of Teiresias' vision; cf. 287), 846 (of Oedipus' learning; cf. 1066), 978 (Jocasta's skepticism about knowing), 1184 (Oedipus' discovery, a line very similar to 1011).

1012 The line contains a specific reference to pollution (*miasma*): "(you feared that) you might incur some pollution from your parents?"

1018–20 The messenger playfully makes a little riddle that takes us back to the computational motif: "not more than I but equal!" "How can my father be equal to one who is nothing?" "Neither he nor I begat you."

1024 Childlessness is also the problem of Aegeus, father of Theseus (*Medea* 669), of Xuthus, father of Ion (*Ion* 65–66), of Hermione, wife of Neoptolemus (*Andromache,* 33–34), of Acrisius, grandfather of Perseus (Apollodorus, 2.4.1; the motif also came up in Euripides' lost play, *Danaë*).

1026 Cithaeron's slopes range along the southern border of Boeotia toward the gulf of Corinth; see also 1090, 1127, 1135, and 1452. **Found** may seem a little misleading, or at least indirect, since at 1038 he will say that he got the baby from someone else. The intervening dialogue certifies that this messenger knows whereof he speaks.

1031–38 This interrogation, and particularly the tone of 1029, seems skeptical. **What ailed me:** if is he testing the messenger, he must remember the pain. Since **pain** translates *kakon* (see on 522–23), he could refer to a scar as well as "pain." Exactly what he suffered is not so clear as **pierced** (also "cutting"; cf. 718, where "pinned" or "yoked" is more accurate) may suggest; the single Greek adjective on which the issue turns is ambiguous. Euripides (*Phoenician Women,* 26–27) indicates the use of "sharp iron," but the play is later and the special form of pinning could be Euripides' invention. Cf. "bonds" at 1350. But we cannot avoid the connection of Oedipus' **name** ("Swellfoot"; cf. 1036) and this wound, whether it was from piercing or binding, and his **disgrace. Rare:** the manuscripts give us "terrible" (*deinon;* see on 514); Eustathius cites the line with "fair," which might be a bitter glance at a scar. If he refers to a mark from birth, that need not mean that he limps. The messenger sees the etymological connection between his name and this event: "So that you were named from this chance (*tychê*), who you are." Oedipus' response (1037) seems to ask whether he was named by his father or his mother, but this is a complete non sequitur, and the commentators argue that the **doing** refers to his mutilation, and that is the way the messenger takes it (1038). A groan (*oimoi*) precedes the question at 1033.

1039a He returns to the questioning of 1025, and both lines (**find** and "found") contain participles from the *tychê* stem (= "chanced on me"; the form in 1025 is, however, an emendation).

1047–51 The question is double: whether anyone knows the shepherd; whether he lives in town or in the fields. How opportune the moment is can be seen from the coincidence noted by the coryphaeus at 1052–54.

1052–54 Oedipus has sent for this **peasant** at 860. Had Aristotle (*Poetics,* chap. 25) made a list of improbabilities, he might well have included the unlikely chance that the sole surviving witness to Laius' death happens also to be the very man who gave the infant Oedipus to a

Corinthian shepherd, who also just happens to be the present messenger. Sophocles sacrifices probability for dramatic economy.

1056–60 By now Jocasta understands, but she has no solid reason to offer against his search (= **hunt**).

1063–64a Thrice slave may be intended literally of a third generation, but more likely in both cases it is simply emphatic. Three, however, is one of those resonant numbers (cf. 162, 283, 716). **Lowly lineage** takes her for a social snob (as at 1070 and 1079).

1064 I entreat you may accompany a suppliant's bended knee. She is desperate, and such appeals are seldom persuasive: see *Aj* 369–69a (Tecmessa's plea), *Ant* 1230 (Creon to Haemon), *El* 427–29 (Chrysothemis to Electra).

1065–66 There is no reference to **chance** here, just a refusal to give up the inquiry. For **clearly** see on 1011.

1067 A secondary meaning of **wish you well** is "understand well," i.e., "with clear knowledge" (Campbell).

1068–69 Repetitions such as that in **best counsel** are common in Sophoclean stichomythia. Cf. 617–19 ("quick"), 344a–46 ("angry" echoes "temper"), 433–35 ("fool"), and 1076–77 ("break out").

1069b Most of the personal names in this translation do not reflect the Greek text. For example, there is no "Jocasta" at 1054a or 1063, nor does she address him by name here or at 1071. **God help you! God keep you** translates a single word that was "ill-starred" at 888: "wretched man, may you never know who you are!"

1071 O Oedipus, unhappy Oedipus: here a doubled cry of grief and an adjective meaning "miserable" or "unhappy" make the referent for **that is all I can call you.** This word (*dustênos*) was "poor creature" at 855 (Jocasta of her baby), occurs in another vocative at 1303 (= "Indeed I pity you"), and is used by Oedipus of himself at 1307 (untranslated there). Sheppard (on line 855) says *dustênos* "confirms the opinion that Jocasta really cared about the death of her child. This word will prove of great dramatic value." Yet the messenger also uses it of Jocasta (note at 1249a–51). This word strikes me as a good example of Greek tragedy's more impersonal idiom and the tendency to view suffering generically. See the notes to *Tr* 1143 and *Phil* 759–60.

This is Jocasta's final exit.

1076 What is **this silence?** Dawe draws an unfavorable comparison with the "genuinely silent Deianeira" (*Tr* 813) and the silent departure of Eurydice (*Ant* 1244–45), both of which exits are explicitly noticed by the chorus. Despite the vocative of 1071, she may address her last lines more to the audience than to Oedipus, more to the Oedipus she has known than to her discovered child and husband. Modern commentators (see

Bain, *Actors and Audiences*, p. 76) do not like asides, but that seems the most obvious way to save the sense of this passage.

1077 Break out occurs metaphorically both of storms and of festering wounds (cf. 1396–97).

1078 The primary sense of **ancestry** is "seed" and "semen," then "origin" and "begetting," as at 1247, where Jocasta is reported to have remembered the "old sowing," and 1405 (in "bred"). Oedipus thinks of a secondary sense such as the translation's, but the allusion to sexual begetting, and so in his case to incest, will attract the audience's attention. The imagery enters the play collaterally in the barren land (25–30), then attaches itself to Oedipus in his own curse on those who hide the murderer (269–72). Later Oedipus thinks of Teiresias as one who "joins with another in sowing/begetting" the plot against him (the sense of "complotter" at 348) and Teiresias counters this charge with "a fellow sower of his father's bed" (459b).

1079a High-flown pride is conventional language, often of the man whose ambitions exceed his mortal nature; Creon accuses both Antigone and Haemon of this vice (*Ant* 477 and 766).

1080–86 In this culmination of the luck theme, Oedipus calls himself **a child of Fortune** (*tychê*: 52, 80–82, 261–63, 945–48, and 977), forgetting, as he styles her beneficent, that she is proverbially fickle (e.g., Euripides *Heracles* 480 and 507–10). In making Fortune his **mother** and **the months** his **brothers**, he virtually equates Time and Fortune; and in noting his affinity with the changing lunar months he implicitly accepts cyclic change (which the translation makes more explicit by adding **now as . . . and now again as**). Fragments of an early fourth-century vase "bear the first representations known to us of the Attic months. They appear as young men clad in himatia [cloaks] and with the sickle of the month above their heads" (Simon, *Festivals of Attica*, p. 5); it is safe to infer that Sophocles' audience fifty years earlier was familiar with such personifications. **Prove . . . false** is in the Greek more ambiguous: "I shall never prove other (than I am) so as not to find my birth" (cf. 1066). While his emphasis is on his ascendancy, his figure recognizes the inevitability of alternation in fortune.

1087–1107 Oedipus remains on stage during this song, the third stasimon. The chorus, like the king, has taken heart and has seemingly forgotten the murder of Laius and the protests of Jocasta. By this time the action has taken a purely personal direction as Oedipus searches for his own origins, which, only seventy lines after this lyric, he will discover to his irrevocable pain. For such moments of deluded happiness immediately prior to the final reversal see the note to *Aj* 693–717.

1087–97 For the choral claim to be **a prophet** cf. *El* 472 and see the note at *Agamemnon* 104. **The sky** is Olympus (see on 867). Most commentators take **limitless** not of sky, but in the sense of "inexperienced," here negated and of **Cithaeron**: "you shall not fail to know from experience that Oedipus honors you." If **tomorrow's full moon** alludes to the Athenian festival known as Pandia, which followed immediately on the Great Dionysia and was held nocturnally at the full moon, then Sophocles has given us a second (see on "dance" at 883–96) extradramatic allusion in this play. **As native to him** personifies Cithaeron as Oedipus' "fellow-countryman." **Honoured in dancing** need not, in this context, be an extradramatic reference, but cf. 896. **King** = *tyrannos* (see the note to 872–82).

1098–1107 By comparison with the second stasimon (863ff.), the chorus's pious confidence is now restored. Oedipus will not only discover his birth but may prove the child of a god. They could hardly be more optimistic, or more selective, in what they have chosen to focus on. The questions ("who is the father?") are adapted from cult, where the worshippers ask how they should name the god. For **nymphs** see *Tr* 215. **Pan** (see on *Aj* 694) is a wild spirit and a father only casually. **Cyllene's king** is Hermes, whose mother, the nymph Maia, lived in a cave in Mt. Cyllene (in northeastern Arcadia), where she was discovered by Zeus (Homeric *Hymn to Hermes* 1–7). The **Bacchants' God** is Dionysus, patron of Thebes (see 208–11). **Helicon** is a mountain in Boeotia, famed for its association with the Muses.

1110 Never met him = "never had any dealings with him" (as at 1130). **Make a guess** also means "measure by a rule."

1115–20 The final interrogation begins with certification of the identity of the witness. Never mind that the messenger from Corinth has not seen the herdsman for twenty years and more. After the messenger's identification the dialogue proceeds with all three characters speaking in units of one or more complete lines until the antilabe of 1173–76.

1126 This man was originally summoned to report whether one or more robbers killed Laius (842–46); now the question of murder has yielded to that of identity raised in the preceding scene.

1133–40 Aristotle discusses various modes of recognition in chapter 16 of the *Poetics*. Reasoning and memory are preferred to marks, tokens, and manipulation by the poet. The repetition of **know . . . knows** may be playful, if less subtle than his first lines (925–26). Cf. Oedipus' play on "fault" (verb and noun from same stem) at 1149–49a.

1144 While some nervous evasiveness may be detected earlier, e.g., in "places near to it" (1127), the double question here definitely marks the herdsman's reluctance to follow the leader.

1152 Without meaning = "he labors in vain," which the shepherd knows is not true.

1153–55 Oedipus' threat is immediately recognized by the old slave as the prelude to torture (= **hurt**). Athenian law not only permitted but required the torture of slaves giving evidence in court, by way of insuring the veracity of their testimony. This "servant of King Laius" (1123) is, more strictly, a slave. Most Athenians owned slaves and would have accepted torture as a part of the interrogation. **God help me** translates the same word rendered "unhappy" at 1071 (see the note there); Jebb compares *Tr* 377 where the same word in exclamation is translated "Oh, I am miserable, miserable!" Dawe, however, would take the word as "a comment on the misguided Oedipus," which seems a risky business for a pinioned slave.

1160 Perhaps this comment on **delays** is accompanied by a gesture indicating the servants should apply more twist to the arm.

1162 Now the investigation has reached the stage of 1039–41 and can proceed to Laius, the ultimate source and link between Oedipus' identity and the identity of the murderer of Laius.

1164 The habit of asking disjunctive questions may explain the double question, but the euphemistic **what house** takes us back to the possibility that the king of Thebes is a slave (1063; cf. 1168).

1167–68 As Jebb notes, it is an ambiguity in the herdsman's reply (**children of Laius** could also mean "children of the house of Laius") that leaves Oedipus in doubt. **In wedlock** means "kindred of Laius."

1173–76 These four lines in Greek are in antilabe (see the note to 626–29).

1179a–82 For the motivation in **I pitied it** see the note to *Tr* 298–306. **To misery** translates Jocasta's word for Oedipus ("God help you!" discussed at 1069b–73; here "a hard lot" seems right).

1184 For the apostrophe to the **light of the sun** cf. *OC* 1549 and *El* 89; for the motif of coming into the light cf. 374a–75 and 1229–30.

1184b–85 Saw the light bred combines two of the most common motifs in the play (Greek *phan-* and *phu-* stems). The Greek is more euphemistic than **accursed** and **cursed**, "I am shown born from whom one ought not to be born, living with whom one ought not to live, having killed whom one must not kill." Of course he is "cursed" in the Greek way of seeing things, but he cannot yet say so (see on 1384).

1186–1223 The second stasimon was marked by doubt and anxiety that divine law and power may no longer be held valid. The third stasimon rang with optimism that Oedipus' birth might even prove divine. Now in the fourth stasimon a third variation is introduced, this time on the theme of mutability, with Oedipus as the paradigm. In the grammar of Greek tragic composition hardly any theme is more common, and there may not be a single novelty in the present example, yet, as so often, the whole is greater than the parts. The song generalizes and moralizes: prosperity and happiness are illusory and evanescent. On the other hand, Oedipus is addressed personally throughout, and peculiar motifs such as conquering the Sphinx and sharing a wife with Laius recall earlier imagery and metaphor. Greek lyric always enjoys an aphoristic and didactic aspect, and in a lament (1219) the work of time (1213) and change on frail mortality offers a perfect ground for the final scene.

1186–96 Generations is chosen because "generation" (1210, but not an echo of this word) has brought Oedipus down. His fall is not directly attributed to a divine scheme; cf. *Ant* 582–84. For man as "nothing at all" see on *Ant* 1321 and *Aj* 126. **I count you:** see Oedipus' reckoning at 843 and the note to 32. **Not at all** echoes and answers Oedipus' question at 1019. **Seeming** and "man as nothing" are prominent in Hecuba's assessment,

I see the work of gods who pile tower-high the pride
of those who were nothing, and dash present grandeur down.
(*Trojan Women* 612–13)

Turning away = "declining," as the sun declines at the end of the day; the verb metaphorically compares man's life to a day. **Oedipus:** the king has departed, but second person pronouns, verbs, and vocatives are frequent. **Pattern:** the Greek word, from which we derive paradigm, has the senses "model," "lesson," and "example" (as in argument). The word for **fate** is *daimôn,* as at 816 (in the compound "hated by the gods"), 829, and 1301 ("evil spirit"). The Greek word for **happiness** is *eudaimonia,* an abstract noun for "getting along with your *daimôn*"; see also 1199. For **luckless** see the note to 962. **I envy not** = "I do not deem happy." Such happiness as man may have comes only day by day (see (*Bacchae* 910–11).

1197–1203c Cf. the similes from archery at *Ant* 1034–35 and 1084–85 and see the note at *Agamemnon* 364–67. Oedipus' triumph over the **hooked taloned maid** (the Sphinx) remains undimmed. For the **tower** as metaphor for protection cf. *Aj* 159 and the note to *Aj* 20. For **he was called** and **he ruled** read "you were called" and "you ruled."

1204–12a More miserable (as at 815) is used by Oedipus in self-reference at 1414 ("my wretchedness") and 1444 ("so wretched"); it is "unlucky" at 1240. As at *OC* 1133, Oedipus is said to dwell in the same house (= **lives with**) as his fate (*atê*). The basic notion in **reverse** is "change," then "exchange" and "barter"; the metaphor echoes the language at 34a (note to 32), 960, and 1110. **Famous:** see the note to 8. **Haven** (= "harbor") combines nautical with sexual metaphor (Empedocles had already equated harbor and womb) while recalling Teiresias' identification of Cithaeron with the womb (see on 420–24a). The commentators, like the scholiast, are divided on whether **father and son** refers to Oedipus alone or to Oedipus and Laius (**both as** reflects the translator's preference for the former view). The Greek follows these two nouns with a word that normally denotes a female attendant in a woman's chamber, but here, as Kamerbeek and Gould suggest, it seems derived in an etymologizing way from "traversing (ploughing) the bedchamber," which meaning, natural to the bridegroom, could be applied equally to Oedipus and Laius. The ambiguity is further intensified by an untranslated verb meaning "to fall," which could allude to falling from the womb (Gould cites *Iliad* 19. 110) and also to falling on someone sexually; our translation represents this with **for generation.** For the woman as **furrows ploughed** cf. Euripides *Phoenician Women* 18; see the notes to *OK* 260 and *Tr* 31–33.

1213–23 Fragment 301 offers another variant on **Time who sees all:**

Then hide nothing, since Time who sees and hears
all unfolds all.

See 614–15. **Against your will** can only mean "you who never willed these deeds," a very elliptical compression; the legal sense is regularly "not premeditated." See the note to 1230. **Marriage accursed** translates "marriage no marriage," the familiar privative construction (note at *Phil* 535); cf. the same sense at 1256. The chorus does not want to talk of incest, pollution, and curses, and so resorts to the circumlocutions of standard tragic diction. **To speak directly** = "to tell the truth." **I drew my breath** suggests both "took life from" and "had relief from" (cf. *Aj* 274), both of which may allude to the conquering of the Sphinx. For **lull my mouth to sleep** read "close my eye in sleep," which suggests the sleep of death (see on *Aj* 833). **With your name** is not represented in the Greek.

1224–1530 The final scene after the last stasimon is traditionally called the *exodos* or *exode* (Aristotle *Poetics* chap. 12). Since murder, death, and suicide are usually excluded from the Greek stage, messengers, here a servant from the house, report the events that have happened within the palace. While the vocal expression of suffering, both in song and in speech, exceeds what is usually found in modern theater, physical violence, against our habit, is greatly repressed.

1224 They are not **Princes** and are not addressed as such: "You who are always honoured by our country."

1225 The servant expects them, and we may suppose the audience, to experience the **grief** as if they were eyewitnesses.

1227 The **Phasis** flows into the eastern shore of the Black Sea; the **Ister** is the Danube. Jebb compares:

Will all great Neptune's ocean wash this blood
Clean from my hand?
                                        (*Macbeth* 2.2.60–61)

Jebb complains of the unnaturalness of the hyperbole. Bloodshed pollutes, and pure water purifies. Oedipus began the day seeking to purify Thebes (99d) and ends it by polluting the palace and city.

1230 **Whether they** (the evils) **will or not** may confuse the sense through an unwanted personification. As at 1214, this language normally refers to agents and "willed" (premeditated) acts; here the adjectives modify the acts rather than the agents, and the meaning is that Jocasta and Oedipus have acted deliberately.

1235 The servant's high style continues with **glorious**, a common Homeric epithet whose root sense is "divine" ("godly" at 298). See on 950.

1242–45 **Tearing her hair** is characteristic of grief and passion (see Aeschylus *Persians* 1056).

1245 After **hands** the translation has omitted a line: "when she entered, she slammed the doors shut." With the line dropped, the slave is saved from contradiction since he cannot report what is said and done behind closed doors. It seems more likely that Sophocles has slipped. Lines 1252–63 certainly imply that the messenger and other servants were in a separate room from Jocasta's, for Oedipus breaks in on them and crashes through the doors of Jocasta's chamber. Then they all discover her. For lament and suicide in the bedchamber see *Tr* 912–31 and the notes there.

1246–49 As at 1255–58 and 1271–74a, these lines are reported, not quoted, in the Greek: "she called Laius, long a corpse, remembering that begetting long ago, from which he died, and he left her to bear a misbegotten brood with his own." My repeated "long (ago)" attempts to bring out a minor variant on the play's concern for time. The same stem occurs in lines 1 ("old"), 109 ("old crime"), 289a ("already" = "for a long time"), 449b, 561, 666 ("to the other troubles" = "to the old troubles"), 907 ("old . . . oracles"), 916 (in "from what was"), 947 (Oedipus "*long feared* lest he should be his murderer"), 973 (in "before now"), 997, 1043, 1215 (where an untranslated adverb "long ago" modifies "begetter and begot"), and 1282. It is not uncommon for something deep in the past to haunt a Sophoclean tragedy, so that discovery of the true meaning of the past becomes either the central problem or at least a major leitmotif in all the plays, except perhaps the *Antigone*.

1249a–51 Cursed and **infamous** introduce a subjective feeling not present in the Greek. The servant, however, adds an (untranslated) "unhappy" of her (see on 1071).

1255–58 This speech is not a direct quotation in the Greek; see on 1246–49. For the **field of double sowing** cf. 1320 ("double"), 1498, and *Tr* 31–33 (note). In asking for a sword Oedipus apparently plans to kill Jocasta, but he is wild, and we are given little time to consider the significance of his demand.

1259 Some god (*daimôn*) = "evil spirit" (1301) and "spirit" (1312); see 1329a–35.

1265 For **cried out** see the note to *Tr* 903.

1270 The self-blinding comes as no surprise to the audience; our earliest reference appears at *Seven against Thebes* 782–85.

1271–74a The messenger does not quote him directly. **Crime** is the neuter of *kakos* (see on 522–23). The word is neither specifically legal nor moral but denotes that which harms physically or socially and so that which degrades a man in his own eyes or in the view of others. The messenger has just applied it to the scene of Jocasta's suicide (1253, the untranslated object of "seeing"); it is "troubles" at 1281, "ills" (1285), "pain" (1286), "ill" (1365), "hurt" (1391), "foulness" (1396), and "evil fate" (1458). In short this common adjective (as substantive) covers as wide a spectrum as "evil," but usually without that word's moral shading. Shakespeare's "evil diet" or his "planets in evil mixture" catches the idea. **Had done upon me** = "suffered" or "experienced": "they would never see what sort of thing he had suffered nor what harm he had done." **Dark eyes:** the translation's apostrophe renders the Greek for "seeing in the dark": "but in days to come in the dark they would see whom they ought not to see, and would not recognize whom he desired to know." Having failed to see and learn in the light, his eyes are bitterly condemned to do their business in the dark.

1280–81 For **it has broken** (the subject is **troubles**) see the note to 1077.

1287 Oedipus' absolute humiliation is vividly present in his willingness, or rather desire, to show himself publicly.

1289 The **word** for incest with one's mother does not occur until the Christian era. The rhetorical figure (aposiopesis) calls attention to a word or phrase by leaving it unexpressed; here the messenger suggestively refuses to say a thing so horrible that only the victim himself has the right to name it.

1294 Sickness may refer to the pollution, but the primary reference is to physical mutilation.

1296–97 Even in the horror of it = "even in one who loathes it." In the tragedies pity is often the natural result of tragic pathos (see on *Tr* 298–306). The abominable Oedipus rouses the disgust, still greater pity, and curiosity of chorus and spectator, an ambivalence at the heart of Greek theater. Note the emphasis on **sight**.

1298–1366 This lyric dialogue (kommos) exposes the gruesome Oedipus, who laments his fate to a chorus that, though sympathetic, thinks him better off dead. This last thought (1368) leads to a speech in which Oedipus defends his self-blinding.

1300 Madness is the time-honored explanation for a mistake or self-harming act: see Oedipus' judgment at *OC* 1535–37. He is, as we say, wild with grief. Since no man voluntarily harms himself, the Greeks viewed these irrational acts as divinely inspired; so here the **evil spirit** (*daimôn*) that has leaped upon Oedipus causes the madness (the figure is Aeschylean: see on *Eumenides* 372–76); cf. 262–63, 1312, and the note to *OC* 1747. Yet the Greeks usually thought of dual responsibility, of god and man steering the same ship, so that it is natural in an admonition for Phoenix to say to Achilles:

> But don't you think in this way [as Meleager thought],
> and do not let the daimon turn you, my friend, in that
> direction.
>
> (*Iliad* 9.600–601; my translation)

On this subject see also the notes to 1307 and 1329a–35. The Greek for **ill-luck** incorporates *daimôn* in a compound; cf. the similar play on words at 1191–94 (note).

1303 Indeed I pity you translates two cries of grief and an "unhappy" (of Oedipus; see on 1071).

1307–12 Oedipus has changed his mask; his face streams with blood as he gropes his way onto the stage. At first he groans, repeating the chorus's cries at 1303, then calls himself "unhappy" (see on 1071) and "wretched" (cf. 1300). The questions and address to the *daimôn* (= **Spirit**) are characteristic of tragic grief; cf. *Phil* 1187–90. **How far:** perhaps rather "from where"; **sprung:** cf. "leaped" at 1301. Early Greek psychology viewed man as the ground of external forces, where divinities, daimons, and irrational impulses forcefully intruded; man might resist but was ultimately subject to their influence, as were even the gods. Something of that feeling for irrational, objective intrusion remains active in tragedy, even though man has become much freer and more personally responsible.

1313–14 The chorus speaks to his last question; answering not the "where?" or "whence?" but "whither?" (his eyes): "to a terrible place neither utterable nor to be seen."

1314a–17 Horror is more subjective than the Greek adjective ("a cloud of darkness *that one would avoid*"); the **visitant** is the cloud of darkness; **ill-wind in haste** translates a single adjective that appears only here and offers in an oxymoron something like Liddell and Scott's "fatally favourable" (for the image see on 691). A double cry of grief, with a self-conscious "again" added, should follow line 1315; Dawe compares Agamemnon's "Ah me, again, they struck again" (*Agamemnon* 1345). **Madness** is interpretative; the Greek coordinates: "stabbing pain of the brooches and the memory of evil deeds have entered me," as if the memory, like the brooches, were external and instrumental. The aspect of the verb is consistent with the idea of daimonic interference but also suggests that the brooches and his memory are one, that memory comes with darkness (and replaces light and seeing), that he is at once the victim of physical blindness and mnemonic sight. **Evil deeds** (= "grief," 1320) is vague and probably includes both the harm he has done and the harm he has suffered.

1325–26 To **know** add "clearly" (see the note to 1011). **Darkness:** Oedipus calls himself "dark," transferring to himself an adjective commonly applied to things.

1327–29 To **do despite** translates a verb with medical connotations: "to cause to wither (or waste) away." **Urged** is more concretely "lifted up," i.e., raised your hand to stab yourself.

1329a–35 Sorrows: see on 840. **Brought . . . to completion** (the *tel-* stem) implies design, but Oedipus' claim has only shadowy validation from our experience of the play. True, Apollo predicted murder and incest and later called for the apprehension of the polluted murderer; not true, however, that Apollo caused the murder or incest, or in any tangible way tempted or beguiled Oedipus to those crimes. Still less true, unless we take 1258–59 more literally than their vagueness warrants, that Apollo had anything to do with the blinding. If Oedipus only attempts to explain why he has abused himself so terribly, we may accept his sincerity but hardly his facts. The dramatic evidence—what we see, what is reported—does not support his claim. As noted above, the Greeks liked to rationalize misfortune by giving a god his due, and the archaic view saw man, psychologically, as the ground for divine action (that is why Phoenix appeals both to Achilles' judgment and warns him of evil daimonic perversity). Still, thinking and saying do not make it so, and Oedipus' case is a far throw from Ajax', where the goddess herself vouches for the origin of the hero's ruin. Here, on the contrary **the hand . . . none but my own** acknowledges personal responsibility, and the question that follows gives a personal reason for his violence. In his next speech (1370–1415) Oedipus elaborates on his motives for the self-blinding, and there is no mention of Apollo. That does not, for the Greek, entail contradiction, only two complementary ways of accounting for the phenomena: the very nature of Greek thinking about the world requires a religious explanation (Apollo); the same thinking, because it posits man as free, responsible, and rational, must also explain the blinding as a reasonable—even reasoned, despite the passion—response to murder and incest. Much criticism of Greek tragedy takes pious explanation for substantive account. Yet the Greeks did not let men off the hook, whether legal, moral, or practical, just because a god might be invoked to account for failure. When, as in the *Ajax, Philoctetes, Heracles,* and *Bacchae,* authentic divine presence is at work, we must bow, as the characters do, to their palpable influence. Not here. Contra: Winnington-Ingram, "Tragedy and Greek Archaic Thought," pp. 32–41; Bowra, pp. 180–86, where "the gods' plan [is] to humble him" (p. 186).

1340–47 Oedipus expects to be sent into exile (for what actually happens see on 1519a–24b). The superlatives translated in **most accursed** and **hates above all** (cf. 1519c) imply that he is completely crushed, but elsewhere (e.g., 1370–71, 1446) we see that he cannot so easily abandon his imperious ways. A man of great passion sees both his heights and depths as extremes. **Hates** (the Greek *echthros* is more objective) simply denotes that which is hostile and behaves or affects one as an enemy would (cf. 816); so fate may be "hateful," as at *Phil* 682 and *OK* 272, where it is "still worse." In our play **accursed** must echo Oedipus' curse on the murderer, but it is also a natural term for abuse (e.g., *Hecuba* 1065, *Medea* 112, and in comedy). As Barrett notes (on *Hippolytus* 1362–63), "Pity and abuse often share their vocabulary." What is pitiable for one is contemptible for another. **Unhappy** (*deilaios*) frequently occurs in self-pity (e.g., "sorrow" at *Ant* 1271 and 1310) as well as in genuine commiseration (*Tr* 763) and became a formulaic cry of "woe is me" in Aristophanes.

1348 Would I had never known you: the wish is virtually equivalent to Oedipus' curse on the man who saved him, since both imply that the king had been better off either never to have been born or to have died an infant. Cf. the wish to revoke a past action at the beginning of Euripides' *Medea,* and see *Phil* 969b–70 and *El* 1131–38.

1353–55 So burdensome = "such a grief" and then "occasion for grief." He says **to friends** *and to myself.*

1358 He does not actually say **mother infamously** but skirts it with "I had not been known to men as the bridegroom of those from whom I was born" (the common plural for singular).

1360–66 Godless means "abandoned by god," i.e., "without the help of the gods." **Impurity** (= "unholy") refers to his marriage. **Begetter in the same seed** translates a single word usually meaning "of the same family or kind"; after which he repeats the circumlocution noted at 1358 ("from whom I was born"). That he is "of the same family" as Jocasta has seemed too drab a comment to some editors, who then emend to get more point (e.g., "begetter in the same bed"), but the self-pity of the present passage does not go beyond the generic (cf. **ill worse than ill:** *kakon* twice).

1367–68 Remedy was good = "that you planned well," as if the blinding were a rational decision. To live blind is elsewhere thought a fate worse than death, and Sophocles apparently took this line in his lost *Phineus* (see on *Ant* 964–74). Teiresias, too, was punished with blindness (Apollodorus 3.6.7), and this is the revenge of Hecuba on Polymestor (see Euripides' *Hecuba* 1044–48). For **better dead** see on OC 1224–26.

1370 Don't tell me = "don't instruct me."

1372 With what eyes would, more prosaically, be "how," but he insists on repudiating his failed vision (1375, 1377). Primitive notions of death describe the surviving spirit's appearance as if it continues the body's condition at death. The poets found this conception useful long after theology had abandoned it. So the blinded Oedipus will be blind in Hades and unable to look with shame upon his mother and father.

1380 The translation has omitted a line in which Oedipus describes himself as "noblest of the sons of Thebes" (Jebb).

1381–83 Criminal is the "unholy one" ("sinner" at 1441). **Since** smooths the construction but is not in the Greek: Oedipus moves, without modifying his grammar, to the events, from his actual decree to what is subsequently discovered. **Proved by God impure** offers a nice example of (his) conventional thinking winning out over (our) experience: the audience has seen Oedipus himself discover the criminal. **God** stands for the Greek plural (with no particular allusion to Apollo).

1384 Guilt was "taint" at 833, a better translation because the word denotes the physical pollution on the murderer; cf. *Eumenides* 787 (note). The context implies as much shame (fear of their reproach) as guilt. The syntax does not break, "Seeing that I have borne witness to such a taint, was I to look directly at my people?" Cf. the sentiment at 999.

1390–91 Neither seeing nor hearing evil, he supposes that he would not think of it. The thought, perhaps a commonplace (cf. *Aj* 554), is hardly worthy of the man who scorned any trouble (= "hurt": *kaka*) at 1077.

1396–98 Fairness . . . foulness/festered: the Greek line of four words opens with an oxymoron (fairness [that consists of] foulness) that is resolved by "festering" (a medical term indicating a sore or boil beneath the flesh) and concludes "you nurtured" (see on 99a). **Sinner** and **Sinners,** like foulness, are forms of *kakos,* with more comment on the harm and degradation of his life than on moral error. Most modern commentators agree on the moral innocence of Oedipus. It is easier, however, to see that he did not intend harm than to be sure he does not feel morally responsible. As we see from "guilt" (1384) and the present lines, the translator thinks of Oedipus as a man conscious of moral failure, whereas Aristotle's linking of Oedipus with Thyestes (*Poetics,* chap. 13) implies that his error (*hamartia*) was merely one of ignorance (on this subject see Stinton). If he feels guilty, it is not because of a bad conscience. **Crossroads:** still in apostrophe, which begins with Cithaeron and continues with "marriages" to 1407.

1400–1401 He speaks as if he had offered his **father's blood** in sacrifice.

1404 The translation has omitted one line (1406 in the Greek): "you bred us, and breeding again sent up the same seed, and you produced fathers, brothers, children, a blood-stained clan, brides, wives, mothers, and whatever is most shameful." The "blood-stained clan" refers to the parricide, an anomaly in this list, but a more natural sense for the Greek than "blood-kinship," i.e., incest (Jebb).

1410–15 Cf. 100–101, where Creon reports that Apollo called for death or banishment. **Your country** is interpretative; it is of course also Oedipus' country. **Throw me into the sea** is not practical for the Thebans; it is added for the sake of a triad (cf. 1427–28) or because it was one of the usual ways of getting rid of a polluted murderer. They are not going to **touch** him because, like Creon (1426–28), they do fear his contagious defilement. Then he bids for their sympathy, a natural request given his shock, but something of a contradiction: no special circumstances free the polluted man from the danger of contaminating those about him. Like "strange evil fate" at 1458, **my evil doom** (simply "my *kaka*") is less mysterious in the Greek than the English may suggest. Creon's reentry forestalls any gesture of sympathy or rejection, and the ambiguous status of the king will hold through this final scene.

1422 An utter liar (*kakos*) simply recognizes that Oedipus has unjustly abused Creon; it is "has abused you most vilely" at 1434a.

1423–28 Laughter and taunting are traditional coin for the man who has gained the upper hand over an enemy (see on *Aj* 67). Creon's sympathy, however, is colored by a careful regard for the shame and pollution that Oedipus represents. The language is traditional: **shame** (cf. *Tr* 596–97), **reverence** (a verb cognate with *aidôs:* see on *OC* 1268) and **pollution** (*agos:* see *Ant* 255 and 776). Cf. Oedipus' "hide me" (1410). The **Sun** as the source of light symbolizes purity. Dawe seems right to suggest that **land, rain,** and **light** are invoked as beneficent influences whose natural work the pollution has corrupted.

1430 In fact he is not taken in quickly at all, and were it not for the magnanimous and cautious attitude of Creon, we might expect him to be driven from the city, according to the terms of Apollo (95–102), his own curse (246–51), and his present request (1410–12 and 1436–37). Davies, observing how protracted and, in terms of exile at least, unexpected this final scene is, notes that both Creon and Oedipus remain true to character. Perhaps the inversion of power between the two men, with a kind of mirror effect from their earlier scenes, attracted Sophocles' dramatic interest: Oedipus is helpless and begs for exile, yet he remains imperious to the last (1524a), while Creon, given power beyond his ambition, will withhold judgment and consult Apollo again (1438–39). Yet in its thematic development the play seems to cry for a final scene in which the king is banished, and many interpretations of the play assume that Oedipus will now (at the close of play) go into exile. But the tradition from epic to Aeschylus had not fixed exile as a necessary consequence, and if the audience expected Oedipus to exit left and out of the city, they did so because of the present drama and not from the previous literary treatments. See also *Phoenician Women* 1540ff.

1433 His **expectation** is immediate exile or death.

1434a **That has used you vilely** gives the superlative of *kakos* a (possible) active sense (cf. 1422); otherwise the word may mean "most vile." Such talk does not imply that Oedipus has discovered in this horror some profound meaning for his own life.

1440–41 **To let . . . die** softens the Greek: "to destroy the parricide, the sinner, me." Apollo's name was popularly connected with the verb *apollunai* ("to destroy"), here in the infinitive form (see the note to *Agamemnon* 1081–83).

1445 What would Creon specify if we asked him for an example of not putting **trust** (in) **the God**? If Oedipus had not trusted the gods, we would have a reason for condemning him.

1446 **Command . . . and will beseech:** for the second verb see 10–13; the habits of rule pass slowly.

1454a **By their decree,** i.e., as if their initial intention might still be fulfilled.

1455–59 These lines offer the best evidence that Oedipus has recognized some special providence in his misfortunes; they may reflect, allusively, his audience's knowledge of his mystic fate at Colonus (see the *Oedipus at Colonus*, 1585–1665). To this, Kamerbeek objects that "evil" is an odd way for the poet to refer to his heroization. **Saved** by whom or what? For the theme see 48, 82, 150, 304b, 1030, 1180, 1351. **Strange evil fate** is "strange *kakon*": the second "fate" is *moira*. See the note to *Agamemnon* 67f. and cf. *Tr* 467–68. Perhaps the tone is more of resignation than insight.

1461 The Greek contrasts the males (**sons**) and the girls, but the addition of **men** should indicate that Eteocles and Polyneices have reached manhood. One tradition made Creon the regent during their youth, and the chorus's introduction at 1418 may imply as much. Euripides (*Phoenician Women* 63) makes them minors at the time of the blinding.

1463 The **two girls** are Antigone and Ismene; see the prologue to the *Antigone*. Oedipus' humane concern for the girls may be compared with Ajax' provision for his son (*Aj* 562–70); see also *Alcestis* 299–319.

1467–68 Again (cf. 1413) the polluted man would **touch** others. **Sorrow with them** = "lament (my/our) troubles (*kaka*)." This reunion will surprise the audience since there is no structural call for it, as will his paternal love and concern, for which there is no more preparation than the fatherly sympathy he offers his people in the prologue.

1470 Three times in this passage extrametrical phrases interrupt the trimeters, a phenomenon regularly associated with heightened feeling.

1477 Dawe points out that the word translated **from old days** may also refer idiomatically to the immediate past: "knowing (anticipating) the immediate delight which has just now come over you."

1479 The first reference for **on your road** would seem to be to his fetching the girls (so "for this course," with some of the Greek ambiguity), while our version picks up the secondary metaphor from "the road of life." The first **God** derives from "may you be lucky"; the second is a *daimôn;* cf. the similar language at *El* 998 and *Persians* 600–602.

1481 His **hands** are also explicitly mentioned in 1467 and 1471. Cf. 1510.

1482–85 In this passage Oedipus refers to himself as a "gardener," i.e., a cultivator (for sexual overtones see *Suppliant Maidens* 592), and concludes with "disclosed a father from whom I myself was sown." Cf. 1257 and 1498 for the verb meaning "to plough" and "to sow." **Turned** has a primary meaning of "acting as a protector (*proxenos*)," which gives the grotesque twist that the hands act to protect the eyes (from seeing) by putting them out. The bitterness is also evident in **knowing nothing** (= "learning nothing" and "observing nothing").

1486 An adverb indicates he also weeps for himself.

1489–91 **Before the world** looks to their dependence on others: "what sort of life you will have at the hands of others." **Will you make one** and **gay company** ("festivals") elaborate the same idea: "how will you (dare) join the common gatherings and feasts of other people?" They will not escape the infamy (1494) touching him and his parents.

1494–96 It is the **infamy** that will **bring hurt. Those that marry with them** appears to be a translation of Arendt's conjecture in this much emended passage. Some editors keep the manuscript reading: "infamy that will belong to my parents and you alike." No one will want to marry either of them for fear of being implicated in the family's shame. On marriage see *El* 164–67 and *Ant* 865.

1497–99 Curse is the serviceable *kaka* (see 1271–74a). **Sowed . . . sprung:** see 260 and 1485 for notes on this language.

1500 For the imagined future insult see *Aj* 501.

1506 The compression and lack of parallelism reflect his feeling: "do not allow them (to be) beggars, husbandless, (though they are your) kin, wanderers."

1509 On counting and equation see the note to 424b–25. He has just said, at 1498–99, that he got them from an equal ("even," i.e., the same) source as himself.

1509a Before **for you can see** add "pity them."

1510 There is no indication that Creon ever does **touch** him, and his response is cool if not cold. The translation should be "Touch me with your hand."

1513–14a Although Sheppard would have **opportunity** (*kairos*) mean "due measure," which is the lesson he has learned, the banality of that didacticism is not worth the strain on the idiom. Apparently he says no more than "accept whatever life's occasion gives." For the prayer for a **better life than . . . father's** see *Aj* 550.

1515–30 The meter changes to trochaic tetrameters, with all the lines save the first and last divided between the speakers. The same meter and similar division occurs in the false ending at *Phil* 1402f.

1517 In season = "opportunity" (1514: *kairos*); with this echo Creon mocks him mildly.

1518 Since **what conditions** contradicts "I must obey" (1516), Dawe punctuates the former line as a question.

1519a–c Send me out: see on 1436. **Gift . . . of the God** refers to his intention to consult the oracle again (1438–43). All life is the gift of the gods (cf. *OC* 710), but in tragedy such gifts are regularly double-edged (see the note to *Seven against Thebes* 719), and in fragment 646 (the *Tyndareus*) we hear of "the gift of an evil daimon that in a brief time overturns complete prosperity." Creon's insistence on reopening the case before Apollo, like his refusal to send Oedipus into immediate exile, leaves the play with an ambiguous ending. Neither the epic tradition nor contemporary dramatic practice compelled Sophocles to send the king into exile; in both Aeschylus' trilogy and the *Phoenician Women* he has remained at home, cared for by his sons whom he nonetheless eventually curses.

1520–24b The question is what happens now? Does Oedipus go into the palace? Does he, alone, go off into exile? Does he remain on stage while Creon leads the children off? Unfortunately, the sense of 1520–21 is not certain: **consent then** may also mean something like "this is your last word?" with reference to Creon's insistence on asking the god. Creon's response (**What I do not mean . . .**) is also equivocal. Does he tacitly bow to Oedipus' argument (1519c–d: the man hateful to the gods will be condemned to exile by their oracle)? Or does he firmly stick to his previous decision ("I've said it once and intend to keep to my word")? Because a change of purpose at this late stage would seem contradictory in Creon, I incline to the second interpretation. Oedipus, then, is refused his request, which does not mean he must enter the house. **Lead me away from here** will mean "take me in," to which Creon responds "come on, but let go of the children" (reverse the order of our translation: Creon bids him follow, but alone, without even the support of the girls). See Taplin (pp. 45–46) for an argument for Oedipus' entry into the palace. I would not rule out the possibility that he is left alone on stage while Creon and the girls exit. The absence of a curtain should not dissuade us from considering such a staging, and it is perhaps only our desire for illusion that makes it seem necessary to take him in or off to the country. The prologue to Euripides' *Trojan Women* requires Hecuba to come on stage, take her place, and pretend not to hear the prologue. No curtain protects the actor being seen as he assumes Hecuba's prostrate tableau. The audience was accustomed to seeing such stage business and would have found a silent, solitary, perhaps fallen, Oedipus completely appropriate here.

1524c–30 A number of editors have condemned these lines. They are flat, commonplace, and not altogether coherent without emendation. The first two lines are virtually the same as those at *Phoenician Women* 1757–58 (lines spoken at the end of the play by Oedipus, to whom 1524c–30 are attributed by the scholiast). Greek poetry often admonishes its readers to judge a life happy and prosperous only when it has reached its term:

> It's vain to say that any man alive
> Is in the true sense happy. Wait and ponder
> The manner of his exit from this stage.
> *(Andromache* 100–102)

Diction and phrasing in this passage from the *Andromache* are also too close to that at *OK* 1528–30 for accident; 1524–30 are accordingly suspected to be an actor's interpolation, though the case is hardly closed. For the commonplace "look to the end" see the note to *Tr* 1–3. **Masterful** echoes "master" and "mastered" (1524a–b). **Not a citizen who . . .**: the line is emended and translated along the lines of Jebb's text; for **envy** see on *Tr* 185. **Breakers of misfortune**: for the "flood of evil" (*Persians* 599) see on 24–24b.

Oedipus at Colonus

*F*OR the story of Oedipus and some comment on the events of this play see the introduction to the Theban plays. It should perhaps be emphasized that the three plays are not a trilogy, i.e., were not presented together in a single production; the *Oedipus at Colonus* is the latest of Sophocles' extant tragedies and was produced posthumously.

The translator's introductory note might suggest that Apollo's oracle named the place where Oedipus was to die; actually, it described the sanctuary and the omens (see 96–98).

Scene: For the **statue of Colonus** see lines 59a and 65. For the flat rock see 192–93.

1 Unobtrusively the poet plants a number of themes and motifs in these opening lines. Oedipus' dependence upon Antigone and Ismene, true and dutiful daughters, will be contrasted with his attitude toward his sons (see, e.g., 337–60). Both his age and his blindness are much stressed in the play, so he naturally depends upon the child for support (see 21) and perception (e.g., 14a–18, 28–29). He has spent his life begging (4–5) and carries the traditional beggar's bag, and if we can believe his son, looks the part of a dirty, wild outcast (see 1258–62).

6–8 The commonplace that **time** and **suffering** bring understanding is illustrated by Prometheus:

> Time in its aging course teaches all things.
> (*Prometheus Bound* 981)

See also the variant "learning through suffering" (*Tr* 142–43). **Kingliness** = "well-born" (76); it is the quality of nobility that Oedipus sees in Theseus (569 and 1042). The motif of instruction finds dramatic extension in several passages: at 150–202 Oedipus is instructed in local propriety by the chorus; three times (the first at 265–74) Oedipus argues his moral innocence; in the final scene Oedipus prophetically reveals to Theseus "what is appointed for you and for your city" (1519).

10 A **consecrated** place, such as Antigone perceives this one to be (16), might be forbidden to strangers or to any use save specified religious rites (cf. 36–40). Holy ground, however, naturally offers the suppliant more security.

15–18 Sacred enclosures were very common in the Greek world. Apart from the statue of Colonus (59a), Antigone would recognize the holy character of the place from altars and dedications. Jebb compares *Phaedrus* 230b, where Socrates describes a sanctuary dedicated to the Nymphs and Achelous and the statuettes and images found there.

21 Readers have reacted variously to Oedipus: Is he a beaten old man to whom age has brought grace and dignity? Does he, even from the prologue, display the temper known from the *Oedipus the King* and still driving him later in this play (see the tirade at 337–52)? How well does he know his own fate, and how confident does that knowledge make him? This translation inclines toward the dignified Oedipus and so tempers the imperatives of the present line with **Help me.** Note his submission at 14 ("do as they direct"), the slight impatience of line 25, the quick resolution of line 45. Cf. his requests for advice and help at 170–80.

30–35 The **stranger** is a native of Colonus who immediately recognizes that they have violated holy ground (36–37). **Fortunate** means it is a happy omen for them that a friendly person has chanced by to offer help.

40–43 These **daughters of darkness and earth** (**mysterious** is an interpretative addition) are the Furies (Erinyes), who in their benign aspect are called the Eumenides (= **Gentle All-seeing Ones**). See on *Agamemnon* 59 (for Fury) and *Eumenides* 1041 (for their benevolent role). Aeschylus (*Eum* 321) makes them children of night. In this play we find them as both spirits of vengeance (see 1299 and 1434) and as benevolent protection for the suppliant (see Oedipus' prayer at 84–110; 457–60; and the instructions for expiation at 466–90). It was not uncommon for divinities, and especially those beneath the Olympian status, to go by different **names** in different places.

44 As soon as he hears their name he understands that this place is destined to be his burial ground; he immediately announces he is a **suppliant** and utters a wish that the local spirits will accept him with pity (= **may they be gentle;** cf. "Be merciful, great spirit" at 1480).

Suppliant drama always focuses on a victim, but the very nature of supplication puts the victim under the power of a divinity and thereby lends the helpless suppliant a kind of power. By entering a sanctuary, touching an altar, or otherwise putting himself within the power of the divine, the victim shares that power insofar as violating the person of the victim also violates the power of the god. In this play the helplessness of the suppliant is intensified by his blindness, age, and, above all, by his parricide and incest (it seems unlikely that Oedipus has ever been formally cleansed: see on 1132–37). On the other hand, his power is augmented by the prophecies of Apollo (see 86–95 and 389–405) and by the acknowledged power of his curse (784–90 and 1375–93). This paradox of suppliant power is the thematic cornerstone of the play, and the occasion for Theseus' intercession, for the appeal and retaliation of Creon, and for the failed supplication of Polyneices. A number of passages keep the suppliant theme before us: 49a–50, 90, 142, 237–53, 275–77, 284, 634, 923, and 1009.

47 Ordained will be explained by 86–95.

49a–51 Bear with me now = "don't dishonor me" (by ignoring my supplication). As so often in Sophoclean dialogue, the response incorporates a word from the same root (**discourteous** = "refusing honor"). **Wanderer** is repeated at 165, 746 ("never at rest"), 949 ("exiles"), and 1097. A synonym will be found at 5, 123 ("vagabond"), and other variations at 20, 99, 303–4, 345–52, and 445. Greek ambivalence about beggars and vagabonds is thoroughly evident in the *Odyssey*, where Eumaios the swineherd expresses the popular piety:

> Stranger, I have no right to deny the stranger, not even
> if one came to me who was meaner than you. All vagabonds
> and strangers are under Zeus.
>
> (*Odyssey* 14.56–58)

When the evil suitor Antinoös has thrown and hit him with a footstool, Odysseus, disguised as a beggar, mildly reminds him of the danger:

> if there are any gods or any furies for beggars,
> may Antinoös find the consummation of death before marriage.
>
> (*Odyssey* 17.475–76)

Antinoös retires with a threat, but the other suitors echo a universal superstition:

> Antinoös, you did badly to hit the unhappy vagabond:
> a curse on you, if he turns out to be some god from heaven.
>
> (*Odyssey* 17. 483–84)

Like the suitors, the stranger does not want to take a chance with a vagabond who has so readily "violated" the sanctuary.

55 The **god of the sea** is Poseidon, who is specifically mentioned in the Greek text (cf. 889a). **Prometheus** is called the **firecarrier** because he stole fire from the gods and gave it to mortals. An annual torchrace from an altar to Prometheus in the Academy near Colonus to the acropolis honored this god.

58 Homer has Zeus speak

of Tartaros
far below, where the uttermost depth of the pit lies under
earth, where there are gates of iron and a brazen doorstone
(*Iliad* 8.13–15)

So any place that offered an entry to Hades might be described as having a **Doorsill of Brass;** it is from this place that Oedipus departs for the underworld (see 1591–1603).

59–60 In Greek *colonus* means "hill," but the place is, typically, named for a hero and founder, who is called **horseman** to associate him with Poseidon's gift (see also 668 and 714a–16).

65 The Greek says the **clan** "takes its name from that god"; Colonus is one of those dead heroes who have become gods, i.e., receive sacrifice and worship (see the note on Amphiaraus at *El* 837). In English we have the word "eponymous" from the Greek for someone who gives his name to a thing. This play makes more of naming than any other play of Sophocles: 41–43, 108, 265, 301–5, 486–87, 527–28, 667, 1320–24.

69 For **Theseus** see the note to 549a.

72 This first allusion to the suppliant's ability to be useful introduces the theme of reciprocity (see on 92–93).

74 Oedipus' blindness becomes the occasion for a number of variations on sight and blindness: e.g., the Eumenides are "all-seeing" (43); the stranger is called a "watcher" or "scout" (untranslated at 34–35); he has a "blind step" (182); and though he is a sorry sight, he brings more profit than a fair form would (576–78). See on 138–39.

76 Though obviously unlucky means "except for (your) *daimôn*"; see on 1337 and 1370.

84–110 The prayer is in part narration, argument, and appeal. Similarly, the opening lyrics of Aeschylus' *Suppliant Maidens* call on Zeus Protector and Savior (lines 1 and 23) to "receive these suppliant maidens" and at the same time includes narration and exposition.

84 Whose eyes are terrible glances rather euphemistically at spirits whose look can paralyze; they are compared to gorgons at *Eumenides* 48; cf. Euripides *Orestes* 256–57 and 261.

87–88 The **oracles of evil** are apparently those pertaining to Laius and Jocasta (see *OK* 789–94a). These signs concerning his final resting place are not mentioned in *Oedipus the King*.

90 The word for **home** is a rare compound that underscores the idea of hospitality for a stranger (the *xenos* motif occurs at 260–63 and in Theseus' ready acceptance of Oedipus at 561–66 and 631–37). **Sacred** translates *semnai,* one of the names given the Eumenides in Athenian cult (see on 457–58).

92–93 Antithetical clauses contrast **benefit** and **curse** (= "harm"; the curse is the means by which he will do harm; see 865). Reciprocity and retaliation are fundamental ethical and social concepts that supply the dramatic ligaments of this play. Gifts and favor (e.g., 540, 576–79, 628, 635), salvation (e.g., 277, 380–81, 390, 460–63), and care and nurturing (e.g., 337–52, 427–60) provide more specific examples of these concepts. Cf. his antithesis ("savior" and "woe") in the concluding line at 460.

94–98 These **portents** will come at the end of the play (1460–1504). **Thunder** and **lightning** are the most majestic signs by which Zeus (= **God**) makes his will known (see, e.g., *Tr* 436 and *Iliad* 8.68–77). **Smiling** is an interpretative addition. An **earthquake** would usually be a sign from Poseidon. **Feathery influence** is a reference to omens from the flight of birds.

101 The Greeks often poured a libation of wine at sacrifice, but the Furies received a mixture of water, milk, and honey (*Eumenides* 107). Sophocles did not think it necessary to account for Oedipus' knowledge of their cult. The coincidence of like chancing on like (**who drink not . . . love not wine**) has something of the divine about it, as Melanthios says of Odysseus and Eumaios,

> Now surely the vile leads the vile,
> as a god always leads like to like.
>
> (*Odyssey* 17.217–18; my trans.)

Henrichs suggests that the participle translated **who drink not** is simply an example of a transferred epithet. Oedipus knows of ritual offerings without wine and is represented as a prospective participant in it. So the phrase is transferred from the ritual to the person who will participate in it. This interpretation is more plausible than those that worry about Oedipus' poverty or depression.

104 The **unearthly voice** is, more literally, "the voice of Apollo."

107 They are **sweet** because he would have them be sweet (the proleptic adjective).

109a Poor carcase and his ghost means "this poor ghost (shadow) of himself." For the metaphor see *Aj* 126.

113–16 As in the *Electra* (80–88), the characters of the prologue retire as the chorus enters. There is less dramatic point in Oedipus' hiding than in the hiding of Orestes in either of the Electra plays, but, on the other hand, his anxiety seems natural, and as Nestle (p. 67) points out, the following lyric dialogue is particularly realistic.

117–253 The parodos begins with lyric strophe (117–37) and antistrophe (150–69), with a brief dialogue intervening (138–48); the second strophe (176–91) and antistrophe (192–206) are responsive lyric dialogues, as is the concluding epode (207–53). The discovery of Oedipus within the sanctuary, his decision to leave it, the chorus's horrified discovery that he is the polluted Oedipus, and Antigone's appeal for mercy are sung in a parodos that is probably the most emotional and dramatic of the extant plays (contrast the emotional but more formally structured parodos of the *Electra*). It is in effect a lyric scene motivated by the interview with the stranger, who has summoned the men of Colonus; the scene leads naturally to Oedipus' argument of 258–91.

120 The single superlative translated by **impious, blasphemous, shameless** would suggest to the Greek ear the excess and outrageous behavior associated with *hybris*.

127 The **inviolate thicket** is the "consecrated park" of line 10 and the "wood" of 114.

128–31 **Those** are the "maidens," i.e., the Furies. **Avert our eyes . . . without conversation** translates a trio of alpha privatives (*without* a look, a sound, a thought). A Greek would salute and perhaps offer a prayer when passing the sanctuary of most divinities, but the Furies are generally so malevolent that it is best to let them sleep.

132 The ancients seem to have prayed, as they read, aloud, but an audible prayer might awaken these divinities.

134 **Alien fool** is too strong; they only know that someone has failed to revere the place.

138–39 Lines 146–48 indicate that Antigone helps him and imply that he is approaching them. He has probably not been out of sight of the audience. **Sounds are the things I see:** "I see (understand) by means of sounds." Apollodorus (3.6.7) reports that when Teiresias' mother Chariclo asked Athena to restore her son's sight, the goddess could not do so, "but by cleansing his ears she caused him to understand every note of birds." In a similar way the seer Melampus, although not blind, was able to understand the language of birds and termites (Apollodorus 1.9.11–12).

142 **Please** is the language of a suppliant; see on 44 and cf. 241–50.

145 **My masters** = "guardians" (of the land).

154–58 **Curse** refers to the hostility of the Furies that may result from his trespass. Aeschylus (*Eumenides* 417) has the Furies call themselves Curses, and Sophocles seems to allude to that identification at *El* 111. Their warning is friendly but anxious. The grove is **still** because speech is forbidden there. In a sacred grove the grass would not be harvested. Water and milk mixed with honey were the liquid offerings (**libations**) given the Eumenides (cf. 101).

170–80 His manner is compliant, even diffident, and in return for his voluntarily leaving the refuge the chorus reassures him that his appeal as suppliant will be honored. With **drive you away** understand (an untranslated) "unwilling," a promise they soon want to break (see 226–36).

180–85 Metrical deficiencies imply that three or four short verses are missing here.

186–87 "Love thy friend, hate thy foe" is an old moral maxim for the Greeks, and one that is acted on with a vengeance in this play. As Pindar puts it:

> Be it mine to love my friend,
> but against the enemy, hateful indeed, turn with the wolf's
> slash,
>
> (*Second Pythian* 83–84)

Cf. 460. The verb **held,** however, suggests "nourishing," "rearing," and "caring for" (e.g., it is "breeding" at 920 and "keep" at 943) and touches on one of the most important themes of the play; see the note 337–60.

191 **Necessity** often means "the force of circumstance" and can usually be referred to a concrete restraint or compulsion, in this case their obvious helplessness; Jebb compares *Ant* 1106.

192–93 This **platform** must be distinct from the "rough stone" on which he sat at 19; apparently the chorus directs him to the boundary of the sanctuary, out of danger but near enough to claim its sanctity for his supplication. Here, too, Oedipus is eager to comply.

199 The interjection **Ah, me!** may indicate he has stumbled.

200–201 **It is I who love you** overtranslates the Greek, which simply means something like "lean on this arm of mine, your familiar support." Antigone's gestures vouch for her love and care.

202 Schneidewin also takes this exclamation to refer to his **blindness,** but the Greek is more vague, e.g., "Ah, this disheartening ruin."

207 With **exile** he identifies himself as a man "without a country."

213 **Star** freely renders the Greek *phusis,* an abstract noun meaning "birth" or "descent"; thus at 270 the same noun occurs in the phrase "evil *in myself,*" i.e., "naturally." At 1295 *phusis* designates the one "younger *by birth.*" Translate here "my birth was unspeakable."

216 **God help me** is the translator's version of a groan sometimes rendered "Ah!" With his question cf. 225.

221 **Labdacidae** means the "family of Labdacus," who was the father of Laius.

223–24d For **ruined** see "miserable" at *OK* 1204. **Accursed** translates a word that from Homer on means "unlucky"; thus Antigone uses this same word (*dusmoros*) of the sisters and father as "partners in sorrow" (1109c). See the note to *Phil* 1062. It does not indicate that Oedipus feels he lives under a curse. Both **dreadful** and **fearful** translate cries of surprise and fear.

227 He refers to their **promises** at 176–77.

228–36 Their argument is that, because they were **deceived** into receiving a suppliant whose true condition (that of a polluted parricide) they did not know, they need not fear divine retribution for violating their promise of sanctuary. The lyric puts this sentiment in a mannered style (**punish** and **injury** play on the same root; **deceivers** and **deceived** appear in a grammatical pattern of a b b a) and does not refer explicitly to pollution (**Wind no further your clinging evil upon us** may also be translated "don't attach any further debt to our city"). The pious Athenian would have found a certain sophistry in the chorus's argument: a suppliant has put himself under the god's protection; let the god care for his condition. Euripides has Ion deplore criminal supplication:

> The unjust should not have the right of refuge
> At altars, but be driven away. For gods
> Are soiled by the touch of wicked hands. The just—
> The injured man, should have this sanctuary.
> Instead both good and bad alike all come,
> Receiving equal treatment from the gods.
>
> (*Ion* 1314–19)

The issue is somewhat clouded by the allusiveness of **evil** (= "debt"; on Oedipus' pollution see the note to 1132–37), but the chorus's revulsion can only be motivated by the feeling that he is polluted and thus polluting.

237 Antigone intercedes in behalf of her father as she will later intercede with Oedipus in behalf of her brother (1181–1204). The authenticity of this speech was doubted by some ancient critics, and Sophocles could certainly have moved directly to Oedipus' plea without it. Dramatically, however, Antigone and Ismene serve as counterexamples to Eteocles and Polyneices; by giving her a suppliant's prayer the dramatist plants the contrast between sons and daughters firmly in the plot.

Of reverent mind appeals to the same quality that is translated as "mercy" at 246 (*aidôs:* see the note to 1268).

238–41 I would prefer to translate: "Since you cannot endure my father and the story of his involuntary deeds, take pity on me." Our translation follows the construction of Jebb, which takes the text to mean that they won't listen to Oedipus because they have already heard his tale. **He never knew what he did:** for the argument see on 265–74.

243 His blindness and the fact that she sees for him are noticed several times (there is an untranslated phrase referring to "using another's eyes" at 147–48; cf. 182, 867, 1200).

248 Or: "Grant us an unexpected favor" (she does not deprecate their harshness).

251–53 For the idea that a man cannot escape divine influence see the notes to *Phil* 1316–20 and 998–99a below.

260–62 Athens is often celebrated as a place of **refuge;** cf. Adrastus' appeal (for the suppliants and for protection of the dead) at Euripides, *Suppliant Women* 163–92; Theseus' invitation to Heracles, *Heracles* 1322–37; Aegeus' invitation at *Medea* 727–30; perhaps the most famous suppliant for Athenian sanctuary was Orestes (see *Eumenides* 235–43 for his appeal at the temple of Athena).

265–74 This is the first of three passages (see 521–49, and 962–99) in which Oedipus defends himself. The key points in his defense are that he was a victim, ignorant of whom he killed and what he did and unwilling to have committed such crimes had he known the facts. In his role as victim (267, 270, 274; cf. 547–49a and 991–99a) he exonerates himself on the grounds of self-defense and thereby transfers the blame to Laius and even to Jocasta if line 274 means that in failing to kill him when he was a baby both parents knowingly **ruined** him. **Retaliated:** retaliation and retribution are highlighted in the diction and motivate much of the action of the play (cf. 953, 959, 1189–91, 1202–4, 1306–7). Both Oedipus and Polyneices desire retribution from their enemies; Antigone stands against this primitive eye-for-an-eye justice; Theseus strikes back against Creon's violence, who has acted in response to Oedipus' curses (951–53). See the note on reciprocity at 92–93. **Even had I known:** this argument applies only to the killing of Laius and not to incest with his mother. **Those who wronged me:** Jebb takes this of the exposure of the baby Oedipus on Mt. Cithaeron (see *OK* 717–20); Jocasta is implicated in this charge by the plural (**those**), but Oedipus cannot pursue that argument, as he knows (see 979–84b). His logic in effect blames his parents for not killing him as a child.

275–77 **Beg** renews the suppliant's plea, and **move me** refers to the gesture of raising the suppliant and thereby accepting his plea.

278 **What is theirs** means "their function" as protectors of suppliants. Textual problems have necessitated emendation here, and Dawe's text would yield "and by not honoring the gods don't count the gods fools" (i.e., insensitive to the fact that your manners belie your words).

In the following lines the essence of his argument is that they ought to leave judgment to the gods.

284–85 Honest petitioner means "the suppliant who is able to give surety." As at 227, where "made" means "put down on deposit," Oedipus uses a commercial metaphor. The next line (285) translates two verbs ("rescue and guard me," Jebb), the first of which is sometimes used commercially of redeeming a debt by paying surety (see the note to *OK* 310–14).

285–86 The demand **honor me** may seem presumptous; the Greek offers a familiar double negative: "do not dishonor me."

287–91 I cannot find this sort of personification of **Nature** in Sophocles. Translate: "For I come to you, holy and reverent and bring advantage to your citizens." See on 1477. "Holy" probably means "under divine protection," whether he alludes to the protection of the Eumenides (Jebb) or to the auspices of Apollo that now seem realized because his oracles concerning this place have been fulfilled. "Advantage" picks up the theme of "benefit" (note to 92–93 and cf. 308–9). **Some lord** means "the lord of this country, whoever he may be" (Jebb). **Be careful to be just** = "do me no harm"; he has said that he is not "evil" (270–71); now he says "don't be evil (*kakos*) to me."

297 The **father** of Theseus is Aegeus.

306–7 End-line rhyme for the Greek meaning **rest** and **quickly** may be brought out by something like "though he be at rest, he'll do his best."

309 The self-interest of **The good befriend themselves** would not offend the Greeks. The tutor in *Medea* asks:

> Have you only just discovered
> That everyone loves himself more than his neighbor?
> (*Medea* 85–86)

There is no break or ellipsis between the sentences, and we need not take the generalization as apologetic.

310 The preceding conversation naturally leads us to expect Theseus, but it is Antigone's sister Ismene who now appears, thus postponing Theseus' entry. The three-actor "rule" tacitly advises the audience that Theseus cannot appear until one of the three present speaking parts has departed.

313–14 The **Sicilian pony** and **Thessalian sun-hat** seem to have no point beyond specific realism. Jebb says that the horse is not seen by the spectators, but why should she not enter on it?

316 Dreaming echoes the motif of wandering ("does my mind make me to stray?"); cf. 303–4.

324 She probably has not heard their **voices**—certainly not Oedipus'—so the Greek word may mean "names": "father and sister, the two sweetest names I know."

327 Old is the same word (*dusmoros*) discussed in the note to 223–24d ("accursed"); it is translated "unhappy" at 332. This exchange begins six lines (in the Greek) of antilabe (through 334a).

329d My children . . . and my sisters: the punctuation may suggest a reluctant consciousness of shame and guilt. What we have is a stock circumlocution for "person" (Long, p. 124), which, literally translated, means "seed of the same blood." At *Tr* 1147 the same two words occur:

Call together all my *children*, your *brothers*.

Polyneices addresses his sister with the same formula (OC 1275), and the son certainly has no reason to bring up his father's incest! On the other hand, the primary sense ("seed": see the note to *OK* 1078) occurs in tragedy and has, inevitably, double meaning for Oedipus. It may be that Sophocles looks for some poignancy from Oedipus' natural use of a phrase that for him has unhappy ambiguity.

330 People translates the word (*trophê*) discussed at 337–60; here, as at *OK* 1, its literal meaning "food" may be used idiomatically as a term of affection. So Constance, Arthur's mother, describes her absent son:

My life, my joy, my food, my all the world!
(*King John* 3.4.104)

334c The **one person** is explicitly recognized as a slave of the house.

335–36 His question would not seem to imply complete estrangement from them, but see his speech that follows. Her answer attempts to deflect the subject.

337–60 As Jebb suggests, Sophocles may have borrowed the comparison from his friend Herodotus: "In character and custom the Egyptians are altogether different from other men. Among them the women go to the market place and do the shopping while the men stay at home weaving" (Herodotus 2.35). In **bred** and **business**, however, and then in **childhood** (344) and **sustenance** (352), Oedipus stresses tendance and nurture, the care naturally owed by his unnatural sons and given in full by his daughters (the Greek *trophê* occurs three times and a cognate word once). Cf. 442–49. This is a world-upside-down, where women do the work of men and fathers roam as beggars while their sons enjoy the security of home. Sophocles' thematic emphasis is clear from Ismene's response: at 361–62 we might also translate "searching out you and your way of life (*trophê*)." His way of life (rather than "father") is the object because it causes her so much anxiety. The root sense of *trophê* pertains to nurture: Polyneices knows his failure "in not *supporting* you" (1266); Oedipus condemns Polyneices for not sustaining and supporting him (at 1363–67, where the *trophê* stem occurs three times in six lines and is stressed by end-line position); the girls' care naturally comes to their father's mind when he says goodbye to them (1614).

These verbal markers anticipate and underlie the dramatic conflicts. Polyneices and his absent brother are condemned beforehand; the only question is whether Oedipus will forgive them (1326–29). Less expected is Creon's attempt to persuade Oedipus to come "home," which concludes with a bad case of foot-in-the-mouth (see the note on "nurse" at 760). De Kock (p. 14) reminds us that this very word motivated the curse in Aeschylus' *Seven against Thebes* (see the note on "tendance" at *Seven* 782–91). Sophocles has transformed what was probably a literal and particular incident in Aeschylus (e.g., the sons may have failed to give Oedipus his due portion at the table, or they may have given him a forbidden portion) into the thematic and dramatic substance of his drama: we *see* the care of Antigone and Ismene, the appalling physical wreck that is now Oedipus, and his violent, unforgiving curse on Polyneices. Other notes on this theme will be found at 760, 805, 1262–66.

342 They "keep the house at home"; this sort of wordplay is constant. See the notes to 544–44b and 611.

353–55 We know nothing of what the **oracle** had to say about Oedipus during the years of his wandering, and Jebb is probably right to say that "they are invented merely to create a pious office for Ismene."

362 For the thematic connection with his speech see the note to 337–60.

365–72 At the end of *Oedipus the King,* Creon has assumed the regency, though the young sons are apparently of age (see *OK* 1460–68). Despite the fact that **desire** is a contested emendation, the meaning of the present passage points to an initial acquiescence by the boys in yielding the throne to Creon, then later demanding it for themselves. Their first line of reasoning, that they themselves, as products of an incestuous marriage and sons of a parricide and regicide, would continue the city's pollution (**defiled**), has peremptory force. Nonetheless, "an evil rivalry from the gods and their own sinful purpose have now come upon them" (my version of **But then . . . for power**). Greek myth often reveals this sort of conflict between essentially incompatible ways of looking at the world: the metaphysics of pollution, which is absolutely binding and irrevocable, is pitted against social and political realities, e.g., the usefulness of legitimate succession, in such a way that the incommensurability of two world views is highlighted. For example, in the archaic and heroic version of Oedipus' own story he is permitted to remain on the throne, a situation clearly incompatible with the notion that he defiles his house and city. A dramatist may prefer one view or the other or take the reconciling stance of Aeschylus in the *Oresteia*. Ismene's antithesis approves their earlier withdrawal from political power and condemns the present rivalry. For another explanation of this passage see Grene's introduction to the translation of the plays (pp. 1–2).

377 This is the traditional version, i.e., that Polyneices went to **Argos** where he recruited an army to help him reclaim the throne; see Polyneices' report at 1302–7.

379 In the Greek, Ismene alludes to his new alliance by marriage to the house of Adrastus, king of Argos; Polyneices married Argeia, Adrastus' daughter.

381 **Eternal glory** euphemistically substitutes the fame they will win for the alternative to victory.

391 Oedipus' skepticism (cf. 393) about his power to bring benefit seems to contradict his confident assertion at 287–89. At 404 he understands.

392 The **their** refers to the Thebans, whose strength depends upon Oedipus (see the note to 405 for the theme of power).

394–95 **Sustain** means "set you up," to which Oedipus responds that it is a small favor to lift up an old man who "fell when he was young."

396 **Creon** is Oedipus' brother-in-law; the line naturally leads us to expect his appearance onstage—will he or Theseus appear first?

399–400 **Have you at hand** = "have control over you." That they do not want him across the border implies anxiety that the parricide and regicide may pollute the land.

402 **Burial** does not refer to the rites of burial but to the tomb.

405 **Where you'll be free** means "where you will be your own master." Five times in the present passage Sophocles marks a significant theme by the Greek word *kratos* ("power") and verbs formed from it: the sons struggle for power (373); the oracle declares Oedipus' "strength" (392); Ismene tells him that the Thebans want "power over you" (400); Oedipus must try to keep "power over himself" (405); and finally he says that they will never "hold me in their power" (408). Some later lines in which the *kratos* stem occurs include 646 ("I shall prevail"), 839c ("enforce"), 1208 ("power"), 1381 ("overmastered"), and 1386 ("master").

Sophocles dramatizes this theme in a variety of ways: Oedipus appears to be helpless, but the oracle promises power; his help is sought by Thebes and by Polyneices; Creon abducts the girls and is only restrained by Theseus and the Athenian cavalry; Polyneices repents and seeks his father's aid, only to be cursed by Oedipus, so that he departs feeling that his cause is hopeless; the suppliant, traditionally a victim, promises strength after his death to his host city.

407 Blood indicates that they still fear the pollution. In his resentment of their self-serving concern, Oedipus ignores this issue; see on 1132–37. The party that controls the hero's grave controls the sacrifices and prayers at that grave. While the Greeks felt that the dead, and especially the heroized dead, had power from the grave, they also felt that such power was limited by the presence or absence of offerings and by the intention of the person making the offering, who of course is expected to pray only for his own good. In the *Electra*, Clytemnestra sends offerings to her murdered husband's grave (*El* 406) in the hope of appeasing his spirit. The Thebans would like to have Oedipus' grave in the neighborhood to keep their enemies from invoking his spirit against Thebes. See also the note to *Libation Bearers* 84–105. **Bitter** echoes "perilous" in 403.

410 There are physical and spatial limits on the power of the dead; the Thebans need fear him only if they come within range of the place he is actually buried. For his **anger** see on 855.

417 Polyneices confirms her report (see 1331–32).

418–19 Campbell summarizes: "It may seem unreasonable in Oedipus to expect his sons to disregard the interest and the law of Thebes. But he is absorbed in his own destiny, and is full of indignation at the thought of being taken to the borders of his country without being restored to it. . . . He regards the oracles as expressing the intention of Phoebus to glorify him at the expense of his countrymen if they persist in rejecting him." Jebb suggests the sons might have argued that Apollo has "virtually condoned" the pollution of a "father's blood" (407). Oedipus does not intend to look at this problem from the point of view of Thebes or of his sons.

421–22 He makes a wish that the gods may never quench their *fated ambition* (= "itch for power" at 372).

431–32 One of the odd aspects of the conclusion of *Oedipus the King* is that Oedipus, who has cursed and condemned the slayer of his father to exile, though he vehemently desires exile, remains in Thebes while Creon promises to seek Apollo's advice (see *OK* 1410–15, 1436–39). The following passage explains the contradiction between his attitude at the end of that play and his present bitterness in exile. **Clemency** = "gift"; this motif occurs in 4a as "charity," in 540 as "reward," in 647 as "blessing," in 710 (see the note), and in the first stasimon (694b–719b) in the list of gifts that the gods have conferred on Athens and Colonus.

437 Jebb detects a medical metaphor in **cooled** ("in reference to the subsiding of an inflammation"), as at *Tr* 728.

438–39 His **punishment** was the self-blinding. The Greek makes the rage "someone who punishes" and also acknowledges that **what I had done** were "wrongs" or "mistakes."

441 Harsh (Greek *bia*) is a frequent word in this play; e.g., it denotes the manner of Creon: 815, 845, 866 ("cruelly"), 875 ("strength"), 904 ("roughly"), and 916 ("violence"). It also appears in the English phrases "against my will" (657 and 943).

442–43 By repeating "father" (**who begot them**) the Greek, as often, emphasizes the filial obligation. The translation emphasizes **helped,** which is certainly also the point.

445 The **like** isn't in the Greek; its presence may soften his vehemence a bit.

446–49 Unaided = "so far as their nature enables them" (Jebb). If their ability is limited, yet all their natural disposition (*phusis*) is bent toward providing their parent with **food and shelter** (= *trophê:* see on 337–60). **Their father** translates a verbal form of *phusis*. With **throne** and **being king** compare the phrasing at 373 and the note to 405.

453–54 The other prophecies are those he speaks of at 87–93. In the Greek he says "Apollo fulfilled them."

457–58 The Eumenides/Furies, here given yet another familiar name, the Semnai (= **holy and awful;** cf. 90 and see on Aeschylus *Eumenides* 1041), are said to **consent** because they have taken him as suppliant.

460 The antithesis of **savior** and **woe** frames the line in the Greek: "a savior you shall have, and for my enemies woe." The theme of salvation appears in various guises, but the Greek stem found here is especially frequent: see 261, 277 (in "give me this shelter"), 385 ("deliverance"), 489 (see the note), 725 ("protect"), 796 ("good"), 1117, and 1345. This is another theme that is readily dramatized: e.g., the helpless Oedipus finds his aid sought; Theseus saves Antigone and Ismene; Oedipus refuses to save Polyneices; Athens will be saved by the daimonic presence of the dead hero. Note how the chorus's response echoes his claim (463). See the note to 92–93.

464–65 Burton (p. 260) compares the chorus's instruction of Electra at *Libation Bearers* 106–23. As a foreigner Oedipus does not know the formalities of local ritual. In line 465 he explicitly likens himself to a foreigner who would follow the guidance of his patron (*proxenos*).

466 The **expiation** (*katharmos*) is the necessary ritual for purifying the place, which has been violated by Oedipus' intrusion. It is not calculated to purify him so much as to restore the sanctity and purity of the sacred enclosure. By laying to rest the anger of the offended Furies, Oedipus makes ready his own last resting place; if he is to be buried here, the divinities that rule this ground must be well disposed to him. The detail of the ritual (469–90) is remarkable and doubtless familiar to the audience.

469–71 The word for **libations** is normally used for drink offerings to the dead (cf. 1599); the Erinyes are spirits of the dead. **Runs forever:** running water will be pure and so clean (= **holy**).

474 The wreaths or **chaplets** are usually made from olive rather than myrtle; here the Greek simply says **springs**.

477 Temples face the east and sacrifice would naturally seek the sun's purity and avoid ill-omened shadows.

481 For **no wine** cf. 101 and the note.

486–89 The etymological play on **Eumenides . . . gentle of heart** might be brought out by "we call them genteel from their gentle hearts." We have a Greek word for "saving" (see the note to 460) here, and in the manuscripts it is in the singular, thus suggesting that Oedipus is the **suppliant** who saves. The translation apparently takes this word as passive (**his wish,** i.e., "to be safe"); some editors emend to make "saving" modify the Eumenides, but the ambiguity is better preserved with the singular.

489b For the silence cf. 129–32. Since a mere glance may disturb the sleeping spirits, the one who sacrifices retreats without looking back.

498–99 The chorus has just hinted (489a) that one of the girls may perform the ritual, which is to say that the ceremony has its own integrity and inherent purpose. Elsewhere Clytemnestra sends Electra (*Libation Bearers* 84a–105) and Chrysothemis (*Electra* 406) with libations intended to placate the dead Agamemnon, and Helen attempts to send Electra with offerings for the grave of Clytemnestra (*Orestes* 95–97).

500–501 Exile, solitude, and crippling infirmity are common to Oedipus and Philoctetes; for **alone** see on *Phil* 286.

508–9 The motif of work/labor/suffering (*ponos*) is closely linked to filial piety—what the girls have and their brothers don't: the *ponos* stem occurs in 335, 341, 343, 384 ("distress" of Oedipus), and 460 ("woe" for his enemies, i.e., the hard suffering he has endured). Here the stem occurs twice: "for parents, even if one labors hard, one ought to ignore the labor."

510–49 This section is sung by both parties and represents two pairs of responsive stanzas. The coryphaeus wants the truth; for Oedipus the recitation is all pain and yet another chance to defend himself.

515–16 **Kindness' sake** reminds them of their duty to a guest and friend. In the manuscripts the object of **do not open** is "deeds"; the translation's **my old wound** interprets freely. The text is corrupt, but the metaphor may be from opening a book or letter or in a general way from opening up to the light that which has been covered.

519–20 The translation interprets this as the scholiast did, but it is more likely that the chorus refers to a request already granted: "Give me my wish, for I have given you so much as you request." I assume that they refer to his request for sanctuary.

521–23 For **not willed** cf. 240. **I would have abhorred it all** is simply a variant on the preceding line, i.e., "there was nothing willed or voluntary in my action."

525–26 In **joined** we have the image of binding, i.e., "the city bound me to destruction." **Fate** translates *atê* (see on 532). We would say the city bound him to a doomed marriage; the Greek idiom says that the city bound him to the doom (that consisted) of a marriage. Thus Jocasta speaks of

> Doom [*atê*] brought by your wedding.
> (*Phoenician Women* 342)

528 **With whom the thing was done:** the euphemistic English translates a similarly oblique Greek reference, "the bed we don't want to name"; at *Aj* 913 the same word is translated "ill-starred."

532 He calls the sisters two "dooms" (plural of *atê:* Creon speaks similarly of them at *Ant* 533). In this variety of metonymy the person who brings or embodies the abstraction is said to be that concept.

539–41 **Unspeakably** translates a word of uncertain meaning (see the note on *alastos* at 1481–85); perhaps "unforgettable" (Jebb). **You sinned . . . sin:** the Greek does not supply an object for a verb that simply means "to do *something*." Oedipus cuts off the sentence before the coryphaeus can pass judgment: "you did . . . I did not . . . How not?" The single Greek line is divided into four parts, two for each speaker, the most extreme form of antilabe (cf. 546–48 for another four-part division). Cf. his argument at 266–67.

540–41 **Reward** is "gift." Apollodorus' version of the story implies that Oedipus waited until the reward was posted to answer the riddle of the Sphinx:

> When many had perished, and last of all Creon's son Haemon,
> Creon made proclamation that to him who should read the riddle
> he would give both the kingdom and the wife of Laius. On hearing
> that, Oedipus found the solution, declaring that the riddle of the
> Sphinx referred to man.
> (Apollodorus 3.5.8)

The translation follows Jebb, but the text is suspect and a satisfactory emendation has not been found.

544–44b There seems to be some remarkable punning on **father,** the exclamation **God in heaven,** and **strike** (*patros; papai, deuteran epaisas* is the Greek sequence). The Greek exclamation (*papai*) is very like the word for "papa" (either *pappa* or *papa* in vocative), and after father (*patros*) that secondary reference would easily suggest itself. Strike (*epaisas*) puns on a verb of exactly the same form that means "you play the child," i.e., "you jest."

548–49 I did not know him: cf. 271–73 and 525 (the same word). **He wished to murder me** translates an emended text (the sense remains uncertain; the translation's interpretation takes us back to Oedipus' argument at 273–74). **Before God** is interpretative: there is no oath here and no invocation of deity. **Innocent** means "pure," "undefiled by the guilt of murder."

549a The lyric exposition is terminated by the appearance of Theseus, son of Aegeus, or of Poseidon (*Hippolytus* 1169a–70). Theseus is the founding father of Athens, its most popular hero, and a frequent character in Greek drama. See on 260–62.

560–61 Since Theseus knows Oedipus' "crimes" and yet enters disposed to grant his petition, he assumes that the man is pure and personally acceptable as a suppliant.

561–66 For the argument from similarity compare 1334–39a. Theseus was born in Troizen where his mother Aethra was the daughter of King Pittheus. When he was grown he took the sword and sandals that Aegeus had left under a rock as tokens and went off to Athens in search of his father. Along the road he fought a variety of local monsters (Periphetes, Sinis, Procrustes, et al.) before he reached Athens and was eventually recognized by his father (see Apollodorus 3.16 and the *Epitome* 1.1–6). Line 566 may also be translated: "and be turned away and refused safety" (for "safety" see the note to 460).

567–68 For the sentiment and the motif **only a man** see *Aj* 124–26 and *Tr* 473.

576–79 Grace = "benefit" at 92; the idea of profit is uppermost (cf. its use as "good" at 1421). Theseus continues to probe this offer with an (untranslated) synonym for "gift" in 581. Both men have in mind practical, reciprocal aid; cf. 627–28 and 636–38, where the first word for "favor" commonly means "tribute," and so here "payment for services rendered."

586 A **brief favor** is one that can be managed quickly.

587–88 Theseus' **trouble** responds to an untranslated word (*agôn*) with which Oedipus anticipates a "crisis" or "issue" (cf. *El* 1491–92). If we keep the reading of the manuscripts, Theseus says: "do you refer to an issue affecting your children or affecting me?" Dawe keeps this reading and thinks that two or more verses have dropped out after line 588. In either case Theseus asks a leading question that we may not altogether expect from Oedipus' request for burial.

589 Some manuscripts give a more vigorous "Those people will (try to) compel you to deliver me up."

590 The theme of **exile** has already figured prominently (207, 428, 440–41, 445, 561–65) and its evils are proverbial (see the note to *Agamemnon* 1668). Oedipus now explains his untypical choice.

592 Childishness = "you fool" (cf. *Aj* 1375, *OK* 433 and 435). **You are surely in no position** = "in trouble temper doesn't serve one"; for his temper cf. 434, 438, and *OK* 914–15.

596 Curse is less euphemistic than the Greek (the same word is "misfortune" at 255).

605 This confident assertion is based on Ismene's report at 410–11, but Sophocles also portrays the passionate old man as something of a seer in his own right.

606 Given the prolonged Peloponnesian War and the intensity of Theban animosity toward Athens, this must be one of the most naive questions in Greek tragedy.

609–18 Cf. "Time brings all things to pass" (*Libation Bearers* 965). This grandiloquent discourse on mutability offers epanaphora (**wastes away** begins successive clauses in the Greek), half-line clauses, parallelism, oxymoron (**pleasure sickens** = "bitter pleasures"), polyptoton (**unmeasured** and **numberless** translate the same word in different cases), and punning antithesis (**Faith** and **distrust** have the same *pisti-* stem).

621 All for a trivial word means "on a mere pretext" and does not refer to any particular historical event.

622–23 Since the Greeks poured liquid offerings to the dead, the poet blends the idea of libations with that of blood drenching the ground. For similar assurance of aid from the dead see Euripides *Heracleidae* 1028–35.

624 Or: "If Zeus is Zeus and Phoebus the son of Zeus speaks clearly." Cf. 792–93 and *El* 1424. There is no lacuna or break in the sense after this clause.

629a–30 Promise probably refers to Oedipus' words at 287–91.

631 Friendship translates a word from the same stem as "Eumenides" (see 486–89).

632–33 Nothing in this play or in the stories of Oedipus makes him an ally with ties of **hospitality** (= guest-friendship) to Theseus and Athens. They have never met before, and it appears Sophocles invented this tie, perhaps to expedite the rapid and unexpected naturalization of Oedipus (637).

634 He has asked grace, i.e., he has come as a suppliant.

646 On prevail see the note to 405.

647 Blessing = "gift" (see 431–32 and 540–41). A verb from the same stem has preceded in lines 640 and 642: "I give it to you to decide." "May Zeus give his blessing to such men."

652–57 Five lines in antilabe stress the nervous apprehension of Oedipus and Theseus' impatience. **I know what to do!** = "don't tell me what I must do!" The language of this scene has accented instruction and learning (468, 560, 575, 594; see the note to 6–8).

656–60 Menace, threats, and **bluster** translate the same stem (four times in these lines). **Against my will** = "by force" (see note to 441).

663 With the conventional image evoked by **sea of troubles** compare the elaborated image at 1240–44.

665 Or: "If Apollo in fact sent you." The conditional clause does not doubt the truth of Oedipus' claim; Theseus simply reminds him that he has a powerful divinity behind him.

Theseus must depart with his guard because he has no place in the interview between Oedipus and Creon that will follow the first stasimon. While Oedipus' anxiety may occasion some dramatic tension, the audience knows that Theseus is ready in the wings.

668–719b The first stasimon, an interlude in the drama, praises Colonus, the olive tree, Athens, and, obliquely, Athena and Poseidon, whose gifts have made the country great. In the first two stanzas (668–94a) we have a common rhetorical topos (ecphrasis) on the theme of the pleasance (Latin *locus amoenus*). Curtius (p. 195), who discusses the Latin forms of this topos, describes the typical pleasance: "It is, as we saw, a beautiful, shaded natural site. Its minimum ingredients comprise a tree (or several trees), a meadow, and a spring or brook. Birdsong and flowers may be added. The most elaborate examples also add a breeze." The present passage lacks a meadow and a breeze but adds the Muses and Aphrodite as compensation.

Such descriptions of beautiful places have their roots in epic poetry. At the end of his description of the shield of Achilles, Homer tells how Hephaestus made

> a meadow
> large and in a lovely valley for the glimmering sheepflocks,
> with dwelling places upon it, and covered shelters, and sheepfolds.
> (*Iliad* 18.587–89)

Among the fabulous places Odysseus visits is the orchard of Alkinoös, which has five kinds of fruit trees:

Never is the fruit spoiled on these, never does it give out,
neither in winter time nor summer, but always the West Wind
blowing on the fruits brings some to ripeness while he starts
    others.

(Odyssey 7.117–19)

Such landscapes are either the gift of divinities or inhabited by them:

At the head of the harbor, there is an olive tree with spreading
leaves, and nearby is a cave that is shaded, and pleasant
and sacred to the nymphs who are called Nymphs of the
    Wellsprings,
Naiads. There are mixing bowls and handled jars inside it,
all of stone, and there the bees deposit their honey.

(Odyssey 13.102–6)

Cf. Plato *Phaedrus* 229a–30d and Aristophanes *Clouds* 1005–8.

668 The last stanza returns to the motif of **horsemen;** both this stanza and the last begin with the superlative of *kratos* ("strength": see note to 405): here it modifies "land" (and is translated **most secure**); at 707 it modifies "praise." The Greek begins with an address to Oedipus ("Stranger, you have come. . . .").

673–75 Jebb is right to say that the god is Dionysus. The **vale** is his because of his association with **ivy** (see *Tr* 220) and **untrodden** because it is sacred to the god (cf. 127). For the **nightingale** see on *El* 148–49b.

679–80 For **Dionysus** and the **maenads** see *OK* 208–15.

683–85 The scholia also identify the **great ladies** with the Erinyes (**whom we fear** is an interpretative addition alluding to them), but the dual number, after **narcissus,** a flower associated with the rape of Persephone (Kore), makes it more likely that these "great goddesses" are Demeter and Persephone. **Garland** may not refer to some practice of cult, but perhaps recalls the fact that Demeter's daughter was picking flowers, narcissus and crocus among them, when she was carried off by Hades (the Homeric *Hymn to Demeter* 8 makes the narcissus the specially grown "snare" that attracts the innocent Kore).

687–90 The **river** Cephisus (specifically named in the Greek text) is praised for its never-failing water (**unthinned forever**); cf. "beside the sweet flow of Cephisus' stream" (*Medea* 835).

691–92 Sophocles does not use erotic imagery of this kind (**perpetual lovers**): "but always it moves each day, across the plain, swift to bear fruit, with a pure flood, across the breast of the earth."

693–94a The **Muses** are usually said to be daughters of Memory (Euripides *Heracles* 679), but the Athenians had an altar to the Muses as daughters of the river Ilissos (Pausanias 1.29.6); and in the nearby Academy, Pausanias also saw "an altar of the Muses and another of Hermes, and of Athene and Heracles inside, and an olive tree said to be the second that appeared" (1.30.2). We do not know, however, of an altar or precinct of Aphrodite (**the divinity of love**) in the immediate vicinity of Colonus. The **gold reins** may allude to her chariot:

> [Aphrodite]
> left your father's dwelling place and descended,
> yoking the golden
> chariot to sparrows, who fairly drew you
> down in speed aslant the black world, the bright air
> trembling at the heart to the pulse of countless
> fluttering wingbeats.
>
> (Sappho 1.9–12)

On the other hand, such compound adjectives are common in Greek poetry from Homer on, and this particular adjective is elsewhere applied to Ares, Artemis, and Demeter. For similar reasons the compound adjective translated "with its yellow ray" (687) may be ornamental, although some commentators point out the association of gold with the underworld, a link we are bound to notice in a context of Persephone's abduction to Hades. For ornamental adjectives compounded from "golden" see *Aj* 846, *OK* 208 and 1269, *Tr* 637 and 925; for vivid metaphorical value see *El* 838.

694b–706 From praise of Colonus the song turns to praise of the olive, symbol of strength, independence, and fecundity. The olive was Athena's gift to Athens when she and Poseidon vied for honor from the city (Apollodorus 3.14.1). Herodotus, having reported the same story, tells how the sacred olive on the acropolis was burned by the Persians when they took the city in 480 B.C.: "nevertheless on the very next day, when the Athenians, who were ordered by the king [Xerxes] to offer the sacrifice, went up to that sacred place, they saw that a new shoot eighteen inches long had sprung from the stump" (Herodotus 9.55). So it is a tree **no hand tames** and, as emblem of the city, **terror of our enemies.** As a gift of Athena the olive signifies guardianship (706), and its bounty enriches the city, whose chief wealth is its children (701). Sacred olives, found in public groves and on private lands, were under the special care of the state, which sent commissioners around periodically to make sure the trees were not abused; the epithet modifying Zeus alludes to this supervision (**Zeus the Father** would be more strictly translated "Zeus who watches over the sacred trees").

704a–b Zeus "the all-seeing" (cf. 1086 and *Ant* 184) often appears in Greek poetry. **Pallas** (Athena) has been described since Homer as having **sea-pale eyes.**

707–19b Having praised the olive and its divine benefactor Athena, the chorus self-consciously (cf. *OK* 895–96) turns in this final stanza to praise of Athens and Poseidon.

710 Rather than a vague reference to **Destiny,** the phrase allusively anticipates the name Poseidon, which in the Greek is postponed for six lines. We may translate: "praise . . . (that derives from the) gift of a great *daimôn.*"

711–13 The triple anaphora in the repeated **land** represents three adjectives beginning in *eu-* (*euippon, eupôlon, euthalasson*) and defining the **pride** (i.e., Athens can boast of her horses, her foals, and sea-power). Jebb prefers to see in **sea** and **sea-farer** an allusion to a spring of salt water found on the acropolis near the olive of Athena (see on 694b–706). This spring was created by Poseidon as a token of his power and claim on the city when he and Athena contended for honor and worship. The single word in Greek (*euthalasson*) is sufficiently indefinite and evocative to suggest both meanings.

714–14a These two lines are the translator's embellishments. **Son of Time** translates a phrase meaning "son of Cronus" (Poseidon, who is now addressed by name); while time (*chronos*) and Cronus (*cronos*) offer a possible pun in Greek, there is little reason to find such a pun here.

715 This praise of Poseidon gives him credit for inventing **a bit** that is a "healer" for horses, i.e., the horse's bit is a physician (here translated **to discipline the stallion**). Poseidon's association with horses is probably pre-Greek (see Guthrie, *The Greeks and Their Gods,* pp. 94–99) and certainly very ancient, and in classical times he is the preeminent god of the sea. Hence the final description of **long sea-oars.**

719b The **hundred-footed sea-wind and the gull** are, more literally, the Nereids, sea nymphs and daughters of Nereus, who traditionally number fifty (*Theogony* 264).

727 Since the play was written when Athenian political and military power was on the decline, and produced after the city had finally lost the Peloponnesian War, such praise of Athens as we find in the preceding lyrics and in **nation's strength** naturally has the look of Sophoclean encouragement for his fellow Athenians. Cf. 733–34.

728 Creon, like Oedipus and Antigone, enters from the direction of Thebes (stage right, if we use the convention I have followed elsewhere in this commentary); in the other direction is Colonus and Athens, whence the stranger, the chorus, Theseus, and Polyneices enter. For comment on the significance of this staging see Taplin, "Sophocles in His Theatre," pp. 158–63.

732 He speaks more euphemistically ("I have not come planning to do anything") and probably does not intend a veiled threat since he flatters them and speaks of persuading Oedipus (see the note to 736).

736 **To bring him** means "to persuade him."

739–39a As Oedipus knows (see 766–70), his sympathy is proven false by this late offer of comfort.

740 **Poor Oedipus** = "poor tired Oedipus" (Antigone at 14a).

743 **Worst of men** puts the condition in the same language Oedipus uses at 270 ("evil in myself"). Creon's language is that of standard tragic commiseration; it is only the disparity between what he says and what he does, and has done, that reveals the hypocrisy.

757 **Father's** should be a plural (fathers': the gods of the Labdacid family); cf. *Ant* 837, *Phil* 933 (also a plural), and *El* 411. **Listen:** "be persuaded."

759 From the report of Ismene (see 399–403) Oedipus knows, and so does the audience, that Creon will not take him to city and home.

760 For a last word he could not have chosen a worse word (**nurse:** *trophos*); it takes us back to the topic of nurture and care (see the note to 337–60).

761 For the rebuke in **brazen rascal** (= "daring anything") cf. below 1030–32 and see the note to *Tr* 582–84.

763–64 In the Greek the wordplay of **take . . . taken** frames a single line.

765 **Private** means both "my own" and "of my house."

774a–76 There is an oxymoron in **cruel** (= "hard") and **soothing** (= "soft"). Though it is not in the Greek, the play on **amiable** and **amiability** is true to the style; cf. "charity no charity" at 779b. **Do not want** recalls the motif "willing/unwilling" (first at 240). Reciprocity is a keynote here; Creon and Thebes fail in their timing.

777–82 The phrasing suggests the introduction of an argument from an example, but in fact its terms clearly refer to Oedipus' past and present situation.

782 There are other contrasts of words and deeds (**in reality**) at 382–83, 761–62, 817, 861–62, 873, 881–82, 1001–2, 1036–37.

784–91 He knows Creon's real purpose from Ismene's report of the oracles; see 399–411. **Curse** in the Greek is somewhat euphemistic (= "may escape without harm from this land," i.e., from any trouble Thebes might have with Athens). The oracle did not name Athens or speak of troubles between the two cities; Oedipus has inferred from Ismene's report (410–11) and from the signs pointing to burial here at Colonus (87–102) that hostility between the cities must follow (607–24). **Vengeance** translates the Aeschylean word for "spirit of revenge" (see notes to *Aga-*

memnon 1507f. and *Tr* 1236); whether he actually believes that his daimonic presence will be felt so far from his burial ground is open to doubt.
He is mad, very sarcastic, and will say anything to turn the tables on the
conniving Creon. **So much room as they need to die in:** the thought, if
not the language, points to the curse of Oedipus upon his sons (see the
note to *Seven against Thebes* 729–33):

> Yes, he allotted them land to dwell in
> as much as the dead may possess.
> (*Seven against Thebes* 731–32)

792–93 In the *Eumenides* Apollo proclaims that

> Never, for man, woman, nor city, from my throne
> of prophecy have I spoken a word, except
> that which Zeus, father of Olympians, might command.
> (*Eumenides* 616–18)

794–95 The punning in **speech** and **whetted** is in the first place
etymological (*stoma* . . . *stomôsis*), but the second word is an abstract
noun for "the hardening of iron to steel," so that there is some tension
between the apparent identity of the words (the resemblance in sound is
the rhetorical figure called parechesis) and their semantic referents. The
artificiality of the phrasing is intensified by the fact that the Greek says
"Your mouth came here with its tempering."

799 There is considerable bitterness in **pleasure** (for the third time
in this speech: cf. 775 and 766, where "lightly" translates the word
rendered "amiable" in 775).

803 Wheedle and **fool** translate the same verb (= "persuade").

805 You shame your age = "you nurture (the) stain (that is your
reproach)," with an acid allusion to the pollution Oedipus incurred by
killing his father; see also on 854–55.

806–7 Oedipus abuses Creon as if he were a Sophist; Protagoras,
e.g., claimed to be able to teach men to argue equally well both sides of
a question (see Aristotle *Rhetoric* 2.24.9).

813–15 Calling on men or gods **as witnesses** of real or alleged abuse
is common in Greek tragedy (see the note to *Tr* 1248), but Creon has
slight legal claim on Oedipus, and the new Athenian citizen naturally
assumes that he will use **violence.** What follows is about as much violence
as one finds on the Greek stage.

817 Brag = "threat" (as at 658); there is another variation on "words
and deeds" here (see on 782).

818–19 Jebb observes that Creon may have seized Ismene prior to
this scene or that he may have just now signaled a guard to go and do so.

In either case the hypocrisy of his persuasion is now revealed. The girls are merely hostages; it is Oedipus he wants (860).

822 His appeal to **friends** corresponds legally to Creon's call for witnesses (813). **This thief** means "this impious man." The antecedents for this scene, in which an evil character is resisted by an aged chorus, include *Agamemnon* 1577–1673 and Euripides *Heracles* 252–315. This scene is the most vigorous, both for its dialogue and action. It appears from 858 the chorus physically restrains Creon.

830–34a By putting his hand on her (**touch**) he makes a further legal claim to have the right of possession and control (see on 856–60). The scene may recall the effort of the Egyptian herald to carry off by force the daughters of Danaus (Aeschylus *Suppliant Maidens* 825–910); there the local ruler arrives in time to forestall the abduction. Sophocles lets the guards take Antigone off (847) before Theseus arrives to save Oedipus.

834b–43 Antilabe, part-lines, and dochmiac rhythms indicate increased excitement. The responding antistrophe runs from 876–86.

838–39 War: Oedipus refers to his prophecy at 616–24.

839d Let go means "to slacken the reins," a common equestrian metaphor.

844 Antigone's appeal, like Cassandra's at *Agamemnon* 1315–17, has legal connotations: the victim must summon aid if she expects a charge of violence to be accepted in a court of law.

849a-b Sticks = "scepters" (used in 449 in the phrase "being king"), and so sarcastically of the girls. Cf. Oedipus' affectionate use of the same word at 1109b ("my staff and my support"). Cf. *OK* 457.

852 For the motif **later . . . you'll learn** see the note to *Ant* 1270.

854–55 Given Creon's recent violence, the taunt in **against your friends** is triumphantly ironic. **Anger** is certainly his vice (cf. *OK* 806 and the note to 335), but **sin** must be understood, like "shame" at 805, as snidely suggesting that Oedipus willfully perpetuates and indulges the defilement he brought on himself by parricide and incest.

856–60 In half-line and one- or two-line parts **chorus** usually = coryphaeus (leader of the chorus). In scenes such as this we can hardly imagine that the actors remain on stage while the chorus is segregated in the orchestra. **Booty** suggests "pledge" and "reprisal" (see on Aeschylus *Suppliant Maidens* 312–14 and 407–11), i.e., that which is seized in token of a legal claim. Harrison (vol. 1, p. 22, n. 3) thinks that Creon claims to be master of Antigone because "she is regarded as the illegitimate daughter of Jocasta and falls under the power of her mother's nearest male relative, her brother." The language here and at 830–34a would appear to support Harrison's interpretation, but since Creon advances this claim only after he fails to persuade Oedipus to return voluntarily, and then only allusively, we may doubt whether even Creon feels he has a cogent case.

861 A terrible thing to say is a cliché of tragedy (cf. the same adjective in "What repartee!" at 806), and here it seems best to take it sarcastically: "that would be pretty fierce (if there were anything to it!)."

864b–67 For Creon's reaction to the **curse** see 952. **Powers** refers to the Eumenides. **Cruelly** = "by force." Because Greek idioms use "eye" as a term of affection, Oedipus can pun on the loss of the girl who served as his **eyes.**

868–70 For the function of **sun god** (Helios) see *OK* 660 and *Tr* 94–99. For the wish/curse and the motif of "like for like" see the note to *Tr* 1036–40.

874–75 Although Creon is a sneak and in the wrong, his indignation and frustration need not be questioned. **Alone:** he has sent all his bodyguards off with Antigone (they would be a dramatic embarrassment if they were present when Theseus arrives). **Strength:** see on 441.

880 Euripides makes Theseus talk in similar language:

> And if the little man is right, he wins
> Against the great.
> *(Suppliant Women* 436–37)

884 Criminal translates *hybris,* which was a criminal offense in Athens; Creon's answer repeats the word *hybris* and thereby affirms it, "yes, but you must bear it!"

889a The great god of the sea is Poseidon (cf. 714a).

895 Oedipus calls Ismene and Antigone "my only pair of children" ("pair" is a metaphor from a team of horses or a chariot team).

900–901 This topographical allusion may have been precise enough for the Athenian audience, but we cannot tell whether Theseus refers to a junction within a mile or so of Colonus or one in the foothills above Eleusis and below Oenoe, farther along on the road to Thebes.

903–4 For the motif in **laughing-stock** cf. 1339a, 1423, and the note to *Aj* 67. **Roughly** (*bia*) is "violence" (916), occurs again in 922 (untranslated), and in 935 is "under close guard."

912 Your own people means Creon's family; so **nation** is not redundant. For triads see on *Phil* 1018, and cf. the three questions at 887–88 above.

913–18 For a longer discourse on the rule of law and its benefits contrasted with tyrannical violence see Euripides *Suppliant Women* 428–55 (Theseus). See also *Ant* 175–91.

939–40 The first two lines of his speech respond to Theseus' accusations at 917–18.

942 Citizens = "kin." Creon might in fact, under Attic law, have some claim for legal custody of the girls, if their father were not alive. **Love** means "cherish/care for" (*trephein*: see on 337–60). **Against my will** once again uses *bia* ("force"), as at 854.

945–46 Unholy = "unclean" at *OK* 823 (note). Here **parricide** defines; incest is not a topic so readily discussed (see on 962).

948 The ancient Athenian court known as the **Areopagus** had as its chief province trials for homicide; see notes to *Eumenides* 566 and 683 ff.

950–55 Prize = "quarry"; for the metaphor from hunting cf. 1025–26. **Curses:** see 864b–70. **Reprisal** appears again as "answerable" at 959. In linking **old age** and continuing **anger** Sophocles would seem to think of Creon as an evil double of Oedipus; cf. 874–75 and 930–31.

960–65 Arrogance echoes "bold man" at 877. **Insulting** ("treating hybristically") reflects his anger at Creon's comparison of himself to Oedipus who, unlike Creon, was a victim and never willfully hurt anyone. **Deaths:** Greek tragic poetry often uses plurals for singulars, and in this line (962) all three words are in the plural (**incest** is "marriages"). **Calamities** may simply fill out, somewhat redundantly, the usual triad or may refer to unlucky accidents that tied together murder and incest. **By fate** translates the adjective *talas* (see note to *Phil* 339a) and is a stock word for someone who is pitiful or wretched. Here, as often in the *Philoctetes*, it describes the speaker himself and so has the quality of an interjection: "I suffered them—poor me!—against my will!" This word belongs to the language of lament and commiseration: Antigone describes Ismene with it ("Ah, poor child," 318) and later uses it of herself ("You break my heart," 1439). **God's pleasure . . . him** translates plurals in another stock phrase from tragedy (cf. *Phil* 390 and "hated by the Gods" *OK* 1519c). Like our "God's will be done," this phrase acknowledges divine power in the affairs of men and at the same time recognizes that god's way is often mysterious to man. The addition of **perhaps our race had angered him long ago** may allude to Laius' rape of Chrysippus (Apollodorus 3.5.5).

966–67 The lines are a little complicated by the fact that **evil** translates a phrase which might be rendered "blame for error" while **sin** translates a verb cognate with "error" (*hamartia*). So the sense may be a bit circular: "you could not find in me a fault on account of which I committed a crime (fault) against myself and my own kin." The Greeks noticed that vices such as *hybris* and greed often led to even greater vices of the same sort. Both the immediately preceding and following lines argue that a divine malice against his family existed prior to his birth; he, then, is but the innocent victim in a larger snare.

968–70 For these **oracles** see OK 850–56.

976 He did know **that he killed** someone (see OK 810–13). The line is slightly redundant and may be translated "all ignorant what I was doing and to whom" (Jebb).

In book nine of the *Laws,* Plato discusses various kinds of homicide and proposes penalties. Besides surveying the categories of voluntary and involuntary homicide, he takes for granted the murderer is polluted and so must be purified. The penalty will often entail one or more years of exile. Remorse and regret in the culprit are required for rehabilitation, which is the aim of his penology, but the constant emphasis on pollution and the vehemence with which he describes the parricide's crime probably reflect Athenian sentiment:

> "If anyone gets into such an ungovernable temper with his parents
> and begetters that in his insane fury he dares to kill one of them,
> and . . . he is not let off [i.e., forgiven by the dying parent], the
> perpetrator of such a crime will be indictable under many laws.
> He will be subject to the most swingeing penalties for assault, and
> likewise for impiety for temple-robbery—he has plundered the
> shrine that is his parent's body, and deprived it of life. Conse-
> quently, if one man could die many times, the murderer of his
> father or mother who has acted in anger would deserve to die the
> death over and over again. To this one killer no law will allow the
> plea of self-defense; no law will permit him to kill his father or
> mother, who brought him into the world."
>
> (Plato *Laws* 869)

Plato does not discuss the unlikely case of a son killing his father in ignorance, but he does consider self-defense, unintentional or involuntary murder, and regret as extenuating factors. For Plato's views of incest see *Laws* 838, where the crime of Oedipus is explicitly mentioned.

978 Unmeditated = "unwilling," as at 987–88.

984–87 In the Greek, successive lines begin with repeated verbs and participles: "she bore me, bore (me) . . . / (me) not knowing, (she) not knowing, and having borne me. . . ." Jebb compares, for style and thought, OK 1402–8. The repetitions are continued in **not . . . willingly / Nor willingly** (987–88), which are preceded by "willingly" (= **content** at 985).

998–99a Forced is too strong: "with the gods leading me on," per-haps with some latent suggestion that the gods trap him. He can say this without personal incrimination, if he thinks, as at 964–65, of himself caught in some scheme to ruin the family.

1003 Some form of **accuse** occurs five times in this speech (966, 971, 984b ["shame"], 990). Like much else here, this word draws attention to slander and blame rather than guilt, which is more evident in his vehemence than in direct confession.

1009 In my time of prayer refers to Oedipus as suppliant.

1018 Worthless means "weak" or "feeble."

1019 For **You can be my escort** prefer the reading from the manuscripts: "I can be your escort." "Escort" often, as at 1547, describes Hermes as conductor of souls to Hades; Theseus enjoys a grim jest at Creon's expense.

1025–27 The captor is now the captive: the taunt has more bite in the Greek for being summed up in two forms of the same verb (*echôn, echei*). Earlier Creon declared Oedipus his "game" (= "prize" at 950); cf. 1088–92.

1028–31 Others points to the characteristic Greek suspicion of treason. The **reason for . . . confidence,** then, is "someone in whom he trusts." Daring and **insolence** (*hybris*) are linked by excess, rashness, and irrationality (lack of prudence).

1034a–38 The question and Creon's response may imply a certain sullen indifference in Creon's manner; **threaten** implies that Creon's tone backs up the sense. So we should perhaps not see him as whining at 1018.

1044–96 In this second stasimon the chorus imagines the fight with the Theban abductors of the girls; the ode concludes with a prayer for divine aid (1085–94). Greek choral lyrics do not use rhyme schemes.

1044 The chorus's wish to see the fight gives this song a personal cast that is seen in the presence of several first person verbs and pronouns (here, at 1055 in an untranslated "I think," 1075, 1080–84). A single compound adjective produces **shout and brazen sound** in a synaesthesia ("brass-braying"). Cf. the brazen compounds at 58 and *El* 491; for the description of **war** (Ares) see *OK* 190–91. Two sites for the engagement are imagined, one nearer Athens and below a temple of Apollo at the pass of Daphne (**on Apollo's sacred strand**); the second site is at Eleusis itself. **Torchlit** ceremonies, processions, and a night-long pageant celebrating Demeter's search for Persephone were well known features of the September festival at Eleusis.

1050–53 These lines digress briefly for an allusive glance at the Eleusinian mysteries, which offered, under the sponsorship of Demeter and Persephone, purification and a happier existence after death. An alternative translation: "where the holy ones (Demeter and Persephone) tend the sacred rites for mortals, on whose tongue the golden lock (key) of the ministering Eumolpids comes." One of the chief priestly offices at Eleusis belonged hereditarily to the Eumolpid clan. The **golden key** metaphorically alludes to the vow of silence imposed on initiates.

1059–62 The first antistrophe begins here, and the first word is another "or" (cf. 1046–47) as the chorus names yet a third place for the engagement; the **snowy mountain** is specifically named Oea, which the scholiast says borders on Mt. Aegaleus, across which the pass of Daphne went. Yet **snowy** hardly fits the hills of Aegaleus, while putting this place above Eleusis on the road to Thebes seems implausibly remote.

1063–65 Perhaps we can take **the god they fear** (= Ares) as subject and translate: "it will be joined, the terrible war of our neighbors (the Thebans?), the terrible strength of Theseus."

1068–71 Besides a shrine of Colonus of the Horses (see 59a), Pausanias (1.30.4) mentions altars of Poseidon of Horses and Athena of Horses at Colonus. Such references must have raised, if only a little, the hearts of the conquered Athenians (the play was not produced until after the defeat of 404). The **god of the sea** is identified as the "dear son of Rhea, he who holds the earth" (this last phrase translates a traditional epithet which probably refers to the sea holding and embracing the earth). **Loves forever / The feminine earth that bore him long ago** is more literally "the dear son of Rhea."

1072–78 We have no particular reason for thinking that "separate voices" took individual parts for the following lines (not four stanzas but a strophe and antistrophe in the Greek). **Presentiment enchants my mind** = "my mind woos me" (a metaphor from courtship by proxy).

1079–79a Zeus is specifically mentioned: "Zeus will accomplish, will accomplish, something today." This line is treated as a refrain through the rest of this lyric, but it is not repeated in the Greek text.

1080–84 For the claim to mantic **forevisioning** see *El* 472. The wish expressed in **Would I could be a soaring dove** is a variant on the escape motif discussed in the note to *Tr* 953–61. In most examples of the wish to fly away (e.g., *Ion* 796–98 and *Helen* 1479) the speaker desires to escape trouble; here, more positively, the chorus desires an aerial view of the battle. See Aristophanes *Birds* 1337–29 for a Sophoclean wish put to the uses of comedy.

1090–94 Athena (**Pallas**) is invoked as daughter of Zeus, patronness of the city and warrior. Apollo ("who wears the fine quiver" *Tr* 209) and his **sister** (Artemis) both hunt with the bow.

1097 Their prayer for divine aid is immediately answered by the appearance of the rescued girls. **Not . . . lied** echoes the claim to "forevisioning" (1080).

1099a–1110 Their excited reunion is reflected in repeated vocatives, exclamations, questions, and antilabe. Because Theseus will have a speaking part, Ismene is mute.

1113 For the metaphor of implanting or grafting in **be rooted in your father's arms** see *OK* 299. There is a wordplay: "rooted" in the father who "planted" them. Fragment 949: "every evil is rooted in advanced old age." See also on 1672–73. Perhaps the present metaphor is elaborated from "my sweet children" (1109), where Oedipus refers to his children by a common poetic metaphor as "shoots" or "sprouts" of a plant.

Boyes compares Shakespeare's,

> How they clung,
> In their embracement, as they grew together.
> (*Henry VIII*, 1.1.9–10)

1116 **So tired** is sympathetic, but in fact he says "so young." Cf. 1181 for her admitted youth.

1129 At 873 he has only **words** with which to requite wrong; now only words for gratitude.

1132–37 This is a crucial passage for understanding the guilt of Oedipus and his attitude toward it. The plain meaning, and particularly the implications of **no stain of evil in him,** is that Oedipus still feels polluted by parricide and incest. **Stain** (*kêlis*) is the "smear of mortal infection" with which the Furies threaten to plague Athens (*Eumenides* 787); it is the "deadly taint" Oedipus sees on himself (*OK* 833) and the "guilt" of *OK* 1384; cf. also *El* 449, where Clytemnestra's bloody hands are stained from the murder of her husband. There are similar connections with pollution in Euripides: see *Hippolytus* 819–20 and *Iphigenia in Tauris* 1200. Despite his repeated arguments for his own innocence (first at 265–74), he has not convinced himself that he is free from the personal taint that makes a man dangerously contagious to those who receive or touch him (see Orestes' comments on this topic at *Eumenides* 443–50). Some scholars have argued, however, that Oedipus must have been purified, else Theseus and the Colonians would not have granted him asylum. For Howe, the present passage speaks more of Oedipus' personal sense of unworthiness and guilt than of the old miasma. Although Sophocles does not make it clear that Oedipus has been purified, Howe (following Linforth) takes his successful supplication as an implicit testimony to ritual cleanliness (Howe, p. 141; Linforth, pp. 107–9). This analysis, based to some extent on argument ex silentio, stumbles on the fact that Greek sanctuaries did receive as suppliants those who were as yet unpurified; otherwise the passage from Euripides' *Ion* cited in the note to 228–36 would not make sense; Latte (p. 25) also cites Polybius (4.35.3): "It must be remembered that the holy place secured the safety of anyone who took sanctuary in it, even if he were condemned to death." It also ignores the horror the name and presence of Oedipus stirs in the chorus (226–36). Oedipus has chanced upon the sanctuary of the Eumenides and gained its protection before the locals could prevent him from violating its sacred space. Once a suppliant there, he is in the power of its divinities: it is theirs to protect him or to punish him. As murderer and suppliant his spiritual status is altogether ambiguous, and that ambiguity is reflected in his extreme vulnerability (the blind, impoverished, neglected exile) and his professed power to help those who give him sanctuary and burial.

This interpretation leaves us with unresolved ambiguities: Oedipus has argued his innocence on moral and legal grounds, but now he steps back in horror at the thought of touching (and so infecting) a friend, and this horror is based—not on moral or legal scruples—on the ancient taboos affecting parricides and the physical contamination that attends them. Although he has seemingly rationalized his action, and particularly the murder, and repressed his guilt, that guilt now confounds him (perhaps we knew it would, for he has argued too passionately and too often for us to believe that he has convinced himself). Howe's argument (p. 141) would cut the knot by seeing Oedipus' present reaction as one of psychological shame, i.e., a personal guilt that has superseded the ancient sense of physical pollution. Her view is attractive in that it makes the crooked straight, but Sophocles' language and the ambiguities of the plot bid us view his gesture in the ancient light. See also Parker, *Miasma*, pp. 310 and 316.

Cf. the dialogue of Heracles and Theseus at Euripides, *Heracles* 1229–54 (Heracles has killed his own children); for an explanation of guilt as the remorse of conscience see the dialogue between Menelaus and Orestes at Euripides *Orestes* 385–415.

1149 **How I found them, how I took them** would have furnished the substance of a messenger's speech, had Sophocles taken that path.

1156–60 Theseus has been told of the arrival of Polyneices. Why has the son **thrown himself in prayer** at the altar? He has some reason to fear his father's anger, and now the suppliant will himself be supplicated. **Praying** and **pray** translate words referring to his posture ("sitting") at the altar. He seeks an audience and, as a foreigner in a strange land, guaranteed safe-conduct. Even in these preliminary touches Sophocles has been careful to put the best light on Polyneices' conduct and manner.

1171 Ismene (377) has mentioned Polyneices' exile in **Argos**.

1178–79 **To me** = "to (his) father." The motif in **yield** occurs in Antigone's appeal (1184 and 1201) and in Polyneices' language at 1328 and 1334, where "give up" and "comply" carry the idea of yielding. See also *Ant* 1095 for this motif.

1179a–80 Just as Oedipus' reception depended on pious regard for the suppliant, so now he must consider if he too is not bound by the same sacral rules. Sophocles makes both Theseus and Antigone more humane than Oedipus.

1182 **This man** is Theseus who, as ruler, is obliged to see that religious proprieties are observed. It is a mark of his regard for Oedipus that he has framed the preceding statement so deferentially. **Conscience**, if it implies a personal moral standard distinct from religious and social values, is a rare concept even in the late fifth century. I would prefer "purpose" or "intention," with that being defined by **give the gods whatever he thinks their due.**

1189–91 A Greek would normally consider the child's obligation to the parent greater than the parent's to the child; Antigone boldly argues the contrary. The theme of reciprocity (see the note to 92–93) also concludes her speech (1201–4).

1194a–b The translation misses a common medical metaphor from the use of spells and incantations: "yet by the charms of friends they are charmed out of their nature" (thus Liddell and Scott, keeping the Greek play on the cognate noun and verb). So Pindar says of Chiron, the centaur famous as a teacher and physician:

> Some he treated with guile of
> incantations,
> (*Third Pythian* 51)

It was natural to connect the medical function of spells (e.g., charming off evil spirits) with magical persuasion. Prometheus can say of Zeus:

> Then not with honeyed tongues
> of persuasion shall he enchant me;
> (*Prometheus Bound* 173–74)

Other notes on this metaphor at *Aj* 582–83 and *Tr* 999–1003; cf. Euripides *Hippolytus* 479–79a.

1196 **Fate** = "suffering."

1199–1200 **Wrath** repeats "anger" (1193) and has the same stem as **reminder** ("reminder of your *mania*" would be a little closer to this wordplay).

1201 **Yield** also began the speech (1184). The wordplay on **importunate, hard, obdurate** is typical of the Greek text, even though the Greek cannot offer the kind of Latin/Saxon pun found here.

1204a **Pleasure ... pain** makes an oxymoron (more literally, a "heavy pleasure"). He does not yield in principle, only to the person. **Power over my life** (for power see on 405) once again implies anxiety.

1210 Theseus leaves, we suppose to fetch Polyneices, but only the son returns. Theseus' protection is not required by the plot, and the third speaking part now goes to Polyneices.

1211–48 The third stasimon is triadic, with strophe, antistrophe, and epode. The tone is sympathetic; the content abstract.

1211–23 From Homer on, poets and moralists lament the miseries of old age. Homer's description of Laertes, father of Odysseus, offers a much more concrete sense of age's ills:

> and he had a squalid tunic upon him,
> patched together and ugly, and on his legs he had oxhide
> gaiters fastened and patched together, to prevent scratching,
> and gloves on his hands because of the bushes, and he was wearing
> a cap of goatskin on his head, to increase his misery.
>
> (*Odyssey* 24.227–31)

The point of **desire the world** is that man desires more than a moderate, and thus satisfactory, portion of anything, including life. After **a decent age,** i.e., a moderately long life, a man should give it up. **Pile up (a drift** is interpretative) suggests depositing money in the bank, and so the idea that the savings of many days brings the interest of so much more pain. In line 1221 Hades (**underworld**) explicitly qualifies **man's heritage** (= "man's lot," his *moira*), and this noun is modified by three privatives (**no epithalamion, no music, and no dance**) .

1224–26 For the commonplace the scholiast cites Theognis.

> Of all things it is best for men not to be born
> nor to look upon the rays of the piercing sun.
> But when born it is best to pass as soon as possible the
> gates of Hades and to lie under much earth.
>
> (425–28)

Sophocles was possibly paraphrasing these lines; Van Groningen lists twelve citations of Theognis' lines in ancient literature. **Not to be born:** variations on this motif at *Aj* 1192–97 and *Persians* 914–15.

1230 Feathery follies is not a fowl metaphor but rather the easygoing and vain pleasures of youth.

1239 The generalities of the strophe and antistrophe take a more personal form at the beginning of the epode. **Blind and ruined** translates a single adjective that was more literally rendered "poor man" at 203.

1240–43 This is a formal simile: **Think of some** = "as" and **It is like that** = "so." The finite verb (**make stream this way and that**) is repeated immediately in the application of the image to Oedipus. **In the north** means "facing the north" and so "struck by the north wind."

1245–48 The quadruple anaphora is true to the Greek. In the last line **the north** translates the proper name Rhipaean (mountains), which are said to lie beyond the boundaries of Scythia.

1250–51 Since the characters wear masks and some of the audience sits at a great distance from the orchestra, details such as **eyes swollen with weeping** are reported.

1254a Creon, feigning solicitude, entered with a guard and eventually seized the girls; Polyneices enters alone and immediately laments the misery of his sisters and father. Both need Oedipus' aid. The audience, alerted by Oedipus' fear (1207–8), may wonder if he too will prove a fraud. For the question **what shall I do?** cf. *Phil* 895.

1259a **Rotting** is strong, but the entire description vividly suggests a wild, filthy appearance (cf. 1596). See Electra's description of herself and her house at Euripides *Electra* 304 ff. Commenting on 1256–66, Easterling ("Oedipus and Polyneices," p. 6) says: "The style of this passage brilliantly suggests a tone of uneasiness in the speaker; not, I think, hypocrisy, but a kind of awkward frigidity. . . . Some of the detail in this passage is quite offensive, in particular the highly mannered and artificial description of the filth on Oedipus."

1262–66 A possible ambiguity in **food** calls attention to Polyneices' failure as a son. The Greek word is cognate with *trophê* (discussed in the note to 337–60) and may mean, as in the following passage from the *Works and Days*, "what the child gives back to the parent in thanks for his rearing." Hesiod describes the deteriorated society in the fifth age of man:

> Men will deprive their parents of all rights
> as they grow old,
> and people will mock them too,
> babbling bitter words against them,
> harshly, and without shame in the sight of the gods;
> not even
> to their aging parents will they give back
> what once was given.
> (*Works and Days* 185–88)

Since, however, Polyneices goes on to affirm as a witness against himself that he has been negligent **in not supporting** (again the *trophê* stem) Oedipus, he may use the word in ironic self-depreciation. **All this I learn too late:** see on *Ant* 1270.

In his speech "Against Timarchus" Aeschines tells how Attic law denies right of speech in the assembly to those who abuse their parents:

> Who then are they who in the lawgiver's opinion are not to be permitted to speak? Those who have lived a shameful life; those men he forbids to address the people. Where does he show this?

Under the heading "Scrutiny of public men" he says, "If any one attempts to speak before the people who beats his father or mother, or *fails to support them* or to provide a home for them." Such a man, then, he forbids to speak. And right he is, by Zeus, say I! Why? Because if a man is mean toward those whom he ought to honour as the gods, how, pray, he asks, will such a man treat the members of another household, and how will he treat the whole city?

(Aeschines, translated by C. D. Adams, p. 27; my italics)

Aeschines' "fails to support them" parallels the language of 1266 (*trophê*). Easterling (p. 7) also points out that "contempt" in 1277 may have legal overtones. She cites Solon's law: "If someone does not support his parents, let him be held in contempt (*atimos*)." On this topic in general see Lacey, pp. 116–18.

1268 Another version: "Shame (*Aidôs*) shares the throne with Zeus." The personification is traditional (e.g., Pindar *Seventh Olympian* 44); Pausanias (1.17.1) saw altars of Shame, Rumor, and Impulse in the Athenian marketplace. Jebb favors "compassion" for the translation, and Liddell and Scott "Mercy," but the traditional meaning of *aidôs* remains valid here: the word is often linked with fear and supplication and denotes an inhibiting power, social and religious in origin and authority, that stays man from violence (see *El* 243–50) and makes him tend to his duty (see *Aj* 1071–75). Cf. 246 ("mercy") and 237 ("reverent mind") and see the note to *Libation Bearers* 896ff. Polyneices anticipates his father's anger and attempts to restrain it ("shares the throne" echoes the language that describes his posture at the altar of Poseidon; see also the echo in "supplication" at 1380).

1271 The question is a partial line and implies a pause as Oedipus turns away (1272). For such questions in rejected appeals see *Phil* 804.

1275–79 For the formality of his address see the note to 329d. Some of the frigidity Easterling detects (see the note to 1259a) may be seen in "unapproachable" (an untranslated adjective) and **implacable**, polysyllabic adjectives that virtually fill an entire line. **Such contempt** echoes an untranslated verb in 1274, both of which imply not only personal "dishonor" but may also allude to the partial loss of civic rights that was the Athenian penalty for abuse of parents (see Harrison, vol. 2, p. 175). **On pilgrimage** refers to his standing before the altar of Poseidon (1158–59 and 1285–89). He is not very hopeful.

1280 Once again Oedipus refuses to speak and turns away. His rejection of the plea implies a little silence before Antigone encourages her brother.

1290 Stranger should be "strangers" (Theseus is not present).

1293 For **eldest** cf. 374. These brothers belong to a familiar type in ancient myth, i.e., the twins whose fates are intimately bound to one another, usually for ill (Cain and Abel, Romulus and Remus, Pelias and Neleus), but sometimes for good (the Dioscuri, Zethus and Amphion). In Euripides' *Suppliant Women*, Polyneices is a voluntary exile who wants to escape his father's curse; for the quarrel see *Suppliant Women* 150–54.

1299–1300 Since in this version Oedipus did not curse his sons before going into exile and Polyneices does not know the curse uttered at 421–27, the **Furies** would seem to allude to the curse on the Labdacids.

1301 The punctuation suggests agreement with Dawe that some lines have dropped after 1301; I would prefer to think that 1301 is a gloss to be deleted.

1302 The Dorian land is Argos, which is here styled "Apian" after the ancient founder Apios. **Adrastus** is king of Argos.

1309 The **prayers** are explicitly "suppliant."

1313–24 The following list of captains is the same given by the messenger in Aeschylus, *Seven against Thebes* (376–626, with descriptions of each and Eteocles' nomination of opposing champions). Cf. *Antigone* 141 ff. (the champions are not named) and Euripides, *Phoenician Women* 1104 ff., where Adrastus is substituted for Eteoclus. **Amphiareus** is able to understand omens from the flight of birds (**ways of eagles**). In Aeschylus' play he is described as the only pious, temperate warrior among the seven, who are raging maniacs. **Tydeus**, the father of the Homeric Diomedes is another exile claiming Adrastus' aid. **Eteoclus** may have been an invention of Aeschylus. **Capaneus** is traditionally represented as god-defying; he is blasted by the bolt of Zeus as he scales the Theban walls (Euripides *Suppliant Women* 497). **Parthenopaeus'** mother **Atalanta** took part in the Calydonian boar hunt during which the hero Meleager fell in love with her (Apollodorus 1.8.2–3). In the Greek, line 1322 says his name is derived from his mother's cherished virginity ("son of a maiden"). His father was Melanion or Ares; cf. Aeschylus *Seven* 537 and Euripides *Suppliant Women* 899.

1324a–25 Evil fathered me means "born to an evil lot." If Oedipus will not own him, he is cursed with an evil fate.

1326 Now comes the formal petition. To avoid possible Christian overtones in **soul** we may translate "in the name of your own life." He speaks in behalf of all the expedition (**we**).

1331–32 These **oracles** may be either his own (1300–1301) or those Ismene has reported (389–90). Creon's trip was clearly sponsored by the same motive (**power**). **Bless** prematurely daimonizes Oedipus: it is here simply a question of which side Oedipus will join.

1333 Streams, rivers, and **fountains** are sacred and usually inhabited by a local divinity. Cf. *Ant* 842 and *Aj* 862. Plutarch (*Demosthenes* 9) reports Demosthenes' oath in the public assembly: "by earth, by fountains, by rivers, by streams." See on 1767.

1334–39 By drawing an analogy between himself and his father (both beggars and exiles) Polyneices hopes that Oedipus will forget and forgive as he thinks how Eteocles **luxuriates** on the throne (for this censure of the tyrant see the note to *Agamemnon* 919). But **paying court** (= "flatter" at 1004) is the way of the son, not the father. **Fate** = *daimôn.* **Insupportable:** see on *talas* at 960–65.

1341 Such a promise might tempt Oedipus, were his memory not so long.

1342–45 Force (*bia*) against force. Easterling ("Oedipus and Polyneices," p. 8) comments on **If not, I can't be saved:** "There is undoubted pathos . . . but Polynices has given absolutely no indication that he is motivated by a genuine regard for his father or even by a proper sense of his filial duty rather than by the desire for power. He is perfectly frank, despite his attempts to present the case as well as he can; what he is in effect saying is 'I have come to save you, because you can save me.' " This analysis ignores the promise of 1341 (can Polyneices actually fulfill such a promise?) and ignores his remorse, but on the balance it is true that Polyneices has no case, save in his father's charity, of which he will find precious little.

1354–56 Discrepancies among the various accounts concerning how and why Oedipus left Thebes (see 367–76, 427–30, 599–600, 1291–98) have troubled some scholars, but Easterling ("Oedipus and Polyneices," p. 9) thinks the present alteration made "for the greatest possible dramatic effect, not as a sign of unfairness and misrepresentation of the facts." The "dramatic effect" seems calculated to underscore anger and vindictiveness rather than rationality and charity.

1357 Homeless means "without a city." For the Greek the two fundamental social determinants are city (*polis*) and home (*oikos*); see *Phil* 1018. For this frequent word in the play the translation has sometimes used "country" (234), "state" (432), "land" (930), "town" (1013) and "Athens" (1509).

1359–59a He accepts Polyneices' equation (1334–35) but not his argument.

1370 There are eyes that watch: the Greek personalizes this with "a *daimôn* watches."

1374 All bloody means "defiled," as at *Ant* 171, where Creon describes the brothers killing each other. This refers to the pollution (Greek *miasma*) gotten from killing blood kin.

1375–76 Before this apparently refers to the curse at 421–27, which, as Campbell notices, is not so much a formal curse as an accidental, however violent and sincere, wish that they may come to a bad end. The curse is invoked as an "ally" (**fight for me**), a common formula when one calls for supernatural aid: cf. 1011–12, *Aj* 90 and 117, and *OK* 274.

1378 Though your birth was such as it was translates "such sons," which probably alludes to their evil character rather than to their incestuous origins.

1380–82 He says that the curses "overmaster your supplication and your (ambition for a) throne." **Still has a place** = "if Justice (*dikê*) still sits by ancient law jointly with Zeus." His argument responds to Polyneices' personification at 1268. Aeschylus speaks of the "high altar of Justice" (*Agamemnon* 383–84); see also on *Ant* 451.

1385–89a The audience knows the truth of this curse, i.e., that according to legend the brothers kill one another before the gates of Thebes.

1390–93 The Greek adds "paternal" to **hated underworld**, but what does "paternal" mean in this context? An allusion to Laius is almost inevitable (as in the adjective's use at 989a and 1196), so that Oedipus calls down a curse that makes Polyneices' hereditary right a hateful home in Tartarus (= **underworld**). **Powers** (cf. 1444c, 1480, and 1566) are the local daimons as spirits who fulfill curses (for the equation of Furies and Curses see the note to *OK* 418–19). The **Power of furious War** = Ares.

1397–1400 Segal (see pp. 368–69) calls the road (in **coming and journey**) "the single most dominant spatial metaphor of the play." Cf. 1433, 1506 ("lucky coming").

1400–1404 Polyneices fatalistically accepts the curse as efficacious, much in the manner of his brother in Aeschylus' *Seven* (see 653–719).

1407–13 What will quiet me means the proper rites of burial. The passage refers to the *Antigone*, where the action is triggered by Antigone's decision, against the edict of Creon, to give her brother burial. It is hard to feel, with Jebb, that this allusion is "lightly and happily made"; concern for burial is too remote from present events. **Serving** echoes the theme discussed at 508–9, which also surfaced in 1368 (as "faithfulness": Jebb renders "true service").

1417 Or: "Do not destroy yourself and the city."

1418–19 Aeschylus' soldier king also feels bound to continue an ill-omened expedition:

How shall I fail my ships
and lose my faith of battle?
(*Agamemnon* 212–13)

1420–26 Anger may refer to his hatred of Eteocles, but this word (*thumos*) often connotes any irrational passion that is pitted against good sense and advantage (= **good**; it is "benefit" at 92); Oedipus uses it twice of himself (434–38). Cf. *Medea* 1078–80. **Shameful** and **laughing-stock** point to traditional values of the soldier hero. As Dover notes (*Greek Popular Morality*, p. 237), "saving face" was still killing honorable men in the fifth century (see the case of Nicias, Thucydides 7.48.4). **Give way** is a variation on yielding (1179).

Linforth (p. 112) rightly notices that Antigone's argument "implies that if Polyneices abandons his plan, it is possible for him to escape the fate with which he is threatened." Linforth also suggests that Polyneices speaks scornfully of the curse as no more than the wish of Oedipus, but he also says that "by adding 'his father's Erinys' [1434] Polyneices acknowledges that the curse is something more than a wish." The issue is largely one of tone: Sophocles wanted a resigned, fatalistic brother, more to be pitied than censured; such a role does not admit a scornful rejection of the curse as a mere wish. Cf. the reaction of Eteocles when he has grasped his fate:

alas, my father's curses are now fulfilled.
(Aeschylus, *Seven against Thebes* 655)

1436 This line is probably spurious.

1437–38 Here, as above (cf. 1405), Polyneices speaks of both girls, though only the one responds; both should join in the scene.

1447–99 In the mixed lyric and spoken verse of this section the first three stanzas (strophe, antistrophe, strophe) are each followed by five lines of iambic verse divided 2 : 1 : 2. The perfect symmetry is interrupted by Theseus' entry (1499). Thus only the final set of five lines is wanting for absolute responsion.

1447–55 New event refers to the last scene; **forms of terror** = "hard fortune" at *Phil* 1094, which is less mysterious but more literal.

1456 The director may have used a tympany for the **thunder**; the **lightning** seems out of the question for the Greek theater. Similar effects are assumed for *Bacchae* 576–95. Daylight production in an open-air theater would have made sensational effects of this sort difficult, if not ridiculous, even if the Greeks had had the technical means.

1472 Appointed = "predicted"; it is explicitly the **end** *of his life*. Cf. the similar language at *Tr* 1149–50.

1478 Neither Sophocles nor Euripides offers a certain example of **Nature** personified; according to Heinimann (p. 105), *phusis* was not personified until the last quarter of the fifth century. Jebb translates: "Ha! Listen! Once again that piercing thunder-voice is around us!"

1481–85 The lines are freely rendered; e.g., neither the **sword** nor **the Furies** are explicitly mentioned. Apparently fearing that Oedipus is both cause and target of the atmospheric bombardment, the chorus prays to separate itself from such dubious benefits as the blind stranger may bring. Another version: "May I find you [the *daimôn*] gracious; and may I not, because I have looked on this miserable man, find for my portion a favor that brings no profit." In an instant the chorus thinks both of Oedipus' tainted past and of the favor (*charis*) he has promised the city. That favor brings no profit (the oxymoron in a phrase of two words highlights the idea), if they are destroyed by the god's lightning.

1487–88 The repetition of **mind**, with a change in meaning, may be offensive, but the sense is perhaps "why would you want (just now) trust in the clarity of your mind?" (West, "Tragica III," p. 115).

1489–99 Immediately Oedipus reasserts the benefit he will bring (a **blessing** is a *charis*), and the chorus, apparently more impressed with his power for good, returns to the favor in 1497–98. To bring out this third use of *charis* in fourteen lines we may translate: "For this stranger thinks it right that you, the city, and his friends should have a just favor in return for the kindness he has had." For this theme in the *Colonus* see Kirkwood, pp. 244–45. The word has occurred in 248, 767, and 779b; for the reciprocal nature of *charis* see *Aj* 522 ("kindness").

1496 **This strange man** is simply "this stranger."

1508 For the metaphor **sinks in the scale** see *Tr* 83.

1516–17 Although Theseus (606) doubted that trouble would come from Thebes, Creon came to fulfill Oedipus' prophecy.

1520–23 Despite the lack of pre-Sophoclean evidence for a cult of Oedipus at Colonus, it is hard to believe that the poet would have made whole cloth a play about the hero's burial in the Attic deme. In later times Pausanias (1.30.4) found a shrine to the hero Oedipus at Colonus, which need not be exactly identical with the site of burial. The actual site may have been a mystery or a carefully preserved secret (1530–34a), since stealing and transferring the bones of heroes was a familiar practice in antiquity. Sophocles has taken every step, short of an epiphany, to invest the passing of Oedipus with solemnity and mystery, and that is the way of staging the exodos. Needless to say, such solemnity does not entail apotheosis. Talk of transcendence and transfiguration is not to be found in Sophocles (on this topic see Gellie, p. 181).

1530 **Keep it secret** = "save it": as Theseus has saved Oedipus, so the secret place of burial will be preserved to protect Athens. Some priesthoods were hereditary and tended by specific families.

1534a The Thebans are **the dragon's sons** (Spartoi) because they all descend from the teeth of a dragon. Cadmus killed it and sowed its teeth, which were born again as the Spartoi.

1535–37 The notion that divine retribution may move **slowly** but will come sooner or later is as old as the *Iliad:*

If the Olympian at once has not finished this matter,
late will he bring it to pass, and they must pay a great penalty.

(4.160–61)

1539 The same verb meaning **teach** began this speech ("disclose" at 1518).

1540–42 Even though there is no word corresponding to **voice** in the Greek, it seems fair to understand that some inner premonition advises him that this is the moment forecast by the old oracles.

1544a That the sightless man can lead others certifies the truth of his prophecy and the presence of something divine. Note that the procession reverses the order of the first scene, when Oedipus entered led by Antigone.

1547–48 **Hermes** conducts the souls of the dead to Hades and so may be called **the angel of the dead.** Cf. *Aj* 832. **Persephone** is the consort of Hades; cf. 1556–57 and *Ant* 894.

1549 Since this **light** may refer either to the sun or to his life (Greek idiom equates light and life), we have both a "life without light" and "a sun that gives no light." With this farewell cf. *Aj* 856–59a and *Alcestis* 244–45.

1556–78 In this brief lyric, technically the fourth stasimon, the chorus prays to the powers below that Oedipus may have a safe and easy passage to the underworld. This song gives the actor playing Oedipus time to retire and assume the role of the messenger who will describe Oedipus' passing.

1556–61 The **Lady** is Persephone (see on 1547–48). The **master of night** is Hades, here addressed in two vocatives with the familiar name "Aidoneus." **Hell** is the Christian analogue to the Greek Hades but an imperfect one inasmuch as for the Greeks Hades houses all the dead and is not reserved exclusively for the damned. It is not associated particularly with either fire or **cold** (the translator's interpretation).

1565–66 Editors have suspected these lines for grammar and sense. The chief problem is in **unmerited and untold,** the word for which is often rendered "in vain" (see 1451). If the manuscripts are sound, the sense is "though many sufferings all for nothing were his, yet may some just god relieve him from distress."

1567–78 The powers are feminine and so probably the Furies/Semnai; The **tameless** (= "unconquered") **Beast** is Cerberus, the three-headed dog who guards the gate to the underworld. Cf. Euripides *Heracles* 20–25. **Of the strange hosts** is, more literally, "that [welcomes] many strangers." Punctuate with a full stop after **say**. **Death** is not explicitly mentioned, but someone is addressed as "child of Earth and Tartarus" (= **offspring of Earth and Hell**); the scholiast thinks Cerberus is intended, though his parents are said by Hesiod (*Theogony* 304–12) to be Typhon and Echidna. In Greek myth Sleep and Death are brothers, and the comparison of death to sleep is already common in Homer. Since the last line (1578) invokes "the giver of sleep," **Death** is probably correct in 1573. Cf. *Ant* 510.

1585 Mercy is not a notable quality of the Greek gods. Jebb translates: "Ah, how? by a god-sent doom, and painless?"

1590–95 We should probably assume that the topographical references in this passage would have been familiar landmarks to Sophocles' audience. **Road** is the reading of most manuscripts but modern editors prefer "threshold," with an allusion to the "Doorsill of Brass" (58 and note): "When he came to the sheer threshold rooted in the earth with steps of brass." This, together with Theseus' and Pirithous' covenant, marks the place as one of many entrances to the underworld. Theseus and his friend the Thessalian hero Pirithous made a pact to have daughters of Zeus for brides. When Pirithous chose Persephone, the two went down to Hades to carry her off (Apollodorus *Epitome* 1.23). This pair, as well as Oedipus and Adrastus of Argos, had shrines at Colonus (Pausanias 1.30.4). The **stone bowl** may be, as the scholiast suggests, a natural hollow in the rock. The **place of stone** is specifically identified as the "Thoric stone," but the significance of this name for the present passage is not known. The scholiast also says that some put the rape of Persephone here (ordinarily that spot is near Eleusis); the **pear tree** may have marked that site (Erineos, the place mentioned by Pausanias [1.38.5] means "wild fig"). We cannot identify the **tomb.**

1599 He will clean and purify himself. For **libation** of water cf. 469–81.

1600–1601 Demeter nourishes young crops and cereals. At nearby Eleusis, a spring festival to Demeter the **Freshener** (*cloê*, a cult title) commemorated her care for the new crop.

1606 The god below is *Zeus chthonios*, i.e., "Zeus under the earth," a mode of describing Hades known to Homer and Hesiod. The timing of this thunder, coincident with the completion of his ablutions, reaffirms the divine summons.

1617 Love suggests to the Greek ear not only affection but also care for all those within the circle of family and friends. The wider range of the Greek concept is illustrated by *El* 981 and *Aj* 680.

1632 For the **hand** sealing a **pledge** cf. *Phil* 813–16 and *Tr* 1181–91, where, as here, the dying hero exacts a pledge of post mortem responsibility; but Heracles' claim is personal and selfish, whereas Oedipus sees to the care of his daughters.

1644a To see = "to learn." It is not simply witness but also knowledge that is crucial (cf. 1518–34a). There is also, however, a fearful sight (1650–52).

1653–54 Just as Olympian Zeus has summoned Oedipus with thunder and lightning and chthonic Zeus with thunder (1606), so now Theseus pays homage in a single prayer to the Earth and the Olympian gods (= **powers of the air**).

1655–65 The messenger surrounds the passing of Oedipus in mystery but never goes so far as to deny that he **perished**. Thus a certain ambiguity remains, a marvel (**wonderful**), but more mystery than miracle. **Some attendant** (cf. 1547–48) would seem to allude to Hermes, but the possibility remains that he proceeded unattended into the darkness that opened with benign favor (= **in love**) for his passing.

1669–69a It may be worth noting, in connection with the entry of Philoctetes (see note to *Phil* 201–20), that the **sound of weeping** is heard before the girls enter from the parodos and that the messenger announces them by referring to their lament rather than to their actual appearance. Although we do not know exactly when the song begins (as they appear or only after they have reached the orchestra?), in this case I would have them first make their way to the center of the orchestra.

1670–1750 This entire section is in lyric meters and sung; it is a lament (*thrênos*, as Theseus calls it at 1751; cf. *Aj* 891–973 and *El* 89–250).

1670 Cries of grief precede **Now we may weep.**

1672–73 Or: "lament the blood of our father, implanted and accursed." It is the family **heritage**, firmly rooted in the blood and ineradicable, that they lament.

1675 Horror is, rather, "burden" (*ponos:* see on 508–9).

1678 Bewildering mystery means something unintelligible or irrational, i.e., what they cannot account for (1679a).

1680 With sea cf. 1660.

1681–83 Too much mystery: "The unseen plains (of the underworld) snatched him away in/by some invisible fate." There is no question of **up or down**. Similarly, at 1701 the Greek has the (untranslated) phrase "beneath the earth."

1684–87 They mourn their own lot. **Deathly** may belong to the girls rather than **night**; if so, translate: "For us who belong to death, Night . . ." (West, "Tragica III," p. 113). **Lives** brings back *trophê* (note at 337–60).

1694a–b For this commonplace see on *Phil* 1316–20.

1697 The antistrophe begins here and repeats the parts responsively and in the same order of singers.

1704a–5 The antilabe of these lyrics responds to the verse at 1678–79b.

1711 There is no **terror** in the Greek.

1717 **Lost our father** emphasizes their loneliness and repeats a word from 1714 ("lonely"); cf. 1734–35 and see the note to *Phil* 286 for the motif.

1724a The second strophe runs to 1736: questions, exclamations, interrupted phrases, a staccato of alliterative interrogatives ("why?" "what?" "whom?"), and simple diction turn the mourning to a frenzy.

1726 She says, perhaps referring to his resting place, "to the hearth (or altar) of the earth." Schneidewin suggests that Ismene does not understand because she thinks of the altar where Theseus was sacrificing.

1737 In the second antistrophe the chorus replaces Ismene in the dialogue and sings the lines responsive to Antigone's in the strophe.

1740 To their **A place . . . unharmed** (implying sanctuary in Athens) she responds "I understand," (not **No**).

1745 The Greek love of antithesis contrasts what was hopeless with, hyperbolically, what is beyond hopelessness.

1747 **Great God!**: Zeus is addressed with a vocative. **Powers that rule our lives** = *daimôn*. Another version: "To what hope (expectation) does the *daimôn* still drive me?" The phrasing echoes the older world (cf. *Aj* 505–6, *Libation Bearers* 1061–62).

1751–53 The interpretation of these lines is controversial, but **night** (an emendation) is to be rejected. **Benediction** is *charis* (see on 1481–85) and **of earth** reminds us both of his burial and of the Eumenides whose ground he now inhabits. Linforth ("Notes," p. 75) offers a paraphrase of the meaning: "There should be no lamentation for one with whose buried body has been jointly laid away in store the benevolence of the lower world." "Laid away" plays on the burial of Oedipus and the storing of treasure, so "benevolence" (*charis*) looks at once to the manner of his death, which was, as we say, "full of grace," and also the favor his daimonic presence will continue to bestow on Athens. The same metaphor from storing away a treasure may be present, more faintly, in "what is appointed for you" (1519). **Retribution** (*nemesis*: see on *El* 792) implies that the gods may resent excessive and misplaced mourning.

1754 **Fall on our knees** marks yet another supplication.

1760 Cf. Oedipus' instructions at 1640–44a.

1765 **Preserve . . . from its enemies** echoes "will never wear away" (1519a: a single word in the Greek).

1767 Zeus is the oathkeeper, i.e., the god whose special province it is to oversee good faith in oaths; Agamemnon prays,

> Father Zeus, watching over us from Ida, most high, most
>   honoured,
> and Helios, you who see all things, who listen to all things,
> earth, and rivers, and you who under the earth take vengeance
> on dead men, whoever among them has sworn to falsehood,
> you shall be witnesses, to guard the oaths of fidelity.
>
> (Iliad 3.276–80)

1771–72 Another (see the note to 1407–13) allusion to their presence in Thebes during and after the seige of Polyneices' army.

1775 For his sake: the last *charis*.

1779 In the hands of God: this is the interpretation of Jebb and others, but the actual wording does not mention god: "all these things are confirmed" (by Theseus? by the gods? or, more vaguely, "all the events of the play are accomplished"?).

Antigone

ANTIGONE was the first of Sophocles' three Theban plays to be produced, probably in 442 B.C. As the play begins, Antigone and Ismene, the only surviving children of Oedipus, discuss an edict prohibiting the burial of their brother Polyneices, who has been killed in battle while attacking Thebes, leading an Argive army against his brother Eteocles. Creon, their uncle, is the new ruler of Thebes and has determined to leave Polyneices' corpse unburied as an admonition for anyone else who would attack the state. Antigone is set on giving her brother proper funeral rites, even though her sister will not take the chance with her. Successful in burying Polyneices, Antigone is apprehended by Creon's guards when she returns a second time to tend the corpse. Her capture sets the stage for a series of confrontations, first between Creon and Antigone, then between Haemon, Creon's son, and his father, and finally between Creon and Teiresias, the old Theban seer who announces that the gods are offended by Creon's refusal to grant burial to the fallen warriors. Shaken by Teiresias' prophecy, Creon attempts to undo the wrong. It is too late, however; Antigone, interred by his order in a sealed tomb, has taken her own life, and Haemon upon discovering her death kills himself. (For the story of Antigone's parents see the note prefatory to the Theban plays.)

Creon is much censured in criticism, called "stupid" by Kitto and "godless" by Linforth. Because it is difficult to imagine how the fullest dramatic and tragic qualities of the play will be realized if he is played as a tyrannical, stupid, godless wretch, an attempt is made to cast a sympathetic eye on him in these notes. Others, of course, have gone so far as to call him the "hero" and tragic protagonist of the play, a path which, if clearly wrong to the majority, nonetheless indicates that he has some potential for sympathy. Wrongheaded is not "stupid," however, nor is "spiritual blindness" godless blasphemy, and we want to find the fine line of characterization that permits sympathy for him in the last scene of the play; otherwise the audience must simply rejoice in the devil getting his due. When the gods speak through the omens of Teiresias, Creon, thoroughly shaken, responds—too late. A truly godless tyrant would laugh Teiresias off the stage and wait for news of his son's suicide.

Creon tries to correct his error; that he is capable of such a change ought to be read back into his character by the director. See Nussbaum, pp. 51–67.

Scene: In the prologue (1–99) Antigone seeks Ismene's help in burying their brother and is rebuffed. The time is early morning (see on 16). The girls come out from the palace (there are no interior scenes, played as such, in Greek tragedy). Since Creon also lives in the palace, privacy motivates their meeting here (see 18–19). Each identifies the other with her first address, and though the scene's dramatic point is the testing of Ismene and the resolution of Antigone, a number of details defining the initial situation are subtly introduced (e.g., at lines 7, 13, 15, 27–29).

The prologue repays comparison with *El* 938–1057: one woman urges her sister to help her in a plan that strikes at established power (Electra would kill Aegisthus to avenge her father); the weaker sister refuses and argues that, though justice is on the side of the plan (*El* 1039–42), mere women (*El* 996 and *Ant* 61–62) must acquiesce. Electra and Antigone remain resolute, while Chrysothemis and Ismene retire. Among the shared motifs are the recognized danger (*El* 945; cf. *Ant* 74), piety as a motive (*El* 969a; cf. *Ant* 74), the virtue of an honorable action (*El* 973–83; cf. *Ant* 96–97), noble birth demands noble action (*El* 989; cf. *Ant* 39), and a bitterness that shouts "denounce me" (*El* 1031 and *Ant* 86–87). Electra admits that she did not expect Chrysothemis to help (*El* 1017–18; cf. *Ant* 69–71), but, like Antigone's hard sarcasm, this remark may stem more from bitter disappointment than cynical lack of confidence in her only friend.

1–3 Family ties and family loyalty are primary themes: who are your friends (10, 11), and how will you treat them? See 73, 99. The brothers have already died fighting for power; Creon, Antigone's uncle, has sided with Eteocles. Before the play is out three more members of the family will die. **Father** is Oedipus, who is mentioned by name in the Greek. **Suffering:** Antigone uses this word (*kaka*) three times in this speech (also 6 and 10: "trouble"); she refers to the misfortune and degradation that now culminate in the proposed desecration of Polyneices' body. **That Zeus does not achieve:** cf. the last lines of the *Women of Trachis* and *OK* 739.

4–5 **Nothing free from doom** (*atê:* see the note to 531–33) is illogical and has long been considered corrupt, despite the importance of the concept in this play. The only way to save the logic is to understand this phrase as an appositional gloss on **grievous**, i.e., "there is nothing grievous, (I mean) nothing that is unaffected by *atê*." **Shameful** and **dishonoured** point to social motivation distinct from but not opposed to her religious concern. In this scene honor is stressed: 22–26 (the *timê* ["honor"] stem occurs three times in the Greek), 39 ("noble": are we well-born or base?), 78, 79. For Antigone there are two sides to honor: honoring the dead (because he is a member of the family, one classed as "friend" [*philos*]) and acting honorably (see on 72 and 97).

7–8 For the **edict** see Creon's speech at 192–207. He is the **commander**; her tone is contemptuous (cf. "the worthy Creon," 31).

10 The division between friend and foe will be turned against Ismene when she refuses to help ("hate" at 86, 93, and 94 translates the same stem). The **foe's troubles** means "such as belong to foes," which is Creon's view. Goldhill's reading of the play (pp. 88–106) focuses on language and action related to "friend and foe."

13–17 Aeschylus' *Seven against Thebes* treats the posting of seven champions from each side to each of the seven gates of Thebes (see below 141–48). Eteocles and Polyneices draw the same gate and kill one another. Polyneices had fled to Argos where he raised an Argive army to support his claim on the throne. Euripides' *Suppliant Women* also dramatizes an episode following this attack. The *Antigone* does not discuss the propriety of his claims, but there is no doubt that he raised a foreign army to invade his native land; cf. the choral jubilation (99–153, the parodos) and Creon's view (198–203). **This very night** may also mean "in the present night," and the predawn darkness may explain the ease with which Antigone accomplishes the first burial. The guard (252) says that the first day-sentry discovered the body buried, and the parodos begins with a hymn to the new day (99a–101).

20 Comments such as that in **clouded** indicate tone, here troubled and "dark": since the characters wore masks, facial expression was fixed, and body gestures and inflection of the voice were all the more significant.

22–26 **Honor** is repeated twice in the same line in a typical antithesis: "honoring one, dishonoring the other." **Just** and **law** suggest customary treatment, not written law; see 450–57.

26 **In pain** = "miserably" (see on OK 1204).

28 **Bewail** denotes the keening at burial: Creon will forbid it ("mourn" at 205), Teiresias will predict it for the house ("wail" at 1079), Haemon (1209) and Eurydice ("wept" at 1302) will give their last moments to lament.

29–30 It seems possible that the true reading for line 29 has been preserved in an interpolation from the *Antigone* at *Phoenician Women* 1634, where Creon himself pronounces the edict:

"Whoever lays a wreath upon this corpse
or buries him, shall find reward in death.
Leave him unwept, unburied, food for the birds."
                    (*Phoenician Women* 1632–34)

If our text is corrupt, line 30, with an image of the corpse as a treasure chest (a "sweet treasury of food" is one meaning), may not be authentic. On the other hand, the ambiguities in the body as a "sweet treasure" (the brother she treasures; a hoard of carrion for the birds), if morbid and grotesque, nonetheless convey more vividly her horror. Leaving a body for birds and dogs is an old threat (see *Iliad* 1.4–5; 22.335–36). Her present intention is to remove the body from the field (see 43); without Ismene's help she must be content to give it formal rites there (see 80–81).

31 **Worthy** is also sarcastic at *Phil* 872 (= "brave"; cf. Deianira's "brave" at *Tr* 540–41).

32 **Yes, yes, I say to** *me* is but one phrase that indicates Antigone's strong *personal* feeling, i.e., there is more than piety at work in her spirit. Note her impatience with Ismene (69–71, 86–87) and her insulting defiance of Creon (469–70).

37 We hear no more of **public stoning** (cf. *Agamemnon* 1117f.).

39 For the contrast between **noble** and base (**fallen**) see Ajax' "Let a man nobly live or nobly die" (*Aj* 479). Cf. *El* 989 and the same language at Euripides' *Phoenician Women* 1621–22. Inflection enables the Greek to make these antitheses crisp and pointed (six words in the Greek). Finley (*Essays*, p. 84) observes that the *Antigone* "is also in style the most antithetical not merely of Sophocles' plays but probably of all extant Greek tragedies." The balance and compression, which Finley sees as typical of the Sophist Protagoras, are to some extent evident in the English of lines 10, 21–23, 73, 78, 88, and 156.

49–54 Since the *Antigone* was produced perhaps fifteen years before the *Oedipus the King,* we cannot turn to that play for background for this one. Oedipus is dead and apparently died at home (contrast *OK* 1519a–c), not in exile, as in the late *Colonus.* He was **abhorred** because he was discovered a parricide and because of the resulting pollution of his native land. **Through his own curse** = "because of the faults he found in himself," perhaps a euphemistic allusion to incest with his mother Jocasta, who hanged herself (*OK* 1263–64) when she found that she had married her son. **Himself:** four Greek words in six lines repeat *self,* as if to underline choice (see the note to 815–23).

59 **Perish terribly** ("vilely"): cf. Chrysothemis' argument that only a "dishonorable death" (*El* 1008) awaits Electra's foolish plan. With **force**

law compare the language at 66–67. While they use the same word for "law" (cf. 25), Ismene clearly refers to Creon's edict. Whose "law" will triumph? For the depreciation of women see *Agamemnon* 594, *El* 996, and variations at *Aj* 652 and *Tr* 1062, 1075.

66 Forgiveness: like Chrysothemis, Ismene never denies the moral and religious propriety of her sister's action.

68 Wild and futile refers not to her manner but to an action Ismene judges is beyond what is called for. Antigone's decision is impractical, so "senseless" (99 and 561–62; see also on 384).

69 Cf. Electra's similar reaction to Chrysothemis' urging that she "learn to give in" (*El* 1017–20); later Antigone will refuse to accept her sympathy and support (*Ant* 536–60).

71 Be what you want to: since the Greek imperatives for "be" and "know" have the same form, this clause may also be translated "know what you want to know," i.e., "think as you do and call that understanding." Because the accent on "what" differed according to the intended meaning, the Greek was not ambiguous to Sophocles' audience. In light of the emphasis in this play on words for knowing, thinking, planning, and the like, I am inclined to favor "know." "You want" is repeated in "you may see fit" (77); cf. Antigone's "I know" (89) and "ill-counselling" (95) and Ismene's "know this" (98).

72 Death is best (*kalon*), that is, death is the noble way; cf. the similar language at 97, where "grace" echoes "best." We may be tempted to detect a morbid strain here, but the emphasis seems rather on the good name to be had from the burial. For her consciousness that death will be her reward see 37, 91, 97, 460–62, 555, and 559.

75 To please the dead may allude to the notion that the dead, and particularly those wrongfully killed or improperly interred, continue to seek revenge and have some power from the grave. Cf. *El* 243–50 and my note to *Libation Bearers* 354ff.

79a Three times (also 90 and 92) Ismene appeals to the same word (here in **cannot**) to express her sense that the business is impractical; see also on 361.

83 Clear your fate conveys the idea of setting something straight (cf. 167), and perhaps "set your own house in order" is our equivalent; a similarly elastic use of "fate" appears at *Tr* 88–89 ("my father's usual good luck").

86–87 Harrison ("Three Notes," p. 14) translates "You will be more hateful to everyone if silent." The construction is in the second person, not the first (I); his version substitutes bitter sarcasm ("we'll all hate you") for the more personal exaggeration of this translation. **Dear God** translates the same exclamation that is "Oh" at 82; its hint of mockery may support Harrison's view. On the other hand, the hate at 93–94 is personal.

94 The awkward Greek is improved by Dawe's emendation: "you will be summoned into court as the enemy of the dead."

95–96 Our sense of Antigone's personality and motives depends in part on the tone she takes. Do we find more intransigence than anger? Pathos of failed hope? Resignation and acknowledgement of her fate? Commenting on **me and my own ill-counselling,** Long (p. 109) says that "Antigone attaches to herself an *alter ego* or force of destruction which she rightly foresees will be used to describe her behavior." He refers to the chorus's judgment at 601 and 875. **Ill-counselling** = "fault" at 1267, where Creon admits his error. **This terror** may mean "this business you think so terrible" (see the note to *OK* 514).

98–99 The last clause is ambiguous and may mean either that (1) Antigone is truly loved by her friend or (2) Antigone truly loves her friends. Why would Ismene want to speak ambiguously? Our version draws attention to her loyalty to Antigone; the alternative emphasizes, and approves (a word meaning "truly/correctly" and modifying "loving" is omitted), the ethical ground of Antigone's action. The second version's antithesis ("senseless but loyal") yields a sharper, more pertinent ethical focus to the last line of the scene. See Goldhill, p. 93.

Ismene returns into the palace. Antigone goes off to the plain (stage right) where Polyneices lies. The chorus enters from stage left (the city).

99a–161 The chorus is composed of Theban elders who have been summoned by Creon (154–61); their song, however, celebrates the previous day's victory, the repulse of the Argive army, and the gods' righteous aid to Thebes. There is no hint of the shadows that hang over the prologue. Although Polyneices' cause is tainted by association with the defeated Argives, the chorus hardly condemns him personally in such a way that we see them clearly taking sides before the sides are drawn. The parodos begins directly with lyrics, with each stanza followed by seven lines (in the Greek) of anapests (in recitative; here they are indented).

99a–104 It is natural to invoke the **Sun** at the beginning of the day (cf. *Ion* 82) and in moments of triumph, as does Euripides' Electra:

O flame of day and sun's great chariot charged with light.
(*Electra* 866)

Since the Greek says that the Sun rouses the Argive host to headlong flight and connects this with a **bridle** (= "bit"), the common idea of the Sun driving a chariot may be latent. **Dirce** is a well known river near Thebes which is often paired with the River Ismenus. **The man** translates a generic adjective ("the white-shielded one"; cf. "covered with white-snow wing,"

113) descriptive of the plain shields of the Argive soldiers. **Shook his bridle free** is the sense we might expect, but the Greek, taken literally, describes a "sharp bit," i.e., a restraint on flight. Lloyd-Jones ("Notes," p. 13) translates "moving him off in a headlong flight by means of a sharply piercing bit" and interprets the bit as "the bit of compulsion":

> but Zeus's bit
> compelled him to do this against his will.
> (*Prometheus Bound* 672–73)

More imagery from chariot racing at 132 and 140.

110–15 The lyric puns on Polyneices' name ("quarrelsome": see *Seven against Thebes* 829–30). **Dubious** means "having two sides." First he is compared to an eagle, then metaphorically identified with it. Several words and phrases, e.g., **screaming shrill, horse-hair crested helms**, "insolent clangor" (130), and "mad attack had raged" (135–36) give this lyric a Homeric cast.

116–22 Above our halls, gaping, and **thirsting spears** modify the subject of **gone** and fuse references to the eagle, a monster about to devour the city, and the blood-thirsty army. The **seven gates** (the same word appears at 99a; cf. 141) are famous in Greek legend. Gods are identified with the instruments and spheres of power: **torch** = Hephaestus; **war** = Ares. **Foe** is a common metaphor from wrestling; the people of Thebes descend from Cadmus and the **dragon** he killed (see *OC* 1534a).

123–33 The most notorious Argive for **boasts** was Capaneus, who swore that not even Zeus would keep him from sacking the city (see *Seven against Thebes* 424ff.); Zeus struck Capaneus with lightning (**hurling fire**) as he scaled the walls (*Phoenician Women* 1172–86). For boasting see *Aj* 766–70. **Top** translates a metaphor from the rope that marked the starting and finishing lines of the race course.

134–40 Raged compares the mad warrior to a maenad, one of the inspired followers of Bacchus (see 152). With the same metaphor Aeschylus describes Hippomedon:

> like a Bacchanal with murder in his glance.
> (*Seven against Thebes* 499)

Line 137 (**He failed . . .**) is corrupt and has not been satisfactorily emended. **First in the war-team** likens Ares to the hard-working, right-hand horse in the team of four.

141–48 It was the custom to dedicate the **arms** of the defeated enemy to a god; **turner of battle** is a cult epithet of Zeus. The **wretches** are Eteocles and Polyneices.

149–53 Victory, often held in the hand of statues of Zeus and Athena, is personified as early as *Theogony* 384; cf. *Phil* 134. She is **great-named** because she brings glory; the adjective is grandiloquent enough for a couple of appearances in Aristophanes. Bacchus is particularly associated with Thebes (his mother Semele is Theban), and so it is proper to offer thanks for the victory to him (see his praise at 1115–51 below). **Thebe,** daughter of the river Asopus, gave her name to the lower city, while Cadmus gave his to the upper city (the Cadmeia).

154–61 The last set of anapests announces Creon, Eteocles' uncle, "the new-made duke that rules the roast" (*Henry VI* 2,1.1.109); with this novelty of rule comes a sense that he must prove his metal (172–77). **Fate** means "fortune," i.e., the way things have chanced out. An omitted noun specifically calls this a **council-session** "of elders," and that fact may bear on their cautious manners (e.g., their response at 211–14). The chorus will offer no decisive advice to either party until Teiresias departs (1090), when it is too late.

162 Creon enters from the palace. Since his edict has already been published (7), it is now a matter of fact which he chooses to justify. Although the chorus has not mentioned the edict, there is nothing to indicate that it comes as a violent shock to them.

Creon is often made out to be a great villain, both a tyrant and a blasphemer. Kells ("Problems," p. 60) is closer to the mark: "he is filled with the commonplace ideas of his day—that the state is above everything, that military virtue is the supreme virtue, that women are inferiors, that sons owe unquestioning obedience to their fathers; above all, that a man— a gentleman—should see friends and enemies everywhere, and devote a considerable portion of his energy to the discomfiture of the latter." On the matter of refusing burial, to take the most pressing issue, Creon would have found a sympathetic hearing from those who put state and politics before all else. As we know from the case of Themistocles (Thucydides 1.138) and Antiphon (*Life of Antiphon* 24), Athenian law outlawed and proscribed burial for those condemned for treason. If Creon goes too far—and the events of the play demonstrate he has—when he leaves the body for the dogs and birds (206–7), he nonetheless has the literary example of Achilles, who refuses Hector's plea that he take ransom:

> So there is no one who can hold the dogs off
> from your head, . . .
>
> (*Iliad* 22.348–49)

Cf. 22.335–36, for dogs and birds. Menelaus (*Aj* 1065) would leave the body of Ajax "to feed the sea birds." Literary texts aside, the savagery of the civil war in Corcyra (Thucydides 3.81) offers ample evidence of how far impiety could be carried by the passion of politics. Yet neither Achilles nor Menelaus nor Creon is finally approved by their respective poets, and normal Greek feeling, which sensed in the dead an extension of the living family, would find Antigone's desire to save Polyneices' body both honorable and necessary. Creon might, for example, throw the body beyond the boundaries of the state and let those care for it who would. He is a man, however, who will have revenge as well as justice, as we discover much later (1080–83) when Teiresias mentions that Creon has refused burial to all the dead enemy. After a battle, Greek military custom regularly allowed for a truce to remove the dead; hence the extremity of Creon's edict may have raised doubts among even the totally political males of his audience.

162–63 Surge. . . set straight is conventional imagery from the "ship of state" (cf. *OK* 24–26 and 104); more maritime metaphor at 178 ("controls" = guides), 189, 541, 583–84, 715–18, 994, 1164, and 1284. Cf. "set . . . to rights" at 168.

171 Defiled because each has shed kindred blood.

175–77 Soul, mind, and **intent** come to character, and especially character as revealed in intellectually determined purpose. This word for mind (*phron-* stem) occurs six times in the play, elsewhere in Sophocles only once (frag. 307). For the shading "purpose" see 208 ("mind") and 458 ("proud spirit"). This intellectual cast of thinking is particularly noticeable in Creon, but Ismene leads off her remonstrance at 49 with the cognate verb ("remember" = "think/consider"). See also the notes to 458 and 1015–16. **Shows his practise of** = "has been tested by," with metaphorical reference to a touchstone: "the test of any man lies in action" (Pindar, *Olympian* 4.18).

178 Controls = "steers" at 1164 (the messenger speaks of Creon).

180 At 504–5 Antigone uses the same metaphor of **fear that locks up the tongue.**

182 As Antigone has defined friendship in terms of piety and personal loyalty, so now Creon offers a political definition that subordinates personal inclination to political good. Kamerbeek observes similar sentiments attributed to Pericles:

> My own opinion is that when the whole state is on the right course it is a better thing for each separate individual than when private interests are satisfied but the state as a whole is going downhill. However well off a man may be in his private life, he will still be involved in the general ruin if his country is destroyed; whereas, so long as the state itself is secure, individuals have a much greater chance of recovering from their private misfortunes.
>
> (Thucydides 2.60)

In his *Politics* Aristotle gives a theoretical justification for this position: "the polis is prior in the order of nature to the family and the individual" (*Politics* 1.2.12).

184 **Zeus** is invoked as the god of oaths (see 304–5 and *OC* 1767).

189–90 For Antigone **friends** are those within the clan, to whom one has ties of blood; for Creon friends are those with whom one has political affinities: political association and security are the conditions for friendship.

191 **Rules** (*nomoi*) = "law" (177) and "rulings" (213).

192 With **brother-edict** Creon puns on an idiom that permits him to refer both to Eteocles and Polyneices and to the "brother" of the sentiments just expressed; we might also catch it in English with "what relates to the relations."

198 **Whom I name** (= "I mean") should not be taken as a formula introducing a denunciation.

200–201 **Burn his fatherland, the gods** is a hyperbolic way of stressing that the attack threatened the homes and temples of the city (cf. *Trojan Women* 15–16, 25–27).

206 **Disgraced** often denotes physical abuse and mutilation, as, e.g., in "mistreat" at *Aj* 110–11. **Dinner for the birds:** Electra (*El* 1487–88) suggests that they throw out the body of Aegisthus for the "grave diggers," which Jebb takes to mean the dogs and kites. A similar "burial" is planned at *Seven against Thebes* 1020–21 and at *Aj* 1062–65 (such plans are always rejected, or at least opposed, in Greek tragedy). Euripides' Heracles promises to cut off Lycus' head and throw it to the dogs (*Heracles* 567–68). Cf. 25–30 and the notes there.

209–10 In repeating **honor** Creon once again "responds" to a theme of Antigone (see on 5). **Well-minded** is from the same stem (*nous*) as "senseless" (99), Ismene's last word on Antigone. "Traitor" (212) continues the stem in a third compound (= "evil-minded," to contrast with "well-minded").

211–14 The reply is noncommittal insofar as the moral issue is concerned, but line 220 recalls Ismene's pragmatism. A neutral chorus leaves the dramatic conflict more tense and evenly balanced; this chorus is an exception to the rule that, in the extant plays, Sophoclean choruses commit themselves to one side or the other, when moral sides are drawn.

219–22 Suspicion of conspiracy and treason, with **profit** (*kerdos*) as the motive, is a commonplace in Greek political literature; see the tirade of Oedipus (*OK* 380–89). Theognis attacks "evil men" (*kakoi*) who subvert justice for their own gain and power (lines 44–50); for the herald in Euripides' *Suppliant Women* a good stable tyranny secures the state against motives of private gain (410–12). Pericles describes himself as one who loves his city and one who is above being influenced by money. A man who has the knowledge but lacks the power clearly to express it is not better off than if he never had any ideas at all. A man who has both these qualities, but lacks patriotism, could scarcely speak for his own people as he should. And even if he is patriotic as well, but not able to resist a bribe, then this one fault will expose everything to the risk of being bought and sold.

(Thucydides 2.60)

Ideas, the ability to express them, patriotism, and incorruptibility: these are the shared values of Creon and Pericles.

223 The guard enters from the spectator's left (the country). The typical messenger hurries with his news (e.g., *Tr* 180, 189–91) and may deliver his report without more ado (e.g., *Aj* 720), but this humorist has made haste slowly, rehearsing his part along the way; altogether unexpectedly we get a self-conscious caricature of the tragical-historical style. Some of the stylistic markers include the pompous "halting in my thought," the interior dialogue in which his *psychê* ("mind") admonishes him ("fool" = "poor devil," as at 82 and 1181, more seriously), paradox, and sententious ramble, all culminating with a less than mystical gloss on "fate."

237 At first Creon seems to humor him: **gloom** is a mocking comment on his "despair."

242 **Shocking** may be right for Creon's facetious tone, but the Greek is limited to **news.**

243 "Strange" is also a possibility for *deina* (**terrible**), which occurs twice in the opening line of the next lyric (in "wonders" and "stranger," 332).

246–47 It is important to note that the first substantive information assures us that the necessary **ritual** for burial, symbolic rites that would placate the dead spirit, are, in the view of this witness, complete. See on 255.

248 On **dared** see the note to 371.

249 The guard's report has sponsored two very different interpretations: the "awe and wonder" school argues the signs of 249–57 truly point to divine intervention; the psychologists see the speech as a subtle characterization of a secondary role (the guard may really believe there is something supernatural in the burial, but we should not read his amazed wonder so much as an argument for a god's hand as an expression of his own hapless consternation). See Kitto, *Form and Meaning,* pp. 153–57 for god's hand; Gellie, pp. 34–35 for the second view. Three considerations weigh against this burial having been performed by the gods. (1) Like humans, Greek gods prefer to avoid the dead and dying:

Farewell, I must not look upon the dead.
My eye must not be polluted by the last
gaspings for breath. I see you are near this.
(*Hippolytus* 1437–39)

Thus Artemis to the dying Hippolytus. (2) We are never given explicit confirmation that the gods have intervened, and at 1017–22 Teiresias reports that the altars are fouled with remains of Polyneices. (3) Lines 426–28 mean, prima facie, that Antigone is horrified to find the body stripped of its dusty cover, and for want of any word from her we must assume that she had previously covered it herself. Against these arguments: (1) The chorus ventures that this burial may "possibly be a god's" (see on 278–79). Clearly they should not suggest something the Greek audience would find inconceivable. (2) The gods of Sophocles do work in mysterious ways, often quite obscure to man (witness Athena's single day of wrath [*Aj* 758–59] and the helpless uncertainty of Hyllus at the end of the *Women of Trachis*), and their justice, if we may call it that, is not man's justice. (3) Just possibly 426–28 might be construed to refer to a corpse that had never been properly covered; in that case she curses those who have prevented anything from being done for it.

Despite the marvelous atmosphere surrounding this burial, and the comment at 278–79 vouches for some intentional dramatic ambiguity, I do not think that Sophocles intended for the audience to believe that the gods had actually buried Polyneices, nor is there enough evidence for the misguided Creon (Jordan advocates this view).

249–51 It would be easy enough to rationalize the absence of **marks** and other indications of human activity (Antigone brought her own dust!), but this fellow's excitement may not justify minute scrutiny.

252 Whoever buried the body did the work in the predawn hours (see on 16). The temporal detail explains human, not divine, success in eluding the watch.

253 Wonder need not connote "miracle," as may be seen from *Phil* 410 or *OK* 1133. **Sick:** elsewhere the Greek word means "hard to take," i.e., of something that causes emotional or intellectual stress.

255 Enough to turn the curse: Jebb's more literal version ("as of one avoiding" the curse) shows the guard offering a tentative explanation, however feeble. "Pollution" (as at *OK* 1427) is preferable to **curse**, but there is some doubt whether the reference here is to the fear inspired by the dead spirit, who, not yet formally consecrated to the nether gods, may work his harm on anyone nearby, or to the pollution attached to one outcast and condemned for having violated the sacred (which seems to be the point of Creon's edict reported at *Seven against Thebes* 1018, where the present term is translated "guilt"). The former motive is the more likely. See Parker, *Miasma*, p. 8. Would the guard talk this way, even with "as if," if he were even covertly suggesting that the gods have protected the body? Would the gods protect the body now, only to leave it to be torn by the birds and dogs later (see 1018–19, 1200)?

260 Bad words is straightforward Greek for "abuse."

264–65 Red-hot iron and **walk through fire** refer to lie-detector tests, but we don't have much contemporary evidence for such ordeals, and the excited guard may be speaking hyperbolically.

274 Typically, markers were put in a helmet for selecting the lucky or unlucky choice. **Poor old** translates a compound from *daimôn* (also at *OK* 1302) that, like the play on **unwilling . . . want** (cf. "want" at *Tr* 198–99), indicates he has not lost his sense for tragical posturing. He concludes with a cliché from the messenger's trade (cf. *Persians* 252 and the dramatic variation at *Agamemnon* 551–55).

278–79 The coryphaeus's suggestion has more dramatic (it provokes Creon's tirade) and thematic (will the gods take sides?) point than the standard two line response to a speech. **Action . . . a god's** (cf. *OK* 255) simply implies some divine impulse or remote origin and is not quite so specific as "did a god do this?"

280 Like Oedipus (see the note to *OK* 335–37), Creon has a quick temper: like Oedipus (cf. *OK* 397–99a), he has a ready, dogmatic confidence in his own thinking.

281–82 Insane = "senseless" at 99; **forethought** contains the same stem (*nous*). **Saying:** the same verb is placed emphatically (at the beginning and end of the lines) three times in his first three lines, as if to say "talk, talk, talk!").

284–87 His argument has a certain cogency, for the gods would certainly have been offended if they had seen their temples sacked (see Athena's attitude at *Trojan Women* 69–71). But in fact the temples were not burned, and the gods at issue, in Antigone's view, are those of the underworld, and not the templed divinities of the Theban acropolis. **Honor:** cf. 210. He is concerned with one kind of honor, Antigone with another.

290 If we interpret the Greek to mean **from the first**, we may be led to ask how long Creon has been in power or otherwise go hunting into the past. But he may refer to the recent past ("I have already noticed that there were . . ."), and the main theme of this tirade (conspiracy for profit) was his suspicion even before the guard arrived (221–22). The **edict** is not explicitly mentioned, and he may refer more generally to his own new authority.

293 Imagery from **the yoke** commonly describes master and slave: see *Aj* 945. Creon's idea of a friend is someone who accepts his place and obeys him.

296–97 Current custom . . . currency aims to catch a pun on a word meaning both "custom" and "current coin." He will follow this at 300–301 with an etymological pun on **infamy** ("villainy and every vileness" would be an English equivalent).

299 Solid citizens are those of "good sense."

304 For the oath cf. 184. He behaves tyrannically in that he presumes the complicity of the guards, who will pay by **hanging** (309) if they don't produce the culprit.

317–19 The wonderful impudence of the guard continues with an odd division ("are you more stung in the ear or the mind?") that makes Creon pause to ask how he allocates pain. The guard's response seems both to exasperate and amuse the king (**quibbling rascal**).

322 Here *psychê* (**mind,** as at 317) may also have the sense "life" (as at 559); such a punning double meaning suits Creon.

323–24 More banter, preceded by a melodramatic and extrametrical **Oh!,** cuts across the serious grain of the scene; **guess** = "think/ suppose." **Pretty up** comments sarcastically on the repeated "guess."

324–31 Either the guard's final comment is an aside, as the scholiast takes it, or Creon exits at the end of his speech (326), and the guard's parting shot is unheard, addressed to the king's back (so Bain and Knox, rightly). **You** (329) is second person singular (not a plural referring to the audience). For **luck** see 1155.

332–72 The chief problem posed by the first stasimon is its dramatic point. As a celebration of human achievement, it may be compared to a number of passages in fifth-century literature that comment on the course of civilization (e.g., it evidently imitates Aeschylus' *Libation Bearers* 585: "Many are the wonders the earth breeds, the pain of fear . . ."). Rhetorically, it takes the form of a priamel, a figure for comparison in which a number of topics or ideas become foils to highlight the primary subject (a list of many wonders serves to cast in relief the greatest wonder, man). Thematically the lyric touches on law (see 365–70 and the note to 354), dwells on human ingenuity (353–64, especially), and warns against daring (371), all of which can be linked to the preceding scenes. Yet its formal coherence and traditional cast of thought do not make its dramatic point more concrete: does the chorus mean to comment in some particular way on the two views of law (*nomos*) represented by Creon and Antigone? If so, why are they so allusive and vague, especially as Creon is offstage and there is no present constraint? Are they not sure of ethical and religious propriety? Surely this would be odd, since the present issue is just the sort that quickly divides even the best of friends. I take them to be of Ismene's stamp, ready to admit the burial is right and righteous, equally ready to call anyone who violates the edict a fool. This is the most obvious meaning of 382–84: they are incredulous that Antigone has been caught in the folly (= "open shame") of breaking the law. While we may find a great deal in this ode that moralizes the play in a general way, only under torture will it yield a decisive dramatic position: the chorus hedges, not so much with studied ambiguity as with anxious generality. And this is altogether "in character" for this chorus, for it will not come off the fence for another seven hundred lines, not until Teiresias' terrible prophecies all too plainly mark the direction the wind has taken. Decent old men, they are not involved and will not be involved if any risk presses; theirs is a sensible pragmatism more useful, or so he may feel, to the assertive Creon than the vulnerable Antigone. For a discussion of the ode's imagery and metaphor in the context of the play see Segal, chapter 6.

332–41 Stranger repeats **wonders** in the comparative form. The Greek word (*deinos* in the neuter) suggests something wonderful and terrible; it is "terrible" in 243 and 323, but it is too common and colloquial for the echo of 243 to be very pointed. The Aeschylean chorus (*LB* 585–651) also turns to the theme of daring (*LB* 594–97; cf. *Ant* 370–71). For the topic of the evolution of civilization see *Prometheus Bound* 442–504, Euripides' *Suppliant Women* 200–218, and Plato's *Protagoras* 320c–22c. The first strophe treats man's triumph over the physical world; the first antistrophe describes his conquest of animals; the second strophe turns to intellectual, political, and medical achievement; and the second antistrophe (362–72) balances praise for human craft with a warning that political prosperity requires regard for divine and human law. **This thing** is man. The **earth** is personified and should be capitalized. **Unwearied . . . wears . . . away** reflects similar punning, alliteration, and assonance in the Greek.

342–52 Gay = "giddy" at 615 (birds aren't so smart and are easily snared). **Salty brood of the sea:** an ample periphrasis for "fish." **Strong:** the manuscripts are divided between "unbroken" (till man harnesses the bull) and "untiring" (in his work); the mild oxymoron of the first may make it preferable.

353–61 The power of **language**, especially persuasive rhetoric, was a favorite topic of the Sophists. For example, Gorgias (frag. 14) says:

"The power of speech over the constitution of the soul can be compared with the effect of drugs on the bodily state: just as drugs

by driving out different humours from the body can put an end
either to the disease or to life, so with speech: different words can
induce grief, pleasure or fear; or again, by means of a harmful
kind of persuasion, words can drug and bewitch the soul."

(Freeman, p. 133)

Like the wind probably refers to the speed of thought (= "mind" at 176,
but a sense such as "purpose" does not suit the present context). **Feelings
that make the town** = "such dispositions as regulate cities" (Jebb); the
Greek (*orgê*) for feelings more commonly denotes passion or anger, but
"temperament" at *Aj* 1153 may be similar. The compound adjective
modifying "feelings" reminds the Greek audience of law (*nomos*). **Shelter
against the cold** comes anticlimactically after this triplet, but then we
might also expect **There's only death** . . . to cap the stanza, whereas the
poet returns to medicine. **He can always help** himself translates a single
compound adjective that in the Greek actually concludes the first sentence.
But the next sentence begins, without connective, with **helpless,** so despite
the negation of **no future,** there is a violent juxtaposition (*pantoporos /
aporos:* try "all-powerful. Powerless" in English; see the note to *Prometheus Bound* 905f.), a momentary paradox that turns to optimism until
only death intrudes. As Sarpedon says:

But now, seeing that the spirits of death stand close about us
in their thousands, no man can turn aside nor escape them,
let us go on and win glory for ourselves, or yield it to others.

(*Iliad* 12.326–28)

362–72 Inventive echoes "beyond all cure" (its privative). **Beyond
all dreams** = "beyond (his proper) expectations/hopes"; both the concision and ambiguity of Greek lyrics may be seen in the omission of simple
qualifying pronouns and adjectives such as my "his proper." **May drive**
is interpretative; the sense is that, though man has all the craft in the
world, he yet sometimes comes to harm, sometimes to good fortune. The
entire final stanza takes this cautionary vein. **Honors** is an emendation
and the likely sense. With **laws** the sentence seems to affirm Creon's
position (177, 191, 213), but Antigone has also invoked law (25), though
the chorus does not yet realize the conflict. **Gods' sworn right** is the justice
(*dikê:* see Antigone at 451) of the gods by which man swears and prospers.
The audience will naturally perceive ironies of which the chorus is as
yet unaware. **High indeed is his city** . . . **stateless** translates two words
metrically responsive to "He can always help . . . helpless" (356–57; see
the note), with the same antithetical edge sharpened by the absence of a
connective. **Dares** may consciously echo Creon's "dared" (248; cf. 449),

but the motif is common (*Aj* 46, *OK* 126, *Libation Bearers* 549ff.) **Not by my fire,** i.e., not at my hearth, the most sacred place in the Greek house (cf. *El* 881).

373 Awful sight refers to their surprise, not Antigone's appearance.

383–84 Law (*nomos*) refers to Creon's edict. **Open shame** is better "folly," a privative ("mindless") of Creon's "mind" (176); the adjectival form is "fool" at *El* 941; the adverb is "senseless" at *Aj* 766. All these passages show the Greek inclination to define error in intellectual terms.

385 The second episode (385–581) begins with the return of the same guard.

386 At the burying = "as she was burying him"; cf. 395.

387–88 Just when he's needed: cf. *Tr* 56–58 for similar self-conscious timeliness. In response to this, Creon's line probably means "What is timely in my arrival?" (rather than **What must I measure up to?**).

389–90 He has had second thoughts (cf. *Phil* 1078, 1270), but he hasn't lost his sense of humor: the Greek of 390 comes to something like "this is the last place I expected to spend an idle hour." Since hope is regularly denigrated, **joy beyond hope** is both hyperbolic and ironically achieved.

395 Burying the dead = "tending to the rites of burial." Cleaning and tendance of the corpse are very nearly as important as the ritual dusting; see *El* 1137–43.

397 His **luck** alludes to Hermes, god of good fortune and happy accident.

399 Prove her = "examine her," "put her to the test." **On this charge** = "from this trouble," no doubt with allusion to Creon's charges of conspiracy.

406 Creon specifically asks "how was she seen?"

410–11 Since there is no undoing the symbolic ritual of burial, **sweeping away the dust** can only offend the living, who, the guards supposed, must be hanging around, hoping to protect the body as best they can. **Slimy nakedness** refers to putrefaction, which we might not expect if the gods had had some part in the burial. Thetis, mother of Achilles, protects the dead body of Patroclus (*Iliad* 19.30–39) and Apollo protects the body of Hector (*Iliad* 24.18–21). Had Sophocles wanted to indicate clearly that the gods have taken an interest in this burial, he might well have used such precedents to put a stamp of the miraculous on it.

416 As readers and students we may be tempted to remember that Antigone performed the rites for the first time before dawn (see 252) and so to wonder what she is doing during the interval stressed **by some time,** but such questions will probably not have bothered the audience in the theater. These messenger speeches remained popular throughout fifth-century tragedy and were evidently not considered mere interludes between the real meat of the dialogues.

417–22 The language of this passage has suggested to some commentators that the guard, whether he realizes it or not, is reporting an authentic omen, i.e., a sign from the gods that the body ought to be granted burial. **Whirlwind** also means "storm" and "thunderbolt" (the weapon and signal of Zeus); **to the sky** translates a phrase that might be rendered "a trouble in the sky" (Jebb) or, more to the point for an epiphany, "a grief from the sky"; **smearing** is a particularly strong verb that usually denotes some kind of mutilation (at 206 it describes the "disgraced," i.e., "disfigured," corpse); finally, **plague the gods had sent** would, on this view, be taken literally (otherwise it might be "a marvelous plague/bane"). While Sophocles may have intended a certain provocative ambiguity such as we find in the choral response at 278–79 he also wanted to explain how Antigone could manage to return to the corpse after the sentries were posted. The guard's storm conveniently provides cover for the girl so that she can be apprehended as she once again covers it and performs the burial service (426–31). Some in the audience might have seized upon these allusions to divine intervention as evidence for just that; others, especially those sympathetic to Creon's arguments, may have smiled at the guard's florid credulity.

423 The guard actually uses vivid present tenses ("see" for **saw**) to describe the scene. **Cried,** as at 29 and 1127, specifically denotes lament for the dead. The comparison to **a bitter bird** may be traced back to a Homeric simile:

> and they cried shrill in a pulsing voice, even more than the outcry
> of birds, ospreys or vultures with hooked claws, whose children
> were stolen away by the men of the fields, before their wings grew
> strong; such was the pitiful cry and the tears their eyes wept.
>
> (*Odyssey* 16.216–19)

Cf. *Agamemnon* 49–54.

426–28 These lines prove that she visited the body earlier; this, together with the body's decomposition (413), seems decisive against divine protection. As for the much belabored topic concerning why Antigone visits the body a second time, the primary fact is that nothing in the play implies her second visit is extraordinary. While in such circumstances religion does not require more than the ritual dusting of her first visit, it may be that she returns to complete the services by making the drink offerings to the dead (**three libations:** offerings were made at the tomb on the third and ninth days after death, and Bradshaw argues that Sophocles has telescoped that ritual into a single day). Yet it is just as likely that she desires to protect the corpse from mutilation, a motivation appropriate to her concern for due honor (see the note to line 5). Her wailing (**groanings**) and indignation (**curse**), the imagery of a bereaved bird and hunted animal (in **trapped her fast**), and her futile effort to cover the body argue an intense despair. She makes no effort to escape, and this report, on top of her defiant manner in the prologue, may even imply a willingness to be caught and to face publicly Creon's accusation. For discussions of the burial see Kitto, *Form and Meaning,* pp. 152–55 and Kirkwood, p. 70; for arguments in favor of divine intervention see McCall.

435–40 The guard remains true to character, tempering sympathy with candid self-interest.

441 Drooping means "nodding" and often denotes assent (to the veracity of the guard's report); in any case the verb does not indicate despondency.

449 With **dared** cf. 248.

450–70 In defending her action by an appeal to unwritten (455) and divine (450–51) law, Antigone puts her iron into a political and philosophical fire that has continued to rage. A century later Aristotle interprets her meaning:

> For there really is, as every one to some extent divines, a natural justice and injustice that is binding on all men, even on those who have no association or covenant with each other. It is this that Sophocles' Antigone clearly means when she says that the burial of Polyneices was a just act in spite of the prohibitions: she means that it was just by nature.
>
> (*Rhetoric* 1.13.1)

(He cites 456–57.) Like a good tragic character, Antigone actually appeals to the gods rather than to nature, and her very last words (943) offer piety as a motive. While the fifth-century controversy over written and unwritten law was probably well underway (for which see Guthrie, *The Sophists,* pp. 117–31), Antigone's defense is securely tied to the language and themes of this play. It falls into two parts: in 450–59a she claims a higher authority than mere human law; in 460–70 she acknowledges that she understood the penalty, accepts it, refers to her family obligation to her brother, and concludes with defiant attack on Creon's "foolishness." The second is clearly more personal, and both the coryphaeus (471–72) and Creon ignore the substance of her higher argument to respond to the tone and manner of the second section. Besides Guthrie, for more detailed comment see Ehrenberg, pp. 28–33.

450–52 Order like "orders" (453) and "warning" (461) echoes

Creon's "order" (447); his "orders" at 31 are styled an "edict" at 192. Since Hesiod **Justice** (*dikê*) has been a daughter of Zeus:

Justice herself is a young maiden
She is Zeus's daughter,
and seemly, and respected by all the gods of Olympos.
When any man uses force on her by false impeachment
she goes and sits at the feet of Zeus Kronion, her father,
and cries out on the wicked purpose of men,
(*Works and Days* 256–60)

Cf. the similar language at OC 1382. She is said to **live with the gods below** because the rights due the dead are at issue, and these laws are ascribed theologically to the divinities of the earth; see also 519a and 521 and the harsher use of the principle at 538.

454–55 The admonition to remember that you are **a mortal man** traditionally warns of human limitations (see on *Tr* 473). **Over-run** (= "transgress"), though a common Greek metaphor for error, occurs in this stem only in the *Antigone*, but four times: "*broke bounds* beyond established law" (481), "can *bind* your power" (602), "who *crosses* law" (663). Both Antigone and Creon speak of "transgressing law," and he connects it with hybris ("insolence" at 480). For **unwritten laws** see also OK 863–71, where too the laws are divine. "The generally acknowledged unwritten laws were those that enjoined reverence toward the gods, respect for parents, requital of benefactors, and also hospitality to strangers" (Guthrie, *The Sophists*, p. 121). The abstract character of the present passage would hardly keep the audience from understanding its particular applicability to the burial. See also Antigone on law at 519a and 909.

458 Proud spirit is possible for this word that has been translated "mind" at 169 and 176 (see the note there) and occurs in Creon's "rigid spirits" (473), so long as the intellectual cast is kept in mind ("purpose"); see also on "think of pride" at 477.

459a As for **the gods' sure punishment**, "sure" is interpretative and while the gods may protest man's barbarity to man, as when Apollo condemns Achilles' brutal treatment of Hector's body (*Iliad* 24.33–54), they are normally quicker to protect their own interests than to arbitrate the quarrels of men. That is, they are more likely to punish Creon if they perceive him as one violating their rights than they are to punish Antigone for not fulfilling religious obligations to her brother. Her claim, however, is consistent with the despair that dominates the second half of the speech.

462–64 Her **gain** answers Creon's charges (219–22, 310, 326). This repetition will be followed by three words from the same stem denoting **grief** (with punning on physical and mental pain and "regret") and then another three playing on **fool** and **foolish** (469–70). Although fifth-century tragic style is readier than we are to accept punning, inflection, antitheses, and other verbal artifice, such figures are less frequent in the later plays. The risk in them is simply that they may seem to reflect more attention to verbal decoration than to ethical substance. The danger, whether we speak of the lawyer in court or of a dramatic persona, is that formal and grammatical qualities of language may seem so studied that the audience's attention will be deflected from meaning. Hence such wordplay is often associated with self-conscious irony. While we may see despair or a touch of the morbid (cf. her lines at 555 and 559–60), the Greek audience probably found the tenor more intellectual and rhetorical than psychological, not less so if they took 460–70 as a variation on the familiar topic "death is better than the present trouble" (for examples see *Aj* 473–80, *Prometheus Bound* 750, and *Alcestis* 935–61). Like wordplay generally, such commonplaces may depersonalize argument if specific details, e.g., "your warning" (i.e., his edict), "gain," and "mother's son . . . unburied," fail to keep us in touch with the real ethical issues.

465 This word for **fate** often denotes "death," as at 489.

466 Something of Antigone's defiance may perhaps be seen in **my mother's son** since a Greek would normally say "my father's son" (cf. 471).

469–70 Her language has legal overtones, as if to say "I am judged a fool by another."

471–72 **Bitter** translates a phrase, the adjective of which ("hard"; three times in compounds of Ajax: "grim" at *Aj* 206) is repeated with **father**. If we accept the manuscript reading, the noun in this phrase means "stock" or "descent," and we have "clearly a fierce descendant of a fierce father," while a preferable emendation yields "clearly (she is) fiercely bold from a fierce father." With either reading, the standard two line comment stresses her tough resolve. On the refusal to yield cf. 47 and 1095 and the note to *OC* 1178–79; Knox, *Heroic Temper* pp. 15–17, discusses this theme in Sophocles. Pericles praises the Athenians with similar language: "You [Athenians] know that the city has the greatest name among all men because she never yields to misfortune" (Thucydides 2.64).

473 On **spirits** see the note to 458.

474–76 For the metaphor from tempering **iron** cf. *Aj* 649–51. **Curbs** (the bit) is taken from training horses; "free running" at 579 is also drawn from animals out of control. See the note to 945–46 for imagery from yoking.

477–85 If a person, like a horse, is reined in and made to understand she is a slave, then she will not be presumptuous (for **think of pride** see the note to *OK* 1079a). To follow this with a charge of **insolence**

(= *hybris*) is conventional, as is the addition of **boast** and **laugh** to the indictment (for boasting see 123; for laughter cf. 647, 837, and the note to *Aj* 368). Consider how much of Antigone's actual manner we may infer from such a tirade. Clearly, she has not acted the slave's part, but, compared to this speech, hers is a model of decorum. **No man and she the man**: see Ismene's caution at 61 and his fuller misogyny at 678–80.

487–89 Creon specifically mentions Zeus as god of the household. Kamerbeek cites Linforth's comment (p. 205): "An altar of Zeus of the Courtyard in every household was the symbol of its solidarity . . . to use the name of the god at such a moment emphasizes his own godlessness." That may be, but Creon certainly does not say it to defy god, nor does he feel "godless" in promising **death and doom** (= "the hardest kind of death": the superlative of *kakos*, "vilest," modifies the noun Antigone use of her "fate" at 465). When Ismene next enters, her appearance will verify the agitation he has noticed (526–30).

502 Greater glory reflects the complexity of her motivation since she refers not to divine approval but to human; cf. 815–16. This motif is connected with honoring her brother (5) and proving her nobility (38–39). The Greek audience probably did not find such mixed motives incompatible or contradictory. For example, Achilles, feeling that he has betrayed his friend Patroclus, accepts death as the price of revenge (*Iliad* 18.98) but is still able to speak of the "excellent glory" (*Iliad* 18.121) he will claim for himself when he has killed Hector and revenged his friend. In a similar way Antigone's piety, loyalty to family, and personal honor may be harmonized.

505 For **mute** see the note to 180.

506–7 Tragedy often uses "tyrant" and "tyranny" as synonyms for **king** and kingship, but here Antigone's taunt and rebuke of the quiescent chorus imply a meaning such as the Athenian democrat found in "tyrant." The parentheses indicate the translator takes these lines as an aside, but their sarcasm suits her hostile manner.

508–10 Since Greek choruses do defy tyrants, usurpers, and assassins—the last scene of the *Agamemnon* is a celebrated example—we should not suppose that dramatic convention rather than dramatic purpose keeps them silent now. While the course of events and Haemon's arguments (690–95) imply some truth in Antigone's contention, it is hard to believe that Sophocles would not at least let them protest a little if Creon were the godless despot his more severe critics have made him.

511–12 The two lines translate a single line of Greek. **Children** is the so-called poetic plural. The Greek does not emphasize **mother's**.

515–17 Your act of grace: Creon puts this sentence as a question: "how can you render honor to the one that the other (Eteocles) must consider impious?" He then repeats **honor**. **Criminal** and **crime** echo (in negative forms) "serve" (512); they are usually rendered "impious" (cf. 924–25 and "unholy" at *Aj* 1294).

519a Death = Hades (the same translation at 542 and 777). In this line **equal** is a variant reading; most editors prefer the manuscripts' "these laws."

521 Since Antigone certainly thinks she **knows**, we have some indication of her tone.

522–23 Traditional Greek morality is unforgiving, even in death: see Agamemnon at *Aj* 1371–73 and Electra at *El* 1487–90 (Creon finds himself in a vindictive alliance); see also the notes to *OC* 186–87 and 1390–93. Antigone's rejoinder echoes Creon: **share in hatred** is linked to **enemy**; (share) **in love** is the verbal form of **friend** (*philos*: see the note to line 10). The clash of principle, for Hegel the chief source of tragic conflict, involves the primacy of political loyalty for one and loyalty to family for the other. See *Hegel on Tragedy*, pp. 68, 133, 178.

525 For **no woman rules me** see 484 and the note there.

528 Another version: "a cloud over her brow disfigures her bloodied face." Perhaps Ismene has taken a new mask.

531–33 For this **viper** (*echidna*) see the note to *Libation Bearers* 249. The simile would seem to continue the idea of male and female animosity found in 525. **Sucked me dry** suggests the vampiric habit of the Furies (see *Eumenides* 183f.); **I looked the other way** is more literally "I did not realize that I was raising (nourishing)"; **twin destruction** identifies them with *atê*, which is often personified by Aeschylus as Ruin or Delusion (see on *Agamemnon* 385f.). Although Sophocles is less inclined to use this and other abstractions as daimonic powers, the context and literal sense imply something of the archaic force: "I did not realize that I was raising twin Ruins and rebellions against the throne." Most commentators now take these nouns as idiomatic abstract for concrete, but after "sucked me dry" and "raised/nourished" the traditional notion of a personal, daimonic agent is tempting. Cassandra likens Clytemnestra to a "secret *atê*" (*Agamemnon* 1230); Campbell offers *Andromache* 103: "Paris brought home no bride, no bride but folly and ruin (*atê*) . . . Helen"; cf. especially *El* 784–86 where "draining" is the same verb we have here in "sucked me dry" and "evil" is a traditional synonym for *atê* (see note to 1103–4 below). *Atê* and Erinys (Fury) are close linked by Aeschylus at *Ag* 1433, and both are prominent in the next stasimon (582–623; see the note to 582–91).

538–47 The following argument has occasioned critical controversy because of Antigone's harsh rejection of Ismene's belated support. Some scholars, following the scholiast, have thought Antigone is trying to save

Ismene; this line of thinking saves her from cold egotism, but nothing in the text insures this view, and Antigone's attitude at the end of the prologue implies irrevocable division between herself and Ismene. **Justice** (*dikê,* as at 451) would surely allow whatever Antigone wishes it to allow. Since **the dead** (542) are literally "the witnesses below" (with allusion to legal witness), and since the distinction between **words** (543) and deeds is both traditional and contrary to the spirit of 523, and since **honor** is not the greater for being shared, she seems to reject Ismene as "enemy" (as at 93–94).

548 Friend keeps the *philos* theme before us, but here the common sense "dear" is more to the point: "How can life be worthwhile without you?"

549 Love is a misreading; translate "Ask Creon." **Kinsman . . . care** translates a single noun that means "relative by marriage" or "guardian." Ismene's response (550) indicates the mocking tone.

551 I also suffer accepts the view of Jebb and others that "the taunt sprang from anguish, not from a wish to pain." Winnington-Ingram, on the other hand, thinks that line 549 is "vicious and sincere" (p. 135). Jebb and the maidenly school of interpretation give us a loving Antigone who only hurts her sister to protect her or in a momentary aberration. Closer to the truth is Kells' argument: if this line expresses a concern for the feelings of Ismene, it is virtually the only line in the play in which Antigone expresses "tenderness for any person other than herself" ("Problems," p. 53). We don't expect that kind of inconsistency. In brief, Kells interprets Antigone's pain as coming from her sense that Ismene has violated family honor and, in refusing to help with the burial, has removed herself from the family and thus from any rightful claim to join in its defense. **Laugh,** as Kells observes, denotes that familiar triumphant mockery of the old heroes (he compares *Aj* 79b–c), here scored as Antigone sarcastically sends her sister off to Creon's house (549) since she no longer belongs to Antigone's. Antigone means "It is to *my* hurt that I score off you, triumph over you—if I do triumph over you—that is, *if I bother to!*" (Kells, p. 55).

552 Service echoes "good" (550) and appears below in "to help" (560). If Ismene does refer to some previous service, it can only be her advice for restraint, or perhaps, as some critics suppose, she has come out to deflect Creon's anger or to persuade Antigone to back off. Whatever construction we put on line 551, 552 does not follow well.

555 As often, the English tempers the antithetical edge of the Greek: "You chose to live, I to die." She uses the same construction in 557, where the antithesis is enclosed by the phrase "think well /nobly," so that the line begins with "well (nobly)" and ends with "think" (*phronein*), with the contrasting "some . . . others" in between. This dismissive and alienating antithesis then occurs for the third time in 559.

565–66 **Wickedness** and **wicked** respond to "deep distress" (all from the *kakos* stem). For Ismene it has the familiar meaning "trouble," for Creon it is moral.

569–70 **Your own son's** refers to Haemon and foreshadows his appearance in the next scene (624). **Furrows for his plough:** similar language appears in legal contracts for marriage and in a variety of poetic contexts (see on *Tr* 31–33). **Closeness that has bound** more explicitly suggests intimacy and affection than the Greek, which offers a poetic word for betrothal: "No, not as he and she have been bound (betrothed)."

572–76 The majority of modern editors assign 572 to Antigone, against the manuscripts, which are of little value in such matters. The issues are interpretative rather than textual: Ismene has introduced the issue of their marriage and may be expected to follow her own argument; on the other hand, Antigone is engaged to Haemon, whose love for her will motivate his subsequent actions; if she loves him, this is the only line that expresses that love, and his fervor may imply some reciprocity (the references to marriage in her song at 813–14 and later are generic to lament). No doubt greater pathos is to be had from assigning the line to Antigone, but the present scene does not seem shaped for that tone: Antigone has been hard, even cruel, to her sister, and it seems more in character to both if we let Ismene play the tune of romantic love.

577 **You helped determine it** = "It is determined, for both of us." As Jebb says, Creon means that he has made up his mind and no pleading will change it. Often the coryphaeus has a brief comment at the end of stichomythia: cf. 764–65, with two subsequent lines; *OK* 631–33, where the three lines mark a transition within the scene; *OK* 1074–76.

578 **Slaves** they are, but for English readers that word assures them of Creon's despotic manner, whereas all Greek household "servants" were slaves. At 1187 the feminine form of the same word is "my women's." The form is Homeric, and Euripides uses it a number of times without reproach (e.g., "slaves" at *Medea* 1138).

582–623 If, as seems likely, Creon remains on stage during the second stasimon, his presence may intimidate the chorus, which might otherwise praise the burial. Thus the chorus only obliquely and ironically sings of the dangers he risks. Several of the traditional and moralizing admonitions, most immediately applicable to Antigone, will prove apt for Creon, and his presence during the song draws attention to their ambiguous point (see Kitto, *Form and Meaning*, p. 165). Sophocles evidently had the second stasimon of Aeschylus' *Seven against Thebes* (720–91) in mind when he composed these lyrics. That song reacts to Eteocles' likely fulfillment of the curse of Oedipus. In the present lyric the house of Labdacus falls victim to a doom (*atê*) sent by the gods, whose instruments are Folly and Fury (601), madness, and vain hope. All this is traditional enough, but even some particular images (see on 600–601) seem to have influenced Sophocles. This larger context (the fate of the house) may surprise modern readers, especially if they are looking for choral comment more intimately linked to the play. Whereas Aeschylus' chorus takes its cue from immediate events and a specific curse, Sophocles' ode generalizes and distances.

582–91 The lyric begins and ends with commonplaces on mutability and the power of the gods. Cf. Theognis, 1013–14: "Blessed, fortunate and prosperous is he who without experience of trouble goes to the black house of Hades." **House** (cf. 592 for the particular application) is a more common focus in Aeschylus than Sophocles (see the note to *Tr* 866–67). With **shaken by the gods** cf. Creon's "gods who shook the state" (162); the verb is used of earthquakes and Poseidon is "the shaker of the earth." **By the gods** suggests that doom (*atê:* see on 531–33) is the personalized agent (Ruin/Infatuation) that does the work of divinity (*atê* is the leitmotif of this ode: 601, 622, 623). So Aeschylus calls the Fury (cf. 601) the "house-destroyer" (*Seven against Thebes*, 722). The image of the **wave** surging from the north (Thrace) and churning the sea to black with sand aptly describes the confusing, blinding effects of *atê*. For imagery of sea and wave see *OC* 633 and 1240–48, *Tr* 112–21, and *Seven against Thebes* 758–62. **Cry** usually denotes human groaning and lament.

592–601 Labdacus is the father of Laius. Cf.

Old is the tale of sin I tell
but swift in retribution
to the third generation.
(*Seven against Thebes* 742–44)

I know means "I see," i.e., "I witness." While there is no explicit reference in this play to a curse on the house, the shadow of this thinking will hang over any choral lyric touching topics such as these. Creon is not, strictly speaking, a member of the Labdacid dynasty, and **Oedipus** also directs our attention to Antigone rather than Creon. **Grief** is "suffering," and the ambiguous Greek may mean "pain from the dead" or "pain for the dead." The line (593) is riddled with p's,

pêmata phthimenôn epi pêmasi piptont'

Will strike is actually a present tense ("strikes"). The last three lines (**So now the light . . . have done this**) have provoked, because of uncertainties of syntax and the mixed metaphor, much discussion, despite general agreement on the basic sense of the passage: Antigone and Ismene, the surviving stock and last hope (**light**) of the house are now cut down. Scholarly argument focuses on **knife**, which is an emendation for "dust" (all manuscripts). "Dust cuts (harvests) the root" may be a violent metaphor, but it has the advantage of alluding to the burial, and **Folly** (from the same stem [*nous*] as "senseless," 99) and **Fury** (the Erinys, who brings on *atê*) clearly refer to Antigone. The Greek text modifies dust/knife with "of/for the gods below." Another version: "For now that light which had extended over the last root in the house of Oedipus the bloody dust for the gods below cuts and harvests—this dust and folly in speech and a Fury in the mind do this." "Folly in speech" must refer to Antigone's defiance; **Fury** (Erinys) brings on the delusion (*atê*) that is manifested in the speech and act (burial), as in Agamemnon's famous apology:

> but Zeus is [responsible], and Destiny, and Erinys the mist walking
> who in assembly caught my heart in the savage delusion [*atê*]
> (*Iliad* 19.87–88)

The metaphor is milder if the verb "cuts" actually represents a homophone meaning "cover" (the light); "cover the root" is also possible, but "dust cutting/harvesting the light" is not too harsh for the occasion.

602–13 Madness = "trespass": see the note to "over-run" at 454–55. **Who ages all** is suspect because Sleep, though the brother of Death, is not usually thought of as weakening. Given Sophoclean repetition, **unaged** is no objection to it. "Snares all" and "beguiles all" are suggested emendations. **Greatness** is an emendation. After **law** (*nomos*), we might expect a statement with more explicit moral content, and most interpretations find here a variation on the commonplace "prosperity is dangerous." The repetition of **doom** (*atê;* cf. 623) also implies thematic connection, but the relevance to Antigone is slight.

614–23 The antistrophe is linked to the preceding strophe by an introductory "for." **Hope** leads man on and deceives him:

> But here is how we men, be we good, be we evil,
> think. Each keeps his own personal notion within
> until he suffers. Then he cries out, but all until such time
> we take our idiot beguilement in light-weight hopes,
> (Solon frag. 1.33–36)

In polar expression such as that in 614–15 the second clause or idea is usually emphatic. Here we have "hope is for many a help, for many a deception (*apatê*)." On this concept see the note to Aeschylus *Persians* 93–101 and compare "disaster from treachery" (*Tr* 850, another passage where love, deception, and *atê* are associated). **Quarry:** there is no hunting metaphor here: "Hope/Deception comes on the unwary." **To him a god would doom** = "to him whose mind a god leads to doom (*atê*)." This is a variation on a theme best known from a fragment cited by the orator Lycurgus:

> whenever the anger of the gods would hurt someone,
> this is the first thing: it takes away
> the good sense from his mind. Then it turns his purpose
> to the worse, that the victim may not perceive in what he errs.
> (Kannicht and Snell, vol. 2, no. 296)

Cf. 1103–4. **From under doom** = "outside the range of *atê*." While all this moralizing may explain, as the chorus sees it, Antigone's self-destructive folly, **loves** foreshadows the arrival of Haemon, Antigone's betrothed (see the lyrics at 781–800 for more on infatuated love), and **doom** (*atê*) will prove the exact word for Creon's error (see 1258–61).

624 The chorus announces the arrival of Haemon; the third episode begins and features the (anticipated) interview between father and son. **Your one surviving son:** the Greek phrase means that he is the last and so the youngest. **Tricked** echoes "tricks" (615). Else (p. 50) notes that Sophocles ignored much of the tradition about Haemon in order to get the character he wanted: "He had to ignore the explicit testimony of the *Oidipodeia* [epic "Story of Oedipus"] that Haemon had been killed by the Sphinx, and the even more damaging evidence in the *Iliad*, IV 394 (more damaging because it would be better known to the Athenian public), that a son of his, Maion, took part in the war of the Epigonoi. (In Euripides' *Antigone* Haemon married Antigone in order to beget this Maion)." From 569–75 and 614–23 the audience is led to expect an appeal from a young lover, but Sophocles has cast Haemon as a wise counselor, as Else observes, while giving Creon the more passionate temper. Corresponding to this inversion of roles is the inverted order of the speeches: Haemon's appeal, which would naturally begin the scene, follows his father's defense. It is clear that the son plays a part (the political friend) in order to effect more personal ends, but that does not mean his argument (683–723) is insincere or untrue.

632–34 **Vote:** cf. the same word at 60. **Maddened against your father,** like Ismene's protests (569–75), implies a strong affection and leads us to expect quite a different line from that which Haemon takes initially. **Friends:** see on 182.

635–38 There is more ambiguity in Haemon's expression than the English offers; so also "when (if) your judgment is good" and, since **kind** is also "fair" or "noble," "your leading when (if) it is best" (cf. "best" at 72).

639 After prefatory statements of four lines each, Creon and Haemon each have speeches of exactly the same length (forty-two lines). To Haemon, Creon speaks of duty in the sententious way of a father preaching the accepted pieties; of Antigone he is more personal, and we sense an animosity deeper than present events.

642 For a father's expectations see *Tr* 1177–78, where "obedience" = "discipline" of *Ant* 676.

644–45 Friends: see 634 and 652; for the morality see on OC 186–87. **Will not help** means "is without profit/use"; cf. his thinking at 310–14.

648 Lust is more sexual than this mild word for "pleasure" (sometimes sensual pleasure) normally suggests. Here Creon takes off on the old theme of a bad wife:

> for while there's nothing better
> a man can win him
> than a good wife, there nothing more dismal
> than a bad one.
> (Hesiod *Works and Days*, 703–4)

652 Friend no friend is the oxymoron "harmful friend" (*philos kakos*).

654 For the motif **marry somebody in Hades** see 813–1⁄ and 1240–41.

658–59 For **Zeus who guards the kindred** see the note to 487–89.

659a Allow is "nourish/raise" (as at 532).

661–62 In an argument a fortiori Creon reasons that "the man who is good (acts properly) at home will surely be just in his city." If a man deals strictly and equitably with those he is most likely to favor (his family), he can be counted on to act similarly in public life.

663–71 Seidler transposed 663–68 (663–67 of the Greek text) to follow 671. Though not necessary, the transposition offers some gain in clarity and coherence.

668 Even when it's not: Creon's most autocratic line may be compared to a single line from Solon,

> Obey the rulers, whether right or wrong.
> (frag. 27 Diehl)

We do not know the context of this line.

672–78 At the beginning of the *Seven against Thebes*, Eteocles tries to quell the excited chorus, frightened by the army besieging Thebes:

Obedience [= **Discipline**] is mother to success,
and success is parent of rescue.
(*Seven against Thebes* 225–26)

This section begins with *anarchia* (**Disobedience**) and ends with *peithar-chia* (**discipline**). **Wrong** is "harm/evil" (*kakon*). **Live decently** = "guide their lives rightly" (as in "set it straight" at 163). For **beaten by a woman** see on 484.

681–82 A two-line comment is standard after a speech (724–26 translates two lines). **Sensible and right** translates the adverb from the *phron-* stem (the weight is on sensible thinking).

683 Had Sophocles made Haemon's love for Antigone more than an adventitious theme, it might have muddied, or at least diluted, the central issue of the play, for then Antigone must either be torn between love for brother and fiance, or she must clearly prefer one to the other. As the action goes, Haemon takes the line of a devoted son rather than a passionate lover, and we need not believe him hypocritical even if, in this first instance, he is prudent enough to repress his personal feeling. He acknowledges his duty to his father and offers his warning and advice as a personal and political friend: he has heard the commons grumble (692–700; 733) and urges Creon to relent. It is worth noting that his arguments bear more on expedience and Creon's character ("a wise man knows when to take up sail") than on the moral and religious themes of the play (but see 745 and 749). Tacitly approving Antigone's act of burial, Haemon puts his case in terms of good sense and a flexible disposition. Thus much in his plea is ad hominem, but in a general and benevolent way. The dramatic point illustrates just how intractable Creon is (note the plea to yield extending from 707–18); now, too, we begin to see the isolation of Creon.

Good sense (= "mind" at 648) and **possession** (again at 701 in "good") ought to be effective appeals to Creon's rationalism. **Only sure** = "highest." For the emphasis on himself as son see 688 and 701.

690–91 Frightens corroborates Antigone's opinion at 504–7. That the tyrant inspires fear and sycophancy is a commonplace.

695–704 Glorious action echoes Antigone's "greater glory" (502). **Golden prize** simply means "shouldn't she receive the highest honor?" Haemon will not refer to what is due the gods until these personal and political arguments have failed. Since he is conceding honor and glory to Antigone, he insists that he is personally interested in his father's honor (= **greatest good;** the father's welfare brings honor to his son) and **fame** (from the same stem as "glorious" at 695). So the unstated conclusion is that the honor she has won need not mitigate Creon's own honor (few Greeks would see how Creon could back down without some loss of honor). **And so a father . . . faring:** this sentence reverses the terms of the previous clause to emphasize reciprocity ("what loveliness in life for a son outweighs a father's fortune and fame?"). His argument is that his own standing is intimately connected with his father's, which should assure his father that the son has only his good to heart.

705 Mind is *êthos* (perhaps "intellectual disposition"), which occurs again at 746; see on *Aj* 599.

707 Wise and **mind** seem redundant; perhaps *psychê* (mind) has the meaning "courage" (Müller).

709 Come the unfolding metaphorically refers to the opening of a letter or scroll.

710–18 Both the coryphaeus and Creon (471–72 and 473–78) comment on Antigone's unyielding manner, and now Haemon argues, with an example from a river in flood and another from sailing, that rigid spirits must perish or be overthrown if they cannot learn to bend. Creon's examples (474–76) emphasize the breaking and curbing of insolent pride; Haemon's suggest that intransigence will result in the tree (also a common symbol of a house/family) being uprooted or a ship sailing on upside down (**ends the voyage** misses this irony), and nautical metaphors inevitably remind us of the ship of state and Creon its captain (162–63, 189). For **learning** see 1271; it is repeated as the last word in the speech at 723 and again in "take his lesson" (725); cf. 727–28.

727–28 To school my mind = "learn to think."

729–30 The play on **actions** moves from the sense "matter/business" to Creon's retort "is there some *need* to respect disorder?" **Disorder** earlier at 659a.

732 Disease is used metaphorically of various afflictions. The notion of moral and intellectual error as a disease probably originated from madness (e.g., *Aj* 59b, 66), which seemed an aberration caused by daimonic possession. At 1015 the state is sick because sacrifice fails and the omens are evil (cf. 1140); at 1052 Creon's intellectual folly is styled a disease.

737 Haemon's democratic bias is a a familiar anachronism; see Aeschylus *Suppliant Maidens* 366ff. (with references) and cf. *OK* 91–95 for the proper attitude.

740 Bain (*Actors and Audiences*, p. 72) argues that this line is directed to Haemon. Comparing *Tr* 1238, he views the third person as reflecting Creon's exasperation.

742–43 Try conclusions has legal connotations; we might say, "taking your father to court." Haemon's **unjustly** responds to this.

744 Unjust: the emphasis falls rather on a repeated (from 743) verb meaning "err" (For this word see on 1256–60 and 1261).

745 With **tread down the gods' due** (= "their honors") cf. "trample on the right (*dikê*)" at *Aj* 1335.

746 Poisoned means "disgusting" or "filthy" (*Tr* 987).

747 On **yield to shame** Jebb comments that "it would have been shameful if he had allowed fear or self-interest to deter him from pleading this cause." But this is defensive, and at this stage we expect pointed hostility; we should consider "beneath/inferior to shame," i.e., "acting, as you have, in manner beneath the normal limits of shame."

751 Creon takes **bring another** for a threat against himself, but it seems that Haemon, although perhaps only vaguely as yet, refers to himself.

754 Past due, sharp lessons: you will cry through your lesson, seeing you are so mindless. For the motif cf. 727–28.

755 Mad (*phron-*) plays on **brain** (*phrên-*) of **754.** The ambiguity of the present line derives from the same phrase meaning "you aren't sane," "you aren't prudent," and "you aren't well disposed (toward me)." The last is easily the most snide, but seems out of court in light of Creon's response, which purports to find some claim to filial regard in Haemon. Creon is certainly hotter than his son.

759a–60 Hateful creature (cf. *Phil* 991) may be less contemptuous than this idiomatic abstract noun suggests; here perhaps "hateful baggage." Creon forgets that people aren't killed on the Greek stage, but the threat incisively closes the scene. The tyrant Lycus in Euripides' *Heracles* thinks to incinerate his hostages on the stage (*Heracles* 240–45).

764–65 Such a man refers to his youth. **Hard** = "heavy," so "resentful" (Jebb).

771 At 546–47 Antigone denies Ismene's right to share in the deed.

773–77 He modifies the original penalty of his edict (see 35–37). His reason for relenting just so much would seem based on the fear that killing someone in his own family might bring **guilt** (*miasma:* "pollution") on himself and the city. See also 885–90. Giving her a bit to eat leaves her death to nature and Hades (**Death**), who, he sardonically suggests, may answer her prayers. A problem not faced by our translation is the meaning of the Greek word *agos* (see on "curse" at 255), which refers to the food and apparently, against its usual meanings, signifies "a propitiatory offering." *Agos* denotes that which is dedicated to a god, and so is sacred to the gods; here he thinks of both the girl's food and the girl as given over to Hades. What is properly said of the girl may also be said of what is hers; the noun *agos* may be transferred from her—the person truly dedicated—to what is hers.

780 Kitto (*Form and Meaning*, pp. 167–68) argues for keeping Creon on stage; he returns at 881.

781–800 The third stasimon celebrates the power of love (*eros* is the first word, Aphrodite is the last word in the Greek ode). It is clear that the chorus believes Haemon is motivated by love for Antigone, and the chorus is not mistaken (see 1223–41). But the universality of love's power naturally leads to general statement, and perhaps only "mad" (790) links this lyric explicitly with the preceding argument.

781–90 For the power of love see the note to *Tr* 441–44 and compare the lyric at *Iphigenia in Aulis* 544a–89. The Homeric *Hymn to Aphrodite* begins with praise of Aphrodite "who drives sweet desire on the gods and conquers the tribes of mortal men and flying birds and all beasts" (lines 2–4). **Havings** = "possessions"; the banality of the Greek phrase has attracted numerous conjectures, none of which particularly pleases. **Rest** = "sleep on/pass the night on." **Men** are **of a day** in contrast to the immortality of the gods, whose happiness is unchanging. **Mad** translates the same verb as "rave" at 763.

791–800 The power of love can turn **the just** off their natural course, make them unjust, and so leave them **ruined**. Blaydes compares *Libation Bearers* 597–601: "The female force, loveless love, drives aside and conquers married union of man and beast" (my adaptation of Lattimore). **Made** = "stirred/troubled," as in "disturbs" at *Hippolytus* 969:

> when love disturbs the youthful blood in them.

Desire looks clear: this sentence begins with "conquers" (cf. 781): "triumphant and clear is the desire from the eyes of a lovely bride." For the power of the eye to instill love see the note to *Agamemnon* 416–19. **Power as strong as the founded world** is a free but reasonable rendering of "Desire that sits in the power/office of the great laws." The principal image (**Desire enthroned**) is familiar in the poets, e.g.,

> they cultivate
> her who sits beside Zeus of hospitality, Themis,
> lady of salvation.
> (Pindar, *Eighth Olympian* 22–23)

The idea is either that desire/love is a counsellor and assessor coequal with the laws, or that desire preempts the place of the great laws. The **goddess** is explicitly named (Aphrodite), and her name (she is often coupled with *eros*) along with **fight** (as in 781) takes us back by ring composition to the beginning of the lyric.

801–81 With the appearance of Antigone a kommos begins. "For the first time in the play we have a genuine interchange between actor and chorus" (Else, p. 58). She sings; the choral responses are anapestic (first pair) and iambic. The antiphonal form is not only poetic but is also characteristic of popular funerary laments, and a glance through Alexiou's monograph will show how many of the motifs are shared by the popular and dramatic traditions (farewell to the Sun, youth cut off, death as a journey, and marriage denied are some of the most common). But, as Creon says (882–84), this is a dirge before the fact, and so, while Antigone sings her miserable fate, the chorus keeps some distance, reminding her that she has chosen death (821, 875) and that she has won the fame she wanted (815, 834). Her defiance gone (we may wonder if she would sing thus if Creon were present), she seeks consolation, which the chorus gives in small portion. So small that she feels mocked (837). With her victory and defeat in hand, Antigone reveals a more human, that is, a more vulnerable aspect. There is more pathos that way. A second kommos will cry the fall of Creon's house (1261–1300).

801 **Carried beyond all bounds** is a metaphor from horseracing, where at the turn there is danger of not staying on the course. More surprising is **bounds,** which translates the same word rendered "laws" in the note on 794. But context and sense seem to change radically here: the chorus says "Now *even I* am carried outside the law," which the commentators take to refer to Creon's edict. If line 794 means desire has supplanted (for Haemon) all other laws, then the present line may follow ("I, too, like Haemon, find myself off the path of law because of my pity for Antigone"). Lines 801–4 signal more sympathy than Antigone feels she gets.

804 **Where all men sleep:** again at 810.

805–14 Cf. the last words of Ajax, with a farewell to his country (*Aj* 859a–61), to the sun (*Aj* 857–58), and his prayer to Hermes, guide for the last journey (*Aj* 832; cf. *Tr* 875). The **river underground** is **Acheron** (the proper noun appears twice here), which Euripides represents as a lake (*Alcestis* 443–44). Charon is the boatman who ferries the dead across the Styx and into the well-watered underworld:

> There Pyriphlegethon and Kokytos, which is an off-break
> from the water of the Styx, flows into Acheron. There is
> a rock there, and the junction of two thunderous rivers.
> (*Odyssey* 10.513–15)

A gravestone reports a girl's early death: "This is the stone of Phrasideia. I shall always be called a maiden, having gotten this name from the gods rather than marriage" (see Lattimore, *Themes,* p. 192; Alexiou, pp. 105 and 155). Antigone dwells on "unmarried": 865, 876, 891, 917.

815–23 **Praise** was her prize (502; cf. 834). She dies neither from disease nor a violent death (the **sword**) but by her own law (**of your own motion**): the Greek word *autonomos* (autonomy) combines the common word for "law" with "self" (she has made a law to match Creon's). These compound adjectives (with *auto-*) denoting what is self-chosen, voluntary, or personal occur fifteen times in the *Antigone,* nineteen times in the other six extant plays, and seven times in the fragments.

824–31 Translators tend to avoid the proper names often favored in Greek poetry: "I heard that the Phrygian stranger, daughter of Tantalus, perished most pitifully on the height of Sipylus." She refers to Niobe, who came to Thebes from Phrygia in Asia Minor. She married Amphion, king of Thebes, and when she bragged that she had more and more beautiful children than Leto, Apollo and Artemis, the children of Leto, killed all her children. In her grief she was transformed into stone on Mt. Sipylus in her native Phrygia. Both Aeschylus and Sophocles made tragedies on Niobe's tale, which survives most notably in book six of Ovid's *Metamorphoses.* At *El* 150–53 she is a type of patient grief. Antigone's prospective entombment makes her think of the ossified Niobe; as the chorus will point out, the analogy is tenuous. **Covered her over:** "the rocky shoot conquered her." **Companion her** = "never leave her"; at this point the Greek includes a parenthetical "as the story goes." **Pouring down:** this sentence fuses, through ambiguous words like "neck/ridge" and "brow/eyebrow," the images of woman and rock: "(she) soaks under tearful brows (her) neck" (the Greek sentence has five words). **Has planned** gives the god (a *daimôn*) too much credit; "me, so similar to her, a *daimôn* puts to sleep." If the rocky end is the ostensible connection and all Antigone asks us to think on, yet beneath that lies the more poignant loss of dearest kin; such a point would have been more sensible to Sophocles' audience, which no doubt still remembered vividly the famous silent grief of Aeschylus' Niobe.

832–36 Since Tantalus was the son of Zeus, Niobe may be called a god. The antithetical mode is better seen if we translate **We are born to death** "but (we are) mortal and mortality's children." **Yet** attempts to offer some consolation, which for Antigone (see 837) is as slight as the logic is for us (**gone like a god to your fate** means "obtained the same lot as the demigods").

837–51 For **laughter** (= "I am mocked") see 551 and 647. **Affront ... in my face** translates the verbal form of *hybris* ("insult"). For **Dirce** see 102. Like "warrior-joy" at 149a, **armored** is a compound adjective that means "glorious for her chariots"; both are generic and ornamental, especially in the present case. The apostrophe to people and places is so common that we might overlook it, save that the call to **witnesses** reflects the appeal to justice of any wronged person who must, under Greek law, invoke those present at the time as witnesses to the crime; see the note on

Agamemnon 1315. An **alien** (*metoikos*) is a person living in a foreign place without full political rights. With **no friend's mourning** cf. 881.

852–55 Daring does not usually commend or console (cf. 248 and 371), so the possible ambiguity of **fell** at the **foundation of justice** (either you "fell before it as a suppliant" or you "tripped over it") seems resolved by the context; secondly, as Linforth also observes (p. 223), Antigone has hardly played the helpless suppliant. Furthermore, while the idea that children may pay for the sins of their fathers is found in Herodotus as well as earlier in this play (1–3), it only revives painful memories for Antigone, and the chorus cannot imagine otherwise, however much they merely seek to explain. Aegisthus says of the murdered Agamemnon:

> Now that I see this man—sweet sight—before me here
> sprawled in the tangling nets of fury, to atone [= **pay**]
> the calculated evil of his father's hand.
>
> (*Agamemnon* 1580–82)

For Aegisthus, Agamemnon has paid for the murder of Thyestes' sons by Agamemnon's father Atreus. Sophocles' **pain** is vague by comparison, but the Greek audience would be sensible to the possibility that Antigone "must be accounted a victim of the family curse" (Lloyd-Jones; for his argument see *The Justice of Zeus*, pp. 113–15).

862–71 My other's marriage bed (in apostrophe) is to be taken with **Destruction** (*atê;* cf. 533) since the harm comes from the marriage to her **husband-son** (translating the impossible "intercourse self-generated"). She describes herself as "pitiful" or "poor." Line 864 means "I was born wretched." **My curse** in this context suggests a curse on the family: "I go to them, accursed, unwed, an alien" (this last word occurred at 850). **My brother** is Polyneices rather than Eteocles; he married an Argive princess and thereby won the help of Adrastus, king of Argos, for his expedition against Thebes: "you found an ill-fated marriage." "The dead are killing the living" is a riddle at *Libation Bearers* 886; Kamerbeek compares *Aj* 1027–29, *El* 809 and 1419a–20, *Tr* 1162–63, all variations on this theme.

872–75 Jebb's translation better reflects what he calls the "purposed vagueness": "Reverent action claims a certain praise for reverence." But even that version explains the three Greek words, which to use their translation at 924–25 might be "To act piously is a kind of piety," faint praise indeed. **So we for you** is the translator's interpretation. The antithesis contrasts piety and **power**: "but power, for him who cares for power, is not to be transgressed." **Self-sufficiency** = "a self-willed temper." Cf. 821 and the note.

876–81 Road = "journey" at 806; **No longer . . . sun:** cf. 806; **no**

wedding-song: cf. 813–14. Repeated word and motif at the end of the lyric define ring composition; formal considerations preempt a response to their last judgment. Twice in this stanza she describes herself with an untranslated "wretched"; at 40 and 56 ("poor") it describes another party and not the speaker.

885 Take her away: he speaks to slaves or guards accompanying him. An omitted verb suggests "enfolding/covering" her, perhaps, as Kamerbeek suggests, a sinister variation of his original idea of stoning anyone who defied the edict.

887 Choose, which is not read by all editors, cynically anticipates that she may prefer the rope.

888–90 For **no stain of guilt** see the note to 775–76. **Exiled** echoes her "alien" (850); ever a "resident alien," she is now stripped of that.

891 The apostrophe is threefold and the O occurs three times in the line. Similarly **dear** (898–99: *philê*) occurs three times in the Greek.

894 Persephone is queen of the underworld; cf. 1201 and OC 1548.

895 Ill-fated = "most vilely" (from the *kakos* stem) and probably refers to the manner of her death (it is "terribly" at 59). "How the mighty have fallen" is a theme as much of the victims as of the observers (see OK 1397–98 and the note). The nobleman deplores his degradation more than his suffering; hence Antigone's sensitivity to mockery, Oedipus' to the humiliation of his family (OK 1500, 1509–9a).

899 Because at 903 she turns in address to Polyneices ("And now, Polyneices . . ."), most commentators take **brother** to mean Eteocles, though we would expect the unadorned singular to refer to the corpse at issue, and she certainly has not prepared Eteocles for burial. There is some ambiguity, but I do not see that the vocative at 903 precludes Polyneices here.

902 For the **libation** at the tomb (wine poured into the grave) see 431.

905–20 These lines were known to Aristotle in the next century, and he cites 911–12, approving the argument:

> Where any detail may prove incredible, then add the cause of it; of this Sophocles provides an example in the *Antigone,* where Antigone says she had cared more for her brother than for husband or children, since if the latter perished they might be replaced,
> > But with my parents hid away in death,
> > no brother, ever, could spring up for me.
>
> (*Rhetoric* 3.16)

We also know a story from Herodotus (3.119) in which the wife of Intaphrenes, when the king gives her a choice of a single relative to be saved from the executioner, names her brother, rather than husband or child. She explains:

> My lord, she replied, 'God willing, I may get another husband, and other children when these are gone. But as my father and mother are both dead, I can never possibly have another brother.
> (Herodotus 3.119)

(For an interesting variant on this argument see Eric Auerbach's *Mimesis*, p. 208.) Such direct and indirect evidence might seem to vouch for the authenticity of these lines, which have nonetheless been condemned as an interpolation by many modern scholars and do not appear in some translations. The reason for suspicion is simple: in arguing that she would not have crossed the state's decree save for a brother, Antigone contradicts her own principle (450–59) that burial is demanded by the justice of Zeus and the gods below, for religious piety cannot quibble on the availability of another husband or child. In short, Antigone repudiates, though she does not recognize it as such, the religious ground on which she has been standing. It may be added that her present reasoning is just as devastating to those interpretations that see her primary motivation stemming from personal and family honor; in matters of honor, father, child, and brother are all one. Given the contradiction, we may excise the passage (Jebb and others) or try to final some rationale for her failed logic (this may well be an overrated problem: neither she, nor the chorus, nor Creon says that she now fails in piety, but then the Greeks were more sensitive to facts than to feelings of the heart). Lesky's view has its adherents: "This is the expression of a basic trait of Greek character: some intellectual reason has to be found for a feeling of the heart" (*History of Greek Literature*, p. 282). That is, Lesky does not deny the contradiction but sees it as the rather bad result of a rationalizing habit—and no play of Sophocles is more rationalistic than this one. Critics must always be uneasy with solutions derived from ethnic, racial, and religious generalities, even when they are true. The other direction stresses the psychological side: she is victorious but vulnerable, and, having failed in the preceding kommos to win the chorus's sympathy, "In this moment of desertion she marvels at her own act, and in a state of mind approaching to delirium, tries to account for it" (Campbell, *Paralipomena*, p. 34). If the syntax is too lucid for "delirium," we can still believe that the girl so conscious of a friendless life (876, 881, 919) and a thankless death (unvindicated, as she realizes:

921–29) may suffer a flagging will, and with it a drooping logic, for a moment (her last lines strike me as a return to the earlier defiance).

In the kommos Sophocles let his heroine be influenced by the traditional pathos associated with premature death. While the burial required strength and purpose against odds, popular feeling and the genre call for the unmarried bride of death to inspire pathos and sympathy. The audience readily accepts this change because (1) Antigone *is* a young girl now denied marriage (a secondary function of Haemon's scene) and (2) the chorus fails to fulfill its usual role of consolation. Even those who sympathize with Creon's position may generously pity the niece and feel all the better for it. And the kommos leads naturally enough to this speech, in which despair and bitterness bring on dubious logic (at least the wife in Herodotus has a man to save!). After all, Ismene did not feel obliged to bury her brother; that Antigone did feel bound simply means family ties are profoundly more important for her. So there is some truth in Hester's rude summation: "Surely in her last moments, when she has nothing to hope for, it is her true feelings we can hear; the rationalization came rather in lines 450 to 460; family and honour are her first thoughts, and her last" ("Sophocles the Unphilosophical," p. 37). At the root, if the trail is radically pragmatic, Ismene has been more "rational" than Antigone, and perhaps we should not be surprised that Antigone's reasons, when she belatedly looks for some, are less cogent than her action.

905 Wise continues the argument about right thinking, and right may also modify it: "those who think rightly."

908 State's decree repeats Ismene's phrase "against the citizens" (79a); cf. also 59.

914–15 Crime is "error" at 927 and "are wrong" at 928 (all verbal forms cognate with *hamartia*). See on 1258–61. Since this is not a technical term for crime, and may be as innocuous as "be mistaken," she may be mocking Creon a bit; **dreadful daring:** last at 852.

919 Struck down by fate (*dusmoros:* see OC 224b–c): this word modifies "father" at 864 and has the same force as "in my misery" (922). Such words are the staple of tragic self-pity.

921–25 Disobeyed = "go across/transgress," similar to Ismene's "try to cross" (60); see the note on "over-run" at 454–55. Since the Greek gods are not moral enforcers, they do not take such questions as blasphemy. Nor should we say the gods have abandoned Antigone: it was her cause (**my pious duty**) in their name, not their commission. Piety (forms of *sêbô*) reflects the language of 512 ("serve"; note at 515–17), 872, and 943 ("respected the right" = "piously regarded piety"). The concept covers both moral and religious responsibilities.

926–29 Righteousness is, more generally, "fair/right"; she ironically offers a variation on "learning through suffering" (see on *Agamemnon* 176–78). Creon will "learn too late" (see 1270–71). For her final wish see the note to *Phil* 278.

929a–30 Tempest = "blasts" at 136; cf. their similar comment on her "temper" at 875. If these lines refer to the content of her speech, rather than her manner, they don't tell us much.

934 Creon's two lines in the Greek have a more legal and pompous ring: "I cannot encourage you to be confident that this is not ratified for her."

935–43 Cf. the apostrophes at 841–45. The formality of these anapests may also be seen in a more literal version of **I am led away at last:** "I am led away and am no longer on the point of going." For **respected the right** see on 921–25.

Exit Antigone. She goes off left by the parodos to the country. Though the following lyric addresses her (946, 984), she is certainly not present for the last vocative. I would prefer to hear her last verses in place, before the procession begins, with the lyrics beginning after she has departed.

944–84 The fourth stasimon is, in terms of dramatic relevance, the most problematic in the play, if not in all the extant plays. Some sort of entombment or imprisonment (Danaë, Lycurgus, and Cleopatra are the examples) provides a formal connection with Antigone, but a deeper relevance to either Antigone or Creon is hard to find, not least of all because the allusive lyric and our knowledge of the Cleopatra story do not readily harmonize. Winnington-Ingram's cautious examination of this ode serves as a prudent survey (pp. 98–109).

944–53 Danaë is the daughter of Acrisius, who, learning from an oracle that his daughter's child would kill him, locked her up in a **brass-built chamber** in order to prevent a pregnancy. Zeus found a way, however, in golden rain, and Danaë gave birth to Perseus (see Apollodorus 2.4.1). The Greek says she was "yoked" in the tomb, and this is the first word in the antistrophe ("and yoked/bound, too, was the son of Dryas"). The Greek repeats **child,** which validates the interpretive **poor. Held and kept** suggests that "she held and dispensed" the seed and ironically inverts the imagery, since from Homer on Zeus is known as the "steward/dispenser" of good and ill. **Terrible** is repeated in "terror" at 957 (this is the word *deinos* discussed at 332–41). The **you** (952) does not refer to Antigone (the Greek sentence says "neither wealth, nor Ares (**war**), nor . . . can outrun it"). The **ships** are modified by ornamental adjectives "dark, sea-struck."

954–63 The **son of Dryas** is Lycurgus, the king of the Edonians (and so identified here), a Thracian tribe. He was the first to reject the worship of Dionysus (the god is mentioned by name here). Apollodorus (3.5.1) reports that Lycurgus "was the first who insulted and expelled him. Dionysus took refuge in the sea with Thetis, daughter of Nereus, and the Bacchanals [the **dancing women**] were taken prisoners together with the multitude of Satyrs who attended him. But afterwards the Bacchanals were suddenly released, and Dionysus drove Lycurgus mad. And in his madness he struck his son Dryas dead with an axe, imagining that he was lopping a branch of a vine." The Greek suggests Lycurgus was "yoked by/because of his mocking temper" and so at Dionysus' command was "encased" (= **pent**) in a rocky prison. **Slowly went down:** if this verb is transitive here, we get "Thus he drips away the terrible, foaming/blossoming strength of the madness." It may be more intelligible to think of the strength of the madness trickling away, as the translation apparently takes it. **Learned:** the text seems to mean that he recognized the god from his taunting assault on him. It seems possible that madness is the medium through which Lycurgus comes to know, too late, the divinely mad Dionysus. An adjective meaning "taunting/mocking" is repeated for the second time in this stanza. The **dancing women** (Bacchants) are inspired and possessed by the god (see *OK* 208–15 and notes; see 1126–51 below); here they are called "Muses" (= "those who love **songs and flutes**"). The **fire** actually refers to the cry *euoi* (see *Tr* 219) of their revel.

964–74 The last two stanzas take up the story of Cleopatra, daughter of Boreas, though she is never mentioned by name. (Sophocles wrote two tragedies entitled *Phineus*, and the lyric clearly counts on the familiarity of the story.) She married **Phineus**, king of **Salmydessus** on the Black Sea. He put her away and married Eidothea, who blinded the sons of Cleopatra (**blinding wounds**). The **savage god** is Ares (these Thracian tribes were infamous for their barbarity). **Terrible** is "cursed." **Looked to avenge** means that their eyes cry out for vengeance. Apollodorus says that Phineus blinded the boys after his wife had falsely accused them of attacking her (the same motif we have in Euripides *Hippolytus*). The **shuttle** is a sharp, pointed instrument used in weaving.

975–84 **Settled when they were born:** because they were the children of a mother whose marriage went awry. **Cleopatra** is not mentioned by name, but the allusion is clear from "she traced her descent from the ancient line of Erechtheus." Her mother Orithyia was carried off by the god of the **north wind** (Boreas). At last we have a **cave**, but it is not a place of imprisonment. The last line is literally, "the long-lived Fates also attacked her, child."

985 For **Teiresias** see on *OK* 284–86. After Ismene and Haemon he is the third voice to oppose Creon, and with augeries and threats so terrible that Creon will—but only when he departs—relent.

994 For the nautical metaphor see 162–63 and 189. The tense of the verb may suggest a longer rule than Creon has actually enjoyed, but he has belonged to the ruling family and can fairly be said to have been a "helmsman" of the state.

996 The image of the **razor's edge** goes back to the *Iliad* (10.173). The present phrase is "on the razor of chance (*tychê*)"; Teiresias thinks that there is still time to correct Creon's error.

1000 The nautical imagery is continued with "the harbor of every bird." Cf. 1284. Pausanias (9.16.1) says Teiresias had an observatory.

1003 Goaded by madness: the image is taken from the sting of the gadfly, such as hounded Io (*Prometheus Bound* 565–66); madness is the typical result (cf. *Tr* 1254). Because exceptional knowledge and power are attributed to birds, that they should turn on one another implies an extraordinary disturbance in nature.

1008 A clean, complete incineration signals an acceptable offering (cf. 1019a–20). The offerings were of bones, fat, and entrails (hence the **gall**, included with the intestines). Having been warned of the ill-omened antics of the birds, Teiresias orders a sacrifice. Its failure to burn indicates divine displeasure and also presents a second ill-omened event, since the Greeks practiced divination from the manner and appearance of the burning offerings. As Kamerbeek says, the failure to get a sign is itself an evil omen.

1015–16 This is a single sentence: "the city is sick because of your decision." **Decision** = "counsel" at 993; this word (*phrên*) repeatedly directs our attention to intellectual decision: "mind" (648, 1064, 1090, 1094), "good sense" (299 and 683), and "heart" (1261) are some examples.

1017 Two types of **altars** are mentioned, one for sacrifice to the gods, the other for heroes, with the purpose of stressing the universal calamity.

1022 Greasy blood makes one queasy. The Greek compression, from which we get "fat of the blood," is idiomatic in tragic diction. More prosaically, "gorged on the fat and blood of the slain."

1023–33 It would be difficult to find a better example of the intellectual cast of Greek ethical thought. Motive and purpose are put aside: Creon has made a mistake (**err, error**: the *hamartia* stem) and can, if he will not remain intractable (**stiffness, stubbornness**), correct (**cures**) his mistake. There is no question of repentance, remorse, or straightening out one's religious thinking, but intransigence in the face of a recognized mistake is stupidity. **Think** (*phronô*) is echoed in **for your own good** (i.e., Teiresias is well-intentioned). **Fool** echoes words such as "ill-counselling" (95) and anticipates "counsel" (1097, 1243) and "fault" (1267). **Nor yet unfortunate** implies that the error corrected will be inconsequential (Creon may yet save the prosperity he enjoys). **Cures** is a common medical metaphor and sees the city's ills (1015) as his responsibility. **Stubbornness** = "obstinacy" at *OK* 549c (see the note there), for which yielding is the cure (see on 471–72 and cf. 1095). To bring out the legal metaphor we may translate: "Stubbornness incurs the charge of stupidity" (see the note on 469–70 for the same figure). **Goad him,** as if the body were a horse to be spurred. **Use** = "courage." **Learning:** cf. 1087 and 1270. **Profitable** (*kerdos*) is for Creon a characteristic way of looking at things (222, 310–14, 1036–47, 1061; cf. 462–64).

1034–35 Teiresias will respond to **bowman** at 1084–85. For the metaphor cf. *OK* 1197–99.

1036 Item in your accounts: cf. the commercial metaphor at 1063–64. He means that he cannot "be bought and sold" by those who would take bribes for their political loyalty (cf. 221–22). **Lydian silver-gold** (electron) refers to the famous mines on Mt. Tmolus near Sardis in Lydia.

1040–44 Eagles are the peculiar birds of Zeus. Creon's anger may divert us from a reasonable argument, one also urged by the Athenian hero Theseus:

No mortal man can stain what is divine.

(Euripides *Heracles* 1232)

Commenting on this line, Bond says the line "exhibits a new rationalistic spirit." Creon and Theseus may have the better theology, but the **pollution** (*miasma*), the failed sacrifice, and the evil omens are facts of more concrete concern for the pious Greek, and Creon himself will finally give way.

1049–50 Creon is not wrong to expect a cliché: Haemon has already used one variant "sense is better than cents" (see 683–84), and there is a fine example in the coryphaeus's comment at *El* 1015–16.

1056 Add "shameful" to **gain,** but is Teiresias saying anything more than "you're another"?

1058 Helped you save the town apparently alludes to Teiresias' advice, during the recent siege, that, because of the wrath of Ares, a member of Creon's family must be sacrificed to appease the god. At 1302–3 the "older son" who died to save the city is called Megareus; in Euripides' *Phoenician Women* (911–14) Teiresias pronounces this son's (there called Menoeceus) fate.

1059 Wickedness is from the *dikê* stem ("wrong" at 791).

1060 Unspeakable alludes to prophecies at 1065ff.

1063–64 Mind (*phrên*) is "decision" at 1016 (note) and here suggests "purpose." **Sell it . . . buyer** is the same metaphor as at 1036–37.

1065–67 Days seems to give Creon time, more than he actually has. The **sun** is imagined as making its **course** in a chariot, and so Creon will not realize "many racing circuits of the sun" before he pays in kind, corpse (Haemon) **for corpses** (the unburied turn out to be more than the single body of Polyneices: see 1080–83).

1068–69 Confused, i.e., "you have thrown down one who belongs above" (Antigone). In 1069 the translation omits "dishonorably" (the *timê* stem), which Jebb translates "ruthlessly." Kells ("Problems," p. 57) suggests that it may refer to depriving Antigone of her civic rights. Creon has failed to understand proper honor.

1071 A triad of privatives suggests the corpse is "without its proper lot," "without due rites," "unsanctified."

1072–73 Can claim him now, i.e., since he is dead, he is of interest neither to you nor to the gods on high, and your action does violence to the rights of the gods below. **The nether gods** is not expressed, and some editors take **rob** ("treat violently") to refer obliquely to the polluted altars of the Olympian divinities; though the Olympians are apparently offended, it is the gods below who are outraged, and they also fill out a triad.

1075–77 The **pursuing horrors** are the Furies (see on *OC* 40–43). With **lie in wait** cf. "ambush" at *El* 490 (also of the Furies). These spirits of vengeance are often equated with "curses," and since they are also called "late-destroying" (cf. *Agamemnon* 58 and *Libation Bearers* 383), we naturally think of the anger of the maltreated dead. Yet Müller rightly notes that the play makes no mention of the anger of Polyneices, as Aeschylus surely would, and as Sophocles will in his *Electra* (243–50, 483). **Will even you:** "you will be caught in the same evils," which will not be exactly the case; apparently this is a vague, and so more threatening, allusion of the sort we have in "corpse for corpse" at 1067.

1080–83 For the first time in the play we learn that not only Polyneices but the other dead allies have been denied burial. Since this information is irrelevant as well, the lines have been suspected. The story, however, was well known, and Herodotus reports that in their claim for a post of honor at the battle of Plataea the Athenians include the following boast:

> Again, when the dead Argives were left unburied after their attack upon Thebes with Polyneices, we marched against the Cadmeans, recovered their bodies and gave them burial within our own territory at Eleusis.
>
> (Herodotus 9.27)

Euripides' *Suppliant Women* also celebrates this Athenian exploit. **Had burial** translates a verb that means "to devote/consecrate by burning"; the transfer to birds and dogs violently condemns Creon. **Move against you now:** the sons of the slain warriors (known as the Epigoni) avenged their fathers by marching against Thebes and destroying it. Teiresias forecasts truly if hyperbolically.

1084 As you said: see 1034–35. Teiresias says that the arrows are aimed at the heart and that Creon will not escape the "heat" of them.

1086 For similar observations on the **rage** of Oedipus see *OK* 344a and 364.

1095 Apart from Philoctetes, who accepts a divine command, Creon is the only prominent character in the extant plays who changes his mind and yields to force of argument and circumstance; for the motif see on 471–72. **Stand against him** should be taken with **strike:** "but if I stand against him, I strike my spirit dreadfully with destruction (*atê*)."

1097 For **counsel** cf. 1050 and 1243.

1098 What must I do?: for this question stressing a moment of decision see *Tr* 385 and *Phil* 895.

1100–1101 The order of the two clauses may suggest "first do one, then the other," but in the event he goes to the body first.

1103–4 More literally: "Swift-footed Disaster (*blabê*) from the gods cuts down misguided men." "Swift-footed" signals the personification of Disaster (here, as at *Tr* 842, a synonym for *atê*). **Misguided** = "those who think badly/harmfully"; the ambiguity seems to look both at the issue of right thinking and, in a secondary way, at the harmful consequences of Creon's thinking for those around him.

1106 For the motif **fight necessity** see on *OC* 191.

1107 He might naturally leave the actual work to his servants, but Sophocles plans to bring his wife Eurydice onstage, and Creon would be in the way of her scene.

1109a–10 Why take axes? For cutting wood to burn the body (1204) rather than digging Antigone out of her tomb (1214–15), though in neither case are axes mentioned or needed. **That overlooks us** would seem to refer to the high plain where the body was left; Jebb suggests a gesture (left), and we have at 412 a hill on which the guards were stationed.

1111–14 Overturned = "turned/changed" (in its course); he is not putting responsibility on the chorus or anyone else. Jebb would have us believe that "at this moment his foremost thought is of saving Antigone. If she dies, his son must die (1067). Therefore, while he glances at the burial rites by telling his men to bring axes, he describes his own part by his most *urgent* task,—the release." But if Creon has defined Teiresias' threat so exactly, why does he in fact take time to provide rites for the body before going on to the tomb? If the **her** (1112) were expressed, we would have no choice but to believe Jebb. Since, however, the **her** is not expressed and line 1112 may mean "What I've done I'll undo," and since **laws of old tradition** will bring to mind, in the first instance, the religious issue, and not her protest, we should not tie Creon in Jebb's knot. Both tasks are imperative. Freeing Antigone will be, psychologically and socially, the more difficult. Yet this is not the moment for that subtlety. For the play she must die, and a degree of ambiguity may be intended. There is more ambiguity in 1113–14: **hold** = "save," with the secondary suggestion that preserving the laws brings a **life** (hers) to its **end.**

1115–51 With an abrupt change of mood this lyric (the fifth stasimon) celebrates Dionysus the healer (1140–41), whose epiphany in his native city will signify triumphant release. While the song touches only briefly and allusively on the preceding dramatic events, it clearly springs from a joyous sense that disaster may be yet averted. As at *Aj* 693–717 and *OK* 1087–1107, the spirit of optimism prevails, only to be dashed immediately by the messenger's report (1152; in both the *Ajax* and the *Oedipus* messengers enter directly after the songs, but in the former case the news is ominous but not final, while in the *Oedipus* the messenger takes part in the stichomythia, brings what he thinks is happy news, and becomes a crucial agent in the final unraveling of the plot). We may with Kranz (*Stasimon,* p. 213) call this dramatic retardation, but the deeper rhythm of the play is against optimism. Less ecstatic but equally mistaken is the lyric at *Tr* 633–62, where hope struggles against metaphor.

1115–25 Gods answer more readily to their proper names; so Dionysus is summoned as **Semele's golden child** (= "glory of the Cadmeian nymph") and **child of Olympian thunder** (= "of Zeus the deep-thunderer"). We should accept Dawe's conjecture Oechalia (see *Tr* 354) for **Italy:** Oechalia (on Euboea: 1132) is connected to Thebes through the adventures of Heracles; Italy has too little to do with Dionysus. **Eleusis,** home of the mysteries (**where all men come**), is north of Athens on the coast; **Demeter** (here called by the rarer "Deo") and her daughter Persephone preside there. **Bacchus,** the most common name of Dionysus, brought his worship first to Thebes because his mother Semele was a native (see Euripides *Bacchae* 1–10 for the god's own report). The **wild Bacchic women** are the ecstatic retinue of the god, the night-long dancers of 152–53 (see 1126), and the Maenads ("the mad ones") of 1150. For the children **of the dragon seed** see *OC* 1534a, *Ant* 122.

1126–35 **You** is the first word of the antistrophe. The lyric turns to Delphi, where Dionysus shared honors with Apollo. Towering above Delphi is Mt. **Parnassus;** the **double mount** refers to two peaks beneath the summit. Cf. *Eumenides* 24–26. **Glaring flame** describes the torches of the Bacchic dance (cf. 1143–44). The nymphs are called "Bacchic, Corycian" (for the famous cave above Delphi). The **Kastalia** flows from the peaks above Delphi; its water was used at the sanctuary (see Euripides *Ion* 95–101). The **ivied heights** belong to Mt. Nysa on Euboea (the mountain rather than the island is named in the Greek). The stanza amounts to "come to us, whether you are now at Delphi or on Euboea."

1136–42 For Thebes above all honors (and is **honored** by) you. **Miracle-death** is translated at *Bacchae* 7 "lightning-married mother": Semele received Zeus disguised as a mortal and was at length tricked by the jealous Hera into demanding that the god appear to her in his full glory; when the god reluctantly appeared in thunder and lightning, the poor girl was incinerated (the fetus was saved and sewed in the thigh of Zeus until its birth). **Grim disease** = "sickness" at 1015. While **healing** is hardly the primary attribute of Dionysus, there is some evidence (cf. the purifications of the Bacchic chorus, *Bacchae* 76). **Moaning sea** would, in the context of Delphi and Euboea, refer to the turbulent currents separating Euboea from the mainland.

1143–51 Cf. the references to nocturnal worship at 1126–27. The **Maenad maids** (literally Thyiads, a name for these inspired women that Aeschylus uses three times, Euripides not at all) "dance for you all night long, (calling you) Iacchus the steward" (the translator seems to have missed a line here). Iacchus is usually connected with a verb "to shout," so a possible meaning is "Lord of Cries" (Dodds on *Bacchae* 725); he is called "steward" because of the gifts he brings.

1152–1352 Only the *Oedipus at Colonus* has more episodes (seven) than the *Antigone*. An unusual feature in this final scene is the introduction of a new character, Eurydice, Creon's wife; Aeschylus has already brought on the late newcomer Aegisthus in the exodus of the *Agamemnon*.

1152 The same actor who played the guard takes this role; there is nothing to indicate that they are the same character. The formality of the opening line quickly passes into a sententiousness that only accidentally, it seems, alludes to Creon. When a direct question is put (1171), he prefers a riddle (1172), and it would seem from his last line before Eurydice's entrance that he does not intend to give a particular account; at any rate, it is only her request that prompts it.

Amphion ruled Thebes for a time with his brother Zethus after they had avenged the wrongs done their mother Antiope by Lycus. Amphion is credited with building the walls of Thebes, the stones of which followed the music of his lyre to their proper place. The brothers ruled during the minority and exile of Laius (see Apollodorus 3.5.5–7).

1155–56 Luck (*tychê*) points to the theme of mutability (see *OK* 611–15 and 1080–86 for this topic) which dominates this speech. The *tychê* stem also appears in **happy** and **unhappy**. **Sets it straight** suggests the metaphor "road of life" as well as steering straight (see 1164).

1160 For skepticism about **prophecy** see *OK* 496–512; for **envy** see the note to *Tr* 185.

1162–64 Saved this city is hardly literally true but points to the generality of the entire speech; by contrast see *OK* 48. **Sons** links Haemon and Megareus (see 1058).

1166 Happiness is commended in the well-known lines of Simonides:

> What is desireable in life for men,
> or what power, without happiness?
> Without that not even the life of the gods is enviable.
> (Simonides frag. 71; my translation)

1170 For **smoke's shadow** see on *Aj* 126. The metaphor is commercial: "I wouldn't pay the price of smoke's shadow for the rest, compared to the value of happiness."

1172 Cf. the riddling servant who flees Orestes:

> I tell you, he is alive and killing the dead.
> (*Libation Bearers* 886)

1174 Antigone, though dead, is not important to the messenger or the house. **One of his kin** is, as the response indicates, ambiguous and may also mean "by his own hand."

1176 Himself: with emphatic stress (see the note to 49–54) that echoes "his own" in 1174; cf. 1314. **His blood is on:** more literally, "angered at his father for (her) murder."

1180 We may see the doors open at 1174 since she says that she has heard something of this conversation (1186). On the other hand, her appearance in the midst of the stichomythia would split the focus, and the circumstantial account (1183–91) is characteristic of unexpected entries (cf. *Phil* 542, where **by chance** also occurs).

1183 She begins with a vocative ("all you citizens").

1184 Pallas is Athena; so Jocasta reenters (*OK* 909) to offer prayer to Apollo.

1186 Of my own sorrow = "of the house's trouble."

1191 With **grief** she apparently alludes to Megareus: "I shall listen as one not inexperienced in grief."

1194 For **soft** speech cf. *Phil* 629a. The messenger at *Tr* 351 also vouches for his firsthand knowledge.

1201–2 The **goddess of all journeyings** is either Persephone or Hecate (they are sometimes identified). **Pluto** ("the wealthy one") is another name for Hades.

1209 Unblest means "without proper funeral rites."

1210 Heard confusion crying = "heard the unintelligible sounds of a pitiful cry."

1214 So far as we can tell, Sophocles' **tomb** seems to have been below ground, with a passage leading to the entry proper. That passage would have been slightly declining, and filled with rock after Antigone was imprisoned. Haemon has torn away the rock from the outer end of the passage.

1217 Tricking: were they tricking him, it would be more innocent than Athena's deception of Ajax (*Aj* 51–67). When a Greek misunderstands or fails to perceive something correctly, he attributes the error to the gods, even if the mistake is relatively trivial.

1221 Jocasta also hangs herself (*OK* 1264); Eurydice (1282–83), Ajax (*Aj* 865), and Deianira (*Tr* 874–83) use a blade. Only the last three of the surviving plays are without suicides.

1223 In the compression of the narrative, Sophocles has neglected to tell us when Haemon takes the body down, as he must if corpse is to lie on corpse (1240).

1224–25 As Müller sees, we have a triad in **bride's destruction, father's actions,** and **marriage,** but the first and third seem redundant; so take "bride's destruction" as simply referring to her grave (that bed, not the marriage bed). Unfated (*dustênos*) is discussed at *OK* 1071; at 380 it is "unhappy," at 1283 "poor soul." There is similar language in Creon's (untranslated) address to Haemon at 1228 (see on *OK* 962). A second *dus-* compound follows at 1234 ("unhappy"). These clichés of tragic diction are offset by the vivid direct discourse (1228–30) and the rapid, pregnant narrative.

1230 Beseech is the language of supplication.

1232 Spat: cf. 653.

1235 Again we are given little time to reflect on the motives of his anger: even if his immediate impulse for suicide is remorse for striking at his father, and not desperate love, the entire context argues his love for Antigone (contra: von Fritz, pp. 233–34).

1240–41 For the motif **marriage in Hades** see 524–25, 654, 876, 891, 917–18, and 1207.

1243 Counsel: see 95 and l097. **Crime** (*kakon*) means "harmful." For the moralizing cf. *El* 1383–84 (Electra's prayer).

1244–45 Cf. the exit of Deianira **in silence** (*Tr* 813–14).

1246 Her silence is no more ominous than his **hope,** a motif of desperation in Greek tragedy (cf. 614 and *OK* 835–36).

1250 His phrasing echoes Eurydice's at 1191: "she is not inexperienced in judgment, so as to go astray" (the *hamartia* stem, at once euphemistic and anticipatory: see 1256–60).

1253–55 There are two reasons for taking the messenger off: Creon's grief is not to be shared; someone must report Eurydice's suicide.

1256–60 Anapestic verse announces the king's arrival. **His own hand**

argues that Creon, not the attendants, carries the body. In the kommos that follows, the whole point, now asserted by the chorus and fully accepted by Creon, is that his error has caused all the suffering. Here that issue is tied to the *atê* theme (notes at 531–33 and 582–91): "his own hands carry the telling token—if it is right to speak of it—his and no other's folly (*atê*), for it is he himself who has erred (the verbal form of *hamartia*: see on 914–15 and 1261)." Despite *atê*'s association with daimonic infatuation, which **doom** misses, chorus and Creon subscribe to his personal responsibility.

1261 The second kommos (see 801–81) begins; Creon's failure and suffering are the central focus, while Antigone and Polyneices are forgotten. Nothing mitigates the king's guilt and sorrow, which are swelled by the announcement of Eurydice's death. This scene is altogether less probing and problematic than Antigone's final scene, more of pure lament since Creon, unlike Antigone (891–929) and Oedipus (*OK* 1370–1415), is not given an iambic speech in which to rationalize his actions. He sings throughout in four sets of responsive lyrics (1261–67 = 1284–94; 1271–74 = 1296–1300; 1305–10 = 1324–31; 1316–21 = 1340–42); the coryphaeus and messenger have spoken iambic trimeters. The dochmiac rhythms of his lines are irregular and agitated. Sixteen times Creon speaks one or more exclamations of grief (**Oh** and **Woe** when they are translated). While the translator has passed over much of this lyric groaning, it is characteristic of the tragic kommos (see the final scene of Aeschylus' *Persians*).

1261 **Crimes** echoes "crime" (1258: *hamartia* stem). **Wicked heart** = "misguided thought" (the cognate *phron-* and *phrên-* stems: see on 175–77 and 1015–16).

1264–67 Both **planning** and **fault** echo "counsel" (1243).

1270 For **justice** (*dikê*) see on 365. For the motif "late learning" see 1023–33 and 1087–90. Creon is a prime example in Sophocles of the Aeschylean "learning through suffering"; see on *Tr* 708–11 and *Agamemnon* 176–78.

1271–74 For the imagery of the god **who has weighted** my head see on *OK* 1300 and *Agamemnon* 1660 ("struck by the heavy heal of a *daimôn*"). When the intellectually disposed Greek finds himself morally culpable, he looks to a divinely induced aberration for the cause.

1275 There is no need for a side door of the palace. It is sometimes argued that comedy of this period used more than one entrance on stage, but, although comedy and tragedy took place in the same theater, few commentators think that the tragedians used two or more entrances.

1284–85 The metaphor in **harbor** is also found at 1000; cf. *Aj* 682 and *OK* 1208. An untranslated adjective meaning "hard to purify/expiate" modifies harbor; it is transferred from the deaths, for which he must take responsibility, to the place where all the dead gather. **You have destroyed me:** this is actually a question ("why, why do you . . ."). **Horror the tale you tell** should also be phrased as a question.

1295 The trolley (*eccyclema*) is pushed out through the opened doors; on it the body of Eurydice is displayed.

1296 Surely no fate: another (cf. on 1284–85) question with double interrogative ("What then, what fate . . .").

1300 Woe: in this set of lines four words are exclamations of grief and three (two of himself, one for his wife) are generic for "miserable/ pitiful."

1301 In a similar way Deianira goes to the household altar before killing herself (*Tr* 904).

1302 Her older son is named (Megareus: see on 1058). Strictly, she "lamented the noble fate of Megareus" (with Bothe's emendation); he died to save Thebes. **Cursed** is probably the sense, although the verb suggests a litany ("chanting a hard lot for the child-killer"). Cf. the lament of Jocasta *OK* 1246–51.

1305 The Greek metaphor in **mad with fear** is "take wing/flight from fear" (of her last words); cf. *Aj* 693–94 and "what fear gives you wings?" (frag. 355). Oedipus too asks if someone will not kill him (*OK* 1411); cf. Euripides *Heracles* 1149–52.

1311 Jebb detects legal overtones in **held you guilty** (= "you were denounced as responsible").

1314 At her own heart: add "with her own hand" (for the emphasis see the note on 815–23). The **suffering** (*pathos*) is "shrilly-lamented."

1321 That a man is **nothing** is a common idea (e.g., *Phil* 951; *Aj* 1231–32 in abuse); "less than nothing" perhaps conveys the thought more clearly.

1322 Good (*kerdos* twice) has been "profit/gain" (see on 1033) and is a bitter word for Creon. He stands over the bodies of Haemon and Eurydice, and the Greek says "brief is best when evil (*kaka*) is at our feet."

1324 Let me go = "Let it (death) come."

1335–36 The doom prepared for him: against the constant insistence on human responsibility (e.g., 83, 1311, and 1316, where "guilt" = "responsibility") tragedy also asserts the "fated" character of action. When Croesus charges the oracle at Delphi with deceit, the priestess responds that "it is impossible even for a god to escape allotted destiny" (Herodotus 1.91). Cf. Philoctetes' acknowledgement of his "great destiny" (*Phil* 1466) and *Hippolytus* 1436 (fate) and 1390 (character causes Hippolytus' ruin).

1340–42 For **frantic** (= "rash/acting in vain") see on *Tr* 587. **Against my meaning** = "unwilling." In an omitted phrase he adds that he killed his wife as well, and then he says "I don't know which way to look nor where to lean (for support)." **My life is warped past cure** = "Everything in my hands has gone awry." **My fate has struck me down** = "An unbearable fate has leapt upon my head" (cf. 1271–73 and "blows" at 1351).

1343–52 **Wisdom** (the *phron-* stem; see 1261) stresses, as the entire play has, the first and necessary basis for happiness. For the retribution that falls on them who boast see 123. **Comes:** "Great words *teach* wisdom to the old."

Ajax

SOPHOCLES' *Ajax* draws on a particularly rich literary tradition. His hero (Aias in the Greek form) appears often in the *Iliad* where he is reckoned second only to Achilles in valor. Later, on his voyage home, Odysseus speaks to the shade of the dead Ajax when he visits Hades. At least two of the cyclic epics, the *Aethiopis* and the *Little Iliad,* treated the contest between Odysseus and Ajax for the armor of the dead Achilles. Aeschylus wrote a trilogy in which the contest for the armor and the suicide of Ajax were the central events of the first two plays. References in the lyric poet Pindar also testify to the popularity and variety of the legends concerning this lord of Salamis.

Apart from the literary tradition, Sophocles has taken a hero with special local claims on the Athenian audience. His home, the island of Salamis, had been incorporated into the Athenian state in the sixth century. When the tribes of Athens were reorganized by Cleisthenes late in the sixth century, Ajax was named as the patron hero of one of them. Not only was he revered in Athens but he was also worshipped by Athenian youth at annual games on his native Salamis. Myth often reflects politics, and well before Sophocles' time Ajax' father Telamon had been identified as the brother of Peleus, father of the Homeric hero Achilles. This identification linked the son of Telamon to Aegina, home of Aeacus, father of Peleus. On the west pediment of Athena's temple on Aegina, Ajax was represented defending the body of the fallen Achilles. Something of Athenian feeling for this hero may be seen from their dedications after the naval victory over the Persians at Salamis. Three Phoenician ships were dedicated from the spoils: one at the Isthmus to Poseidon, another at Sunium to Poseidon, and the third on Salamis to Ajax, whose help, along with the heroes of Aegina, was invoked before the battle (Herodotus 8.64, 121). Clearly, Ajax was dear to the Athenians.

The legend behind our play is simple, the variations in its treatment complex. When Achilles was killed in battle, Ajax and Odysseus rescued the body. At the funeral games his armor was offered as a prize to the warrior judged the greatest after the dead hero. Odysseus and Ajax were the finalists, and Odysseus was awarded the armor. Ajax, ashamed and dishonored, committed suicide. Odysseus tells how he met Ajax in the underworld:

Only the soul of Telamonian Aias stood off
at a distance from me, angry still over that decision
I won against him, when beside the ships we disputed
our cases for the arms of Achilleus. His queenly mother
set them as prize, and the sons of the Trojans, with Pallas Athene,
judged. And I wish I had never won in a contest like this,
so high a head has gone under the ground for the sake of that
armour,
Aias, who for beauty and for achievement surpassed
all the Danaans next to the stately son of Peleus.
(*Odyssey* 11.543–51)

Ajax' anger is such that, though addressed by Odysseus in a friendly way, he stalks away in silent anger. The resentment is natural to a Homeric hero, for whom second in any rivalry is humiliating. And perhaps that anger gave rise to the early tradition of his madness, his attack on the army, and even greater chagrin when that revenge is frustrated. Homer's "disputed our cases" leaves open the manner in which the contest was decided: the epic tradition told how spies beneath the Trojan walls had heard the Trojans themselves rate Odysseus higher and, alternatively, how Trojan captives had been pressed to judge. Homer's "sons of the Trojans" may more naturally allude to this second version, which it seems likely Aeschylus also used. Sophocles is not quite silent on the propriety of the judgment: both Ajax and Teucer claim ballot stuffing, with the clear implication that the Greeks themselves gave judgment. But we can hardly take these partisans at their word, and the poet has not chosen to make an issue of it.

What must be considered, however, are the changes Sophocles effected. Chief among these is the character of Ajax. In the *Iliad* he is a model warrior, brave, pious, even a useful speaker. We may assume that the earliest story attributed his suicide to the public humiliation of coming second to crafty Odysseus. But the early epics had introduced the theme of madness, and soon he turned his resentment against the army. In epic any extraordinary event such as Ajax' failed effort to murder the Greek chieftains demonstrates the power of the gods. In the early versions Athena saved the Greek host, acting, we imagine, more to save her friends, and especially her client Odysseus, than out of animus toward Ajax. Sophocles has taken the causality one step further. His play begins with the goddess triumphant over the still-demented hero: we witness Athena taunting a man who recently went beserk and is still so deep in his hallucination that he supposes the slain cattle in his tent are the dead and tortured bodies of his former comrades.

Great poetry and dramatic surprise are to come, but the prologue is the key to *Ajax*. Yet how thoroughly Sophocles has reimagined Ajax is not revealed until the prophecy of Calchas midway through the play. Now we learn that Ajax was ever one to dismiss divine aid: unlike his Homeric prototype, Ajax has arrogantly belittled Athena's aid in battle (770–79). Thus we learn that Athena's malice has, for Sophocles, roots much deeper than his attempted murder of the Greek princes. Her triumph in the prologue is revealed as personal; the madness of Ajax now seems the flowering of a deeper *hybris* that the Greeks identified with man's refusal to accept his mortal limits. Athena's timely aid is transformed into a long delayed revenge.

The boldness of Sophocles' conception is hard to overestimate. Aeschylus had dramatized a debate between Ajax and Odysseus over their respective merits, and it seems likely that both his raid and suicide were reported in messenger's speeches. The second play of his trilogy, in which the suicide was announced, was probably given over to a great lament for the dead hero. By dramatizing in the prologue the immediate aftermath of the raid, by pitting the demented hero against his real adversary, Athena, Sophocles makes his protagonist's insanity more ambiguous and his fate more problematic. When we are forced by Calchas' prophecy to link his dismissal of Athena's ironic appeal for pity (111–13) with a deeper ethical perversity, we see his brutal way with Tecmessa and the dominating egotism of subsequent scenes as aspects of an almost daimonic self-reliance. As for his fate, in the tradition Ajax was condemned to burial rather than the usual cremation. In making him the outrageous enemy of the gods as well as of man, Sophocles has raised the issue of whether he deserves any burial at all. His mortal enemies would throw him to the dogs; in his case the gods cannot be expected to intervene. Yet the Athenian audience cannot be denied one of its most renowned eponymous heroes. How will the poet resolve this dilemma of his own making? The answer lies in the ever serviceable Odysseus, who has learned Athena's lesson (127–33) and returns in the final scene to win burial, if not reconciliation, for the dead hero.

It is hard not to admit that the play falls off rather badly after the appearance of Menelaus. For all the late polemics, this is tepid stuff, mean-spirited and stiff. Menelaus and Agamemnon are a sorry lot, unworthy of their titanic foe, willing to do a favor for Odysseus, but in Sophocles' ethical conception unable to bend any more than they are able to reach. The true dramatic problem, however, may not be so much our modern lack of interest in the rites of burial or the banality of the secondary characters as in the powerful opening scene and the fascinating, even enigmatic, Ajax. Some will think that Sophocles never composed greater speeches than the final two he gives Ajax. When that solitary giant dies, there is little that even Sophocles can do to save his play from a great emptiness.

Scene: A modern production may find it convenient to use a second door, even though there is no certain evidence for its existence in the fifth century. It is not necessary for this production. The "structure" is the scenic building used for all the plays in the competition. Sophocles may have decorated its front with canvas or panels to suggest a tent, but the theater and circumstances of production put obvious restraints on realism. In this play we have a change of scene (815) which the ancient theater cannot manage with our curtain, and I doubt that Sophocles broke the rhythm there by sending on stagehands with bushes. Gods may appear from the wings as well as on the "high platform" (the roof of the scenic building), and Taplin (*Greek Tragedy in Action,* p. 41) suggests that Athena follows Odysseus unseen until "I cannot see you" (15), after which he turns and speaks to her. The effect of her interview with Ajax is lost if throughout the scene she is a disembodied voice from offstage. It would be appropriate for her to appear on the roof and let Odysseus discover her after some initial surprise. He enters from the parodos and is not moving "across the stage" so soon, assuming that there was a stage platform in the time of the *Ajax.*

1 In Homer the special affinity between Athena and Odysseus is already well established. For example, see *Odyssey* 1.45–90 and their conversation at 13.187–440, a scene that reveals Athena as the divine alter ego of the hero. For the world's assessment of their mutual regard see Diomedes' comment at *Iliad* 10.242–47.

2 The hunting metaphors (**stalking**) are elaborated extensively; in this prologue see 5, 7, 18–19, 26–28, 32–34, 39, 59c, and 94. Here, as at 1057, the text suggests a "trial/attempt" against the enemy.

4 **Last place** designates the place of honor on one flank; in the *Iliad* the camps of Ajax and Achilles are on either flank.

7 Laconia, in the south central Peloponnesus, was famous for its hunting dogs. The chorus says of Cassandra that she is "keen scented like some hound" (*Agamemnon* 1093).

13 The note of instruction in her last line will come, in her concluding lines (127–33), to more than practical advice. The curious malice of

Athena in this scene derives from the fact that for her Ajax' madness is a spectacle for derision.

15 The context does not indicate why he **cannot see** her: she could be at a distance (the opposite parodos), or in the shadow of the building, or on a platform above him. In any case, the subsequent dialogue implies, as Stanford says, an intimacy that suggests he soon sees her.

17 As at *Eumenides* 567, the Greek text explicitly describes the **trumpet** as Etruscan.

19–20 Man I hate = "my enemy." Since the enmity is professional and not personal (cf. 121–26 and 1332–45), "hate" may bring the wrong tone. Homer makes the huge shield of Ajax his distinctive armor:

> Now Ajax came near him [Hector], carrying like a wall his shield
> of bronze and sevenfold ox-hide. . . .
>
> *(Iliad* 7.219–20)

See the play on "shield" at 59c and also 159 and 577–79.

22–24 Staggering horror strains a phrase that may be no more than "an inconceivable business." Similarly, **If it all can be believed** overheats "if he has in fact done it." **Floundering** = "at a loss."

25 Odysseus says that he has, as a volunteer, "yoked" himself to the task; we can catch something of this with "I've taken it on myself."

29 Notice that the slaughter of the **guards** will not become the central issue, i.e., the generals will not worry about murder so much as about the attempt on themselves.

34 How can these tracks be his? = "I cannot tell whose they are" (a more literal version that seems inconsistent with what he has said about tracking Ajax). Prefer the sense: "I cannot make out where he is."

35 Just as I need you is echoed in "to some purpose" (39a; both *kairos:* in a timely, opportune way). For the motif see on 120.

41 Aggrieved = "weighed down by anger" (as at 744). The same idea occurs in "galled" (*Tr* 269) and in Achilles' description:

> and gall, which makes a man grow angry for all his great mind,
> that gall of anger that swarms like smoke inside of a man's heart
> and becomes a thing sweeter to him by far than the dripping
>   of honey.
>
> *(Iliad* 18.108–10)

43 Fouled (= "polluted") is not what he intended but her view of what he has accomplished.

44 Whole should be deleted.

46 Daring is often a pejorative charge; cf. *Tr* 582–84, *Ant* 248, and *OK* 533.

47 Stealthly denotes the cunning and deceit traditionally associated with Odysseus, not Ajax. So Helen describes Odysseus as a man reared

> to know every manner of shiftiness and crafty counsels.
>
> (*Iliad* 3.202)

See also *Odyssey* 13.291 ff. (Athena praises him for cunning) and *Phil* 86–97 (on "treachery"). Even before Athena checked him, Ajax' behavior was abnormal for him; the Greek audiences would remember that in the only night raid of the *Iliad,* Odysseus and Diomedes slaughter the sleeping Thracians.

48 The redundancy of these questions is typical of this play; dialogue is less economical and pointed, and the speeches are less fluent and more periphrastic than in the later style.

49 The **two supreme commanders** are Agamemnon and Menelaus.

50 Yearned: Homer uses this verb of spears and swords, and Aeschylus (*Suppliants* 895) of a snake ("quivers").

51–52 Since **thoughts of insane** (= "incurable") **joy** may also be taken with **checked him,** a certain ambiguity yields both "kept him from the joy of success" as well as "checked him and gave him the illusion of success." The second version corresponds to what we shall see but hardly excludes the secondary meaning. **Obsessive,** more literally "unbearable," like **insane,** is medical and occurs at 641–42 of the calamity (*atê*) that afflicts him. Cf. "diseased delusions" (59b) and "madness" (66); see also 81, 206–7, 217, 271–72 (his "joy" in distress). The Greeks naturally think of a daimonic or supernatural cause (244, 278–80).

59c Net plays on a second meaning "wall" and Homer's description of Ajax as the "wall of the Achaians" (*Iliad* 3.229). The celebrated defensive giant becomes a victim of his virtue. For net as trap see *Agamemnon* 1611; for divine deception leading man into nets see on *Persians* 93–101.

65 Tormenting = "tortures and humiliates"; at 401 Ajax uses this verb to describe Athena's treatment of him. At 111 it is, too feebly, "mistreat."

67 More than anything, the Homeric warrior fears public humiliation. By presenting him as a crazed object of ridicule Athena degrades Ajax, his honor, and former glory. Her malevolence is clear from **publish it.** For public mockery see 79a–b, 198–200 and 383.

70 I'll turn his glance away repeats the verb of line 51 ("checked"). Such framing by repetition of a word or phrase, called ring composition, is a regular feature of Greek style from Homer through Herodotus.

72 In **binding** we have a verb that also means "punishing/correcting," but also of guiding a ship; perhaps "straightening them out" catches her tone.

74–89 The Greek text is composed of single line stichomythia. Odysseus' comic cowardice, teased out by Athena, will give way to the grotesquely triumphant Ajax.

79a My enemy because Odysseus has defeated him in the competition for the arms (1336–38). Nothing in this play will surprise the audience more than the volte-face of Odysseus, even though Sophocles has carefully prepared us for it with 121–26.

79b The Homeric vaunt over the fallen warrior often mocks him or his friends; see, e.g., *Iliad* 13.414–16 and 446–54. Hence **to laugh at your enemies** proclaims your own superiority and taunts the opponent with defeat and public dishonor. The motif rests on social values and occurs in all the plays.

81 The **madman** is not merely a lunatic but someone gone

beserk, so that no one can match his warcraft against him.
(*Iliad* 6.101)

The warrior's hands are said to "rage" (*Iliad* 16.244–45) and he attacks in such a fury that even the gods are not safe from assault. Despite Athena's promises (70), Odysseus knows that a daimonicly possessed Ajax will care nothing for her. So she repeats her assurance (83, 85).

90 With **ally** cf. 117 and the rejection of her help attributed to him at 774–78. This particular point is not Homeric; in the *Iliad*, Athena favors the Greeks but not Ajax in any special way. It continues her mockery.

91 The portrayal of Ajax is a delicate problem. Arrogant and cruel, gloating over his supposed triumph, yet mad and potentially ridiculous, Ajax' character may be particularly repugnant to modern audiences less sensitive than the Greeks to honor. But we see the way of playing the role from the reaction of Odysseus: frightening and repulsive as he may be, yet Ajax is pitiful (121–22). The production ought to aim to rouse this ambivalence in the audience. Emphasize the mad joy rather than the cruelty and sadism. From Tecmessa's description at 301–5 we have some indication of his manner: he rushes out, speaks in a wild, incoherent manner, and exults with laughter at his triumph.

93–94 It was the Greek custom to dedicate to the gods **trophies** . . . **from the spoils** of battle or hunt; see *Tr* 237–45.

99 Slight = "dishonor"; for the theme see 425 and 440 ("shamed" = "dishonored").

100 My armor, i.e., the prized armor of Achilles.

101 Laertes' son is Odysseus.

103 Sneak is literally "fox."

111 Mistreat = "torture" (see on 65).

112 A prudent man does not dismiss divine appeals in this manner. Cf. at 770–78 his (reported) reaction to her offered assistance.

118 Do you see: Seale (pp. 144–48) stresses the significance of literal and metaphorical vision in the prologue. Her power is demonstrated in the failure of his attack and in her malicious teasing. Ajax is a blind *theomachus* ("one who fights against god") and can expect full payment:

> If gods give ill, no man may shun their giving.
> *(Seven against Thebes 719)*

119–20 The Homeric Ajax is not distinguished for his judgment (**foresight**). **To act with judgment** carries the idea of timely, opportune action (*kairos*). The theme is Sophoclean, not Homeric. Such supposed virtues only serve as foils to her power.

123 Other metaphors from yoking at 736 and 945. See *Agamemnon* 217. **Blindness** (*atê*) here seems to have the old sense of "infatuation/ delusion," precisely right as the cause *and* condition afflicting Ajax. See the note to *Agamemnon* 385f. *Atê* is "ruin" at 195 and 307; at 363 it is translated "ill disease."

124 I think of him . . . myself: his attitude anticipates his later intervention; cf. 1365. The empathy is remarkable, especially from Odysseus, but there is ground for it in *Odyssey* 11.543–67, where he reports on having seen Ajax in the underworld.

126 Dim shapes . . . shadow: "shapes" (*eidôla*) often describes the shades of the dead and so stresses the transient mortality of human striving:

> We are things of a day. What are we? What are we not?
>   The dream of a shadow
> is man, no more.
> *(Pindar Eighth Pythian 95–96)*

For the motif see *Agamemnon* 82; cf. the thought at *Ant* 1169–70.

127–33 Odysseus is hardly the man to need an admonition not to boast (**speak no towering word**); nor have we had a straightforward boast from Ajax, even if his manner is arrogant enough. But from the chorus's warning at 387 and his own self-conscious reference at 422 we can see that Sophocles conceived the character in this familiar heroic mold. Perhaps, then, we should be less surprised at the late report (762–78) of an old brag that mightily offended Athena. For the commonplace "don't boast!" see *Ant* 123 and *Persians* 828. **Hand is weightier** refers to the physical strength of a great warrior, and the generality of her statement is further underscored by **great wealth,** which is irrelevant. **One short day** begins another tragic aphorism (see on *OK* 438) that, like boasting, will gain more dramatic point from the messenger's speech (see on 756). **Balance** is an Aeschylean metaphor from the scales of fortune (see *Tr* 83 and *Agamemnon* 206). Read **sink** and **rise** again: although he dies, Ajax' fortunes will rise again in the second half of the play. **Steady sense** (the *sôphron-* stem) is naturally opposed to madness, but here the opposition is less precise: **proud** (*kakos*) denotes "mean/bad/vile," and while its use here may be an early example of moral condemnation, this word would never have been applied to Ajax prior to the present calamity. The same word is "terrible," i.e., "harmful," at 123. "Base" (319) and the context there give a good idea of its moral/social significance and how far a normal Ajax would stand from such description.

We may ask why Athena speaks as she does, and to whom? Is it possible Odysseus requires this lesson? Can this be her personal admonition for him: Ajax crushed, humiliated and displayed so that Odysseus may learn the gods' power and the dangers of boastfulness? When did he not know these lessons? Certainly, there is no question in the prologue of Odysseus scorning divine power or of Odysseus the vainglorious. If she speaks to him, the message is not for him. For the audience it is too familiar—we think of the "yoke of blindness" on Xerxes and Agamemnon—to have dramatic force, at least not the dramatic force just witnessed in the mockery of the demented hero. Though she moralizes and draws a lesson for Odysseus (cf. the emphatic **yourself** at 128), the speech is in reality a vaunt. She has displayed her power, mocked her enemy, and now she draws the moral for all. There can be no reply to such a divine boast. We have witnessed the kind of divine wrath that Euripides saves for the middle of his *Heracles;* Iris speaks of the madness about to fall on Heracles:

> Let him learn what Hera's anger is,
> and what is mine. For the gods are nothing,
> and men prevail, if this one man escapes.
> (*Heracles* 840–42)

In the *Heracles* Madness herself opposes Hera's vendetta, and, as here, the demonstration of divine power and malice has the dramatic effect of turning the audience's sympathy to the victimized protagonist. For a useful comparison of Heracles and Ajax see Furley, "Euripides on the Sanity of Heracles."

134 The chorus enters to anapestic rhythms until 172, when a triadic lyric extends to 200. After Tecmessa's entrance (201), a lyric dialogue follows until 263. Of the extant plays this one alone has a chorus composed of dependents of the protagonist. Thus they are more vitally involved in his fate and fully sympathetic when their worst fears are realized; until his death, Ajax is surrounded by family and dependents. Since, however, they are ignorant of the true situation and consider the charges against their lord mere slander, the parodos may be said to interrupt the dramatic rhythm, which Tecmessa's appearance takes up again.

Ajax' father **Telamon** is an offstage figure throughout the play: 181, 204, 461–72, 508, 569a, 763, 848, 860, 1009a, 1299b are some of the explicit references. Fathers and sons make an important thematic complex in the *Iliad:* Achilles and Peleus, Hector and Priam, Nestor and Antilochos come to mind immediately. In the *Ajax* the range is extended by the addition of Eurysaces and by Teucer's consciousness of Telamon's censure (the central event in Aeschylus' final play in the Ajax trilogy), a subject Sophocles dramatized in his own *Teucer.*

135 Salamis was Athenian in Sophocles' time (see 203) but not in the earliest stages of heroic legend. This play makes Telamon an independent king while asserting the kinship of the two peoples.

138 The fury of Zeus is the "blow of Zeus" (as at 279 and *Agamemnon* 367). Originally literal, the lightning bolt of Zeus becomes, like the leap of a *daimôn,* a metaphor for deranged action. Cf. Ajax' language at 452 (Athena . . . "sent me sprawling") and 456–57 ("when a god strikes harm"). The blow would be the cause, the **slur** the secondary effect, so that the disjunctive **or** would more logically be "and."

139–40 More literally: "I fear like the eye of a winged dove." Cf. the imagery at 166–71.

142–43 Rumors . . . wretched and shameful are "dishonorable" (*El* 1008); cf. the concern for "insult" (153), "ignorant clamor" (163), and Ajax' fear of "mockery" (368). The hero's dearest possession is his reputation, which, unhappily for him, is in the hands of others. Cf. 463–66.

153 Insult = "treat hybristically"; *hybris* is "outrage" at 196, "indignity" at 368, and "criminal heart" at 1061. This last version is not good: the Athenians had a law against *hybris* and spoke of the hybris of plants and animals (see on *Agamemnon* 763–71).

154–56 The Persian counsellor Artabanus, speaking to Xerxes, offers a typical piece of Greek thinking on the dangers of greatness:

You see how god strikes with his lightning those creatures that stand out, nor does he permit them to appear great, but he does not disturb the insignificant. You see how his bolts fall on the greatest houses and trees. For god is accustomed to check the great. Thus a great army is destroyed by a small one in this way. When in his envy god throws fear or thunder on them, they perish shamefully. For god does not allow great ambition in anyone other than himself.

(Herodotus 7.10; my trans.)

159 In his only figurative use of **fortress** (= "tower"), Homer has Odysseus call Ajax "a great fortress for the Achaeans" (*Odyssey* 11.556).

163 Clamor echoes "oppressive rumors" (142). Ajax is subject of a passive verb ("you are the object of their clamoring") and this anticipates the screech of birds at 166.

166–71 Ajax has retired and his cowering enemies will chatter, but if he, a great bird of prey among so many starlings, will but appear, they will flee in mute silence.

The subject of **out of your sight** is unstated but assumed to be "your enemies," until the simile (**like a gaggle**) superimposes the image of screeching birds. The **falcon** continues the image but is metaphorically identified with Ajax, whose presence is desired, that he might drive the screeching slanderers away.

172 For "which god is it?" cf. *OK* 1098–1107. Kranz (*Stasimon*, p. 188) suggests that such canvassing for the responsible divinity had its origin in cultic hymns. **Wild, bull-consorting** translates the cult title Tauropola given to Artemis at Halae Araphenides, on the southeast coast of Attica (Kamerbeek). The anachronism is suggested by his attack **against the flocks** (rather "herds of cattle"). Her cult seems to have been orgiastic, and the goddess was invoked as one inspiring madness, all to the point in this context. The **evil Tale** = "great Rumor"; cf. 978 and the personification of "immortal voice" at *OK* 157.

175–77 They speculate that Artemis' anger may have been excited by Ajax' failure to pay tribute after a successful battle or hunt; cf. 98.

178 In the *Iliad*, **Enyalios** is both an epithet of Ares and a personification of battle. **Co-operant** means that the spear gets its power from Ares.

183 Frenzy . . . when the gods will: the noun is the generic word for "sickness/disease" and is modified by an adjective meaning "divine/from god." The phrase also occurs at *Ant* 421 in "plague the gods had sent" (of a dust storm). "Holy madness" (611) is a synonymous phrase.

187 Odysseus' enemies like to taunt him as the bastard son of the rogue **Sisyphus,** by whom his mother Anticleia was said to be pregnant when she married Laertes. Cf. *Phil* 416–17. Perhaps that calumny suggested **supposititious,** in which Jebb finds a metaphor from the mother who takes to breast the child of another; this metaphor occurs again at 482 (in "spurious and alien").

192 Face translates "eye," a common metonymy in Greek, but here we notice that "eye" has now appeared three times in the parodos (139a and 165). The Greeks felt that the eyes reveal character (fear at 139a) and also may have a benign or malevolent influence (the birds flee the eye of Ajax/the falcon at 165). Consequently, although we have here a natural circumlocution for "don't hide in your tent," the lyric ambiguously and unconsciously anticipates the madness that will be evident in his eye. Cf. 51, 70 ("glance"), 1005. Seale (p. 151) offers a different interpretation.

194–95 Forbearing to fight your cause translates an oxymoron that juxtaposes "leisure" and "contest": "in embattled leisure" catches something of it. **Ruin** is *atê* (see on 123), and the clause is bolder: "(all the while you are) making ruin flare to heaven." The victim of divine blindness is charged with kindling, by his inactivity, its flame.

196–98 Their **outrage** (*hybris*) is their laughter; cf. 368.

201 Tecmessa is a slave (489), the daughter of Phrygian prince (210) whose land Ajax has wasted in a raid (516–18). Thus "spear-won bride" (212) means "captive," and her standing may be judged from the reproach Teucer, himself the son of such a slave, imagines his father Telamon directing at him: "Bastard and gotten by the war-spear, coward" (1013). Ajax treats her harshly, not to say brutally (but see 652–53), yet regards her son as legitimate. With her appearance the action gets back on track; the eyewitness corrects the false hopes of the chorus. Both parts are in lyric meters through line 261.

203 Sprung from the Athenian earth = "sprung from Erechtheus," the first king of Athens. Salamis was not annexed by Athens until the sixth century, but two Athenian families traced their lineage back to Ajax' sons Eurysaces and Philaios (the second is not mentioned by Sophocles). As an object of heroic cult and the eponymous hero of one of the ten Cleisthenian tribes, Ajax was revered as a native Athenian hero.

207 Troubling is from "muddy" and so "confused and confusing." **Flood** is from the familiar imagery of winter storms, as when Io speaks of "that storm sent by God on me" (*Prometheus Bound* 643); cf. 255–58 and 351–53.

210 Phrygia is a district in northwestern Asia Minor. Like the slave girls Briseis and Chryseis of the *Iliad* 1, Tecmessa came to the Greek camp as a part of the booty from a raid. See 485–525 for her story.

211 Valiant is a Homeric epithet that means "rushing" and so of one eager to spring into battle. Three times it describes Ajax ("valorous" at 1211, untranslated at 613, where it is transferred from Ajax to Ares); the word does not occur elsewhere in the extant plays and fragments.

215 Accident (*pathos*) is "experience/suffering."

218 In the night translates an adjective modifing Ajax, as if he were a natural phenomenon of the night, i.e., something in and of the darkness.

219a–20 Victims is appropriate to sacrificial offerings. As for an **oracle:** they speak ominously and revealingly of him.

221 Fiery was "bright" at 146 (of his sword) and will be used pejoratively at 1089 ("hot"). It occurs more often of things than persons; cf. the commendatory "a man of fiery spirit" at *Seven against Thebes* 448.

230 Frenzied = "driven off course, as from a blow"; see the note on "fury" at 138.

237 The metaphor in **shore off** is from harvest mowing; cf. Aeschylus, *Suppliants* 635–38.

244 Whatever is done unnaturally is the work of a **demon** (*daimôn*), who is able to put words in our mouths (**taught**) and drive us to do that which otherwise we would never do (see 533–34, where "evil genius" = *daimôn*).

245 Their worst fears realized, the chorus thinks of slinking off before Ajax can be killed (253) by the outraged army.

252 Stir echoes "row," i.e., metaphorically speaks of the Atridae going to the benches against them; cf. *Seven against Thebes* 854–56.

253 The **killing stone** refers to death by public stoning; cf. *Ant* 35–37.

254 The Greek achieves typical metaphorical vividness and compression by transferring the adjective that describes him as "unapproachable" to his **doom** ("fate") so that we might also translate "an unapproachable fate holds him."

255–57 The "doom" is identified with the transitory madness, which is likened to the passing of a storm. Here we actually have a simile in the Greek ("like a southerly storm-wind") in which the ambiguous fusion of subject and referent creates an incisive image of sight and motion. **After** = "without/apart from"; **lightning flash** is also "glare" and flash of the eye (as in frag. 474); **leap** suggests the sudden changing of the storm, but the verb has already described the way Ajax' hand darts to its work (40) and occurs a little later (256 and 301) of the agitated spring of Ajax; **He is calm** translates the verb and final word in the figure and also means "ceases/quits." Efforts to parse the simile run aground in failing to see how thoroughly the double focus permeates the comparison.

268 The line seems to have a more riddling point if we accept Hermann's emendation: "Then we, though he is no longer ill, are now ruined."

271–72 In the marking of the disease motif (*nosos*) the translator has varied the Sophoclean diction: "Madness" (66), "Frenzy" (183), "ill" (268), "mad fit" (271), and "raving" (280) all translate the same stem; it goes untranslated at 274 ("breathes clear *from the disease*"). Cf. the similar concentration of **wretchness**: "as bad a thing" (267), "anguish"

(275), "grief" (277), and "catastrophe" (282) are all from the same stem (*kakos*).

274 Recovered is the same verb that is translated "He is calm" at 257. Already in Homer we find the metaphorical **breathes clear** in the sense "has relief/respite from."

275 Masters may suggest an animal driven to utter subjection by his burden.

283 Swoop down perhaps suggests the fall of a daimonic spirit on him.

288 Pointless, as she supposed.

293 A woman's decency is silence: Bowra (pp. 23–24) cites several examples of this typical Athenian sentiment. Cf. 370 and 528–29.

295 Horrors is too strong. Prefer "I don't know what happened there."

299 Severed with an upward cut, i.e., he cut their throats as if they were victims for sacrifice; cf. 235.

299a Abusing = "tormenting" (65; see the note).

300 Vexing poor dumb beasts is the translator's gloss.

302 The metaphor translated **wild, rending words** may be medical: "drawing up in gasps his speech." The **phantom** is Athena.

303 Ajax has, he imagines, taken vengeance for their *hybris*.

307 For Ruin (*atê*) see on 123. Here Ajax sees the results of his own deluded work.

308 Bellowed is repeated in 334 ("distorted . . . cry"); despite the comparison to a bull at 322, this verb does not specifically denote the bull's cry.

309 Note the etymological figure in **wreckage . . . wreck**. Line 317 contains a similar, though less vivid figure: "wailed a shrill wail."

323–25 Overcome by = "lying in." As at 206 and 426, there is some emphasis on the prostrate, fallen hero; cf. 308–9. Such language suggests the posture and manner of Ajax when we see him again (347).

327 Dreadful = "harmful": he inspires fear.

330 She is mistaken. **Noble** = "such as he." Nestor advises Patroclus,

the persuasion of a friend is a strong thing.
(*Iliad* 11.792)

331 Honored = "child of Teleutas" (21). The verb of this sentence likens Ajax' **frenzy** to that of an ecstatic seer of Apollo.

The exclamation attributed to Ajax in the Greek text hardly justifies "shriek," or any particular tone; Seale (p. 152) curiously accepts the scholiast's "like the yelping of a dog," but we have a surer comparison in 322 and the utter dejection she describes at 323–27.

337 Child: he shouts "child, child," which need not refer to Eurysaces, though it is natural for the boy's mother to think of him. Campbell may be right in thinking he means Teucer, as he makes explicit at 342.

340–41 Dear God and **What shall I do!** are variations on the same exclamation (Greek *talaina:* see *El* 389a).

342–45 His half-brother **Teucer** is away from the camp (see 564–65). **And I here perishing:** such exclamations are typical of grief (see 440, 1002, and *El* 305), as Aristophanes' parodies indicate (e.g., *Acharnians* 163).

344–46 Despite Tecmessa's invitation (329a), the chorus cannot leave the orchestra for the scenic building—they never do.

His call to Teucer strikes them as sensible, i.e., **sane,** so they have no need to fear him; and they suggest that the sight of friends may also inhibit him (**compose himself** = "have some regard for others").

This is a good place to use the eccyclema for a tableau revealing Ajax among the slaughtered animals. In the modern theater a curtain can reveal this scene, without the use of the cumbersome trolley which Greek audiences had already accepted by the time of the *Ajax*. At least for a while, and until line 430 if we take "lie abject" (426) literally, he reclines while singing these lyrics; Tecmessa and the coryphaeus respond in spoken iambics. For a similar tableau see Euripides *Heracles* 1028ff.

351–53 This time the image is explicitly of a **storm** at sea: he likens himself to a ship battered by a swirling wave driven by a murderous/bloody squall. Cf. 207 and 255–57.

356 In the Greek, **insanity** is simply the privative of "being sensible."

361 Help me die = "kill me with these (animals)." Apart from Tecmessa's premonition at 327, this is the first indication that he will take his life; cf. 391, 394–98, and 415. Both Heracles and Philoctetes, suffering physically, ask others to kill them (see *Tr* 1031–40 and *Phil* 748–50; cf. Euripides *Heracles* 1148–52).

363 Worse cure for an ill disease is a variation on a proverbial expression. Cf. 377 and 384. As often happens, a sympathetic chorus is none too profound.

365–68 This sarcastic recognition of his humiliation begins with "do you see?" (= **Here I am**). **What indignity** = "how outrageously I am treated" (see on 153). He is not penitent; he scorns Tecmessa and ignores the chorus.

371 Be more gentle translates the familiar motif of yielding. So Haemon pleads with Creon to "yield your wrath" (*Ant* 718). See below 666–69.

379–83 With a double irony the stanza begins **Spying everywhere** (= "seeing everything"), though of course Ajax has no idea of Odysseus' presence earlier. Then he attributes malicious laughter to his rival, which is also far from the case. Ajax will die without knowing of Odysseus' sympathy.

384 Among other sources for the changing gifts of the gods is Achilles' description of the two urns of Zeus (*Iliad* 24.527–33). Good and ill come from two urns from which Zeus dispenses man's varying fortunes; they are sometimes mixed, sometimes not. For a developed metaphor on this motif see *Iphigenia in Aulis* 1324a–33.

387 The warning not to boast (**no blustering words**) recognizes the unstated threat in Ajax' previous line. In his present condition even thinking about attacking an enemy is extravagant.

389 Father of my fathers: Telamon is the son of Aeacus, the son of Zeus.

394–98 His apostrophe inverts the normal equation of **light** with joy and life. **Take . . . receive . . . keep** translates the same verb twice repeated.

399 For Ajax to say that he is not **worthy** of either human or divine help is indeed a low, as well as a violent emotional fluctuation from the threats just uttered. The word for **humankind** is "men of a day" at *Ant* 790 and is well suited both to his own despair and to the theme of mutability; cf. 130–32.

401 Although the **martial goddess** is Athena, there is no reason to suppose that he is now conscious of the events of the prologue. She is the patronness of Odysseus, and he assumes that Odysseus' work is her work. See on 65 for **cruelly works my ruin.**

410–11 The **wretchedness** she complains of is her own, as in Antigone's exclamation "Then I am lost" (*OC* 1444). It differs little from the single word translated as a question at 372. The contrast between past and present is a central motif, particularly and concretely connected with the sword (see on 815–22).

412 After addressing Zeus (389) and the dark underworld (394) in apostrophe, he turns to the familiar features of the Trojan landscape. With the exception of "friends" at 407, very little in his lyrics recognizes Tecmessa and the chorus.

420 It is odd to find the **Scamander** River, whose tutelary deity gives Achilles such a hard time in *Iliad* 21, described as **gentle to Greeks.**

422 For his **boast** see the note to 127.

427–28 They do not in fact anticipate his pun on **agony.** We might also translate: "and yet I cannot allow you to speak (your grief), you who have fallen in with such trouble (*kaka*)."

430–33 Agony: Ajax (Greek Aias) etymologizes his name from the cry *aiai*, which we have already heard at 370. The connection is fanciful but no more strained than many Greek efforts at finding the essence of a person or thing in its name. At 913 "ill-starred" apparently alludes to this supposedly star-crossed name. See on *OK* 1036. **Fortunes** is the "trouble" or "grief" just mentioned. The **name** (*Aias*) foretells a man who will bewail (cry *aiai*) the evil he suffers. Pindar (*Sixth Isthmian* 49–50) derives his name from "eagle" (*aietos*). Aristotle (*Rhetoric* 2.23) blesses this type of argument, citing, among others, Sophocles' play on the proper name Sidero and iron.

434–37 Telamon accompanied Heracles on a raid against Laomedon, king of Troy. As a **prize**, Hesione, daughter of the king, was given to Telamon, and she became the mother of Teucer (see his account at 1299b–1303). The comparison of father and son is very common in the *Iliad;* as an example, here is Agamemnon's encouraging praise to Teucer:

> Telamonian Teukros, dear heart, o lord of your people,
> strike so; thus you may be a light given to the Danaans,
> and to Telamon your father, who cherished you when you were
>   little,
> and, bastard as you were, looked after you in his own house.
> Bring him into glory, though he is far away.
>
> (*Iliad* 8.281–85)

Agamemnon's "glory" = **praise** (*kleos*); it is ever the issue (see on 142–43).

439a–40 No less a champion = "have accomplished no less work with my hands." **Outcast, shamed** = "dishonored."

442 For the argument "I know how X would judge if he were here" cf. *OC* 999–99a.

446–47 Of most dishonest mind is common abuse for "cheat" or "rogue." The Greek translated **have contrived** is strained; Dawe recommends Hartung's emendation, which would yield "they've sold out to. . . ." It is typical of Ajax that the word for **claims** denotes "power/ victories." Nothing in the play validates his charge of fraud and cheating, which Teucer also urges (see 1137–39), and the audience would not have, from the tradition, a general opinion on this issue.

448 Leapt is yet another instance of the verb translated "leap" at 256, "darted" at 301, with connotations of frantic, impulsive, quick motion. **Whirling** appears to be almost a technical term for the wild, distracted glance of a madman. Sophocles coordinates **eyes and mind,** though the former perverts the purpose of the latter: "my eye and mind, distracted, darted from my purpose." As with "filched"(445), **cheat** is a little more colorful than the Greek: "bring a charge against."

450 Stanford sees in **fierce-eyed** a "disparaging substitute for the

Homeric "grey-eyed," a regular epithet for Athena. More literally, this compound means "having the face/aspect of a Gorgon," as, e.g.,

> while Hector, wearing the stark eyes of a Gorgon.
> (*Iliad* 8.348)

The Gorgon's glance petrifies, and her face may well have inspired madness, (see *Heracles* 880–84a), yet in the same play the chorus also describes the children of Heracles with this very adjective (130–31).

452 Sent me sprawling = "tripped me up," a common metaphor (see *Tr* 293–97) which is, ironically, both literal and figurative in this case. **Distraught and frenzied** = "(she) throwing a raging disease on me." The thought and diction are Homeric; the gods may cast strength, fear, desire, or sleep onto friend or foe.

456–57 For the thought **when God strikes harm** see *El* 697–98.

458 What is to be done?: Such questions are a constant of tragic rhetoric; see *Tr* 385, *Ant* 1098.

459 With **hated by the gods** cf. *OK* 816 and *Seven against Thebes* 692. Bad luck and any misfortune are often assigned to divine animosity, whether or not there is any good evidence. Now he makes a list of options, examines their consequences, and concludes that death is the only honorable way (473). Given the heroic ethos and Ajax' willingness to pursue it to the extremity, his logic is clear and cogent.

463 Jebb aptly compares *OK* 1372–73. The Greek suggests both "how can I show my face to him?" and "how can I look at him?"

465–66 Armed with no glory and **chaplets of men's praise** echo "prize of all for valor" and "sweet praise" (436–37).

471–77 Homer's Achilles, who has been insulted but not humiliated, can contemplate returning home (*Iliad* 9.618–19), but Ajax, who feels ashamed (= **contemptible**) at his failure and sees the possibility of even greater abuse, cannot face his father without appearing a man who has lost his stomach (= **weakling**; Sophocles and Shakespeare enjoy similar diction). **By breed** = "by nature"; the *Philoctetes* also uses the natural similarity of father and son for a paradigm and source of argument (see the note to 79b–85 and cf. 874–75). Death is preferable to an ignoble life:

> Whoever is in trouble and still desires life,
> he is either a coward or insensible.
> (frag. 952)

For the topic cf. *Ant* 463–64 and *El* 1485–86. **Long file of days**: Achilles' famous choice is between a short, glorious life and a long but quiet existence (*Iliad* 9.410–16). **Edging you forward . . . Then back:** Kamerbeek sees a metaphor from draughts in these verbs.

478 Hope is proverbially vain; cf. *El* 1460.

479–80 For the thought cf. *El* 1320–21; the absolute disjunctive suits his uncompromising ethos.

485 It is perhaps only with this speech that the audience realizes how subtly Sophocles has drawn upon Homer. For even though Ajax' sword, the gift of Hector (818), has been mentioned, there is so little similarity between Hector and Ajax that few in the audience will have imagined the bold dramatic comparison that now follows. We must compare *Iliad* 6.390–502, when Hector, having returned to Troy, takes his final leave of his wife Andromache and son Scamandrios. Tecmessa's present appeal is modeled on Andromache's bid to keep Hector from returning to battle. Sophocles' audience would remember how Andromache recalls the death of her father and brothers at the hands of Achilles (6. 414–24), how she begs him to pity their son Scamandrios, and particularly how Hector vividly imagines his wife's fate when, with Hector dead, some Greek will point to her slavery and contrast it with her former life (see on 501 below). Later in our scene Ajax will summon his son and speak to him in a way calculated to recall Hector's farewell to his son (see on 545 below). And yet, while this family scene clearly evokes its Homeric model, the contrasts in situation and ethos still more starkly distinguish it: Ajax has killed his concubine's father (490), while Andromache is a free woman whose family was killed by an enemy; Ajax is in dishonor for having madly attacked his friends, while Hector is the only hope of his city; Eurysaces has been hidden for fear of his father's rage (533), while Hector finds wife and child together and fondly laughs when the boy cries out in fear of his terrifying helmet (*Iliad* 6.466–75). Thus the scene calls us to compare the families and thereby highlights the bitter differences that separate them. The loneliness and despair of both Ajax and Tecmessa stand in high relief against the intimate and loving Trojan family; the bitter and vindictive Ajax, barely civil to his "wife," against the pathos of Hector's hope against all hope, and determination to put honor and country before personal safety, even before those he loves best.

For an analysis see Kirkwood's essay, "Homer and Sophocles' *Ajax*."

486–90 Compelling fortune is one of numerous variants on "necessity" and "luck"; see the first line of Hector's speech cited at 501–5. Her example illustrates mutability. Homer's Andromache remains a free woman, but she too lost her family to a strong hand; both women belong to the regional nobility that has been devastated by the war. The emphasis is on **your strong hand,** which is the instrument of **the gods' will.**

492–94 Recognizing his power, her appeal is essentially that of a suppliant, though one with intimate and friendly connections. **Known peace with me** translates a euphemism for sexual intercourse.

496 Their **bondslave,** i.e., putting me into the hands (power) of your enemies.

501–5 In Homer's scene it is Hector who, imagining "a day when sacred Ilion shall perish," thinks of his wife carried off to slavery:

> all unwilling, but strong will be the necessity upon you;
> and some day seeing you shedding tears a man will say of you:
> "This is the wife of Hektor, who was ever the bravest fighter
> of the Trojans, breakers of horses, in the days when they fought
>   about Ilion."
> So will one speak of you; and for you it will be yet a fresh grief,
> to be widowed of such a man who could fight off the day of
>   your slavery.
> But may I be dead and the piled earth hide me under before I
> hear you crying and know by this that they drag you captive.
>
> (*Iliad* 6.458–65)

The self-conscious pride of the Homeric warrior is evident. There is perhaps more pathos in giving such a speech to the woman, although Hector's fatalism and resolve to die rather than see that day cast an austere gloom over the Homeric scene. **Fate** = *daimôn;* the phrase is similar to that at OC 1748–50 ("powers . . . press me on").

507 **Reproach** responds to "contemptible" (473) and is a nice example of persuasive definition: she argues that abandoning wife and child is more shameful than living with his shameful humiliation.

508 So Hecuba, Hector's mother, begins her appeal to her son with "**revere** and take pity" (*Iliad* 22.82). In that scene Hector's father has just called on him to take

> pity on me, the unfortunate still alive, still sentient
> but ill-starred, whom the father, Kronos' son, on the threshold of
>   old age
> will blast with hard fate, after I have looked upon evils
> and seen my sons destroyed and my daughters dragged away
>   captive
>
> (*Iliad* 22.59–62)

510 Cf. Andromache:

> Please take pity upon me then, stay here on the rampart
> that you may not leave your child an orphan, your wife a
>   widow.
>
> (*Iliad* 6.431–32)

Of course such appeals to pity are common in tragedy, especially in scenes of supplication; cf. 526.

516–18 Since there is no pre-Sophoclean tradition concerning the death of Teleutas and his wife, we cannot be sure that Ajax personally killed them, although that would certainly be the implication if Tecmessa did not speak of **another fate**. This phrase has roused suspicion and so has been much emended; the favored emendations do not spare her from living with the man who destroyed her town and, directly or indirectly, her family. If the text is sound, Sophocles has failed to avoid an awkward dilemma for Tecmessa, to which he may have been led by his model (Andromache's family was killed by Achilles).

521 Gentle thing is "happiness" at 967; "pleasure/delight" is the usual sense, and in this context it naturally suggests the pleasures of love.

522 Kindness (*charis*) as reciprocity is a familiar theme; see 567, 809, 1266 ("gratitude"), OC 779b and 1489–90.

523–24 Forgets, recollection, and **remember** (520) are all from the same stem, with, then, a strong verbal emphasis on "remember." Cf. 1268. **Slips away** is also echoed in Teucer's retort (in "how fugitive" at 1266).

525 Noble: see 479–80, to which her argument responds.

534 Evil genius is *daimôn*.

545 When Hector meets Andromache, an attendant is carrying their son. After a pair of speeches by the parents, Hector moves to embrace his son, but the warrior's armor and plumed helmet frighten him. Hector laughs, removes his helmet, takes the boy in his arms, and prays to Zeus:

> Zeus, and you other immortals, grant that this boy, who is my son,
> may be as I am, pre-eminent among the Trojans,
> great in strength as am I, and rule strongly over Ilion;
> and some day let them say of him: "He is better by far than his
>   father,"
> as he comes in from the fighting; and let him kill his enemy
> and bring home the blooded spoils, and delight the heart of his
>   mother.
>
> (*Iliad* 6.476–81)

It may be well to look ahead to his next speech (644–92), where Ajax seems to have experienced a profound change of sensibility, or at least of intention. Since he claims there (650–52) to have been affected by pity for wife and child, which he has shown little enough of to this point, we may hope to find in the present speech signs of a mollified temper. In his own rough, egotistic way he is concerned for Eurysaces and foresees the mother's joy in his rearing (558b). Yet on the central issue of suicide he remains unalterable (this is a farewell and his purpose is baldly put at 579b). There is certainly no sign of repentance (see 550–51), no change in his hatred of the Greeks (574–76), no improvement in his manners toward Tecmessa (580–81 and the dialogue that follows). On the balance, it is hard to see great change in thought and character, but visually, dramatically, such a leave-taking is bound to win sympathy for this grim, rough hero; even pride such as his takes thought for his son. If his idealism is narrow and harshly indifferent to its consequences for soldiers and wife, he is not exempt from humane concern for the boy and for his parents, or from confidence in Teucer (560–70). There can be, moreover, little dramatic purpose for the scene save that it shows a less severe, less arrogantly self-centered protagonist. Whether its thought and ethos serve as a sufficient bridge to the next speech is less than certain, but it at least points the way.

548 Rugged appears in "grim" at 206 and 883; see on 933.

549 A nature = "breed" (472).

550–51 Vergil's imitation merits comparison. Aeneas addresses his son Ascanius:

"Learn valor (*virtus*), my child, from me, and your true task, fortune from others.

(*Aeneid* 12.435–36)

Base (*kakos*), as at 319. The same word is "misery" in 553, as in the euphemistic "misfortune" at 323.

554–55 Not knowing anything: cf. the thought at *OK* 1390–91. Line 555 is often bracketed by editors as an interpolated gloss on 554.

556 Perhaps we may find in his recognition of the alternation **of joy and grief** the theme of mutability so prominent in his next great speech. But in what follows he tacitly expresses the hope that his son may be an avenger.

559 With **what man's son** cf. *Ant* 471–72 (Antigone is the true daughter of Oedipus).

559a The metaphor **feed on light breezes** may pick up "colt" (548). For the significance of atmospheric conditions and winds on health see the Hippocratic "Airs, Waters, Places," especially section 5 for salubrious moderate breezes.

560–61 It is naive or optimistic not to expect **outrage** (*hybris*) and **insult** (see on 217). One thinks of the fate of Hector's son, thrown by the Greeks from the walls of Troy that he might not grow up to be an avenger of Trojan suffering.

567 Kindness: cf. 522.

569a Since Teucer is his half-brother, he adds "I mean **my mother.**"

570 In **tend and nourish** there is an echo of "feed" (559a); after the child's easy, carefree youth he will assume responsibility for his foster parents (his grandparents). If **"giving your mother joy"** (559b) is "the first touch of consideration that Ajax shows towards Tecmessa" (Stanford), yet he thinks not of the boy's care for her but for his parents. If Sophocles wanted to imply concern for Tecmessa, he has let Ajax do that in the most indirect way.

576 **Destroyer** connotes maltreatment and dishonor; apparently he refers to Odysseus. In this proposed disposition of his arms he remains wonderfully oblivious to his inability to control the future, but that sense of authority is Ajax.

577–78 The **great weapon** is the shield (see on 19–20) from which **Eurysaces** (= "Broadshield") takes his name.

579c **Take the child** is addressed to Tecmessa, who is wailing.

580–81 **What a plaintive creature womankind is** may be proverbial; it certainly belongs to a commonplace on the frailty of women. Stanford compares Euripides *Medea* 928 and *Heracles* 536. The directions for exit should be ignored.

582–85 **Quavers incantations** = "chants his threnody of spells"; for metaphor from quack medicine see on *Tr* 999–1003 and *OC* 1194a–b. **Good** (*sophos*) suggests understanding and intelligence. **Quavers** occurs in 630 and and is virtually a technical term for lament for the dead. The derisive **incantations** suits his imperious tone. He will be a surgeon to his own disease: **knife** is only latent (from a verb that we may also translate "when the malady *calls for cutting*"). **Whetted** sees the cutting edge of his speech. We think again of his sword, already so often mentioned (31, 96, 146, 286).

587 **It becomes you to submit** = "it is right (for you) to be sensible" (*sôphrôn*: cf. 1269, *Tr* 434, *El* 308–9b). He will use the same verb at 675 ("learn place and wisdom"); it is "steady sense" at 133. Moderation is for women.

590 **Owe** = "have no debt/obligation to."

591–99 In the Greek these are four lines in antilabe (split between the two speakers). **What impious words:** cf. 362.

597 **Soften!:** see on *Phil* 629a. This is the last sort of appeal we expect to work on him, but see 650–52.

599 **Nature** (*êthos*) means "disposition/character"; "mind" at *Ant* 705 and 746. Cf. his self-conscious "rugged ways" (548).

Ajax has never left the eccyclema. Now it is pulled in, withdrawing him and the slaughtered animals. All our expectations are that he has made his decision, will take his life, and the next scene will bring a messenger announcing his death. Some critics have Tecmessa exit with the child, as he has commanded, but her last supplication has intervened, in a sense canceling his command. As Seale observes, separation is called for, so we should keep her on, thereby avoiding an awkward reentry (see Seale, pp. 157–58).

599a–643 Instead of a lament for his imminent death, the chorus sings of his continuing madness (e.g., 611, 623, 633–40) and the grief his parents will have from its report.

599a–606 The apostrophe to **Salamis** that is **blest** is answered by an antithetical "But I am wretched" (607). **Time . . . losing count** will be echoed by Ajax' first line (644). The **slow abrasion** is explicitly that "of time." Cf. the emphasis on his mother's age (621–22). The strophe does not end with a question, nor tentatively: "with the hard expectation that I shall come to . . ." In **detested . . . Death** the translation catches the alliteration of the Greek but not the etymological punning in which Hades (the "unseen") is linked with "making something unseen."

607–20 Ajax is likened to a competitor sitting by the ring, waiting to take his turn against the winner of the present contest (our "on-deck hitter" comes to mind). But he is sick (**ill to cure**), lives in the same house with **holy madness** (i.e., "sent by the gods"), in sad contrast to the strong (= **brilliant**) warrior once dispatched to battle. The metaphor changes, and with what we hope is unconscious irony Ajax is compared to a solitary herdsman whose flock is his thought. **Works of his strong hands** echoes the more freely rendered "no less than he a champion" (Ajax at 439a). **Of war** is more literally "of valor" (*aretê*). **Undear, unfriended:** or "thanklessly before the thankless kings." **Friendless** is one of those generic terms and usually means "miserable/pitiful"; Kamerbeek suggests that here it may express some indignation.

621–31 **His mother:** cf. 569a. They make explicit reference to sickness (*nosos*) both here and at 633. With Dindorf's conjecture we have a "sickness that devours his mind." **O lamentable, lamentable:** at *Agamemnon* 121 this cry of grief is translated "sorrow, sorrow." For the **nightingale** as an emblem of grief, see on *El* 148–49b. Beating the breast and tearing hair are standard features of Greek mourning.

632–43 **Better . . . in Hades** concedes that he has threatened to kill himself, but once again they turn away to less immediate concerns. **He keeps no more the steady heart:** Greek psychology and personification tend to disassociate one aspect of personality from another. So here Ajax is said to no longer be stable in the temper (or disposition) which was once his companion, and this metaphor is continued in **ranges in extravagant madness** (= "consorts [with another temper] outside himself"). In this context **calamity** (*atê:* see on 123) may carry the old notion of an external, i.e., divine, infatuation. Then **has borne** (= "has nurtured/reared") implies that he, unlike all previous members of his clan, has cultivated this companion (delusion).

644–92 Some members of the audience will surely have expected a messenger announcing the death of Ajax. Now he returns, and in a monologue—Tecmessa and the chorus overhear him but are not addressed until 683—he ruminates on the theme of mutability. The effect of this speech is to convince Tecmessa and the chorus that he has changed his mind and no longer intends to commit suicide. Yet when he next appears (815) he is preparing for suicide, and at the end of a speech concerned with his death he falls on his sword (865).

The essential dramatic problem is the question of motivation: Has he really altered his purpose? Or does he consciously deceive his friends? What is his motive for a conscious deception? Is he brooding, ambiguously, perhaps only half-consciously, on the possibility of comprising his previous resolve to die? If his mood has in fact turned womanish (652), we are faced with an unusual, perhaps unique, offstage decision of dramatic consequence, not to mention the subsequent change, without notice, back to his original purpose. If he consciously deceives them, the plain-spoken, even brutal, candor of his earlier characterization is transformed, for a single scene, into humane concern. If he has changed his view of himself in relation to the world, are we prepared, dramatically, for such a turn, even if it does not entail an alteration in his decision to commit suicide? Resolving this issue would be easier if the speech were not studded with ambiguities, which any interpretation must take into account.

Three main lines of interpretation have been proposed. (1) Few critics follow Bowra in thinking that, for the moment, Ajax has decided not to commit suicide but rather to seek accommodation with the Greek chiefs. On this view he is sincere now but reverses himself again and commits suicide without comment on his change of intention. (2) Ajax has not changed his mind, but out of pity for Tecmessa and his friends he dissimulates his purpose. Those who, like Lattimore (*Poetry of Greek Tragedy,* p. 71), suggest that he deceives not from pity but from a desire to clear his path for an unobstructed suicide offer a dramatic answer to an ethical problem (i.e., has he so far shown sufficient regard for their feelings to imply that he would now care for their protests?). (3) The most subtle interpretation, advocated by Knox and Sicherl, argues that Ajax debates his resolve in a soliloquy that is overheard and misunderstood by Tecmessa and the chorus. Stevens (p. 328) summarizes this interpretation: "The essence of it is that Ajax' purpose has not changed but that his outlook has been transformed." (Stevens argues against this view.) This interpretation avoids unmotivated, offstage changes in purpose as well as the charge of intentional deception, which does not seem to suit the character of Ajax. Knox sees Ajax as pondering possibilities such as pity, yielding, and accommodation so foreign to his nature that even the language in which he phrases them denies his ability to act upon them. He may, for example, speak of pity, but even in articulating this alien mode, he calls pity "womanish." Thus his friends seize upon that aspect of his speech that promises them relief, and they cling to this hope, even though the last lines (684–92) are the least ambiguous in the speech.

Among other interpretations, Simpson argues that Ajax evolves from a man of deeds to a man of thought and that Tecmessa's arguments have swayed him: "Ajax later admits that he has been affected by his exchange with Tecmessa (650–52). In fact, his awareness of her effect on him has kindled his insight that *all* things change. Thus Tecmessa is, in a sense, responsible for his ascent to a higher vision of reality which becomes his new justification for suicide" (p. 96). Although I cannot find such intellectual evolution in Ajax, there is no denying that this speech so differs in tone (the brutish nastiness has fled) that we feel pressed to find a "new" man. Certainly this contemplation of man's nature at odds with the world gives substance to the hero's stature, which to this point has rested more on defiance than right. The problem is that this is the same man who moments earlier shouted:

> you have a foolish thought
> If you think at this date to school my nature.
>
> (598–99)

If we look ahead, two passages imply, in different ways, that Sophocles had an intentional deception in mind. First the final lines of the next lyric (714–17) indicate the chorus's surprise at what they have heard. Clearly, they too find this volte-face "out of character" but still possible, even plausible. The dramatist could hardly have more candidly admitted what an unexpected turn his protagonist has taken. Secondly, when the messenger reveals to Tecmessa that Ajax on peril of his life must be kept indoors, her reaction ("I have been deceived; he is bent on death": see 803–12) cuts so incisively to the issue that one feels she has known the alternatives all along. In her despair she naturally seized on hope, but the slightest suggestion of something amiss exposes the deception. While she does not say that he *intentionally* deceived her, the unequivocal insight that he is in fact hastening to his death (812) leaves little doubt she now believes that Ajax has meant to take his life. As for his motivation, we must perhaps take him at his word (650–54), even if pity seems an unlikely commodity to sway his nature.

644–47 For **time** see the note to 600–602 and compare the variation at 713. The power of time to change, soften, accomplish, uncover, reveal, etc., is a standard commonplace of tragic poetry. **Brings . . . forth** = "brings to life." **Marvelous** = "unexpected"; the translator's **That man . . . not be** expands this idea.

648–54 **Iron intent** anticipates the metaphor from tempering (651); iron also means "rigid" and "harsh." **Come crashing down** = "is caught" (by madness at 217) or = "taken in battle or in a trap." **No sword dipped** most obviously refers to tempered steel, though there may be a secondary meaning, and ambiguity, that alludes to dipping iron in oil to make it more flexible. The vehicle linking the metaphors of tempering steel and being soft like a woman is a single word (*stoma*), which is here translated twice, in **edge** and in **speech**; cf. "whetted tongue" (585). While a sardonic tone might blunt his "I am (grown) womanish for this woman's sake," it is hard to see how irony can affect **And pity touches me . . .**" even though a secondary meaning is "I am full of pity at the thought of leaving wife and child. . . ." **Widowed** and **lost** would seem to reflect the force of her argument at 510ff.

655–57 His last scene will take place in a **meadow by the sea**. The ambiguity of **cleanse my stains** turns on the literal meaning of washing away the blood that defiles him and a figurative sense of purging/cleansing the stain on his honor by killing himself. Athena's **wrath** will naturally cease with his death.

657–65 Now the **sword** becomes explicitly the ambiguous symbol and instrument of his life and death, the sacrificial weapon with which he will end all contention with god and man (see also 815–22). Since he will dig a hole in the ground and fall on the fixed sword, he can say that he will **hide it** out of sight; but of course it will also be hidden in him. It is **hatefulest** because it was given to him by his great enemy Hector. Disposing of the polluted weapon by burying it does not entail a wish that **Darkness** (= "Night") and **Hades** should keep it safe; he thinks of himself and the sword. Hector,

> bringing a sword with nails of silver
> gave it to him, together with the sheath and the well-cut
> sword belt,
> and Aias gave a war belt coloured shining with purple.
>
> (*Iliad* 7.303–5)

Ruinous = "not profitable/useful." **Gift . . . no gift** translates the popular privative construction.

666 **My rule: Give way** = "I shall learn to yield to the gods (= **Heaven**)." This is not the Ajax of the first scenes; note the repetition of this verb in 669 ("give way"). Following the scholiast, some modern

commentators claim that Ajax inverts normal usage of **give way** and **bow before,** i.e., he should say "give way to the sons of Atreus and bow before the gods." But the usage is not so strict; e.g., "bow before" is "serve" at *Ant* 512 (Antigone of her brothers) and *"constant in respect to* Laius' royal power" (*Ant* 165–66). After **obeyed** (from the same stem as "give way"), a terse question occurs in the Greek ("What else?"). **Dread strengths:** the adjective (*deinos*) repeats "strong" in 647 and 650 (cf. 672) while the noun echoes "rigid" (650). **In turn and deference** = "to honors/ authority (*timê*)."

669a–73 His example from seasonal and atmospheric changes, with the focus on opposites (**winter-summer; night-day**) transformed into each other, had already been noticed by Heraclitus (see, e.g., Kirk and Raven 207, where God, the underlying substance, experiences change in the form of summer and winter, day and night). In the *Heracles,* Amphitryon contemplates mutability in order to gain hope:

> Human misery must somewhere have a stop:
> there is no wind that always blows a storm;
> great good fortune comes to failure in the end.
> All is change; all yields its place and goes;
> to persevere, trusting in what hopes he has,
> is courage in a man. The coward despairs.
>
> (Euripides *Heracles* 101–6)

Slackens and gives peace translates a single verb meaning "lulls to sleep," so that there is actually an ellipsis of "slackens" and a paradoxical and mixed metaphor of a violent gale putting to sleep the groaning sea. **Sleep,** then, is suggested by the preceding verb. **Strong jailer** is literally "all-conquering," a common epithet of the gods.

675 **Learn:** cf. "school my nature" (599). **Place and wisdom:** see on 587. Nature reveals moderating change as the universal law. Can such a rule be transposed into the ethical sphere for Ajax? Can he understand moderation in terms that are ethically and socially acceptable? The ethical relativism of lines 675–81 reflects the traditional wisdom of Bias of Priene, one of the seven sages of archaic tradition. Old men, experienced and naturally cautious and cynical,

> neither love warmly nor hate bitterly, but following the hint of
> Bias they love as though they will some day hate and hate as
> though they will some day love.
>
> (Aristotle *Rhetoric* 2.13)

For an unexpected conclusion to this line of thinking see Odysseus' speech at 1332–45.

692 The ambiguity of **safety** stems from death as a healer and physician and his friends' perception that his recantation may save him. Note the echo of "safe" (660) and the theme of the salvation of Ajax ("saviors" at 779a, "save" at 812).

693–717 Hearing what it wants to hear, the chorus sings for joy that Ajax has, against expectation (716), relented in his anger against the kings. The audience, however, knows that according to tradition, Ajax died a suicide. The dramatists had leave to change such traditions, but we can be sure that the audience will have heard both edges of his argument. Such mistaken hope, here truly euphoria, in a choral song will also be found at *Tr* 633–62, *Ant* 1115–51, and more cautiously at *OK* 1087–1107.

693–705 Joy (*eros*) = "love/desire" (of/for Pan?). With **take wings** cf. "flutter" at *OK* 488. **Lord Pan** is the goat-horned god of Arcadia; hence the reference to Mt. **Cyllene**. His pipes are associated with exuberant song and dance, and sudden seizures are attributed to Pan. The chorus actually calls him by name four times. **Come** (= "appear/be manifest"); **over the sea** is a vocative ("sea-roamer"): "Hail, Hail, Pan! Pan! O Pan, Pan, sea-roamer from the rocky ridge of snow-struck Cyllene, appear O lord dance-maker of the gods, that to me you, present, may send the dances **Mysian, Cnosian,** self-taught." Mysian and Cnosian (Cnosos in Crete) seem to link Pan's dance to those celebrating Cybele, the Great Mother. "Self-taught," i.e., Pan has not learned them from others; the spontaneity of the dance is more effectively suggested by transferring the adjective from the god to his dance. The **open sea** is explicitly the Icarian Sea. Perhaps **Apollo** is invoked as a healer; his paean, among other things, averts evil and celebrates victory.

706–17 The harsh god is Ares (so named in the Greek). As often in lyrics, English must supply personal pronouns where the Greek is more concise; so **from our eyes** may be "from his (Ajax') eyes." Here, as at *Tr* 653–54, the god of war may be substituted for the warrior, who, they feel, has at last seen the light. The (implicit) darkness that has obscured his vision leads to **perfect daylight** and the prospect of a safe voyage home. **Forgets his pain**: the same compound occurs, in "unconscious of pain," at *Tr* 1021; for such forgetting cf. *Phil* 877–78. **With holy rite and due observance**: they refer to "sacrifice," thereby unconsciously foreshadowing his language (see on 815). **Reverent thoughts** translates the verb rendered "bow before" on 667. **Great Time** echoes his opening lines (644–46). **Makes . . . dim** may suggest either putting out a fire or causing something to wither and fade away. **Nothing seems beyond . . . speech**: it is worth stressing that the chorus is as surprised as modern critics by his apparent change of heart. **Has resolved** = "has repented from/changed his mind from." **Amazing** = "against expectation" (it was translated "marvelous" at 646).

718 Seeing this messenger approach, the audience will naturally assume, if only until he speaks, that he brings news of Ajax. The repeated references to Teucer and his absence (342, 562–68, 687) are ample preparation for his return, though few will have guessed the extent of his role or Sophocles' use of it as a bridge to the pivotal persuasion of Odysseus.

720 Homeric **Mysia** is a district southeast of Troy; in later times this name is used of the northwestern corner of modern Turkey.

728 For **stoning** see 253. **Torn and bloody** translates a violent metaphor from combing wool: the stones, like the pins on a carding board, shred the victim.

730 **The thing** is a "quarrel," which implies Teucer's response, although the focus in this report is all on his reception.

732 No specific **elder** is mentioned, but the audience, like the scholiast, might think of old Nestor's attempt to mediate the quarrel between Achilles and Agamemnon (*Iliad* 1.247ff.).

736 Cf. Jebb's more literal version: "for he hath yoked a new purpose to his new mood." They have heard him talk of accommodation, a yoke he voluntarily accepts.

737 **May God help him then!** stands for a cry of grief ("O, O, O," at *OK* 1183).

743–44 **Truest good** = "a more useful purpose." The underlying metaphor in **relieved of the gods' anger** is from commercial or reciprocal exchange, which in turn gives rise to "making a proper arrangement" and so to reconciling one party with another. If the coryphaeus expanded this thought, he would say that by sacrificing (711) and cleansing himself (656) Ajax will appease the angry god. Cf. 657 and 759.

746 In the *Iliad,* **Calchas** is the seer for the Greek army; in book one he correctly assigns the plague to Apollo's anger (see *Iliad* 1.69ff.).

750 **Left the kingly circle** is explicitly "apart from the sons of Atreus"; since Menelaus and Agamemnon will appear in our play, it seems Sophocles had a reason for these more particular references (cf. 620 and 717). There is no Homeric precedent for the seer's special concern for Ajax.

756 The awkwardness of **this now present day** at least fits the emphasis of the Greek (cf. 758). "This day" (779) completes the ring, and the whole passage gives new and particular content to Athena's gnomic utterance at 130–32. For the motif "a single day" see on *OK* 438. Why one day? Divine caprice? Or a grim perception, of which Calchas himself is unconscious, that one day will suffice for his death?

759 Vex = "will be driving" at 506; it is a common verb for divine persecution, as, e.g., at *OK* 28–29 (translated "is on").

759a–61 To **forget man's nature** is to ignore mortality and the limits on human power and ambition which it entails, limits that define the essential distinction between man and god, mortal and immortal, as the Greeks so often put it. Words "kept no human measure" (778) repeats the Greek phrase verbatim. For parallels see *Tr* 473 and *OK* 1079a. **On most untoward disasters** = "from heavy disasters."

762 Now comes, unexpectedly for those who read Homer, evidence of his foolish self-confidence. Although all Homeric heroes welcome the aid of the gods, other heroes like the lesser Ajax (see *Odyssey* 4.499ff.), Idas (*Iliad* 9.556ff.), and Kaineus exemplify men who have put the gods aside and trusted in their own power. See *Seven against Thebes* 529a–32 and Nilsson, "The Men in Their Own Power," *Opuscula Selecta* 3, pp. 26–31. Sophocles made a play about the lesser (Locrian) Ajax who

> would have escaped his doom, though Athena hated him,
> had he not gone wildly mad and tossed out a word of defiance;
> for he said that in despite of the gods he escaped the great gulf
> of the sea, and Poseidon heard him, loudly vaunting.
>
> (*Odyssey* 4.502–5)

The Locrian Ajax had desecrated Athena's temple in Troy, which left him, along with most of the Greek army, in the eye of divine anger (see the prologue to the *Trojan Women*). Our Ajax, as the following report discloses, has a more personal arrogance. What especially surprises us is that Athena's anger is now revealed as longstanding; the present madness is but the shadow of the goddess standing in wait for her man. As often, the Greeks see human stupidity as an indication of divine disfavor. But the gods do not read the human heart; hence a **senseless boast** regularly triggers the gods' reaction.

762–63 The father's advice on his son's departure is already a thematically significant motif in the *Iliad* (see, e.g., 9.252–59 and 11.782–89).

768–69 Triumph echoes **to win** (765), which itself occurs twice in the Greek line. The stem (noun *kratos*) denotes power and so the essential virtue of a warrior (as in 613) and his claims to victory ("war prize" at 444, "claims" at 448). Agamemnon uses the verbal form (in "has the advantage") when he sums up Ajax' problem (1250–52). **Fame** (*kleos*) = "sweet praise" (437).

775 There is no Homeric precedent for this dismissal of Athena's aid.

778 Kept no human measure = "he was not thinking as a man ought" (cf. 759a–b).

783 Deprived me of my hope = "if I have come too late." As in the *Antigone* and *Oedipus,* the seer's knowledge comes too late.

787 The metaphor from the close shave is well established; see on *Ant* 996. For the Greek it signifies an immediate crisis, when there is still some chance of not being cut.

800 Heaven help us! = "O God!" (*OK* 744; see the note). As there, this is an exclamation of self-pity prompted by a sudden foreboding.

803–12 The dramatic pace will not permit further interrogation; she accepts without question the prophet's warning and orders a search, which will clear the stage for Ajax' return. If she does not say that he has willfully deceived her, that is surely the most obvious construction to put on **beguiled of his intent** and **bent on death.** The latter phrase unambiguously declares (her present perception) that Ajax means to take his own life. **Of his intent** does not = "by him" but more vaguely "in relation to him." For **kindness** see 522 (note). **What shall I do?:** for the question see 458 and the note to *Tr* 385. It is perhaps less natural for her and the child to join the search, but the poet doesn't want her even so near as within the tent, and the question and decision to join the chorus underscore the urgency.

815 Elsewhere in extant Greek tragedy the chorus leaves the orchestra only at *Eumenides* 231, where the Furies exit in pursuit of Orestes. When he speaks at 235, the scene is the Athenian acropolis, and the Furies return at 245. Sophocles' reasons for taking the chorus off are less mythic and more particular to this play. Whereas in Aeschylus' version a messenger reported the death of Ajax, Sophocles offers us a unique (for extant tragedy) suicide on stage. Sweeping past the conventions of reported death, the poet isolates the alienated hero, thereby winning for him a sympathy necessarily qualified in earlier scenes by his manners toward Athena, Tecmessa, and the chorus.

The modern director will have no trouble staging this scene because, unlike his ancient counterpart, he has no need to remove the body of the fallen protagonist. In the original Greek production, however, the actor who played Ajax took the part of Teucer in subsequent scenes. Since it is universally agreed that Sophocles used only three actors, we must guess— the text will not settle this problem—how he managed the death, the removal of the body, and its reappearance on stage (the figure remains on stage, certainly prominently displayed, throughout the remainder of the play). Bound up with this problem is the question of how freely the Greeks brought on sets: did stagehands bring on the bushes the translator mentions? (they are derived from the "copse" at 892) or are references such as that at 892 essentially appeals to the spectators' imaginative involvement? Values such as those we attach to realism and illusion are clearly involved. In the first place we must attend to matters of fact: fixing the sword in the ground and falling on it are so emphatically stressed (815, 819a, 821, 833, 899, 907–8) that it seems impossible to hide the sword, even partially, behind the bushes. On the other hand, when the chorus enters, it does not see the body, and Tecmessa's cry of discovery (891) is heard before they see her. They do not see the body until 900. It would appear, though some critics disagree, that both Ajax and Tecmessa enter from the main door, which has previously represented the tent of Ajax, but it may be that she enters from one parodos and remains unnoticed until her cry. In any case he must die at the door, and his body will be displayed at that dramatically central position afterwards. This is a good time to use the trolley (*eccyclema*): Ajax fixes the sword on it, dies in full view of the audience, then (between 866 and 890) the trolley is retracted into the scenic building and returned with a dummy aboard. This staging eliminates the need to bring on sets for bushes and gives the actor full scope for his "swift unconvulsive leap" (833). There is the possibility, not generally entertained by commentators on this staging, that extras came on before 815, set up panels representing bushes and a deserted place, and then returned at 865 to carry off the body. In that case the *eccyclema* could still be pushed forward to return the body. For a different view of the staging see appendix 2 (pp. 131–33) in Arnott's *Greek Scenic Conventions*.

815–17 **Slayer** = Sacrificer"; for a discussion of this motif see Lattimore, *Poetry of Greek Tragedy*, pp. 75–77. The Greek calls attention to placing the sword in such a way or place that it will be **deadliest;** perhaps there is an allusion to the tradition that Ajax was invulnerable save at his armpit. Aeschylus accepted this tradition, accordingly to the scholia on *Ajax* 833, when he had a *daimôn* show the hero how to fall. Cf. 833. **Time** = "leisure"; the tone is sardonic.

818 For **Hector's gift** see the note to 657–65. Their relationship is not strictly one of **guest-friendship;** better "gift of that most bitter foe, most hateful of my enemies."

824–25 The prayer to **Zeus** would be natural enough, even if he were not the ancestor of Ajax' clan (389).

830 **A prize for birds and dogs** is the lot usually feared from the enemy; cf. 1062–65 and *Ant* 206–7. **Prize** is a Homeric word (cf. *Iliad* 1.4) which occurs only twice in tragedy.

832 **Hermes,** protector of all travelers, guides the dead to Hades; cf. *OC* 1547.

833 For the allusion in **unconvulsive** and the desire for a clean death

see the note to 815–17. **Waft me** = "put me to sleep"; for the identification of sleep and death and the wish cf. *Agamemnon* 1448–51.

834–43 In tragedy the Furies (= **Erinyes**) are most commonly invoked as spirits concerned with blood-guilt within the family. As chthonic daimons they naturally come to mind after Hermes. Here, as in the allusion at *OK* 418, they are spirits that fulfill curses; cf. 1390. Although they are given power over Zeus and equal to the Fates at *Prometheus Bound* 516, the Furies do not explicitly watch **the fates of men** in this text. They are represented by Aeschylus as hounds that pursue (**Come with long strides**); their similarity to the Harpies may be seen in **sweep upon them** (= "snatch them up"). For the wish/curse that someone may suffer as the one who curses suffers see on *Tr* 1036–40. It seems unlikely that Sophocles would add, against any known early tradition and in plain contradiction of the tradition, **by loved and kindred hand.** Consequently, this verse (841 in our text) is usually deleted by modern editors. It looks like an inept actor's interpolation or a marginal parallel has ousted one or more lines of the Sophoclean text. **Blood** is interpretative, and **taste** often means "make trial of," but since the Furies are vampires, the translation's expansion seems legitimate.

844–52 The Sun (**Lord Helios**) is often invoked as a witness (e.g., *Iliad* 3.277) and a bearer of tales (e.g., *Odyssey* 8.270–71), but we may momentarily expect Ajax to announce that he is taking leave of the light (cf. 856–59), until the more poignant use of the god as envoy to his parents gives this prayer a special inflection. Although **Poor mother** (*dustênos*) and **wretched** (*talaina*) are almost formulaic, and **grief's note will quaver** ("shrieking" at *Tr* 866) belongs to the standard vocabulary of lamentation, the thought seems to move Ajax deeply. Cassandra uses this language (in "threnody") in her prayer to the Sun (*Agamemnon* 1322–24).

854 Death is repeated: "O Death, Death." Cf. *Phil* 794 and *Tr* 1085 (Hades). **Attend me now** suits Kamerbeek's suggestion that the verb may have medical connotations here and implicitly call up the image of Death the healer.

856–59a For the final apostrophe to the light cf. *OC* 1549, *Alcestis* 244–45.

860–63 Strictly speaking, it is an anachronism for the archaic hero to join **Athens** and **Salamis,** but in historical times an Athenian tribe took its name from Ajax, and the Athenian audience would now be wondering how Sophocles will sort out an honorable burial. **Nurtured** and **nurses** reflect Greek cognates; **streams** and **springs** are sacred and universally associated with life and nurture. **Nurses** = "you who nurtured me"; cf. Philoctetes' farewell to the "springs and Lycian well" (*Phil* 1461). There is, obviously, great pathos in such a farewell, and particularly in the nostalgia for home, hearth, and kin. He has come far from the brute madness of the prologue. The solitude, the alienation from home, and the absence of self-pity and vindictiveness in these final lines win sympathy; comparison with the Heracles of the *Women of Trachis* is instructive.

866–973 The reentry of the chorus, or second parodos, sharply defines the opening of the second half of the play. The divided chorus enters from either side and reunites (866–77). The chorus sings of its frustrated search (878–90) until it hears Tecmessa's cry, at which point a dialogue begins (mixed lyric and iambic verse; this continues through 913). Lines 878–913 constitutes the first strophe, responsive to 925–60; the subject is discovery and lament. At 914 Tecmessa has a ten-line speech ("what will be the fate of the body?"), which corresponds structurally to 961–73, another speech by Tecmessa. The antistrophe (925–60) is given over to lament, first in a choral lyric (925–37) and then in dialogue between Tecmessa and the chorus (938–60). The dirge for the dead is the natural closure for archaic tragedy (cf. the *Persians* and *Seven against Thebes*); here that theme is blended with concern for the fate of the dead hero and the anticipation of his defender's arrival.

866 Toil: the triplet in polyptoton: *ponos ponôi ponon.* It is followed by **where** three times in the Greek. "Labor" (875), "struggling" (878), and "plod" (886) echo "toil."

868 No place . . . secret: this is Jebb's interpretation of a verse editors continue to think corrupt because of the strained sense and syntax. They apparently mean that no place has disclosed the secret location of Ajax.

878–84 The two clauses (**What . . . What . . .**) translate a Greek triplet. They express both question and wish: "(would that there were someone) who might tell me. . . ."

879 Haul = "hunting" (94); their search for Ajax mirrors Odysseus' "hunt" of the prologue.

881–82 Proper names specify **nymph** as "Olympian" (of Mt. Olympus on the border of Mysia) and **river** as "Bosporan," (of the streams flowing into the Bosporus).

883 Grim was "rugged" (548) and occurs in "fierce heart" at 929a; cf. 206. The key element in the compound is translated "savage" at *Tr* 975 (note); "hard/fierce/harsh" circle the idea.

890 Homer applies the adjective here translated **afflicted** to ghosts and dreams; possibly Sophocles offers a bold metaphor likening the undiscovered Ajax to a fleeting, shadowy specter, with ominous foreshadowing of his death, now immediately signaled by the cry of Tecmessa.

894–95 Captive is modeled on the Homeric compound "taken by the spear," i.e., as a captive in battle (*Iliad* 9.343). **Lost in lamentation:**

a similar expression is translated, more literally, as "soaked in sorrow" at *Ant* 1310. The metaphor is from blending.

898–99 Though the body is at her feet, they cannot see it (cf. 912–13). The body might be behind her, but this seems awkward for the shrouding (914). The chorus need not be crowded up to the stage, and their request to see it (912) need not mean that the huddled form is hidden. **Enfolds:** the English here captures a subtle emphasis, already suggested at 829 in the Greek for "fallen on," of the body bent round and enveloping the sword. An adjective in 908 ("on which he fell") carries this figure on to "enfolding" at 915.

900–903 **Oh** is more frequent than the translation suggests. The self-pity is characteristic; cf. 945–46, 966–67, 980. In such laments the Greek relies more on phrase and exclamation than on sentences of any length. For example, for the sake of its concision we might translate here:

Oh, my homecoming!
Oh, you destroyed, my lord,
this shipmate, O miserable!
O miserably suffering wife.

It is not imagery or metaphor so much as the rhythm of intense grief that is the object.

904 The verb **(weep)** recalls the pun on agony at 430 (note); "ill-starred" (913) also refers to his ominous name.

905 **Fate** and bad luck always figure in lament; the same word (*dusmoros*) is applied to Tecmessa at 894 (there translated "poor"). When she uses it for the third time (at 923, in the apostrophe to Ajax), the translation drops it. But much of this language was the lifeblood of Greek popular mourning ritual, and we cut it out or offer variations at the price of authenticity. Cf. "luckless life's share of affliction" (927–28: *moira*) and "my ill-luck" (980: *tychê*).

906–8 We saw the **blade** earlier, when Ajax carefully fixed it in the ground; now we can see it again. Meanwhile the body has apparently come and gone, with the blade. Perhaps body and sword were taken off and brought back on the trolley.

910 **How blind I was!:** the exclamation "Oh, *atê!*" (see on 123) echoes Ajax' own reference to "my *atê* and my death" (847). In both passages the more general "disaster" seems right, and that is the translation of *atê* offered at 976.

912–13 **Let me see him** = "where, where, does he lie?" The question before her speech thus echoes the question "where, where?" beginning the lyric at 867. **Rugged:** the meaning is "intractable" or "truculent." **Ill-starred** refers to his ill-omened name (see on 430).

914–15 For the uncovering of Ajax see 1003. There may be two reasons for covering him. Flickinger (p. 244) suggests that the large cloak held out before and over the body would give ample opportunity for the actor to depart while a dummy is being substituted. This seems to play games for the sake of elusive illusion. Otherwise, Sophocles may think to tease our expectations once more: just as he twice led us to believe that the next scene would offer a report of the death of Ajax, only to bring the hero himself back on, so now the tableau that will eventually (1171 ff.) be organized by Teucer is postponed. Both considerations may be at work here, but I prefer the staging suggested at 815.

918 Wound translates the proper word for "sacrificial slaughter"; see also 815 ("Slayer").

920 For the question cf. 809a and 1024; in both cases the speaker changes the subject abruptly.

921–24 Time, tendance, and **weep** combine to express her anxiety that Ajax' enemies may intervene to prevent proper rites and burial. In Greek tragedy proper burial is such a frequent concern that the audience, even without the preparation already given in the *Ajax,* would wonder how the helpless friends of Ajax will manage this necessary but seemingly impossible task.

925 You were bound = "You intended/were going to." Like 910–11, this stanza (the beginning of the antistrophe) meditates on their late understanding of what was Ajax' purpose even before the ultimate attack on the army. **In the end** = "in time/at length"; the same word is "time" at 934, with its echo of 713.

927–28 Luckless life's share of affliction = "the evil portion (fate: *moira*) of your boundless toil." Though the road to Hades is a common metaphor, **that vast journey** is in this case a gloss.

950 Even may suggest to the English reader something exceptional in attributing human suffering to the gods; it should not.

951 With **overload** cf. "bearing heavily" (980); the weight of grief is to be connected with the heavy *daimôn* that brings man down; see *Agamemnon* 1174–76.

954–57 Waiting, laboring translates a Homeric epithet of Odysseus (it is "long-suffering" in Lattimore's translation). **Insults** (*hybris:* see on 153), here without an object, seems to mean "gloats"; cf. 971. For **laughter** and **mockery** as tokens of *hybris* see 368 and *Ant* 480–83; cf. 961, 969–71, 989c, 1043.

970 His death concerns the gods: this vague phrase may relate to the themes of expiation (656–60) and sacrifice (815), but it cannot be pushed very far, not so far as Kamerbeek's "He has fallen a victim to the gods, not to them."

974 Ajax' half-brother, famed as an archer, Teucer is a secondary figure in the *Iliad* (see 8.266–344, where he joins Ajax in battle). In Aeschylus' trilogy Teucer returned home to Salamis with Eurysaces and was banished by Telamon. Lines 568–70 and 1009a–21 allude to the subject matter of Aeschylus' third play.

The cry **O God! O God!** = "Oh! The pain of it!" (938). Unlike the chorus (891–98), Teucer sees the body immediately upon his entry. I doubt that this cry is heard before the spectators see him, as the translation's stage direction may imply. Seeing the body, he goes directly to it, passing by the usual formalities with the chorus.

976 Straight to the mark is a metaphor from archery; a homonym meaning "guardian/overseer" also comes into play. It is transferred from Teucer to his cry and anticipates his function as protector and guardian of the body.

981–83 Three lines of the Greek text in antilabe. According to the conventions of Greek tragedy, it is not unnatural for the entering character to address the chorus/coryphaeus before addressing another character already present; e.g., cf. *El* 670ff.

989–89a For the lionness who has lost her cub Stanford notes that the grieving Achilles is compared to a lion whose cubs have been stolen (*Iliad* 18.318–20)

996 Trace it = "track it," recalling the hunt of Odysseus (see on 5–6). Ajax is the object of his search, not the **truth.**

1005 Fierce resolve is the "daring" more often deprecated than admired; cf. 46, *Tr* 582–83, *Ant* 367 and 449.

1006 The metaphor "sowing sorrow" is unique in Sophocles; cf. *El* 642.

1009 Cf. Achilles' lament that he failed to defend Patroclus when he was about to be killed (*Iliad* 18.98–99).

1009a–21 Aeschylus' (lost) *Women of Salamis* dramatized Teucer's homecoming and his banishment by Telamon. Though we don't know the date of that trilogy, the present passage would surely have recalled the substance of Telamon's outraged sense of honor. Teucer was **cast into exile** and went to Cyprus where he named his new home Salamis.

1020 In his account: Telamon's abuse deemed Teucer's behavior no better than a slave's, and he treated him the same.

1027–28 The motif of the dead killing the living may have come into tragedy as a popular riddle; see on *Ant* 871 for other examples. For **Hector** see 818ff. **Consider** is second person plural: Teucer, having withdrawn the sword, displays it to chorus and audience; there is no reason to think he speaks more to one than to the other. Reflective and little concerned with anyone now present or with prospective events, Teucer first speaks to his dead brother (995 and 1015), and until 1028 first and second person singular pronouns give the speech something of the intimacy of dialogue; after 1028, he becomes more impersonal, and Ajax becomes "he" rather than "you" (1032).

1029a–32 This **girdle** is the "war-belt" of the quotation cited at 657–65. In *Iliad* 22, Achilles kills Hector before dragging his body to his own camp; since Hector has been wearing the armor he took from Patroclus, Homer cannot allude to Hector's duel with Ajax. Sophocles seems to have invented his own variation, not without a little of the grotesque: **clamping** suggests biting with teeth, and **grating** pictures the body combed, i.e., shredded on a card used for separating wool.

1034 At *Libation Bearers* 646–47, Destiny forges a sword on the anvil of Right; cf. the blade sharpened by fate at *Agamemnon* 1535.

1035 Aidoneus is Hades. **That other one** is the girdle. Hector died first, the "victim" of the one gift, so naturally his gift that kills Ajax is his avenger and thus may be said to have been made by an avenging spirit (**Fury**).

1044 Who means us harm = "rascal" at *OK* 705 (Oedipus of Teiresias), which is also right here.

1045–46 Teucer is still by the body. Although the question lets the coryphaeus announce Menelaus, it also implies that Sophocles will not let Teucer attend to anything else until he is forced to it. **Menelaus** is the husband of Helen, whose seduction prompted the expedition to Troy. In the *Iliad* he plays second fiddle to Agamemnon, who will also be making the decisions here (1221ff.). Given the emphasis on the difficulty of burying Ajax, the audience probably expected one of his enemies to appear to oppose Teucer. Agamemnon, as the more illustrious, would most naturally be anticipated. For a discussion of the following debates and Sophocles' dramatic design see J. F. Davidson, "Sophoclean Dramaturgy and the *Ajax* Burial Debates."

1049–49a Menelaus has no time for formalities as he sees Teucer, who momentarily ignores him, tending to the body.

1049b Since there isn't anything **grand** in Menelaus' style, we might render this "why waste so much talk?"

1051 The invitation to give **some justification** introduces a pair of speeches, accusation/prosecution and defense, more self-consciously than is usually the case in Sophocles. By contrast the defense comes first at *Ant* 450–96 (Antigone, then Creon) and at *El* 514–609 (Clytemnestra, then Electra). Euripidean debates often have the kind of self-conscious formality we find here; see, e.g., *Trojan Women* 903–10, where Hecuba (the prosecutor) actually begs leave for the accused Helen to defend herself. This play will offer a second, and essentially redundant, pair when Agamemnon and Teucer square off at 1225–1314.

1057 Some god: Odysseus has not reported Athena's intervention; cf. the equally generic "God" at 1060.

1061 Criminal heart = *hybris;* it is "insubordination" at 1081, "hot aggressor" at 1098, "outrage" at 1092, "insulted" at 1151.

1063–69 Power, rule, and **hand** all point to his frustration at so long being unable to match Ajax and the work of his strong hands (cf. 616). Violent men at last will have their way with the stronger. **To feed the sea birds:** see on 830.

1071 Poor common soldier introduces an argument that falsely implies a rigorous authority and chain of command, considering the Homeric army, where Achilles is quite free to absent himself from the fighting as long as he pleases. Teucer is quick to deny Menelaus' superior military office (1093–1108).

1074 Fear is the mainspring of **reverence** (*aidôs:* see on *OC* 1268). Note his references to a "city" (1073 and 1083). His talk of law and order and the dangers posed by men who do not fear authority belongs more to fifth-century Athens than to the heroic age of Ajax and Athena. For the mentality see Creon's speech at *Ant* 161–210. On fear and the law see Ehrenberg, p. 40.

1084 For the metaphor of the state as a ship at sea cf. *OK* 24.

1089–89a Hot aggressor repeats (1061) the charge of *hybris,* which is common enough, but when he speaks of his turn to **entertain large ideas,** he sails close to the wind. That phrase is typically translated "high-flown pride" (*OK* 1079, with notes); in most cases the Greek phrase appears in an accusation, not in a boast (see on 1120).

1090 Fall: he has used the same verb of the city/ship falling into the gulf of the sea (1083–84) and of Ajax falling on the cattle (1061).

1091–92 That the chorus will concede **fine principles,** even in the abstract, squares with their criticism of Teucer for being too tough and harsh (1118–19).

1093 Teucer has no trouble refuting Menelaus' arguments, still less sneering at this character, but none of this has the dramatic value of his defiance: regardless of "orders," he will bury Ajax. Since tradition and its own sympathy assure the audience that Ajax will be buried, the question is how Sophocles will resolve the conflict.

1095 Noblest birth: for the topic see 479–80 and 1228–32, where Agamemnon throws much the same stuff at Teucer.

1098 Ally you enlisted responds to the charges at 1052–55.

1100 His own master fairly describes the independence of the Homeric princes, but it hardly grants Ajax license to kill them. Menelaus' triumphant gloating over his present opportunity to "rule" Ajax gives Teucer leave to beg the question.

1112–13 When the princes of Greece courted Helen, Odysseus advised her father Tyndareus to exact an **oath** from each that he would honor her decision and protect the marriage. Consequently, when she ran off with Paris, all Greece was bound by oath to avenge the wrong.

1115 Menelaus is accompanied by one or two **heralds**; he will need more to enforce his purpose.

1116 The **general** is Agamemnon, whose intervention we now expect.

1120 For **bowman** as abuse Jebb cites Diomedes' taunt to Paris:

You archer, foul fighter, lovely in your locks, eyer of young girls.

(*Iliad* 11.385)

Athenian hoplites (heavy-armed infantry) carried spears and swords. Odysseus, famed for his bow, did not take it to Troy. **Quite well of himself** is a litotes that, by substituting "small" for "great," echoes Menelaus' "entertain large ideas" (1089a). Teucer himself will use the earlier phrase at 1125 ("have some boldness").

1123 The **light-armed** archers remained in the rear and had no need for shields and heavy armor.

1127–28 From 1120 through 1141 the single line stichomythia is not broken in the Greek. **Killed . . . living:** see the note to 1027–28.

1129a Teucer's point, which Antigone makes with more force, is that the issue stands between Ajax and the gods; like Creon, and many another Greek, Menelaus believes that a dead enemy deserves just what the kites will give him. See *Ant* 21–30 and 206–7 and the notes there. For the audience Creon has a better case than Menelaus: Polyneices attacks his native city and thereby hands Creon a political rationale; Ajax attacks his personal enemies and, as we know, because of Athena's hostility never had a chance. It might seem that Teucer ought to argue more explicitly for Athena's anger being a sufficient burden for the living, and dead, Ajax, but of course Menelaus might then be led to answer that, in denying burial, he is only doing the goddess's work!

1136–37 The charge of **fraudulent votes** is unsubstantiated by the play. Like the news that Athena's wrath will last but a single day and dates from earlier blasphemy (758–78), this is late information for which the audience's calculus is hardly prepared. Comparable but much more significant dramatically is Neoptolemus' pronouncement on the cause of Philoctetes' suffering and its cure (*Phil* 1325–42).

1143–49b Menelaus makes an allegory from the familiar material of sailing in a storm. **Reckless:** Homer uses this word of turbulent winds.

Quenched, as Stanford notes, often means merely "stopped/checked," without any metaphorical relation to putting out a fire. Here the "hot" talk may vivify the metaphor a bit.

1163 Contest (*agôn*) anticipates Menelaus' return with force (1160).

1165–68 They recommend immediate burial; he prepares to protect the body, as if the proper rites of mourning may somehow yet be assured. Pausanias (1.35.3) reports a tomb of Ajax on the coast of the Troad. With those of the other eponymous heroes his statue was near the Athenian council house. An annual festival in his honor was celebrated on Salamis. The Athenian audience could hardly doubt that his body will be saved, but it could not expect Agamemnon to take a different line from his brother. As for the burial, two different conceptions are combined: on the one hand, Teucer should find a ready-made **hollow** for quick, easy interment; on the other, the **tomb** will be **a signal reminder,** i.e., a great mound such as Achilles foresees as a memorial for Patroclus and himself (*Iliad* 23.245–48).

1169–73 Teucer organizes a tableau around the body of Ajax. The child and Tecmessa, both without speaking parts, will remain near the body until the cortege carries it off at the end of the play. As before, however, all Teucer's attention is for the boy; she is nearly ignored.

Kindred touch and the whole of 1171–72 are a bit soft: "Come here, child, stand near and (like) a suppliant touch the father that begot you." In the former phrase a verb for wrapping the body for burial takes as its object a word signifying both grave and funeral rites, so there is an ellipsis: "clothing (the body for) the grave."

1173–81 The **lock** of hair is commonly offered as a dedication to the dead, but it is not an aspect of funeral rites. Teucer is treating the body as if it already has the powerful protective influence of the heroic dead. At the same time, the **suppliant's** station protects the body since the suppliant has put himself and all that he contacts under the eyes of the gods. Thus the relationship is reciprocal. Finally, in a curse, the clipping of the hair symbolically anticipates the fate of anyone who tears the suppliant from the body, i.e., he will be severed from **all his race.** Cf. the curse of Thyestes, *Agamemnon* 1601f. Jebb points out that those convicted of treason to Athens were not permitted burial in Attica; **unburied from his land and home** may be a mild anachronism. On the scene see Taplin, *Greek Tragedy in Action,* pp. 108–9; on supplication see chapter 8 in Vickers, *Towards Greek Tragedy.*

1181 Inclining is a compound from "fall": Ajax fell on the cattle (374), lies fallen among the slain animals ("relapsed" at 325), finds his great deeds and fame fallen (617), falls on his sword (829, 922), and is one that "falls on disasters sent by Heaven" (760–61). He prays that

Teucer may "lift him up" (827) and Eurysaces falls over him to protect him. Cf. on 1090.

1186 The tableau remains in place. Teucer's departure is a false start: he will return immediately without accomplishing his purpose. The brief lyric continues the lament. For the question beginning a lyric cf. 172.

1192–97 The stanza combines the familiar motifs of the first inventor (cf. *Prometheus Bound*, 440–504) and fantastic escape (see on *Tr* 953–61) with a wish (here hardened to **curse**). Note the opposites: "would that he had disappeared into the highest atmosphere or into the depths of Hades." **Generations of toils be made for us:** the **be** is apparently a typographical error for "he." The Greek is an exclamation, heavy with *p, o,* and *n: ô ponoi progonoi ponôn* ("O toils begetters of toils").

1198–1210 Balance, isometric clauses, parallelism, and anaphora are more significant in the Greek verse than in the English. The last sentence and line of the preceding stanza begins "that (man)" and the present stanza repeats it in the first position. Then follow two parallel clauses, each formed with "neither . . . nor"; both clauses have the same word ("delight") as the postponed object. To see the shape: "That man neither of garlands nor of deep cups gave to me a delightful share, nor the sweet clamor of the flute nor a nightlong, delightful sleep." Greek parties featured garlands and music as well as drink. The repeated **love** is in the genitive case and thus continues the construction "of garlands," etc. But **abridged and interdicted** legalizes a common verb meaning "stop/hinder from": "from love, from love, he kept me." The **dew** may be imitated from *Agamemnon* 560–61, where the herald complains less lyrically of working conditions before Troy.

1211–21 On **valorous** see 211. **Ward and cover** recalls the great shield of Ajax (577–78). **Handed over to** = "devoted/dedicated to," with allusive reference to Ajax as a sacrificial offering (see 815). While the Greek verb may suggest an animal consecrated to the god and left free to wander loose, it is also possible that the Greek is a middle voice denoting "he has dedicated himself to the *daimôn.*" **Joy** occurs twice in the previous stanza. The concluding wish more realistically (than 1192–95) imagines the last leg of a safe passage home (Cape **Sunium** is the southern promontory of Attica).

1224 Hateful = "awkward and stupid," a more scornful tone.

1225 In the *Iliad,* Agamemnon is the recognized leader of a very loosely organized, aristocratic group of princes who do not hesitate to criticize him and go their own way when they feel like it. Achilles' abuse (*Iliad* 1.122–29, 149–71, 225–44) condemns his greed, meanness, and cowardice.

1228 His **slave-woman mother** is Hesione, whom Telamon got as his booty from an earlier raid on Troy. The mockery and ad hominem invective (cf. "slave" at 1237) set the tone for a pair of speeches which seem to thwart any effective resolution of the plot.

1234–36 Menelaus has faithfully reported the sense of 1097–1108.

1238 At least his verbs are vivid. **Bawled** is elsewhere used of the croaking of a frog; cf. "yawp" (1226), which is appropriate to a slack-mouthed dog. "Wound" (1248) may suggest the pesky sting of a bee or wasp.

1252 In Sophocles **sense** is always recommended but seldom seen as the protagonist's virtue. For **advantage** see on 768–69.

1253–54 A small **whip** for a big **ox** looks proverbial; cf. Creon at *Ant* 476. We may think of Ajax attacking the cattle; Agamemnon, however, is thinking of **medicine** for Teucer.

1257 Shadow: cf. 126.

1259 For **learn moderation** see 587 ("submit"); cf. 1264.

1260–63 He returns to his initial topic, Teucer's illegitimacy. There is a mild anachronism here in that Athenian slaves could not **plead** their own cases before a court. **Barbarian** refers to Hesione's foreign origin.

1266 For **gratitude** (*charis*) see 522. **Fugitive** echoes "slips away" at 524. The paradox in **shown to deceive** derives from the fact that gratitude forgotten betrays the dead man's expectation of reciprocity (Jebb).

1269c The following incident cannot be referred to a particular episode in our *Iliad*. When the Trojans do fire a ship in *Iliad* 16, Ajax is beaten back and unable to protect it.

1283–89 Yet another (cf. on 662 and 818) reference to the duel in *Iliad* 7 between Ajax and Hector. There nine captains cast lots to see which will face the challenge of Hector (7.161–69), and Homer adds (7.179–80) that the army prays that either Ajax, Diomedes, or Agamemnon will win the lot. The **clod of moist earth** is the invention of the malicious Teucer and no doubt a familiar trick that the veterans in the theater would appreciate. The scholiast finds an allusion to Cresphontes, who used this ruse to win the rule of Messenia (Apollodorus 2.8.4).

1292–99 Agamemnon's grandfather **Pelops** was driven from Phrygia by Ilus. He migrated to Greece and eventually gave his name to the Peloponnesus. To gain revenge on his brother Thyestes, who had seduced his wife, Atreus invited him to a banquet where the main course was boiled stew of sons' flesh; see *Agamemnon* 1577–1611 for the story. Aerope was the **Cretan mother**. The better known story makes her father Catreus send her into exile when he learns from an oracle that one of his children will kill him. Here Sophocles follows a version that makes Catreus discover her in adultery (**interloping foreigner** dresses this up a bit), for which offense he sent her to Nauplius with orders that he drown her.

Nauplius, however, spared her, and she later married Atreus, father of Agamemnon. Greek myth sometimes treats Cretans as hostile foreigners, as in the legend of Minos, but seldom are they in the same class as barbarian Phrygians.

1299b–1303 For **Telamon, Laomedon,** and the gift of **Heracles** see on 434–37.

1311 **Clytemnestra, wife** of Agamemnon, has nothing to do with this war, but the recent references to adultery in the house may lead to an aspersion on her character. Helen was notoriously abused as the whore of Troy, and Teucer's question puts her and Clytemnestra in the same bag, indifferently.

1315–16 With **just in time** (*kairos*) cf. Teucer's "just in time" (1169) and Odysseus' "just as I need you" (35); see also the note at *OK* 631. Contrast the view of Odysseus at 149–52; the coryphaeus has no new reason to see him as peacemaker, and his reputation as a diplomat is hardly at work in this play. The audience has witnessed his sympathetic attitude at the end of the prologue and is thus better prepared than the chorus and Teucer for his mediation.

Odysseus comes in the nick of time to resolve the dramatic dilemma and avert an inevitable fight. In this capacity he serves as a kind of *deus ex machina.*

1319 **Valiant** = "martial" at 401, a Homeric word that signals his goodwill.

1330–31 As a traditional confidant and **friend** of Agamemnon, Odysseus is well qualified to arbitrate and persuade. See *Odyssey* 11.387–464 for their cordial exchange in Hades and *Agamemnon* 841–42 for Agamemnon's regard.

1334–35 **Vindictiveness** = "violence" (*bia*); **right** is *dikê* (*Ant* 451). With **trample** cf. Haemon's "tread down the gods' due" (*Ant* 745).

1340–41 The sentiment is precisely Homer's:

Among the men far the best was Telamonian Aias
while Achilleus stayed angry, since he was far best of all of them.
(*Iliad* 2.768–69)

1342 **Wrong** is the negative of **right** (1335); "foul thing" (1344) also appeals to *dikê* (i.e., "it is not right"). **To do . . . injury** = "to dishonor."

1344–45 For the **gods' laws** and burial see *Ant* 450–60. Many Greeks would not stick at kicking the dead enemy: Electra recommends throwing out the body of Aegisthus (for the dogs), Clytemnestra and Aegisthus mutilate the body of Agamemnon, and Achilles drags the dead Hector behind his chariot (*El* 1487–90, *Libation Bearers* 439–43, *Iliad* 24.14–18). But just as Apollo protects Hector's corpse, so there is usually in Greek literature an enlightened voice protesting such vindictiveness. Odysseus' appeal is essentially that of Antigone, and his argument from the gods' laws would have about as much chance of success, were he not the friend and henchman of Agamemnon (1353, 1370–73).

1346 In the prologue Athena mocked Ajax by calling herself his ally (90 and 117); now Odysseus "fights on his behalf" (= **take his part**).

1347–49 Fair and **unworthy** appeal to "nobility" (as at 479; cf. "best" at *Ant* 72).

1350 Reverence translates the same verb stem as "bow before" (*Ajax* at 667). To treat the body piously would be to show respect for the dead warrior.

1352 The line applies to both Ajax and Odysseus; more naturally here of Ajax, as Odysseus takes it.

1353 Yield to = "are conquered by," with the not very vigorous paradox after **victory** (*kratos* stem).

1354 Interceding for = "doing a favor (*charis*) for"; again in 1371 ("at your request" = "for you").

1355–57 For nobility see *Ajax* at 479–80. For **greatness** (*aretê*) see on *Phil* 1417–21. Ajax is unable to accept mutability. Now an old foe tries to save him, and to rehabilitate his reputation, by arguing that we must accept change as a necessary fixture.

1361 With **rigid** cf. the same word at *Ant* 473; Creon condemns the "rigid spirit" of those like Antigone. It is "harsh words" at 1119 of this play.

1363 Generous returns to the *dikê* stem (see "right" at 1335).

1365 That necessity is death: we are all going to die and want burial.

1370–73 Although Agamemnon relents and permits the burial, he is not persuaded; his gesture is a favor (*charis*) to Odysseus.

1388–92 Rot is more concrete than the Greek (see on "ignominy" at 218); the same stem is translated **outrage** at 1392, where the verb "to cast out" is also repeated. For the **Furies** see on 834–43 (Ajax' curse). **Justice** (*dikê*) is traditionally the daughter of Zeus; the **Furies** are invoked as the chthonic agents of his will. For the triad of Olympian god, abstract noun personified, and Fury cf. *Iliad* 19.87 (Zeus, Destiny, and the Fury).

1394 Teucer's refusal to let Odysseus participate in the burial can be attributed to regard for the sensibility of the dead, whose anger is not likely to be placated; Kamerbeek compares *El* 431–35. Nonetheless, we may feel that his exclusion strikes a somewhat discordant note in the ethical resolution: Odysseus has saved the form but, in Teucer's view, cannot mend the substance of Ajax' alienation.

1407 The body must be bathed before burial, but it is not certain that the **cauldron** and armor (1409b) need be brought on. No great time should be wasted forming the cortege, but if attendants are ready with the armor, the final spectacle may be more impressive. It is possible that Teucer addresses the chorus and simply anticipates the ceremony to follow the exit. The chorus, which will form up to escort the body out, should not be dispersed for these chores.

1410 Tecmessa is still on stage, but it is the son of Ajax who, as before, is the central figure.

1419a I speak of Ajax is feeble and the line has been condemned. The beginning and ending of plays were particularly susceptible to alteration in later productions and to mutilation in transmission. These anapests (from 1403) have aroused suspicion for various reasons, even though there is little doubt that the play concludes with a procession carrying the hero's body away for burial.

1419b–20 It is hard to disagree with this tag, harder still to find any particular point.

The Women of Trachis

*H*OMER *AND* HESIOD are both familiar with Heracles and a variety of his adventures. For Achilles (*Iliad* 18.117–19) Heracles is the paradigmatic hero who, for all his strengh and divine connections with his father Zeus, still had to yield to death and the anger of Hera. Yet Homer also knows of Heracles' deification, as we see from Odysseus report of his own visit to the underworld:

> After him I was aware of powerful Herakles;
> his image, that is, but he himself among the immortal
> gods enjoys their festivals, married to a sweet-stepping
> Hebe, child of great Zeus and Hera of the golden sandals.
> (*Odyssey* 11.601–4)

Already in Heracles' speech to Odysseus, the theme of the laboring bondman is clearly articulated:

> For I was son of Kronian Zeus, but I had an endless
> spell of misery. I was made bondman to one who was far worse
> than I, and he loaded my difficult labors on me.
> (*Odyssey* 11.620–22)

Apart from Hesiod's "Shield of Heracles" (it is 480 lines long), no long narrative about Heracles has survived, though we know of several poems devoted to various aspects of his labors, including his journey to Hades where, according to Bacchylides (*Epinician* 5.165–75), Heracles asked the hero Meleager if he had a sister whom Heracles might marry. That woman was Deianira.

In the tradition (e.g., Apollodorus 2.7.5), Deianira, the daughter of Oeneus and Althaea, was the second wife of Heracles. He had previously been married to Megara, by whom he had children. Unlike the version in our play, the usual story seems to have made Megara the wife during the time of his labors. According to Euripides' *Heracles*, the hero returned home to Thebes, having finally absolved himself of his debt to Eurystheus, to find his wife (Megara), father (Amphitryon), and children threatened by the tyrant Lycus, who, thinking Heracles dead, intended to kill the entire family. In that play, Heracles arrives in the nick of time, kills Lycus, saves his family, and then, in one of the most stunning reversals of fortune on the Greek stage, is driven insane by the goddess Madness while he prepares to make a sacrifice of thanksgiving. In his crazed condition he imagines his family is the family of Eurystheus, and he kills them all, except his father, who is saved by the intervention of Athena. Some writers in fact put these murders before his labors and explain the servitude to Eurystheus as an expiation for the death of Megara and his children. In any case, the usual version seems to have made Deianira the wife of his last days, after the labors and after the murder of his first family. Sophocles, on the other hand, says nothing of Megara and writes as if all the labors have taken place since Heracles won Deianira (31–35).

One or two other variations deserve notice. First, Deianira's name means "husband-destroyer," and in the tradition she seems to have belonged to the masculine warrior type familiar from the Amazons, the Lemnian women, and Atalanta. Sophocles, however, makes no punning use of this name and portrays Deianira as a thoroughly feminine wife whose murder of her husband is not only involuntary but even the occasion for her own suicide. Second, the tradition connects the death of Nessus, Deianira's supposed love charm, and the drug that kills Heracles (see lines 572–77). We do not know whether Sophocles or an earlier poet closed the circle on Heracles by making the Hydra's blood the means of his death. A fragment of Hesiod's catalogue, however, gives evidence for the charm ("drug" as both poets call it) and its association with the shirt:

> thoughtful Deianira, who overcome by the strength of Heracles
> bare him Hyllus, and Glenus and Ctesippus and Oneites. These she
> bare and she did a terrible thing [when infatuate of mind]:
> annointing a shirt with a drug she gave it to the herald Lichas to
> carry. And Lichas gave it to his lord Heracles, the son of
> Amphitryon, the sacker of cities. And as soon as he received it the
> end of death was on him.
>
> (frag. 25.17–24; my translation)

What was her motivation? Iole, the captive daughter of Eurytus, is already mentioned by Hesiod (frag. 26.31), so it seems even at an early date Heracles' lust led to the sack of Oechalia. Bacchylides (*Dithyramb* 16) certainly connects the arrival of the slave girl with Deianira's "tearful plan." Unfortunately, we do not know whether Bacchylides' poem or Sophocles' *Women of Trachis* was the earlier, but the versions are so similar in content and tone that imitation seems more likely than is usual in such matters (nothing, however, excludes their mutual debt to a still earlier source; e.g., we know that Archilochus wrote of Heracles, Deianira, and Nessus).

Most vase paintings that can with certainty be dated prior to the play show Heracles killing Nessus with his sword or club; it may be that Sophocles introduced, if not the bow, at least the poisoned arrow. This motif connects the beginning and end of Heracles' labors and provides a powerfully unifying symbol for the fire that at once purifies and destroys. Having killed the Hydra, Heracles took its poisonous blood to tip his arrows; thus he adopted guile as much as force for fulfilling his labors, and it is by the guile of Nessus as well as of the innocent Deianira that he dies. Sophocles may have also been the first to bring Iole into the presence of Deianira, a scene particularly praised for the way its pathos highlights the sensitive character of Deianira. The oracle that riddles ambiguously on Heracles' fate (1159ff.) may be another invention of Sophocles; its gradual, piecemeal revelation is one of those elements that leads Jameson (Introduction, p. 65) to argue that it is "the discovery of the end of Heracles that gives the play its unity."

The ancient audience was steeped in these legends. Unlike its modern counterpart, the Greek audience came to the theater expecting a new version of the familiar. One problem for modern readers is that, much as we may know about some myths (especially in the case of such a popular figure as Heracles), we can be sure that the preceding summary, no matter how supplemented from modern learning, would not do justice to the Greek riches. Yet we can be certain that the theatrical experience was a meeting between versions: as in the medieval mystery plays and Shakespeare's histories, the play confronts the audience with a realization of the more or less familiar. The playwright may invent small (Deianira sends Hyllus for news) or significant details (the Hydra's blood as the poison that kills Heracles?), he may ignore versions (what happened to Megara?), he may invert and rearrange (did Heracles send for the robe or was it Deianira's idea?), but he can never either escape the audience's preparation or assume that he is creating a fictional world into which the audience will be absorbed in willing disbelief, or which, to put it another way, is completely integral and dependent upon his own imaginative projection. Hence we cannot accept, however convenient, the rule that what is not in the play and explicitly mentioned by the playwright must not be taken into account. Mikalson states this view succinctly: "If Sophocles had wished to introduce an event so momentous for the understanding of Heracles and Zeus as an apotheosis, he would have done so explicitly. . . . In the *Trachiniae* he chose not to deify Heracles." (note 6, p. 92) In this play there is no explicit reference to the apotheosis; yet every Greek in the audience knew of it. Nor is there any connection between the apotheosis and the pyre on Oeta; yet the pattern of reference, allusion, and imagery finds its only unified meaning in that conjunction. This is not to say that Sophocles is asking the audience to do his work or assuming that it will take his meaning for granted. Rather, dramatic tension in such a play meets at exactly that hypothetical but unrealized intersection of received legend(s) and allusive reference: what the audience may assume is never affirmed, the apotheosis is never granted, and that, too, is part of the reinvented dramatic fabric.

Scene: It is not necessary to bring the nurse on with Deianira. The monologue is not addressed to the nurse, and Deianira's isolation may be more strongly focused by letting the nurse enter only at the end of the speech.

1–48 This is the only extant Sophoclean play to begin with a monologue, a frequent device in Euripides. The speech is not Euripidean in style, however, being more personal, more introspective, and more intimately connected with subsequent events of the play than the typical Euripidean monologue. A comparison with *Andromache* 1–55 will illustrate the difference amid superficial similarities (Andromache's husband Neoptolemus is away; she is persecuted by his wife Hermione; after the monologue she is comforted by a household slave; the theme of mutability is introduced immediately in her speech, as here, but what follows is much more exposition than personal reflection).

1–5 Deianira introduces a commonplace of Greek moral wisdom ("look to the end") as a foil to her personal experience. Solon (see Herodotus 1.32) said that he would not judge a man happy and prosperous until he had seen how his life ended. She has already experienced an evil fortune (*tychê*), yet, as the final lines of the speech will reveal, she is apprehensive of still greater sorrow. For some variations on the theme of mutability see 296–97, 943–46, *OK* 1529–30, *Agamemnon* 928–29. **Death's house** is Hades.

6–9 Pleuron is in the northwestern district of Aetolia. **Oeneus**, father of Deianira and the hero Meleager, is best known for causing the Calydonian boar hunt. When he failed to sacrifice to Artemis, the goddess sent a wild boar to ravage his country. She has lived a life of **fear** (cf. 23, 28–29, 50–51). Cf. Io's "nightly terror" at the prospect of divine lust (*Prometheus Bound* 640ff.). The **Acheloüs** is the largest river of Aetolia. Rivers are regularly also male divinities in Greek religion and myth and are often credited with rape or seduction. Sophocles made a play about one such woman, Tyro, who had children by the river Enipeus (or Poseidon).

11–17 Her fear of marriage is not due to frigidity but to the monstrous form of her suitor. Water divinities (e.g., Nereus, Proteus, Thetis) are particularly adept at sudden transformations.

The spacing between lines 17 and 18, like that between 35 and 36, does not indicate a gap in the text but rather the translator's feeling for a pause in the narrative.

18–26 **Famous** translates the same word Oedipus uses of himself ("great" at *OK* 8); in both cases it refers to reputation won by achievement. The **contest** is described in the first stasimon (503–30). Any divinity who brings victory may be styled **of the contests**. At 515 Aphrodite is called the "referee" because love motivates both contestants. **Zeus,** the most powerful god, brings victory to the stronger, and of course he has a special interest in his son; cf. 140, 200, 238, 275–79, 288–89, and 303 for a few of the many references to Zeus early in this play. **The end** (the Greek stem *tel-*) denotes fulfillment and accomplishment; it introduces one of the unifying themes of the play (cf. 36, 79, and the notes to 155–74).

30 Time and timeliness are prominent themes (notes at 26, 44, 57–60; 228, 247); **night** is an important early motif in this complex (see 94–95, 131, 132, 149).

31–33 Heracles comes home no more often than a farmer visits a remote field. For **sows** of begetting children see *OK* 1257 and 1498; the subject of the narrative (Heracles) and of the simile (the farmer) are fused in the image.

35 In fact he serves Eurystheus, whom Deianira will not mention. Freedom and slavery make a pair of antithetical themes through the play. We have already heard how Heracles set Deianira free (21) and how she remains the captive of fear and anxiety (5, 28–29; cf. 37 and 47–48). Heracles has served both Eurystheus and Omphale (70–73, 248–50); for this second humiliating slavery Heracles swore that he would enslave Eurytus and his family (255–57), and he sends slaves home (245)—ironically, since he himself is "completely vanquished" by love (489). Certain dramatic elements reinforce these themes: the nurse's self-conscious role as slave (52–53); Deianira's sensitivity to that role (61–63); the messenger's willingness to profit from Deianira's gratitude (190–91); the procession of slaves who were once free (301–2).

36 In a typical Sophoclean paradox the **end** of trouble brings the greatest fear. An interest in suspense is implied in her vague apprehension and in the gradual way the murder of Iphitus (38), the length of absence (44–45), and Heracles' last instructions (46) will be linked.

38–39 **Mighty Iphitus** translates a periphrasis in the Homeric manner, i.e., "he killed the strength of Iphitus"; see also 1048–50. For the death of Iphitus, son of Eurytus, see Lichas' report at 270–73. Prior to the murder, they had lived at Tiryns (in the Argolid). Forced into exile, they went north to **Trachis** on the gulf of Malis in southern Thessaly where Ceyx, king of Trachis and cousin of Heracles, the **stranger** (i.e., a host who acts as guest-friend) has given them sanctuary.

43 **Trouble** is repeated in 47 and appears again in a cognate form as "sorrow" in 48.

44 **Time** is critical, as we learn later (79–81, 164–74, 821–30). The Greek actually says "fifteen months" (as at 164–65).

46 The content and true meaning of the prophecies on this tablet remain a question through much of the play. Cf. 77, 79–81, 169–74, 1159–72.

There isn't a play without prophecy; it may be oracular (from Delphi or Dodona) or vatic (Calchas, Teiresias, or Helenus); it is always taken seriously, usually held to be authoritative, and always validated by the events of the play. Seers like Teiresias are more readily doubted than divinely sanctioned oracles. Such prophecy predicts, as in the case of Oedipus' birth and fate, or commands ("rid Thebes of her pollution"; "keep Ajax within for a day!") and may be used to explain (*Phil* 1314–48; invoking Helenus, Neoptolemus expounds the meaning of Philoctetes' lot). Obeying an oracle's command or discovering what it means or if it is true may constitute the primary energy of the play or the impulse for a scene and decision. In the *Oedipus* the veracity of Apollo's predictions gradually becomes the central concern of the king; in the *Ajax* Calchas confides that the day of wrath must find Ajax in this tent, and immediately a search for him begins. In the *Electra* (33–39) Orestes reports a seemingly unambiguous command, but even there we find "if Apollo has prophesied well" (1424), and some readers have wondered if he has. There is nothing equivocal about Teiresias' prediction in the *Antigone* (999–1090), but in most cases every such pronouncement is somehow problematic, uncertain, or riddling. Testing an oracle does not strike the Greeks as impious. The audience may know the truth and wait for the protagonist to discover it, as in both Oedipus plays; or the prophecy may be revealed partially or gradually, as here, so that for a time at least the audience itself is implicated in the riddle. Thus a significant aspect of resolution and closure derives from our realization that the prophecy makes sense; hardly secondary for the Greek is the satisfaction that comes from knowing the gods observe and are involved in the affairs of men.

49 The slave as confidante was a familiar role to Athenian audiences. Cf., e.g., *El* 30–32 (a male) and 80–88 and Euripides, *Andromache* 56, where another slave woman counsels her mistress after an introductory monologue. Similar roles, with more dramatic scope, will be found in Euripides' *Medea* and *Hippolytus*.

54–57 Although we have been told that the whole family is here (39), Alcmena and some of the children are away (see 1151–55). **Hyllus** was a well-known figure among the children of Heracles: the audience knew him as the son who married Iole, continued the line of descent, and led his clan back to Greece to reclaim their rightful heritage. (See Apollodorus 2.8.1–2 and, for their flight from Eurystheus after Heracles' death, Euripides *Heraclidae* 45.)

57–60 At all should not be taken as impudent or skeptical. She is properly deferential; her thought leads to the happy chance of his arrival. Such coincidence is not uncommon (cf. 391–92 and *Ant* 386–87). **Of any value** (*kairos*) means "opportune" and so "timely."

61–62 For the metaphor from dice cf. Aeschylus, *Agamemnon* 32 and this line from an unknown play of Sophocles:

"the dice of Zeus always fall well."
(frag. 895, Radt)

69–70 Cf. Lichas' report concerning his service to Omphale (the **Lydian woman**), queen of the Amazons (248–53). **Service** echoes "serve" at 35; cf. "laborious service" at 356. We may wonder that Hyllus knows of a year's slavery while his mother does not. Sophocles seems to have conceived her as an innocent in a world of monsters. She knows and understands very little but is ready to believe. This innocent credulity will be her undoing, as well as Heracles'.

73 She asks whether he is **alive or dead** because of the ambiguity of **is free now.**

74 Euboea is the long island stretching from the eastern coast of Attica north toward Trachis. **The city of Eurytus** is Oechalia, not so far away as this conversation might suggest (see on 237–38).

76–77 Since there is no indication that the prophecy actually mentioned Oechalia, or any *place* for that matter (see 155–74), it appears that Deianira makes her inference from the temporal coincidence (see 173–74). **True** means "credible."

79–81 Here two *tel-* stems (cf. 26) combine with reference to **life** and **time** to suggest a culminating event or crisis. It also appears in "end" (824 and 825), "last" (1150), and "complete" (1171). The apparent alternative turns out, as Heracles sees at 1169–73, to be no alternative at all, but rather an ambiguous double reference to the end of labor and suffering. Cf. the messenger's terse summary at *Aj* 802: "one day . . . life or death."

82 In the balance is a metaphor from weighing in scales; cf. *OC* 1508 and *Aj* 130–32.

84 This line is omitted because it is thought to be interpolation.

85 As in the *Ajax,* so in the *Women of Trachis:* one fate, one life, one day, everything hinges on the fortune of a single man. Such concentration is typical of the extant plays.

91 Fate here is simply "this business." Exit Hyllus and Nurse, and perhaps Deianira.

94–140 The parodos is composed of two pairs of responsive stanzas with a final epode (132–40).

94–99 As a traveler across the face of the earth, the Sun sees all and can report where Heracles is; cf. *OC* 868–69 and *Agamemnon* 632–33. Night is despoiled because the new light drives off the stars which are her ornaments; despoiled also means "killed" and so with birth suggests a cycle of life and death. The Greeks reckoned each new day from the evening rather than the morning; consequently, night precedes day and can be said to give birth to the sun. The translator (see his note p. 70) accepts Lloyd-Jones' view that sea-narrows and twin continents refer respectively to the Dardanelles and Gibraltar, which are then taken to refer to east and west; cf. *OK* 195–96. Other commentators are content with "on land or sea." Rest suggests leaning or reclining on (or against), and Dawe (*Studies* 3, p. 79) dismisses the notion of a gigantic Heracles bestriding Europe and Africa. The strait of Gibralter is between the "pillars of Heracles." The sense is probably "is he resting at the pillars of Heracles?" Brilliance of lightning = "with brilliant flash/gleam."

103–11 Having heard of Deianira's grief, they come to console her. The unhappy bird may be the nightingale (cf. *El* 149 and note), but see also *Ant* 423–26. Lines 106–7 may also be translated "never lays to rest the longing of tearless eyes," where "tearless" is proleptic, i.e., it anticipates the effect of crying until she is tearless (thus Dawe, *Studies* 3, p. 80). Since lays to bed translates the same verb found at 95, we have an implicit equation: Deianira = Night; Heracles = the Sun.

112–21 The simile, implicitly comparing Heracles to a swimmer at sea, is not altogether congruent. The first image (112–16) asks us to imagine the rolling waves of a wind-driven sea, one huge wave following another, while the second half (the referent is Heracles) suggests less regularity (twisted, an emendation, indicates a turning rather than a rise and fall). Elevated is more responsive to the initial image (he is carried to the top of a wave). If we stay with the manuscript, we have (for "twisted") "one wave nurtures him (in its folds, i.e., carries him down in the trough), while the next elevates him." Campbell compares *OK* 374a where Oedipus says to Teiresias that he is "nurtured by one long night." The ambiguous idea of Heracles hidden away yet cared for suits their optimistic uncertainty. Heracles is not literally **the descendant of Cadmus** but is thus named as the adopted son of Thebes. The **Cretan** sea pounds the south coast of that island tremendously. Lines 120–21 echo the confidence of Hyllus (88–89).

122–31 The stage direction belongs to the translator. The lines imply but do not necessitate Deianira's presence (choruses do address absent characters, but the personal appeal is more to the point if she is present). Hope (**expectation**) and fear are frequently fused at the beginning of Aeschylean tragedy, and the same atmosphere may be found early in the *Ajax* and *Oedipus the King*. Deianira's pessimism resembles, without the fierce aggressiveness, Electra's. The verb is active: "you should not wear away all expectation of good." The **all-accomplishing king** is Zeus, who from the *Iliad* (24.527–33) on is known as the dispenser of good and evil. **Circling** recalls the waves of 112–16 (cf. *Aj* 351–53); it also is used naturally of constellations moving through the heavens (hence the comparison to Ursa Major, the **Bear**). For the "wheel of fortune" see Herodotus 1.207, where Croesus observes that "human life is like a revolving wheel and never allows the same man to continue long in prosperity." **Grief** is the same word translated "trouble" at 43, and **joy** is what the messenger will bring (see on 179, and cf. 135 and 201).

132–40 This stanze is an epode, i.e., a nonresponsive unit outside the pattern of strophe/antistrophe. The repetition of **shimmering night** from the first line of the parodos (94) neatly formalizes the motif of cyclic fortune. **Calamity** translates *kêres*, which in earlier poetry are death-spirits; in Sophocles the singular often = Fate (e.g., "doom" at *Phil* 1164), but the Aeschylean meaning (*Agamemnon* 206) and tone are perhaps still functioning at *OK* 473 (note). **Expectations:** see 125. **Careless:** Zeus's neglect of his children is notorious, but the pious chorus wants to encourage its friend.

142–43 **Learn ... suffering** (in the Greek the two words are adjacent) is a variation on an Aeschylean formula (see on *Agamemnon* 176–78) and a significant theme in this play (cf. 151–52, 582–83, 1145, and *OK* 404). Whitman entitles his chapter on the play "Late Learning."

144 **The young thing:** Thetis compares the growth of her son Achilles to that of "a young tree" (*Iliad* 18.56), and Odysseus compares the girl Nausicaa to a palm tree (*Odyssey* 6.160–68). As she begins, Deianira thinks of the youthful chorus, but it is her own attitude and experience which are reflected in 149–52. **Grows** = "pastures/feeds"; cf. *Aj* 559a.

155–74 Note the concentration of words referring to time and limit. The *tel-* stem occurs in 156 ("last"), 170, and 174 ("come true"). The foreboding of Heracles himself serves to explain Deianira's anxiety. She is sometimes described as timorous, but his manner, since he was usually cocky (159–60), justifies her fears. Everything in the present passage points to an oracle solely concerned with a crucial temporal limit. There is no textual evidence that the oracle specifically mentioned Oechalia.

169–70 There is some ambiguity in the Greek sentence. Cf. "Such, he declared, were the things fated by the gods to be the issue of the toils of Heracles" (Easterling) and "Such, he said, was the doom ordained by the gods to be accomplished in the toils of Heracles" (Jebb, where "in" means "in regard to").

171–72 Dodona in the northwestern district of Thesprotia was the greatest oracle of Zeus. Apart from a tradition of Delphic hostility (see Apollodorus 2.6.2), Heracles would naturally turn to his father's prophets. The priestess (called **Doves**, Greek *Peleiades*) may have interpreted the sound of wind in the rustling leaves of the sacred oak or the flight of birds in the tree (Pausanias 7.21.1 and 10.12.5). See Heracles' report at 1166–71.

177 Cf. "best of all men" (811). The primary meaning of **finest** is martial, not marital.

177–79 In the Greek her last word is **deprived,** which is immediately taken as a bad **omen** by the women, who have spotted the messenger and think her word may be connected with his message. For other exclamations at unlucky speech see *Aj* 362 and *El* 1211. The wreath (**laurel**) on the messenger's head indicates good news, and the Greek actually contains a phrase meaning his speech will be "joyous." Cf. *OK* 80–84.

180 One of the dramatic novelties of the play is the use of two messengers. This one anticipates Lichas and later reveals Lichas' covert deception. For the theme in **free** see 21, 70–72, 248–57. The Greek suggests "release" (as at 1170). **Mistress** need not mean that he belongs to the house. His manner is not excessively deferential. In the interview with Lichas this man aggressively takes over the questioning, with more interest in the truth than we might expect from a stranger (see 335–92). Yet Lichas apparently does not know him (429–30, 434–35).

183 First fruits are the best spoils of battle, selected for sacrifice and dedication to the gods; see 760–62.

191 Profit is the usual motive of the lower classes; cf. 231, *OK* 1006 and Oedipus' offer of reward (*OK* 232).

193–99 The seemingly trivial restraint on Lichas rings a variation on a primary theme (see on 180 and 35). With **Not want . . . want** cf. the similarly playful use of this figure at *Ant* 275–76.

200 Nearby Mt. **Oeta** (above Thermopylae) will be the site for Heracles' funeral pyre (see 1191–99 and the note to 1198–1202). On it was a precinct of **Zeus** (cf. 436–37) which was **unharvested** because it was sacred to the god (at 238 we hear of the founding of such a precinct, the harvest from which is dedicated to Zeus).

203–4 By a common idiom the Greek here reads "eye" (translated **sunshine**), a word often used for anything dear, beloved, or encouraging. Deianira returns to "eye" at 226, thus making a ring around the lyric (see on "night" at 132–40). **Risen high** suggests the rising sun (hence the translator's "sunshine"), though strictly it modifies "eye." **Pluck** (= "harvest" and so "enjoy") comes paradoxically after 200, as if Zeus, in return for the holy meadow, had given a bounty of joy which they now harvest.

205–23 This brief lyric is astrophic and predominately iambic in rhythm. Cf. the song at *Aj* 693, which also follows unexpected good news.

205–15 Joyous shouting translates the Greek verb for "song/shout" at successful sacrifice or victory. Unwed **girls** are often called upon for religious celebration; they would naturally sing for Artemis, Hera, or Athena. **Apollo defender** has a statue in front of houses (cf. *El* 637). His weapons are the bow and arrows, and the **paean** is a song of victory as well as epithet of the god of healing (cf. 221 and *OK* 154). **Artemis**, the twin sister of Apollo, is said to have been born on the island of Ortygia ("Quail Island," near Delos, where Apollo was born; see Homeric *Hymn to Apollo* 16). Cf. *OC* 1090–92 and *OK* 201–7, where brother and sister are also paired. **Torches** are proper to her nocturnal alter egos, Hecate and the Moon (Selene). Cf. the reference to "Malian nymphs" at *Phil* 723. **Nymphs** are female spirits of the countryside. Cf. *OK* 1107, *Ant* 1127, *Phil* 1453.

216–20 As their excitement grows, the chorus invokes Dionysus. **Master of my heart** refers to ecstatic possession (Euripides *Bacchae* 73 ff.); the **flute, ivy,** dance (220), and shout **Euoi** are all characteristic of Bacchic worship.

221–23 As if about to return to praise of Apollo (210), the chorus invokes him as **Paean,** only to see Lichas and the captives approaching. They call Deianira's (**dear lady**) attention to the procession.

226 The Greek periphrasis (cf. on 38–39) represented by **sentinel eyes** draws particular attention to the act of watching (cf. 241, 303–4, 306, 523–25). Long (p. 103) sees such periphrases as this and "accomplished fact" (230)—both noun phrases in Greek, i.e., "guardianship of the eye" and "accomplishment of fact"—as marks of an elevated style. The repeated **welcome** is also at home in the high style.

235 The triple assertion of the same idea, with each unit longer and thus more emphatic, elaborates the thought and leads, in the last phrase, to a definition by opposition ("well, not ill"). As Easterling says, when we see Heracles, **burdened by disease** will precisely describe his condition.

236–38 Since Hyllus reported a rumor (74), the question is legitimate. Cape **Cenaean** extends to the west from the northern end of Euboea. Heracles is consecrating a sacred precinct to Zeus. For **harvest** see on 183 and cf. 200–204.

239–41 Such a **vow,** a promise to honor a god in return for divine favor, was common; see, e.g., Clytemnestra's argument and the notes to *Agamemnon* 931–35. **Women** were commonly enslaved after the sack of a city. Jebb cites Herodotus 6.134 for prisoners of war selected to be temple slaves. In *Iliad* 1, Agamemnon and Achilles fight over slave girls who were given to them as their share of the booty. In the *Agamemnon,* the king brings home Cassandra to be his concubine (see on 329).

248–90 This speech purports to explain the reasons for Heracles' slavery to **Omphale,** queen of the Amazons, and his recent siege of Oechalia. Much of it must be true, but the manner of telling (somewhat offhand, allusive, without regard for chronological sequence) and the omission of Heracles' love for Iole create problems. Lichas was more candid before he reached the palace (see 351–54). What we would like to know is when Heracles fell in love with Iole and how that love affected his relations with her father Eurytus. Since this particular episode in Heracles' story is old, dating from the epic *Sack of Oechalia,* and was probably known to at least some in the audience in more than one version, Sophocles may have been able to presume a little on his audience's prior knowledge. While Lichas does not blatantly lie, he does cover up, and in doing so he may muddle the facts and their sequence a bit.

248–58 Heracles treacherously killed Iphitus, son of Eurytus (270–73). For this crime Zeus (274–80) caused Heracles to be sold into a year's slavery so that he might be cleansed of blood guilt (258: **pure**). He became the slave of **Omphale.** Such punishment is known from other stories; e.g., Apollo killed the Cyclopes and was forced by Zeus to serve Admetus, king of Pherae, for a year (see *Alcestis* 1–10). Humiliated by his slavery to a woman (cf. 1062–63), Heracles vowed revenge on Eurytus (**the author of his suffering**). Since Eurytus can hardly be held responsible for Heracles' bondage, at least not on the evidence we have, this oath was probably no more than a pretext for returning to Oechalia to claim by force the girl Eurytus had refused him. Normally a homicide had to flee into exile and there find someone willing to perform the rites absolving from the crime (see Orestes' report of his own exile and absolution, *Eumenides* 443–52).

259 Strangers means "mercenaries."

261–73 The narrative, having advanced to events subsequent to the Lydian slavery, now returns to the events prior to the slavery. The Greek says that Eurytus **alone of mortals** *shared* responsibility (i.e., with Zeus). **An old friend** alludes to guest friendship from the days when Eurytus had taught the young Heracles archery. An alternative version, found in Apollodorus and probably known to Sophocles, is worth comparison:

> After his labours Heracles went to Thebes and gave Megara [his first wife, whose children he had killed in a fit of madness] to Iolaus [his nephew; cf. 1224], and, wishing himself to wed, he ascertained that Eurytus, prince of Oechalia had proposed the hand of his daughter Iole as a prize to him who should vanquish himself and his sons in archery. So he came to Oechalia, and, though he proved himself better than them at archery, yet he did not get the bride; for while Iphitus, the elder of Eurytus's sons, said that Iole should be given to Heracles, Eurytus and the others refused, and said they feared that, if he got children, he would again kill his offspring.
>
> (Apollodorus 2.6.1.)

In Lichas' speech no reason is given for Eurytus' anger (why did he **thunder greatly?**), and it is only conjecture, based on Apollodorus' story, that he resented a murderer's suit for Iole (as we know from the story of Oenomaus, Hippodamia, and Pelops, fathers do not always want their daughters married, even though the girl is offered as a prize). Or he may have resented the fact that his pupil challenged his teacher (Heracles had previously killed his tutor in music, Linus).

265 Because Heracles' bow and arrows were the gift of Apollo, they were **inescapable.** We should join Dawe and Bergk in suspecting a lost line after 264; in it a verb meaning "to fight" would have given a typical antithesis between words and deeds: "he thundered against him in words and with malice in his heart fought against him."

267 As for speech is Pearson's emendation and refers to the free man Eurystheus ordering about his slave Heracles. This interpretation of a difficult passage does not seem to have won favor, but the general sense of Eurytus' abuse is clear.

268 He got him drunk interprets the text, perhaps too freely, since Heracles is well known for getting drunk without anyone's help. Cf. *Alcestis* 755ff., and 788ff.; in the second passage Heracles recommends, in a world where uncertain chance rules all—drink and love. Did he while drunk make advances to Iole and thus cause her outraged father to throw him out? See 359–60.

274–78 Heracles' treacherous murder of Iphitus is all the worse for the fact that Iphitus is his guest, and this is the essence of his guilt in the Homeric version:

[Iphitus] came to the son of Zeus, strong-hearted,
the man called Herakles, guilty of monstrous actions,
who killed Iphitos while he was a guest in his household;
hard man, without shame for the watchful gods, nor the table
he had set for Iphitos, his guest; and when he had killed him
he kept the strong-footed horses for himself in his palace.
(Odyssey 21.25–30)

In his version Lichas stresses wrongful **guile** (*dolos*) rather than violated hospitality. Neither Homer nor Apollodorus mentions guile, and this motif may have been invented by Sophocles; cf. "treacherous" at 832, "treacherous words," "treachery," and "false-faced" at 838, 850, and 1050. Heracles kills Iole's brother by guile and is himself guilefully killed by Nessus and Deianira.

280 Foul play translates *hybris*, which might be properly said of Eurytus' behavior but hardly of Iphitus. Lichas serves his master as best he can.

282 Hell is not a particularly happy translation of the Greek Hades, the house of all the dead and not merely of the arrogant.

283–85 The lot of these slaves reflects the mutability theme; cf. 301–2. Historians provide numerous examples of a victorious army slaughtering the men and enslaving women and children; see, e.g., Thucydides 3.68.

291–92 For the choral leader's response to a long speech prior to the more interested character's response see *El* 764–65, *Phil* 318–19, *Ant* 278–79.

293–97 Deianira's native anxiety inclines to caution even at good news. That the prosperous man is most likely to stumble (**fall**) is a commonplace. The metaphor is one of tripping or stumbling on a road or course; cf. *Aj* 452, *Tr* 719, 727. Here it follows the running in **keep pace with.** For prosperity tripped up see Aeschylus, *Persians* 163.

298–306 Pity for the captives (cf. 243) leads to reflections on the vagaries of the human condition, then to a prayer for her own children, and finally to the linking of pity and fear. Aristotle (*Poetics,* chap. 6) thinks that it is the function of tragedy "to effect through pity and fear the catharsis of such emotions." As Kamerbeek notes, these emotions are often connected by the Greeks. A sympathetic reaction to the suffering of others leads one to identify with the sufferer and thus to fear for oneself. Cf. Odysseus' reaction to the mad Ajax (*Aj* 121–26), Tecmessa's appeal (*Aj* 510) and its effect on the chorus (*Aj* 526–27), Oedipus' pity for the suppliants (*OK* 58), and the messenger's motivation at *OK* 1179a. See below 1070–71, 1080, 1265–72. In Aeschylus' plays see *Suppliants* 210, *Agamemnon* 241, and particularly the chorus's response to the suffering Prometheus (*Prometheus Bound* 145), which finally leads it to join Prometheus in his suffering.

311 The fullness or redundancy (pleonasm) found here **in the father that begat her** at times will hardly be noticed, as in "crying and groaning" (790–91), where the repetition is natural to Heracles' pain, but in "dead" after "no longer sees" (828–30) the Greek would hear a literal expression for death after a common figurative expression. The redundancy in "dead . . . just been killed" (1130; cf. *Ant* 1282–83) translates an adjective containing essentially the same idea as the verb; the present example translates a noun ("father") and a participial phrase ("the one who begot").

Translators tend to omit pleonastic expression (the phrase in 311 occurs at *Aj* 1296, where it is not translated), in part because English always requires more words than Greek (here five in English for three in Greek), though one seldom senses mere "wordiness" in the Greek usage.

312–13 Something in Iole's manner and appearance excites special pity. Deianira compares Iole to the other captives because she (in another version) "more than the others knows how to control herself." Perhaps she sees no more than "character in manner," as at *Ion* 238–40. If her costume marked her as royalty, and there is no textual evidence for her costume, then Deianira's "intuition" would have more objective grounds.

314–15 He knows very well who she is. His feeble evasiveness does not deceive her.

321 **Great shame** means "misfortune" (as at 243 and 325), a sense that will be appropriate when her true identity is discovered.

325–26 **Weight . . . pangs of labor;** the **like** softens the expression since there is no comparison in the Greek. "Laboring with the weight" will be literally true if Heracles has already taken advantage of his victory. Despite 1226, Sophocles probably thought here of the common metaphorical meaning of "grieving."

327–28 I would prefer Pearson's text: "This state is certainly bad, but it does lay claim to (our) indulgence" (Easterling's translation).

329 The Greek audience must have seen the resemblance in situation and dramatic gesture between Cassandra and Iole. Aeschylus has Agamemnon bring home the captive Trojan princess (*Agamemnon* 782ff.) to be his concubine (954–55). After Clytemnestra and Agamemnon have entered their palace, the queen returns to fetch Cassandra, who refuses to speak to Clytemnestra (1035–68) and only enters the house after a lyric dialogue with the chorus. Clytemnestra knows who Cassandra is

and will kill her; Deianira does not know who Iole is and sympathizes with her suffering.

335 The audience may have wondered that this first messenger did not leave, as he naturally would when his part was finished. The usual stories about Heracles, Eurytus, and Iole would have made the preceding scene transparent to them. As soon as this man steps forward, the audience realizes that Deianira does not have long to wait for the discovery of Lichas' deception.

An alternative staging would take this character off either at 199 or 204 and bring him back in the group accompanying Lichas. For the Greek audience his departure signaled the possibility that Iole would have a speaking role (this actor would take her part). There is obviously some dramatic suspense to be had from this ambiguity. If he went off and returned with the slave women, he might not have been particularly noticeable in the crowd, and of course the audience's attention will be given to Iole and the speakers. In this staging he would now step out from the crowd, and the audience will know him from his costume and voice.

Lichas has suppressed the identity of Iole as well as Heracles' interest in her. Until Deianira knows who Iole is and why she has been brought, there can be no crisis in the action. That crisis turns out to be Deianira's decision to use a magic potion to reclaim Heracles' love for herself. Sophocles leaves her in ignorance so that we can see her sympathy for the slaves; then he reintroduces the first messenger to reveal the truth and to make Lichas confess. Deianira is more a witness than a participant in the interrogation of Lichas, at least until 436 when she manages to reassure Lichas of her goodwill towards him and the slave girl. If we look at how Sophocles might have plotted this scene, assuming that eventually Deianira must discover Iole's identity, we see that the most straightforward method would have let Lichas announce frankly what Heracles has done. Or else the playwright might have given Iole a speaking part and let Deianira discover through dialogue the girl's identity. Both of these options are more direct; both would probably give the wife a more aggressive role in the discovery. As the play stands, Deianira is deceived by Lichas and needs the first messenger; thus she is depicted as a more vulnerable character, more controlled by, than controlling, the dramatic events.

347–48 The contrast is between a *kakos* man (**liar**) and a *dikaios* (**honest**).

351–74 In contradicting Lichas, the messenger depends on the same public report that enabled him to dash on ahead of the official messenger. Perhaps it is not strange that in the earlier scene he did not want to cool the celebration with news of the concubine, but it seems odd that Lichas was so indiscreet in the public gathering (351–53 and 371–73) and yet so nervously evasive before Deianira.

352–57 The messenger flatly contradicts Lichas (254–57). A Greek naturally looks to both a human and divine cause, the second being the cosmic power we see working in the first. Here **Love** is *Eros* rather than Aphrodite (cf. 497 and 516), but there is no practical difference (see the note to 441–44). **Bewitched** is "spells" at 585 (same stem, but the line is suspect) and "beguiled" at 709. **Violence** may be stronger than the Greek; perhaps simply "to go to war."

360 Since **bed** is also used of its occupant (e.g., it is properly translated "bride" at *Aj* 212), we may also translate "for his secret love." As for Heracles' motives, see 475–78.

362–64 The translation has omitted half of 362, 363, and half of 364, which were condemned as an interpolation by Hartung. Although nothing that we need is lost (in 363 Eurytus is said to rule!), interpolations, whether they be from actors or from school glosses, are usually whole lines. See also on 377–79.

368 **Inflamed with desire** is already a cliché, but Sophocles avoids the most common verbs. In this play the metaphor gains some life from the fire imagery attached to Heracles (96–102, 765–66, 840, 1014, 1086, 1198).

373 **Unkind** means "not what you would like to hear."

376 The **enemy** translates an abstract noun denoting "sorrow" (as at 48) or "pain." This Greek idiom, which conveys "strong emotion, generally disapproval" (Long, p. 114), does not readily translate into English, but see 536–40 and the notes there.

377–79 This sentence should be framed as a question: "Is she then truly nameless? . . ." Asking her name would be odd if 364 were kept, where we have the phrase "killed her noble father." Jebb thinks that, in any case, the question may be regarded "as merely continuing her own bitter thought,—not as really asking for information." Three manuscripts give 379 to the messenger, and so would I (His speech would then begin "She is brilliant . . ."). We should also consider the emendation "name" for **looks**. The Greek offers the idiomatic use of "eye" (here **in her looks**) which, though it may denote facial aspect, seems to have the wrong connotations ("dear" and "precious") for the messenger, while "name" provides a transition from Deianira's question to his answer.

380–82 His sarcasm is obvious; commentators have also observed this tone in the phrasing of the Greek in 357 and 359.

383 The usual Greek for these curses is put in the form of a wish ("may all scoundrels perish"); **secret:** cf. 376, 533, 914.

385 Cf. her willingness to listen to the nurse (61–63). It is a mark of her diffidence that she asks them what to do. Cf. Creon (*Ant* 1098), who puts a similar question only after the plain threats of Teiresias. Easterling says "shock" rather than "indecisiveness" accounts for the question.

391–92 Cf. the first entrance of Hyllus and the note at 57–60.

398 Another version: "Do you have regard for good faith and truth?" We should not find diffidence in her question here.

409a–12 The first line is divided between the two speakers, as again at 418. **Honest:** threading two or more lines together on the meaning of a word is a common technique of stichomythia.

422 Such scenes often have the flavor of the courtroom, as **testify** suggests; See also 399, 410–11, 427.

428 **Consort** is the same word used of Deianira at 406. See the note on 1224.

430 The implication of **stranger** is that the messenger is not known by Lichas and is not a domestic servant (see on 180). He is so vigorous in Deianira's behalf, however, that he answers for her.

436–69 Deianira convinces Lichas to tell her the truth. She persuades him by arguing that she understands men and sex and that she, a reasonable woman, can accept Iole as yet another of Heracles' loves (459–60). Like Ajax (*Aj* 644–92), she argues that she can accept the ways of the world because she must. As in the case of Ajax' great monologue, so here we must ask if Deianira intends to deceive, for when the next scene begins (531), she announces that she cannot accept a "shared marriage" (545). The comparison with Ajax (see Reinhardt, pp. 46–47), however, is only partial. His monologue lacks the dramatic integration of the present speech, which is immediate, spontaneous, and responsive to the condemned report of Lichas, itself a conscious deception. Nor is this speech ambiguous, as Ajax' plainly is. Unlike the chorus and Tecmessa, Ajax' audience may read his ambiguities as intended deception, but who will suspect that Deianira's demand for truth is, in any sense, a trick? Moreover, as Jebb notes, she may be sincere in both speeches. Now the urge for truth allies itself to resignation; when she is calm, she rebels at this latest infidelity, and the rebellion is more natural and plausible for her having, apparently, a remedy (555–81). While both Ajax and Deianira are presented as victims, the hero has, until his monologue, defied his fate and rejected any compromise with god or man; Deianira, by contrast, is passive, a spectator, without, so far as we yet know, the will or means to escape, much less defy, her misfortune. See also on 490–96.

436 Cf. her invocation at 200 and her prayer at 303. **Lightning** is invariably the weapon and sign of Zeus (cf. *OC* 1515). The god is honored on mountain tops ("the sheer face of Zeus on Athos," *Agamemnon* 285).

438 Spiteful (*kakê*): this adjective/substantive was "scoundrels" at 383, "villainy" at 384. Below it is "dishonest" (452 and 469) in contrast to "decent." Deianira is well-bred, with a proper self-respect and regard for the morally and aesthetically superior behavior expected from her class.

441–44 Cf. 352–57. Among the many pre-Sophoclean variations on the power of invincible love Romilly cites *Iliad* 14.198–99, where Hera speaks to Aphrodite:

> Give me loveliness and desirability, graces
> with which you overwhelm mortal men, and all the immortals.

At *Ant* 781 *Eros* is "unconquered in fight." In his (lost) *Phaedra* Sophocles wrote that "even all-powerful Zeus cannot resist love, but he yields and willingly gives in to it" (frag. 684.4–5 Pearson). For later, elaborate celebrations of the power of *Eros* see the speeches beginning Plato's *Phaedrus*. The comparison from boxing seems to occur only here in Sophocles. Cf. *Prometheus Bound* 922, where Zeus prepares against himself "a strong wrestler," i.e., love.

Until the next scene, two attributes distinguish Deianira from other Sophoclean protagonists: she sees she must yield to powers greater than herself; she is able to discern the similarity between herself and her "antagonist" Iole.

445–48 Jebb is surely wrong to suppose that Athenian tolerance of concubinage explains Deianira's attitude. Most Athenian women would probably have felt the presence of a concubine both **shameful** and harmful. Cf. Hermione's rage at the concubine Andromache (*Andromache* 155ff.). Love as a **sickness** is commonplace; cf. Euripides *Hippolytus* 476–79a, 766–67.

449–50 Lichas will deny (479–80) that Heracles taught him **to lie**. **Honest** = "noble," "worthy of a noble."

451–52 Cf. the appeal of Io:

> There is no sickness worse
> for me than words that to be kind must lie.
>
> (*Prometheus Bound* 688–89)

456–57 The pause is interpretative, and sensible, although the Greek does not follow with a question (rather, "And if you fear . . .").

459 Her entire speech has argued that truth and right understanding are superior to deceit and ignorance; cf. Lichas' response at 472–74. Heracles often had one or more girls (fifty in the case of the daughters of Thespius: See Apollodorus 2.7.8 for a list) as a reward for his labors.

463 She is utterly absorbed: some editors prefer to understand Heracles as the subject, since it is his passion, not Iole's, that matters. The Greek more naturally supports our translation. At 446–47 she explicitly assumes that Heracles is "love-sick," and she adds Iole, as if she may be too. Jebb takes **absorbed** from a metaphor for "pouring molten wax or metal into a mould, to which it cleaves."

464–65 This is a more explicit, and personal, reason for pity than we had earlier (243, 308–13). Iole is apparently distinguished by her nobility, and now Deianira has better reason for her previous intuition. **Beauty has destroyed her life,** as it once threatened Deianira. Language and thought remind us of Deianira's anxiety when Acheloüs and Heracles fought for her hand (25).

467–68 Committing something to **wind** and water is proverbial for sending it off and forgetting it. The proverb "let it go on the wind" seems to have many applications. The commentators cite Aeschylus *Seven* 690–91, where Eteocles signifies by it an acceptance of his fate:

> Since it is the god who drives this matter on
> let it go with the wind, catching a wave of Cocytus,
> this whole clan of Laius, hateful to Phoebus.
> (*Seven against Thebes* 689–91; my trans.)

In the present context Deianira seems to mean "let all this business concerning Iole go where it will (my real concern is for an honest report from you)." More wind at 815–16, 953–55.

473 For the motif **see things as we mortals must** see on *Persians* 819cff. In Sophocles see *Aj* 124–26, 759a, 778, OC 567–68. It is proverbial wisdom that man should think (and aspire) within the limits of his human nature. When Lichas is convinced of Deianira's reasonableness, he relaxes and tells the truth.

479–80 We shall have direct examples of Heraclean candor when he arrives. Since he has had so many "wives" (460), he could not suppose one more would matter. None of them was invited home, which does make a difference. We need not fear that we are anachronistically civilized and soft in thinking Heracles morally insensitive; Lichas himself was **fearful** that the news would hurt his mistress.

483 **Erred** and **error** translate *hamartia* and a verb from the same stem (a common figure: cf. "learned," "learning," and "lessons" at 449–50, which translate a triple play on the *math-* stem). Similar wordplay in "all blows and all dust" (506: the English translates a pair of compound adjectives).

488–89 This conception of Heracles as the physical master of all his opponents and yet a bondman is not specifically Sophoclean. In Apollodorus and in Euripides' *Heracles* he is struck by sudden madness; sometimes he is sated only by huge quantities of food and drink, or given over to extraordinary lust. In his moral and spiritual life, then, he is often **vanquished**. Greek comedy did not fail to exploit this weakness.

490–96 For those readers who have suspected Deianira of dissembling in 436 ff. the present response offers ambiguous comfort. Despite her professed refusal to fight with the gods (the *theomachos* motif; see *Aj* 118, 759–78), her talk of **messages** and **gifts** implies she has already thought of the charm (575, 584) with which she will fight the goddess of love. Iole and the other slaves are his gifts; her **gifts to match** aim to counteract Iole's and Aphrodite's power over him. As Easterling notes, **match** also means "fit," an ominous foreshadowing of the robe; cf. "apply" at 687 (the same verb). The suggestive vagueness of these lines is very much in Sophocles' manner.

497–530 The first stasimon consists of a single triadic song (strophe, antistrophe, and epode). In reflecting on the power of love the chorus turns back to the contest between Heracles and Acheloüs for Deianira.

Love and deception, futile intrigue, and killing in ignorance link the *Women of Trachis* and Euripides' *Hippolytus*. On Aphrodite's power see *Hippolytus* 525–63, where Iole, the "Oechalian maiden" (545), is offered as a paradigm of love's power.

497–506 Cyprian (cf. "Cypris" at 516) regularly describes Aphrodite (860), who, according to Hesiod (*Theogony* 192–94), emerged from her sea-foam birth on that island. **I would not tell** introduces a familiar figure of thought (Latin *praeteritio*, "passing over"; cf. *OC* 361), in which contrast is heightened by a feigned lack of interest in well known examples that are introduced to serve as foils to the real subject (the erotic contest for Deianira). Here **But for our lady's hand** starts toward the true subject, only to be checked and postponed further by the two rhetorical questions (**who?**). As a result the entire stophe becomes a proem to the antistrophe (507–16), where the climax is finally reached. A less elaborate example of this figure will be found at 1046–50, where Heracles contrasts earlier labors and suffering with his present pain. Cf. the catalogue at 1058–63, where "a woman" is set against giants and beasts. This foil and climax mode of exposition has been given the name *priamel*. **Zeus was tricked by her** on many occasions, i.e., every time he pursued a woman for love (e.g., Alcmena, mother of Heracles), but Zeus is notably and grossly tricked by Hera and Aphrodite in *Iliad* 14 (see note to 441–44). **Hades** fell in love with Persephone, daughter of Demeter, while **Poseidon** got children by a number of Greek girls (e.g., Tyro, Alcyone, Aethra). **Shaker of the earth** is Sophocles' variant of a Homeric epithet; it may refer to waves pounding the beach or to a god of earthquakes. The questions in 503 are of course rhetorical. The idea of contest (**contenders and bouts**) continues through the lyric both in the imagery of fighting and grappling and in specific words (e.g., "referee" at 515, "over whom they fought" at 527). Sophoclean lyrics are much more concise than their English versions. For example, lines 505–6 translate a Greek sentence of six words. The difference is largely due to the economy of the inflected Greek which uses adjectives where the English version uses subordinate clauses (**they who** and **that were**).

507–16 Now we have a fuller, if impressionistic, version of the contest Deianira could not bear to watch (20–26). The river god **Acheloüs** here takes the form of a bull (as in his courtship: see 11); Easterling notes that **looks** also suggests "monstrous," as at 836. Coins from the town of Oeniadae in Acarnania (near Pleuron: see note to 6) depict Acheloüs as a bull. Heracles was born in **Thebes**, which is **of Bacchus** because the god was born there to Semele, daughter of Cadmus. Heracles is more often depicted in art as a bowman than a spearman, and his **club**, which he cut for himself at Nemea (the other weapons are gifts of the gods), comes closest to symbolizing the brute strength of the hero; his victory here, as often, comes in a wrestling match.

517–30 After the antistrophe's focus on the contest as a bout, the first lines of this epode (517–22) describe the wild melee as warrior and bull grapple. As in Deianira's report (21–24), the emphasis here is on her distance from the battle (524–25) and on her as prize (527–28). In the Greek, three different words (**lovely eyes** catches one of them) emphasize the beauty of her face and herself as spectator/prize. "Eye" (*omma* see note on 203–4) is used in the sense "darling" (here **bride**); and the hill is literally "seen from afar." **So the struggle raged** is an emendation of a corrupt text. If we must have something, Zielinski's "As a spectator I have told it" is better, but both are weak. Kamerbeek (with the scholia) thinks the received text might stand; he takes it to mean "I report it as a mother would, i.e., from the heart."

531–33 Her return, alone, surprises us but no more than the news of her jealousy. Now she begins to work in secret (**unobserved** = "secret" at 376 and 384, where the chorus condemns "secret . . . villainy").

534 **Hands** occurs four times in this speech ("arms" at 560). The lustful hands of Nessus (565) give her work to do with her hands (572). Heracles, known for the work of his hands (1046 and especially 1089); "Sheer strength" (488) translates "with his hands." See also Deianira's hands at 602 and Heracles' proposal at 1066–67.

536–40 A **married woman** translates a common metaphor for marriage ("yoked," as at *OK* 825). As Long (p. 119) points out, the Greek makes the two women one ("we two, one hug for"), a single object to be embraced. **Cargo** and **goods** are mercantile, while **outrage** is Homeric and heroic (e.g., "insult" at *Aj* 561; see the note to *Aj* 218) and suggests a shameful insult.

540–41 The tone is certainly bitter, perhaps sarcastic as well (Blaydes compares *OK* 385, *Ant* 31, *Phil* 872, all instances of patent sarcasm), since an untranslated "called" (as in 551) questions **brave and faithful.**

543 With **sick . . . sickness** the translation very nearly manages the Greek framing of the line.

544 **Incapable** is expressed in a typically intellectual manner: "I don't know how to be angry." Cf. 552–53.

548–49 **Eye** is an object of sexual desire at 527 (where "the bride" is "eye" in the Greek); here the eye represents active sexual desire. Cf. "that Zeus's eye may cease from longing for you" (*Prometheus Bound* 654), *Ant* 794, and the note at 102–11. For the eyes (a singular in the Greek, and without the interpretative **of men**) to pluck a blossom is a bolder metaphor, more so because this verb suggests rape ("to snatch by force" as at *Phil* 644), and Jebb mistakenly dismisses comparison with Aeschylus *Suppliants* 663 (see note 663–65 there), where the sexual connotations are certain.

If we look at the frequency of antithesis in the preceding passage (e.g., maiden/married, two/one, her youth/mine, pluck/turn away, husband/man), the agonistic tone comes clear (cf. "defeat the girl" 585). If she does not consciously pit herself against either her husband or Iole, the contrasts define opposition and imply some action that will resolve them, i.e., make her husband her man.

554 This line is emended, but **solution** is secure and continues the freedom/slavery theme; it is cognate with the verb "free" at 181 and "release" at 1170.

556–61 **Centaur** actually translates "beast" (as at 568) and is used of any wild animal. Although the centaurs were half-man half-horse, their bestial nature usually had the upper hand; thus only in a fairy tale would anyone trust a centaur. Their fight with the Lapith clan, which began after the centaurs got drunk and assaulted the Lapith women, is often represented in Greek painting, as is the meeting of Heracles and Nessus at the river **Evenus.**

565–71 Even in antiquity the midriver rape and prompt reaction of the outraged bridegroom bothered realists. That a magically poisoned arrow kills—but not instantaneously—teases the imagination less than her midstream credulity. But if in the fashion of opera he is to make a last bequest, so presciently foreseeing her need—he evidently understands the casual manners of her new lover—we can hardly blame her for listening. Later, on reflection and with some evidence at hand, she sees the implausibility of the gift (707–11).

There are some extradramatic facts that a Greek play will inevitably refer to, which for us will seem fanciful or symbolic. Everyone in the audience knew these stories, in this case knew of the river rape and its consequences. Although Sophocles is at liberty to change details, if he does he may contradict received opinion. If the poet takes the rape out of the river and onto the riverbank, he may satisfy realists, but he will also call attention to his new version. Since the old version has something like the status of history for the Greek audience, a new, perhaps even a more plausible version contends against their assumptions. The result may be a breach of dramatic and ethical illusion. For the world of myth conditioned the Greek response, gave the audience certain expectations, and relieved the playwright of the need for exposition, but if a new version defies the old version, there is the risk that the myth will become—if only for a moment—more important to consciousness than the play. Deianira's naive version corresponds to the familiar story; what must happen according to myth does happen in her account. The kind of clash between myth and drama posed when Philoctetes refuses to go to Troy, although all the audience knows that he did go, does not come into play. The necessity of the myth and rationale of the plot remain one.

572–77 The Hydra's blood was poisonous (714–18, 770–71); cf. Apollodorus 2.5.2 ("he dipped his arrows in the gall") and 2.7.7 (for the effect of the poison). Rather than a periphrastic expression for **Hydra**, Long (p. 103) argues that **monstrous serpent of Lerna** means "the poison which grew in the Hydra." "Poison" is not specifically mentioned, and the periphrasis more literally means "that which the Hydra nourished" in her blood. Nessus gives Deianira his blood, which has itself turned poisonous from venom of the Hydra. Following West ("Tragica III," p. III) we may render the passage: "This blood . . . where he dipped his arrows black with the Hydra's bile, that bile the Lernaean Hydra nurtured."

582–84 Another version: "I neither know nor would I learn harmful boldness, and I hate bold daring in women." **Bold** is a special attribute of Clytemnestra (see the notes to *Agamemnon* 10f., 1237 and *Libation Bearers* 594ff.). Cf. Philoctetes' use of it ("impudence" at *Phil* 985) and its connotations of dangerous excess at *Ant* 371. Blaydes notices a good parallel in Phaedra's speech:

Truly, too, I hate
lip-worshippers of chastity who own
a lecherous daring when they have privacy.
(*Hippolytus* 414–14b)

Phaedra contrasts moderation and secret daring (as at *Tr* 531–33).

587 Rashly = "lustfully" at 565. This is a favorite word of Aeschylus (see on *Agamemnon* 422f.) and often implies vain or futile effort, as in "her cost" at 1149 (where it means "to no good use"). Daring tends to be rashly ineffective and destructive (a sense that suits 565). Once again (see 61–63) Deianira is willing to accept advice.

589 For **acted** understand "planned."

591 In fact she will shortly discover a **test** that proves the charm an evil trick (see 672–704).

596–97 Ashamed and **disgrace** are cognates and thus give the idea the kind of emphasis seen in 483 and in other such verbal interactions. She means that a person does not fall into public disgrace if deeds otherwise shameful are done in secret. That which is shameful may be either harmful (as at 447–48) or defamatory (as at *Aj* 173–74) or both. Embarrassed a little by her own deception, she hopes to achieve **in darkness** what she, no gypsy or witch, would not do openly.

602–3 Since Greek women did the weaving for the home—even royalty like Andromache and Penelope was not exempt—it is natural for her to offer her own handiwork and just as proper for him to offer sacrifice in new robes.

604–9 The centaur's "instructions" (579, 685–86) imply the charm is activated by the **sun:** fire will make fire. Heracles will understand these restrictions as dictated by the need for ritual purity and honor to the gods, who accept only that which is virgin, pure, and unused. **Bull-slaughtering** (see 760) is the grandest kind of sacrifice.

610 A **vow** for safe homecoming often includes a promise to sacrifice or dedicate a personal offering to the god who has looked out for one's welfare (see *Agamemnon* 931–35 and the note there).

613 Jebb sees "unconscious ambiguity" in **to make new sacrifice,** which could also mean "to make a novel sacrifice."

616–19 This concluding admonition, after some emphasis on the **seal,** indicates her mistrust: she does not want Lichas opening the chest before he reaches Heracles.

620 Hermes is the protector of messengers, "the Guide" (*Phil* 133).

623 The last word in the Greek line echoes "match" at 494 (see note on 490–96). Jebb suggests "fitly/duly add" (for our **repeat**), which helps establish the echo. We might try "and to the chest I'll add your words, a fitting match to your gift."

632 The **side entrance** of the translator's stage directions is the parodos by which he first entered.

633–62 The second stasimon consists of two pairs of responsive stanzas. The subject is the long absence of Heracles, whose appearance the audience will now expect momentarily. The four stanzas utilize, successively, apostrophe, proclamation, recollection, and wish/prayer.

633–39 The first strophe begins with an apostrophe to those who live around the gulf of **Malis**. The sentence is not completed until the next stanza. The major landmarks are the gulf of Malis, whose **inmost reaches** are surrounded by land on three sides, Mt. **Oeta**, which rises high and steep above the coast, and Thermopylae, where warm springs and a narrow pass (**Gates**: Thermopylae means "the gates at the hot-springs") offer a natural meeting place. The famous gatherings alluded to here are those of the Amphictyonic Council. The **Maid** is Artemis; **who shoots the golden shaft** alludes to the goddess as huntress (cf. 212).

640–46 More than the **flute**, the **lyre** is associated with cheerful celebration. Jebb cites Pindar's praise of the lyre:

> Golden lyre, held of Apollo in common possession
> with the violet-haired Muses.
>
> *(First Pythian* 1)

Prizes are the spoils of victory, such as the slaves already sent ahead.

647–54 Deianira has said (44–45) that Heracles has been away fifteen months, not twelve. There is no apparent reason for emphasizing his travel **on the sea**—after all, he was not at sea with Omphale—but they speculate (as at 100–102). **God of War** is added by the translator as a gloss. **Stung to madness:** Easterling compares Aeschylus *Seven* 343 ("Ares . . . maddened") and also notes that the sting of the gadfly has erotic connotations (but not always: see on *OK* 1316). **Dispels** may also be translated "frees her from" (as at 181). The sentence is a variety of metonymy, where one name (**Ares**) is substituted for another (Heracles, the warrior guided by the god of war). Campbell compares "Ares has taken a siege of grief from our eyes" (*Aj* 706–7; see the note there), where Ares is substituted for the warrior Ajax.

655–62 **Hearth** is the altar of Zeus of Cenaeum (see 752–54) where Heracles is now sacrificing. Lines 660–62 are metrically irregular and have been emended and interpreted variously. There is little doubt, however, that the chorus refers to the centaur's charm. The Greek actually describes Heracles as the one **dipped** (= "steeped" or "joined in") in the ointment of Persuasion (an Aeschylean personification: see note to *Agamemnon* 385 and *Suppliants* 1039ff. for persuasion's association with passion). Haupt's emendation of "robe" for **beast** enables Jebb to translate, "Thence may he come, full of desire, steeped in love by the specious device of the robe, on which Persuasion hath spread her sovereign charm." **Inducements** (Jebb's "specious device") ambiguously suggests both Deianira's trick and the centaur's deception. It would not be un-Aeschylean to read, "May he come, full of desire, steeped in the anointed pretext of the robe," with the adjective transferred, i.e., "the pretext of the anointed robe."

663 Her return may be a surprise since we are prepared for Heracles' arrival, at least news from Hyllus.

664 With **too far** cf. "too late" (711). In the grammar of Greek tragedy "going too far" is a common metaphor for violating limits set on human thought, passion, and action. Prometheus is a prime example (see *Prometheus Bound* 29–30, 249, and 505).

667 The line is framed by **harm** and **good** (cf. note to 543). The Greek phrasing suggests "great harm done from good hope," as if the one were derived from the other. **Good** = "noble/fair."

668 In the *Ajax* it is the **gift** of Hector that kills Ajax (*Aj* 661–65, 818); in the *Medea* a gift brings "all-devouring fire" (*Medea* 1187). Cf. 871. Hesiod's Pandora is the archetype for double-edged gift.

676–77 With **devoured** cf. 1084; with **eaten away** cf. 771 and 1088.

683 Aeschylus has already used this metaphor, "the tablets of the mind" (see note on *Eumenides* 273–75).

684 Several editors condemn this line as an interpolation.

685–92 The drug cannot bear the light, nor can she use it save **secretly**; when it comes to light (normally this would be a metaphor for survival!), it destroys. Her nature is not secretive, yet she is forced ("beguiled" at 709) to act unnaturally.

693–94 Her excitement is indicated by the present tense and by phrasing which, literally translated, gives "I see a report incomprehensible," i.e., **something unspeakable.**

696 This line also looks like an interpolation.

701–4 There are more similes than usual for Sophocles in this play. This one likens the bubbling **foam** of the poison to the ferment of the newly pressed grape (must has this dark, blue-green color).

705 An interjection (*talaina*) of the common sort is omitted from the translation. When it is translated here, it is some form of "miserable" (790, 1075, 1104). Cf. "unhappy wife" at 713.

707–11 For **beguiled** see the note to 352–57. For the motif of late learning see *Ant* 1270 and *OC* 1263. Learning becomes discovery and then knowledge (see 335–37). For Deianira's readiness to learn see 449–50 and 459 (where "danger" translates the same word as "terrible" at 706), 694 and 749 (where "hear" = "learn"). Lichas formulates the theme in its traditional way at 472–73. Hyllus, too, has late knowledge (932–35) and comes to understand its value (1118, 1134). With Heracles' learning (1145) comes revelation (1149–50).

715 Chiron, the good centaur who was teacher to Achilles and a physician, was accidentally wounded by an arrow of Heracles. When the wound would not heal, he was persuaded to trade his immortality for death. See the note to *Prometheus Bound* 1018–29.

720 Under the same blow means "with the same motion/impetus"; the scholiast imagines she plans to use the robe!

721–22 Deianira puts this impersonally and generically: "It is not bearable for her to live with a bad name who would prefer not to have been born than to be born ignoble." Cf. Jebb's "for no woman could bear to live with an evil name if she rejoices that her nature is not evil."

724–26 Expect and **expectations** return to the motif of hope (667). Bad planning does not commend good hope.

727 In a court of law justice would be tempered by the involuntary character of her act. Hyllus repeats **unwilling** at 1123. Cf. the sentiment of frag. 665: "No man is base because of an unwilling error." Pearson compares OC 977–78, *Phil* 1318–20.

729–30 Cf. Prometheus' similar response to the chorus at *Prometheus Bound* 265–67.

734 Hyllus has the function of a messenger who reports offstage action, though of course one personally affected both by the person whose deeds he reports and by his relation to the person to whom he speaks. To have sent him on his errand may have seemed unnecessary, but to have him available for this role clearly justifies any awkwardness we may have felt earlier. For Sophocles there was also a useful dramatic economy in integrating the messenger into the subsequent action.

734–37 In the Greek text the last line (**three ways**) is the first thus; the three wishes are presented in a preconceived, and so more rhetorical, context. The wish seems based on a proverb to the effect that the fortunate men will get one wish out of three while unlucky men will have only three hard choices.

739–40 The translation omits "on this day."

742–43 Or: "Only what can not fail to be accomplished [the *tel*-stem]. For who could make what has appeared to be unbegotten?" The abstract form alludes to a commonplace: "Not even Time the father of all could undo an accomplished fact" (*Second Olympian* 16–17).

751 Trophies are the captured arms, which are often dedicated to the gods (cf. Heracles' boast at 1102); **first-fruits** are select sacrificial offerings (here the twelve best bulls, 760–61) and not necessarily war-booty (cf. *Eumenides* 834).

752–54 The sacrifice to Zeus at Cape **Cenaeum** has been mentioned at 237–38 and 288–89, where Zeus is also styled **god of our fathers,** a phrase that, since it is in the singular, also suggests simply "(his) father Zeus" (as at 1168).

755 Glad after my longing means "happy because of my longing."

760–61 Perfect victims . . . pick of the booty represents a kind of redundant amplification characteristic of this speech. Of this speech Long (p. 97; I am translating his examples) observes that "Hyllus uses a high style of description. This [the high style] overlaps and contrasts with the vivid horror conveyed by his recital of symptoms (765 ff.), and the simplicity of Heracles' reported speech (797–802). We find amplification, 'trophies and first-fruits' (751), 'he marked out altars/and a whole precinct' (753–54), 'rejoicing in his handsome dress' (764), 'pale brains' (781); periphrasis, 'raised his eyes, distorted' (794); and heavy compounds [all the following phrases translate a single word in the Greek], 'wave-beaten' (752, 780); 'killed . . . his bulls' (760); 'great . . . sacrifice' (756); 'mismating' (791) etc.' " Translations cannot manage all these effects and often purposefully avoid them; e.g., the figure hendiadys, i.e., saying one thing through two, is found in "rejoicing in his handsome dress," which might more literally be rendered "rejoicing in his ornament and dress".

762 The sacrifice of **one hundred** animals, called a *hecatomb,* is traditional for a magnificent offering.

763 The subjective comment of **poor wretch** is more common than our translations indicate. For example, of the three passages Kamerbeek cites, only one brings it into English (*Ant* 1271, "in sorrow"). See the note to 705. Cf. "unfortunate" at 772, "unlucky man" (775), and "wretched" (792).

766 The flame is **bloody** because of the burned sacrifices but also in anticipation of his blood as sacrifice.

769 In sculpture, of course, the robe of the figure is necessarily joined to the skin of the figure. Other comparisons from art at *Agamemnon* 242 and Euripides *Hecuba* 560.

770–71 Since Hyllus does not yet know the ultimate source of the poison, we must suppose that his comparison comes from having seen other victims struck by the arrows of Heracles. The audience, knowing the truth, will appreciate his intuition while not making much of it, for the effect is just as they have expected.

772–84 With the mad violence of Lichas' death cf. Euripides' description of Heracles hunting down his wife and children (*Heracles* 930–1001). The brutality of knocking the innocent herald's brains out will likely make more impression on modern readers than the great man's agony does, but the Greek audience may have been more impartial; cf., e.g., Amphitryon's sympathy at *Heracles* 1042 ff. (he says of the carnage,

"Even a god would weep if he knew it." [1115]). His monstrous strength, so useful for dealing with the likes of Acheloüs and Nessus, destroys Lichas as it destroyed Linus, Iphitus, and the others. Early in his career he mutilated the Minyan heralds who were demanding tribute from Thebes: "he cut off their ears and noses and hands, and having fastened them by ropes from their necks, he told them to carry that tribute to Erginus and the Minyans" (Apollodorus 2.4.11).

788 **Locris** is the continental district opposite Euboea.

792–93 **Marriage** is personified so that it becomes the polluter (**be-foul**) of his life.

797–98 The best of men is not overly concerned for his son. When Creon's daughter Creusa is burning to death from a robe doctored in much the same way as this one, her father throws himself on her flaming body and finds his flesh torn away until he dies (*Medea* 1205–19).

808–12 For similar prayers for revenge see *Aj* 842–43 (the Furies are also invoked there; cf. 895 and 1051–52 below) and *El* 209–10 (Electra calls on Zeus). The present passage is a wish (and prayer) rather than a prediction (so "may they" rather than **will**). **Justice** (*dikê*) coupled with the Erinys (**Fury**) recalls Aeschylus (see the note to *Agamemnon* 1431–34; **right** [*themis*] also appears in that passage). The triple repetition of **right** emphasizes the social and moral censure of his curse, the full force of which is seen in Deianira's silent departure. For **best of all men** cf. line 177. The ambiguity of **shall never see again** will be clear to her and to the audience.

813–14 She must go into the house, not by the side. Deianira's silent departure is comparable to Eurydice's at *Antigone* 1243 (also explicitly remarked by the coryphaeus) and to Jocasta's at *OK* 1073 (where she speaks and exits, and the chorus comments on "this silence"). Since she has already discovered her error and sentenced herself (719–22), to speak now would be redundant, unless she sought to excuse herself to Hyllus. His suffering, however, will be the greater when he discovers after her death that he has unjustly condemned her. Sophocles takes her off without a word, then, leaving her defense to the audience's sympathy. Aeschylus was famous for dramatic silences, and Sophocles has clearly learned from him. It is neither for want of a defense (both the chorus, 841–50, and Hyllus, 1122–23, say what she might say) nor for lack of character that she leaves as she does, but because her shame and sense of propriety inhibit an apology that cannot change the facts. Death is not so fearful a thing as a shamed life is hateful.

815–20 For the imagery from the **wind** see the note to 467–68. Here "wind" is the first word in his Greek sentence, **fair** (for him) the last word. In **name** some commentators have seen an allusion to the meaning of her name ("she who kills her husband"), but the context does not encourage that association here any more than it does at 1064–65. The antithesis is, rather, between word and deed. With the euphemistic but clear wish of 819–20 cf. Antigone's wish for Creon (*Ant* 928–29); see also *Aj* 840–41.

821–61 In this third stasimon the lyric is saturated with imagery and themes from the preceding episodes. The first strophe (821–30) reports the (now understood) prophecy; the first antistrophe (831–40) imagines the dying Heracles in his final bout with Nessus and the Hydra; the second strophe (841–50) recalls the fatal deceit of Deianira; the second antistrophe (851–61) returns to Heracles and his fatal passion for Iole.

821–30 **The year of the twelfth plowing** means "the twelfth year (as measured by the annual plowing)." Though the tradition—and so probably Sophocles' audience—was aware of a prophecy that the end of Heracles' labors would bring him rest and immortality, such a prophecy has not been mentioned so far in the play; cf. Heracles on his two prophecies at 1159–61 and 1164. The reference may be a slip, or the poet may have taken advantage of the audience's knowledge, as perhaps he also does when he lets Hyllus connect the poisoned shirt with the Hydra (770–71). For **end . . . end** see the note to 26 (the *tel-* stem). **True-born son of Zeus** picks up references to "Zeus the father" at 19, 140, 288, and 754; see later 958, 1088, 1106, 1268. Lines 826–30 seem to refer to Deianira's prophecy at 164–68. **No longer sees** is idiomatic for dead. For **servitude** see the note at 180.

831–40 In this stanza note the repeated **treacherous** (*dolos;* cf. 850 and see on "guile" at 278) and **soaked** (cf. the description at 767–71). Ambiguities (e.g., **cloud** also means "net"; **clings** means both "stings" and "anoints"), compression and some textual uncertainty make translation difficult. **Cloud** has been taken as an allusion to the "dark smoke" of the flaming figure (794). That may be, but the net imagery is clearly established and will be used below (see 1051 and 1057). The translation brings out the ambiguity by rendering the word twice (in **cloud** and **trap**). The meaning as well as the reading of 834 is disputed, but the idea is, as Blaydes notes, "that which partakes of anything is often said to be produced by it." So **Death** and the **Hydra** are represented as parents of the venom. **Soaked** in the Greek modifies Heracles: "when he is glued to the horrid apparition of the Hydra." Throughout the stanza Heracles' futile effort to free himself from the burning robe is fused with imagery pointing to his ancient struggle with the two monsters. The focus in the last sentence (837–40) is not on **words**; Easterling translates: "and all mingled together, Black Hair's murderous guileful goads, having erupted, torment him." The goads (*kentra,* here translated **sharp points**) play on the word centaur (*kentauron*) and also suggest that Heracles is the victim driven mad by a daimonic power. Aeschylus has used this imagery (see note on *Suppliants* 101 ff.), and the chorus of Euripides' *Heracles* sings:

Madness has mounted her car;
she goads her team!
(*Heracles* 880–81)

But Easterling's "torment," like **torture,** is too abstract; the Greek verb denotes both physical harm and cruel, humiliating torture (see *Aj* 65, 111, 401). We have, then, the image of Heracles and Nessus inextricably fused through the medium of burning, boiling poison, and yet the beast rides on top of the man, goading him to self-degrading madness.

841–50 Knew nothing of this ironically echoes "agonizing fear" (7): in applying the charm she acted without her characteristic apprehension (Easterling). Greek uses abstract nouns such as **injury** (*blabê*) more freely of persons than English does; here the injury, nearly synonymous with **disaster** (*atê* in 850), is Iole as well as the injury she embodies. The lyric contrasts Deianira's **remedy** (her intention) with what came from another **will** (the effect of her fatal meeting with the centaur). The **doom** (*moira:* "fate") of Heracles **advances and makes clear** (Jebb's "foreshadows" catches a second meaning: the imminent arrival of Heracles himself) the treacherous *atê* (both objective disaster and subjective "delusion": the chorus does not censure Deianira, even though she has used guile and is now manifestly the victim of *atê*).

851–61 Poured upon continues the imagery from "soaking" (833). **Suffering to pity** means "such suffering as never yet his enemies caused, suffering which causes us to pity him." Aphrodite attends upon Heracles, i.e., is his **handmaiden. It is her work** translates the same word used of Zeus at 251.

862 Cf. at *Agamemnon* 1343–71 Agamemnon's death cry (from within the house) and the debate it prompts from individual members of the chorus; cf. also the semichoruses in their search for Ajax (*Aj* 866ff.). Part-lines (865 and 868) break the iambic rhythm.

866–67 Shrieking denotes a cry of lament for the dead, as at *Aj* 851 and *Ant* 29. For the personified **house** see the note to *Agamemnon* 36.

874–75 Motionless translates the final phrase of the sentence which means "without stirring foot" (Campbell). As Easterling notes, this may sound more frigid to us than to the Greek audience. Perhaps she makes a feeble riddle.

876 In the following passage the short lines in the English reflect half-lines to individual speakers in the Greek (*antilabe*).

882–88 Recent editors follow Maas (*Greek Metre,* p. 54) in giving this entire lyric section to the chorus. Maas does not think a slave ought to have lyrics (the exception seems to be the Phrygian slave in Euripides' *Orestes*). If the lines belong to the chorus, question marks must be put after **killed her** and **cut her,** with individual choristers taking the several questions.

888 Awful act translates *hybris*. Here the sense "violent action" keeps us from thinking of "insolence" or "insult."

894–95 Iole (**That bride**) has given birth to (cf. 834) a Fury, as Hyllus hopes (809). So Helen is a Fury (*Agamemnon* 749) because she brings revenge and death on the Trojans.

899–942 Since the maid's report of the manner of Alcestis' death (*Alcestis* 152–98) contains a number of correspondences in detail (the altars, the bedchamber, the lament on the bed, the lament for lost marriage), several scholars have thought one scene must be modelled on the other. There is no agreement, however, on the priority. Lesky ("Alkestis und Deianeira") finds the Euripidean scene more naturally integrated (e.g., Alcestis prays at the house altars while Deianira falls before them; the servant's knowledge of her mistress's last moments fits more perfectly in the *Alcestis*) and so argues that it is prior. Unhappily for such analysis, there is no compelling reason for the "more natural" or better integrated scene being earlier, and it is difficult to believe this play was produced more than twenty years after the *Agamemnon* (the *Alcestis* can be dated to 438).

903 She hides from shame and to escape any interference with her suicide. **Groaned** = "howled" (805) and, rather too feebly, "sobbing" (1072). The word suggests the exclamation of wild, uncontrollable grief, as at *OK* 1265, where "cried out" is weak.

910 Her **fate** is her *daimôn;* cf. the same translation at 1025. Since **call out loud to** = "invoking," and since the evil spirits of Nessus and the Hydra hover over this play, it seems reasonable to interpret this passage in more personal terms.

915 It may be idle to ask why she casts **sheets** on their bed. She has seen Hyllus preparing a stretcher for his father, and her wild grief leads her to a futile mimicry; or she thinks of their married love (920).

920–22 In her apostrophe to the marriage bed Alcestis concludes:

I could not bear to play him false.
(*Alcestis* 180)

932–35 Forced means "attached" or "bound," as if he put it on her; a second metaphorical meaning may be "kindled," as if he started the blaze that led her to it; see Dodds on *Bacchae* 778–79.

Offstage learning is clumsy, but a scene in which Hyllus learns (from a servant, probably the nurse) would deflect the tragedy toward him and away from Deianira and Heracles.

940 **Thoughtlessly** translates a stem that in this scene has been used of the chorus ("mistaken" at 862), of the nurse ("helpless" at 888), and finally in the generalizing conclusion ("does not think," 945). The adjectival form occurs more often in this play than in the other six combined. It ranges in meaning from "rash" through "foolish" to "futile"; apparently these connotations seemed particularly appropriate to this story. Later it occurs at 1118 ("how mistaken") and 1149 ("to her cost").

943–46 West ("Tragica III," p. 111) cites several variants on the commonplace "think only of the day" (*carpe diem* is the Latin formulation, with more hedonistic direction than the earlier Greek maxim). Taking the long view may be commended, and it is only the nurse's pessimistic inferences from today's events that lead her to condemn as futile counting more than one day at a time. For "this day" as crisis see note to 739–40 and cf. 83–85 and 173–74.

947–70 The fourth stasimon begins with the shortest responsive stanzas in Sophocles (strophe, 947–49; antistrophe, 950–52). The preceding report of Hyllus' discovery may have led the audience to expect a tableau (he would lament over the body of his mother), but this lyric equates the twin disasters and, in the second pair of stanzas, turns toward Heracles and the last scene (technically the exodos) of the play. It is remarkable that the second antistrophe (962–70) is given over to announcing the arrival of Heracles on a litter; Deianira is thus eclipsed by her long expected husband.

947–49 Torn between sympathy for husband and wife, the chorus asks which it should first lament. Hoey ("Unity of Hero," p. 13–14) emphasizes the near perfect symmetry of these lines: there are three words in each line of the Greek; the first two lines begin with anaphora (**Which**) and not only have the same meter (iambic dimeter) but also rhyme (with an offrhyme in the third line); the alliteration of the third line gives the effect of a miniature lyric triad (strophe, antistrophe, epode) to the stanza,

potera proteron epistenô
potera telea peraiterô
duskrit' emoige dustanôi.

For **final** (*tel-* stem) recent editors tend to prefer Musgrave's "grievous," which avoids what Easterling calls the "uncomfortably hyperbolic" **more final**. We should stay with the manuscripts and understand the meaning to be "more complete/more comprehensive."

950–52 A similar concern for symmetry is evident here: anaphora and antithesis in the first two lines, syntactical parallelism, and final, capping line and word (**the same**). This last word also expresses the shared and reciprocal nature of the suffering, as well as the chorus's attitude toward it.

953–61 For this type of wish, which in the poets sometimes becomes a wish for personal transformation, see the note to Aeschylus *Suppliants* 779a–82 (examples of fantastic escape) and cf. *Aj* 1192–94 and Euripides *Ion* 796–99. The impulse for the wish is escape; the present wish is less fantastic than those in Aeschylus. For the metaphor from the **wind** see 815–16.

962–70 For the **nightingale** see the note to *El* 148–49b. The announcement of his arrival gives more than the usual time for an entrance; this cortege is slow and dismal.

971 It may be better to bring Hyllus on now, after the litter reaches the front of the palace. If he has come on as the procession arrives, he must withhold this exclamation, and such restraint does not fit well with the old man's attempt to silence him. Though Heracles does not speak for ten lines, he may stir at this cry of grief, and this movement would reinforce the urgency of the old man's tone. The meter is anapestic until 1004.

975 **That makes him savage** is a single compound adjective which modifies "father" in the Greek. The translation takes it as proleptic (i.e., anticipating an effect), and it may be, but it is equally appropriate in an attributive sense ("who is savage-minded"). It is used of Ajax (*Aj* 929a); see also on *Ant* 471.

981–82 Although Heracles is now **helpless** and **under an immense weight**, these lines refer to Hyllus' own feeling of helplessness. Kamerbeek sensibly suggests that **drives me mad** may overstress the idea of rage; he prefers "my heart is full of eagerness (to utter its sorrow)."

993–96 His first word was "Zeus" (983), and even if he were not the son of Zeus, he could legitimately complain that such suffering is a poor thanks for his recent sacrifice at Cenaeum; for blaming the gods see note at 1264–74. For the apostrophe cf. *OK* 1392. The dying Hippolytus, also in great agony, walks in supported by his servants (*Hippolytus* 1347) and calls on Zeus to behold his suffering (1363).

997 The second **you** in this line refers to the altar steps. Heracles dwells on the Cenaean altar for two reasons: (1) he was standing there when he put on the robe and suffered this attack; (2) his thanks offering to Zeus seemingly has this unfair return from the god.

999–1003 **Inexorable** and **exorcise** are cognates with the "charm" of Nessus (575). These three words occur only in these three passages in the extant plays. The verbal irony lets Heracles understand both the power and author of his pain. **Flowering of madness** is an Aeschylean oxymoron; for "flowering" see the notes to *Agamemnon* 659 and *Ant* 954–63. Cf. "blooms" 1089. For the power of song to cast spells and cure physical and spiritual ills, see *Aj* 582–83 and notes to *Agamemnon* 977f. and *Eumenides* 646–50. The **curse** is an *atê* (= "disaster" at 850); here it probably has a more objective sense ("ruin"; see the notes to *Ant* 531–33 and 582–91). For Zeus as the last resort see *Agamemnon* 160–66. **Wonder** also occurs at 961.

1004–42 The preceding anapests (971–1003) now yield to a curiously made lyric passage: strophe (1004–17) and antistrophe (1023–42) are both interrupted by five lines in dactylic hexameter (1010–14 and 1031–40); between the responsive lyric stanzas Hyllus and the old man split five anapestic lines (1018–22).

1004–9 His protests and cries may imply that the bearers are trying to help him, but the nature of his pain—presumably the robe still clings to his burning flesh—precludes certainty. While the old man's words (1018) do not necessarily mean he has been trying to make Heracles comfortable, it will be easier for Heracles to deliver the aria if he is propped up.

1010–14 His view of himself as the civilizing hero who purged (cf. "purify" at 1061) the earth and seas of monsters is traditional. Even Euripides' Madness recognizes his virtue:

He reclaimed the pathless earth and raging sea.

(*Heracles* 851)

He says **beneficial** because either fire or sword will end his suffering; Deianira died by the sword and he will die (?) on a pyre. Hippolytus calls for spear (or sword) to end his pain (*Hippolytus* 1375–76).

1015–17 Dawe (*Studies*, vol. 3, p. 95) asks, "Has any man or god in the literature of any nation ever proposed to terminate his days in such a manner?" Dawe has emended away a similar request at *Phil* 1207. Perhaps not, but Dawe's suggestion that Heracles wants them to hack away his flesh seems at least as grotesque. Despite the metrical problems here (one or more words are missing), the violence of this hero warns us from emending away violence. Cf. "shear me apart" (*Hippolytus* 1376).

1019 **Your strength . . . than I** translates a much emended yet still uncertain passage.

1022 **Such is the will of Zeus** implies resignation; what man cannot understand he refers to the inexplicable management of the gods (cf. *Phil* 1020), just as he gives them thanks for unexpected gifts (cf. *Ant* 330–31).

1025–30 **My fate** = *daimôn* (see note to 910). Jebb compares the same exclamations at *Phil* 1187 ("the God, the God," as the pain returns) and *OK* 1312, where the question "how far have you sprung?" makes the *daimôn* more a personal spirit. Popular belief attributed illness to daimonic influence; incantations and healing or cursing by magic entail a belief that spirits may possess the body. In the next sentence, because the tame **sickness** is postponed, for a moment the spectators see the *daimôn* lunging.

1031 **Pallas** is Athena, the daughter of Zeus who often comes to Heracles' aid.

1036–40 For **godless** see the note to *OK* 254. The wish that the enemy may suffer the same fate may be found at *Prometheus Bound* 972–73, *Phil* 1111–13, *Medea* 163–65 (where "for the wrong" misses the comparison: "and suffer such wrong as they dared to make me suffer").

1041 **Hades**, Poseidon, and Zeus were brothers who once claimed equal power in the world (*Iliad* 15.185–93). Sleep and Death resemble one another and so are brothers (*Iliad* 14.231). For **death** the healer cf. *Hippolytus* 1372; for death and sleep, *Hippolytus* 1376 and 1388.

1048–50 **Wife of Zeus** (Hera) is a much less loaded periphrasis than the **false-faced daughter of Oeneus** (Deianira), since **false** (*dolos*) echoes the deceit theme (see the note to 274–78) and **face** reminds us of Deianira as spectator (e.g., 523–25). Heracles' mistaken assumption, which implicitly likens her to women like Clytemnestra (see next note), is one of the knots the play has yet to unravel.

1050–52 Clytemnestra actually did throw (**fasten**) robes over Agamemnon. The present passage is a complex quotation drawn from two or three passages in the *Oresteia*. Clytemnestra tells how

> as fishermen cast their huge circling nets, I spread
> deadly abundance of rich robes, and caught him fast.
> (*Agamemnon* 1382–83)

Aegisthus comes on to gloat:

> now that I see this man—sweet sight—before me here
> sprawled in the tangling nets of fury.
> (*Agamemnon* 1580–81)

"Nets" (1581) is the common word for "robe" used at *Tr* 603. Cf. Orestes' reference to "casting net" at *Libation Bearers* 492. The metaphor for weaving a deceit goes back to Penelope's trick (*Odyssey* 2.91–110; she pretends to weave a shroud for her father-in-law in order to postpone marrying one of the suitors). Cf. Bacchylides: "Then the irrestible *daimôn* wove for Deianira a clever plan full of tears, when she learned that the son of Zeus was sending Iole" (*Dithyramb* 16.23–29). There is unconscious irony in **Furies**, since Heracles does not yet know why these agents of revenge have been sent on him.

1054 Channels is the Greek word from which we get "arteries," which ancient medicine thought were passages for air.

1057 Fetters continues the motif of Heracles the bondman (see note to 35).

1059 When the monstrous **Giants**, raised by Earth to avenge the Titans defeated by Zeus, attacked the Olympians, Zeus summoned Heracles to assist the gods (an oracle declared that the Giants could be killed only with the help of a mortal). At Phlegra or Pallene (the two are sometimes identified), Heracles shot Porphyrion and Alcyoneus, and thus saved the Olympian order (see Apollodorus 1.6.1–2). Such stories illustrate the mediating function of Heracles: part man, part god, part brute, he lives and acts on the boundaries of experience and never seems fully at home in any one sphere.

1062–63 This sort of misogyny (cf. 1072 and 1075) is common in Greek tragedy (cf., e.g., *Aj* 652, *Ant* 484, and *Libation Bearers* 304), but the sexual themes of this play and its complex links with the sexual antagonism of the *Oresteia* (notes at *Agamemnon* 10f. and 594) lend his complaint something more than generic animosity. Heracles' recent slavery to Omphale and the erotic bonds fashioned so often by Aphrodite make "not again!" seem more appropriate than **alone**.

1064–65 Cf. Hyllus' derision of the **name mother** at 816–17. There is no pun here, only the prelude to his test of Hyllus' loyalty. Heracles quickly passes from punishing Deianira to his own condition and comes back to her in conclusion (1109–11).

1070 How far Heracles has fallen is evident from the appeal for **pity** (cf. 1035 and 1080). The cry for pity does not keep the old Oedipus or the wounded Philoctetes from being hard and willful.

1076–80 So far as I can tell, we cannot say how naturalistically Sophocles may have represented Heracles' wounds. The display is clearly for the spectators as well as those on stage, and the gesture seems to require some bloody horror. Dingel (*Bauformen*, p. 357) compares *Prometheus Bound* 91–95 (Prometheus calls on nature to witness his suffering) and *Hippolytus* 1363–67 (Hippolytus calls on Zeus to witness his suffering). More common are those scenes where another actor or the chorus calls attention to the presentation, i.e., to the visible evidence of suffering (*Bacchae* 1200: the coryphaeus tells Agave to show the head of Pentheus; *Aj* 65: Athena will show Odysseus the mad Ajax). In another kind of scene we become witnesses, as when Orestes displays the robe that made Agamemnon helpless (*Libation Bearers* 980–90), and, in a less specifically legal context, as when the chorus calls on us to contemplate the fate of Oedipus (*OK* 1524–30).

1081 This line and 1085–86 are brief lyric exclamations within the iambic trimeters. Such metrical irregularity reflects the excited passion of his speech.

1082–84 **Tearing** and **shoots** are medical; several passages (767–71, 778, 1053–56, 1082–84) achieve their vividness from anatomically specific language. The realism of proper medical terminology, however, is qualified by typical tragic personification (**in devouring sickness**) and the use of *atê* (here translated adjectivally as **malignant**) to define **tearing** (the "tearing of this ruin"; cf. *atê* as "disaster" at 1104). For the metaphor of the poison feeding on him see 677, 771, 987, 1053–56, 1088. As we might expect, some diction, e.g., "blooms" at 1089, while securely in the poetic tradition, is also found in the medical writers (of the height of a fever).

1086 We have already heard of Zeus' lightning (436), of the flames of love (368), of the sacrificial fire (765), of the boiling heat of the poison (840) ignited by the sun (695–98), and of the scorching pain (1082: same verb as "became warm" 697). All of this imagery, and there is more, looks forward to the pyre Heracles orders for himself (1197–99).

1089 For his now helpless **hands** see 1046, 1066–67, 1102, and 1110. Cf. Philoctetes' "Hands of mine" (*Phil* 1004). Perhaps it is significant for this motif that, in the short list of his labors which now follows, the Nemean lion, the Erymanthian boar, and Cerberus were all conquered by physical strength.

1092–1100 The lion of **Nemea** (just north of Argos) is usually named as the first of his labors for Eurystheus. When his arrows failed—he had not yet poisoned them—he choked it to death. The **serpent** (hydra) **of Lerna** (the swamp is also near Argos) was destroyed by cutting off its heads and cauterizing them before they could grow back. The **galloping army** is the centaurs, whom he encountered while on his way to search out the boar of **Erymanthus** (a mountain in northwestern Arcadia). Apollodorus (2.5.1–4) makes these the first, second, and fourth labors; **the hell hound with three heads** (Cerberus, watchdog in Hades) is last, and **the dragon guarding the golden apples** of the Hesperides is the penultimate labor. Both of these last two labors involve a symbolic triumph over death, while the hydra has provided Nessus (a centaur) with the poison now killing him. Clearly, then, this apostrophe to his hands provides an occasion for retrospective allusion (of which he is unconscious) to the dramatically relevant labors, and Cerberus and the golden apples may be covert foreshadowing of Heracles' apotheosis. **Violent, lawless** is a quotation from *Theogony* 307, where the phrase describes the father of Cerberus, Typhon (for him see *Prometheus Bound* 353–74). The serpentine **Echidna**, half nymph and half monstrous snake, mated with the dragon Typhon to produce Cerberus, but Echidna is mentioned here because the word is also a common noun meaning "viper," which was used at 771 of the hydra.

1104 The grandiloquent **sacked** literally describes "razing a city."

1105–6 **Who claim to be** is a variant on **called** and does not suggest doubt.

1110 He would give her a lesson, but her learning is over, and his is about to begin (1118 and 1145).

1118–21 **Mistaken** means both "futile" and "wrong-headed"; see on 940. The first sense of this adverb suits **craves** (Heracles cannot punish the dead); the second sense suits **feels** (Heracles erroneously believes Deianira was trying to hurt him). This natural ambiguity accounts for **your riddles.**

1123 Deianira's **unwilling error** is hardly a moral flaw (see Whitman, pp. 114–15). In attempting to regain her husband's affection, she has made a mistake in the means employed. If we understand Aristotle's *hamartia* (*Poetics*, chap. 13), with which "error" in the present passage is cognate, as "mistake" or misunderstanding of the relevant facts, Deianira's case seems to satisfy the philosopher's view of the proper cause for tragic reversal. This language appears in "crime . . . committed" (1127) and again in 1136 (a still more positive formulation).

1131 The tone is incredulous and sarcastic: "By whom? What a marvel of bad news you prophesy!" Our translation risks sympathy, which 1133 clearly denies.

Even those who wish us to admire the endurance and authority of Heracles will not claim much humanity for him. He never expresses a word of sympathy for Deianira nor any regret for his wild threats. Completely egotistic, he now follows the thread to Nessus.

1143 The **Woe is me** school of translation has not found a contemporary idiom; there may not be one. The combination of grief, agony, and self-regard makes a rough trail, where, in this case at least, tone is more important than sense. Our translations are much influenced by the Victorian Jebb: "Alas, alas, miserable that I am! Woe is me, I am lost,—undone, undone!" Here, as at *OK* 1183 and *Phil* 38, the predominant tone may be discovery (Lattimore translates "Ahoy!" at *Agamemnon* 24). Two very common adjectives denoting a pitiful unhappiness (e.g., "wretched" at 792, "poor boy" at 932, "miserable boy" at 936, "unhappy" at 713 and 1148) account for **woe** and **miserable.** Some of this is metrically convenient filler, but there is also a significant dramatic and aesthetic point in this language: articulated grief and lament are pervasive in Greek tragedy, and the language denoting wretchedness is shared both by sympathetic observers and the sufferers, who regularly draw our attention to their physical and mental pain by calling themselves "miserable," "wretched," and "unhappy." See on *OK* 1071.

One last point. Heracles' arrogance and egotism may offend the modern audience more than the Greek since we are taught in a tradition that values humility more. In *King Lear,* for example, Gloucester, his eyes gouged out by Cornwall and his heart crushed by Edmund's betrayal, speaks not of his own suffering but of how he has deserved it:

O my follies! Then Edgar was abused.
Kind gods, forgive me that and prosper him.
(*King Lear* 3. 7. 90–91)

Heracles knows nothing of his own follies, never speaks again of the abused Deianira, and cannot even imagine asking forgiveness of god or man.

1146–50 Although it is awkward to summon family who are not at hand, Easterling is probably right to see the solemnity of such a gathering as the dramatic point. **To her cost** means "for nothing" (seeing that Heracles has not profited from divine seduction).

1157–59 For the motif of proving a worthy son see 1064, 1201, 1205.

1159 This prophecy has not been previously mentioned in the play and, so far as we know, Deianira knew nothing of it.

1164 These **more recent prophecies** are those first alluded to at 46 and described in more detail at 156–72.

1166 The **Selli** are the priests at Dodona (see on 170–72); Homer describes them as men who "sleep on the ground with feet unwashed" (*Iliad* 16.235). The **oak** tree is sacred to Zeus; the priest may have interpreted the rustling of the wind in the leaves.

1170–71 Release echoes the theme of freedom and slavery (see on 180), while **complete** (the *tel-* stem) echoes the repeated "end" at 824–25, where it is emphatically associated with prophecy, "final" (948), and "last" (1150).

1173–78 Linforth points out that the plot does not necessarily lead to the pyre or to the marriage of Hyllus and Iole. Now that Heracles has understood the oracles, he might, like Eteocles in Aeschylus' *Seven,* accept with resignation his fate; a procession off, whether or not we learn of his divine prospects, would conclude this play in a natural way. These lines, ominous in their demand for an ally (1175) and insistence on an obedient son, turn toward unexpected matter, and Hyllus' alarm reflects the audience's uncertainty.

1181–90 Demanding an oath and handclasp is a particularly strong gesture inasmuch as a son is bound to follow his father's will in virtually any matter. Zeus oversees oaths (called "the oath keeper" at *OC* 1767); Heracles emphasizes the family connection as well (**who begot me**). The oath is blind, a blank check made out to the authority of Heracles.

1191 The ultimate thematic reason for previous references to **Mount Oeta** (200 and 634) becomes clear in Heracles' revelation that he is to be burned on a pyre there. The place was sacred to Zeus and from ancient times the site of a fire cult. The incineration of Heracles offers an explanation for the events and place of this fire festival (an *aetiology*, as it is called).

1196–97 The **oak** is sacred to Zeus, and he is also guardian of the olive (see on *OC* 701–6), though the Athenians more readily associate it with their guardian, and Heracles', Athena. The **wild olive** is said by Pindar (*Third Olympian* 11–15) to have been brought from the north by Heracles, who made a wreath of it the victor's crown at Olympia. The Greeks mistakenly thought that the wild olive was male (= **lusty**) and the domestic olive female. Hoey ("Ambiguity in the Exodos," p. 282) suggests symbolic association with Heracles and Deianira respectively.

1198–1201 Burning his father alive would have horrified any Greek son, and were it not for the authoritative tone of the whole passage and the specific instructions to forgo tears and mourning, Heracles might be thought mad. But he speaks as one who knows the divine will, which must be fulfilled even to the penalty of the father becoming an avenging spirit and **curse** on his son; cf. the **curse** of Oedipus on Polyneices (*OC* 1375–93) and Clytemnestra's threat that she will curse her son (*Libation Bearers* 912). For the power of such cursing and references see also on *Agamemnon* 1601f. Since Heracles will not explain either this command or the command to marry Iole (1221–29), we are left with Hyllus to wonder, but the audience has this advantage over Hyllus, namely that it knows of Heracles' apotheosis. Despite the absence of specific reference to that event, it seems certain that the combination of prophecy, pyre, Oeta, Zeus, and manner of the hero imply such a destiny. Friis Johansen ("Heracles in Sophocles' *Trachiniae*") offers some compelling arguments for interpreting the character as "hero/god": before he understands his fate we see a man of "no moral feelings at all" (p. 53), who, although greatly admired by others, possesses only limited power and knowledge; after Heracles understands the meaning of these prophecies, the "divine element in Heracles is heavily predominant" (p. 59), with the result that limitations imposed on the mortal hero yield to a "full and true knowledge" and a nearly "supra-human spiritual authority which complements his knowledge" (p. 59). Logic might bid us interpret **even below** as implying that Heracles has no expectation of immortality ("final end" at 1256 has also been adduced as evidence), but it is easy to understand an unstated premise that the son's failure to perform the rites might frustrate successful ascension, and secondly, a powerful threat is required to make Hyllus take such unnatural and impious orders.

1207 Hyllus will become, he naturally feels, **polluted,** and thus an outcast from family and community. Pollution is the physical and social stigma attached to anyone who has shed blood, no matter what the circumstances. His scruple at 1214—he will do everything but touch the fire to it—shows how significant the purely physical element is.

1208–11 Heracles offers a paradox (his killer will be his **physician**) and deflects Hyllus' request for an explanation. The paradox, however, is a tragic commonplace: see *El* 1170, *Hippolytus* 1372.

1212–16 Legend told that Philoctetes or his father Poeas actually set the torch to the pyre (see *Phil* 725–27). Another tradition, much later attested than that of the *Philoctetes,* reports the poisoned robe itself, ignited by the sun, started the fire. Sophocles' audience almost certainly knew the first version, which is not to say Heracles' prophetic knowledge is itself so specific. Friis Johansen (p. 60) argues, however, "Heracles could not make such a concession if he did not know what was going to happen to him. He knows that it is of no consequence who lights the pyre—and the audience knows that Hyllus' not performing the task did not impair his father's divinity—; this being so, Heracles quite naturally avoids the superfluous trouble of compelling his son on this point."

1221–29 Pre-Sophoclean tradition made Hyllus and Iole the parents of descendants of Heracles. Since the audience would have shared Hyllus' appalled reaction to this second command, Jebb thinks the dramatist introduced this topic to explain how it happened that Hyllus married a woman implicated in his father's death. They may have been curious on that score, but the dramatic reason for this second, striking command should be more organically related to the plot. Once again we must look to the new authoritative tone that has followed Heracles' insight into the meaning of his oracles. He offers no explanations but speaks firmly and dogmatically, quite indifferent to Hyllus' feelings and apparently equally forgetful of his own suffering. The dramatic point, then, would seem to be the reassertion of that heroic authority which in his mad suffering he had lost. His emphasis on obedience anticipates Hyllus' response. **Wife** means wife (as at 428 and 650), not "concubine," as some have suggested.

1230 For **to argue** prefer "to be angry."

1236 By implication Heracles suffers a daimonic attack when he asks such a thing. **Avenging fiends** probably suggests the Furies, since a man who lives compatibly with anyone responsible for his father's death would very likely be subject to their vengeance.

1238–40 **Due** is *moira,* and so "lot" or "portion," perhaps with allusive overtones of "what is granted by the gods" (= "doom" at 849; cf. *OK* 376). **Curse** is the same threat he made at 1202. The parallels in the two injunctions are based on Hyllus' fear of pollution, his father's threatened curse, and medical metaphor drawn from healing the sick. Of course Heracles is actually ill; the metaphorical extension plays on the topic "death the healer" and on "sick" thinking.

1245 Deianira has learned; Heracles has learned; but Hyllus will leave the stage acting on an uncertain faith, never understanding his father's will.

1248–51 Calling the **gods to witness** makes their oaths reciprocal. Religious and legal concerns meet, as when Orestes invokes the sun to "be a witness for me in my day of trial" (*Libation Bearers* 987). The point is perhaps more forceful if we translate lines 1249–50 "I shall do it then, and I shall not forswear, since I may show to the gods that the deed is yours." This is more literal and responds more directly to the use of Heracles' oath as evidence. For this legal motif in the play see lines 351–52, 421–22, 899–900.

1252 **End** (also 1256 and 1262) and "accomplishment" (1257) introduce a concentration of words from the *tel-* stem and echo the motifs connected with the prophecies and with time. **Mercy** (*charis*) means "act of kindness" ("favor" at 1229).

1259–63 **Is stirred** may be transitive; if so, he asks his soul "not to stir up again the sickness"; thus he calls on himself to control the enemy within, personifying the disease in a manner similar to lines 1053–57. The image of the **steel bit** (for a horse) is more remarkable for an untranslated adjective meaning "set with stone," which converts the bit into a steel clamp that holds stones close set. Thus in this mixed metaphor his spirit is likened to a rider curbing a horse so that his mouth will clamp back any shriek as firmly as a steel clamp holds stones together. The paradox in **unwanted, welcome** derives from telescoping an unwanted task with its welcome completion. His last word epitomizes his life.

1264–74 Hyllus' last words have excited much comment, but they are in fact a commonplace of Greek tragedy, namely blaming the gods. For a collection of examples see the note to *Agamemnon* 1485–88. In Euripides' *Heracles* Amphitryon is given a lengthy (339–47) abuse of Zeus:

Your love is even less than you pretended;
and I, mere man, am nobler than you, great god.
. . . .
You are a callous god or were born unjust!
(*Heracles* 341–42; 347)

Because the Greek gods are more concerned with power than with pity, they are bothered very little by such criticism. The antithesis between **much compassion** and **little compassion** may also be translated, "grant me forgiveness for this [i.e., for obeying his father's orders] since you know the lack of feeling the gods have shown in these matters." That the gods and particularly Zeus look upon our suffering is a commonplace (see the note to *Agamemnon* 1270). **Called our fathers** rings a final variation on "Zeus, god of our fathers" (see on 752–74) and the final, ambiguous, allusion, unconscious so far as Hyllus is concerned, to the apotheosis on Mt. Oeta. Consequently, **No one can foresee** is true of the speaker, perhaps untrue for the dying Heracles, whose oracular knowledge does not seem fully divulged, untrue for the audience insofar as its knowledge external to the play is concerned, and a teasing open closure in that Sophocles has refused a definite answer to "When has Zeus been so careless of his children?" (140). The thought of 1270 also concludes, less appositely, the *Ajax* (1419b–20); its ambiguous fitness to this play is beyond doubt (see Hoey, "Ambiguity in the Exodos," pp. 273–76).

1275–78 The manuscripts and editors are divided on the attribution of these lines: Hyllus, the coryphaeus, and the chorus all have their champions. If Hyllus speaks them, this play would uniquely, among the extant plays of Sophocles and Euripides, give the final lines to a character (Kranz, p. 205). Jebb's view that "it seems dramatically right that [the choral] silence should be maintained in this last scene" may accord with modern taste, but ancient practice should probably carry the day, though we should note that Clytemnestra has the last words in the *Agamemnon*. Cf. Lesky (*Greek Tragic Poetry*, p. 193): "His son accuses the gods: It is a disgrace that they let noblemen suffer! But the chorus immediately cancels such an accusation in their final words: There is nothing in all this that is not Zeus!" **Maiden**, then, is singular for plural, as the chorus calls itself to attend to the procession that will now carry the body of Heracles from the stage to Mt. Oeta. **Nothing here which is not Zeus:** for the thought cf. *Agamemnon* 1485–88.

Electra

•

ELECTRA is the daughter of Agamemnon, leader of the expedition against Troy. With his army gathered at Aulis but unable to depart because of adverse winds, Agamemnon sacrificed his daughter Iphigeneia to appease the divine anger. The army departed, and ten years later its victorious leader returned home to find a wife (Clytemnestra) who had not forgotten her dead daughter. Clytemnestra killed Agamemnon and together with Aegisthus, Agamemnon's cousin and her seducer, ruled the land. The only son, Orestes, had been sent into exile before his father's death. In Sophocles' version two daughters, Electra and Chrysothemis, remain at home. The one lives on hatred and hopes of revenge, the other causes her mother less concern and pain. Meanwhile Orestes waits and plans vengeance for Agamemnon's murder.

Sophocles' play dramatizes Orestes' return and revenge. Over forty years earlier Aeschylus had treated the same events in his *Libation Bearers*. Euripides' *Electra* was probably staged within ten years of Sophocles' play (both are usually placed between 420 and 410 B.C.), but we cannot tell which was prior. Although Aeschylus introduces Electra and gives her a significant role in the first half of his play, it is Orestes, and the killing of Clytemnestra, that are of paramount dramatic interest. Both Euripides and Sophocles greatly expand the role of Electra, and for both, perhaps inevitably, she is the suffering victim of Clytemnestra's malice and fear. Euripides, however, sets the scene in the country, where Electra has been given as wife to a farmer. It is there that brother and sister are reunited, and from there they plot their revenge, in which Electra and an old family retainer play leading parts. Sophocles, like Aeschylus, sets the scene before the palace, and again like Aeschylus, brings Orestes on in the prologue. Here similarity in plot ends, for Sophocles' Orestes has no sooner announced his purpose than he retires, not to return for a thousand lines. Clearly, the revenge of Orestes is but the context for this play, not its dominant thematic or dramatic point.

From the end of the prologue, when Orestes pointedly passes up a reunion with his sister, until the recognition scene, the character and personality of Electra give the play its focus and dynamics. Perhaps more than any other play by Sophocles, this is a character study. Oppressed and abused, Electra reacts bitterly and vindictively. A series of scenes with the chorus, Chrysothemis, and Clytemnestra are all more calculated to explore her suffering and reaction than to advance the action, which is of course qualified from the start by the resolute, pragmatic hero. Thus all Electra's despair ("Will Orestes never return?"), grief (the lament for her father continues), and determination to have revenge (she urges Chrysothemis to join her in revenge after she thinks Orestes dead), are included in an ironic plot that victimizes her one last time, for her brother has arrived and will kill their enemies as coolly and expeditiously as one could imagine.

Two questions seem to occupy much modern criticism. The more significant turns on the morality of the play and on the place of religion in Sophocles' conception. While Orestes has consulted Delphi, and apparently has the blessing of Apollo, he seems little troubled by his task, and as Sophocles has designed the plot, there is no place for remorse and guilt at the end. Electra lives her hatred and seems only to regret that Clytemnestra and Aegisthus cannot be killed twice. Thus righteous revenge is taken, but without the troubling moral dilemma—can a son kill his mother?—posed by Aeschylus. Winnington-Ingram has studied references to the Furies, which are several, but they not only do not materialize at the end of the *Electra*, but Orestes seems unconscious of them. Consequently, this may seem the least "religious" of all the extant plays because the divine seems here less the focus of thought, less the motive for action. That is one problem. Another is the question of the tragic character of the play. Those who are ready to accept it as melodrama, first-rate psychological melodrama, will find no problem. Our answer will depend in part on definition, in part on how we describe the moral and religious tone of these events.

The only scenic props required are statues of the gods (see 1374–75), particularly Zeus, Hermes, and Apollo, whose image should be conveniently placed so that Clytemnestra (637) and Electra (1376) may pray before it.

Greek children were cared for by household slaves like our Paedagogus. He fled the house to save Orestes (11–14), who was too young to remember his father's house and country.

1 **Once general in Troy** occupies the entire first line of the Greek text; Haslam has presented strong arguments for thinking it spurious. It is inflated and irrelevant, not at all in the manner of this character.

4 Mycenae stands on elevated ground at the north end of the plain of Argos. It is the Homeric home of Agamemnon and about five miles

from the town of **Argos,** which Aeschylus makes the scene of Orestes' return. The **Inachus** river flows into the plain from the northwest. His **gadfly-haunted daughter** is Io, who suffered the love of Zeus (see *Prometheus Bound* 561–887 for the gadfly and her torment).

6–7 **Wolf-killing** offers an etymological interpretation of **Lycean** Apollo; a different meaning is present at *OK* 919–21.

8 The **famous temple of Hera** (the Heraeum) is about two miles south of Mycenae. For the first eight lines the Paedagogus is looking away from the palace and pointing toward the landmarks in the valley below.

9 **Golden Mycenae** is a Homeric phrase (*Iliad* 11.46).

10 **Pelopidae** is a patronymic form here expanded to mean "the descendants of Pelops." The revelant genealogy of the house is

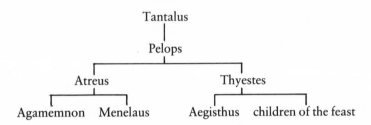

Tantalus
|
Pelops
|
Atreus   Thyestes
| |
Agamemnon   Menelaus   Aegisthus   children of the feast

The house is **death-heavy** because of the various crimes committed by its rulers. Attempting to trick the gods, Tantalus killed his son Pelops and served him in a stew to the visiting divinities. Restored to life, Pelops killed his charioteer Myrtilus. Atreus, seeking revenge for the seduction of his wife, killed Thyestes' sons and fed them to their father. Aegisthus seduced Agamemnon's wife and helped her kill the king.

11–17 In Aeschylus' version Clytemnestra has sent the boy Orestes to Strophius of Phocis (*Agamemnon* 877–80; cf. 44–45 below). **Pylades** (a mute role in this play) is the son of this Strophius (see 1110); in the *Libation Bearers* he has three lines, but they are crucial (900–902). The **sister** is Electra, who is here treated as an older sibling (for her age see 164–72). For her part in saving Orestes see 297–99 and 1130–33. **To be the avenger:** the Greek phrase describes him as an avenger and does not set it as the Paedagogus' purpose.

18 We do not know how early in the morning the Greek productions began, but both the *Agamemnon* (16) and *Antigone* (100) begin before dawn and make dramatic use of the darkness. Cf. Electra's invocation at 89.

21–22 **Parley . . . action** (*logos* and *ergon*) will occur several times as "words and deeds." The play is built on the contrast of what is actually the case, the fact that Orestes is alive and present, and what Electra believes is the case, the report of his death. Orestes dissembles the truth with a false report (59a–60), never reckoning the effect of the fiction (1217) on his sister. Her despair ("you killed me with your words," 1359b) leads Electra to vow a personal revenge, a plot that is aborted when the disguised Orestes reveals the "sweet reality" (1360). This ironic plot, with its happy ending for the avengers, victimizes Electra with a false report while promising, as the audience knows all along, an ultimate triumph over her enemies. In a secondary variation on this theme mother and daughter abuse one another for ugly, shameless words and deeds (see 612–29). Some passages highlighting this antithesis are 287, 319, 358–59, 935–36 (a double irony since Chrysothemis has good news and is persuaded not to believe the truth), and 1372–73. **High time** (cf. 1338) reflects another motif, that of occasion (opposed to "talk" at 1258) or "chance to act" (1368), hitting the mark (31) in timing action. Words, as Orestes says, may ruin opportunity (1291–92). Two words (*kairos* and *akmê*) mark this motif; see also 39b, 75–76, 386, and 1338.

25–27 Comparison of men and animals is common in Homer. Paris, for example, is like a stallion that has broken from his stall and races across the plain (*Iliad* 6.506–11). **Break his spirit** echoes Homeric phrasing, and **His ears still erect,** which probably does not comment on the paedagogus's mask, typifies the Homeric simile's freedom from context.

30–32 This request for advice and correction is more than good manners if lines 83–88 belong to his servant (see the note there). In any case this old man has a larger part than might be expected since he not only plays the messenger's role (660–73) but appears a third time (1326) to rebuke Orestes and Electra for their foolish loitering. Nothing troubles Orestes' resolution; it is not ethical advice he solicits but rather, more pragmatically, timing.

33 Pytho's place of prophecy is Apollo's oracle at Delphi.

34–35 His purpose was fixed when he approached the god: he asks how, not if. Offering several examples from contemporary Greek literature, Sheppard argues that the Greek audience, equally sensitive to the rule of law and to the evils of matricide, would have been quick to sense that Orestes could not so easily escape moral responsibility: "You could not, by consulting oracles, get rid of your own moral responsibility, and if you framed your question disingenuously, then acted on the answer without thought, you had no right to blame the gods when things went wrong" (p. 4). Kells ("Sophocles' *Electra* Revisited") supports this perspective on the play. The chief difficulty for this view seems to be that in this play there is relatively little attention to conscience and moral scruple; neither Electra nor Orestes gives us much reason to think that they experience a moral dilemma in killing their mother.

37 Apollo's (**Phoebus**) response at *Libation Bearers* 269–96 is more threatening in that it anticipates Orestes' ambivalence. In Sophocles there is no dilemma, no need for threats if he should balk at killing Clytemnestra. Cf. Euripides *Electra* 971–81.

38 Craft . . . **stealth** (*dolos*) is also the advice in *Libation Bearers* (274) and the way of Orestes in Euripides. It was by guile that Clytemnestra killed his father (124–25, 196, and 279). See also 1229d–e, 1392, and 1397.

40–43 Even Electra will not recognize the paedagogus (1346–50). The intrigue, well planned and straightforward, is delayed only by the appearance of Electra.

44–45 A mountainous district in central Greece, Phocis is north of Boeotia. This **Phanoteus** was the ally of Clytemnestra and Aegisthus. His brother Crisus was his enemy and the father of Strophius, father of Pylades and friend of Agamemnon, who gave sanctuary to Orestes (see 1110–11).

48 The **Pythian games** were held every four years and were second only to the Olympian games in renown. The story is elaborated at 680–763.

51–53 Later Chrysothemis will discover these offerings and infer the presence of Orestes (892–904). The **libations** are milk (895); for the offering of **hair** see *Aj* 1174.

55 The **urn** will contain the ashes of the dead Orestes (58–59 and 758–59).

58 Besides **tale of lies,** there is emphasis on the verbal nature of the deceit at 43, 50, 59a, 61, and 63.

59a–60 For the antithesis **die in word** . . . **in deed** . . . **alive** cf. 1229d–e. **Glory** (*kleos*) is the standard heroic motivation; cf. *Ant* 502–3. Yet **no word is base** . . . **profit** is more the ethic of Odysseus (*Phil* 79b–85 and 99d: "it is the tongue that wins and not the deed") than of Ajax and Antigone. His readiness to let the paedagogus forswear himself (47) is another gratuitous pragmatism (the messenger will not take an oath; none is required of him). **Base** (*kakon*) is perhaps ambiguous: Jebb takes it to mean "ill-omened" because a superstitious person would avoid allusion to his own death. Kaibel protests "base" (ethically bad) on the grounds that only the sense "harmful" gives a satisfactory antithesis.

62–65 Orestes' **wise men** may be an allusion to Pythagoras or the Thracian Salmoxis (Herodotus 4.95), who feigned death in order to reappear and thereby gain authority for their teaching. If such are the allusions, they are a little strained, and might be taken by some in the audience as cynical reflections on pseudoreligious teachers.

68 Homer, e.g., *Iliad* 22.26–32, has similes likening heroes to baleful stars. Here the Greek verb translated **glare** means little more than "shine," and Orestes' point seems simply that he will be alive.

69 The *Libation Bearers* begins with a prayer by Orestes.

69c–70 A major difference between this play and the *Libation Bearers* turns on **purifier**: in Aeschylus he comes to avenge his father, and in killing his mother he pollutes himself and his house and so is driven once again into exile. Then he seeks purification from Apollo and in the *Eumenides* he is absolved of guilt and pollution. In this play the problematic nature of revenge against kin is hardly raised (see 1424, 1498–99). The **justice** (*dikê;* cf. 39) of revenge is an accepted fact.

72 Rich from of old time refers to possession of his patrimony; cf. *Libation Bearers* 301.

76 Greatest master is a political metaphor, i.e., "chair-man/president," and is ethically neutral. The Aeschylean Orestes constantly thinks of himself as under the guidance and tutelage of the gods (see, e.g., *Libation Bearers* 405–9 and 583–84).

78–88 We should take seriously Sandbach's suggested attribution of these lines:

> *Paedagogus:* Inside the house some one of the servants,
> I think, is crying. Might it not be the unfortunate
> Electra?
> Do you want us to stay here and to listen to her cries?
> *Orestes:* No, Nothing must come before we try. . . .

With this change, the decision to put revenge before reunion becomes Orestes'. Although the manuscript attribution, accepted here, can appeal to the young hero's deference at 28–32, Orestes' manner in the preceding speech is all business and definitely that of a man in control. He has a plan and will pursue it, and to give the servant this dramatically momentous decision undercuts his authority. **For your father** is no objection because the *your* is not expressed in the Greek and so may be "for my father." For **lustral offerings** (apparently = "libations" at 52) see on 435.

89–250 The parodos begins with a lyric solo (monody) that is followed by responsive lyrics (121–235) and concluded with another song by Electra (236–50). Formally this is similar to the parodos of Euripides' *Electra* (112–212), where Orestes in hiding overhears the song. The essential subject of the initial song is the pathos of the protagonist, and this is characteristic of such lyrics; cf. *Aj* 394–409, *Hecuba* 59c–98. The responsive lyrics are more expository: the chorus attempts to console and restrain Electra while both voices reflect on the death of Agamemnon and her present circumstance. Unconsolable, assured of the loyalty of the chorus,

Electra concludes (236–50) with a cry for revenge and justice. The chorus should come on with Electra.

89 For the apostrophe to the **light** see *OK* 1184 and cf. *Aj* 394. **Copartner:** because air and light share the realm above the earth.

90 Euripides' Electra sings of

> ripping my flesh with sharp
> nails, fists pounding my clipped
> head for your dying.
>
> (*Electra* 147–49)

Greek lament was violent and unrestrained, and Electra is no novice in grief. "Bring me again the sweetness of tears," says Euripides' Electra (126), who is typically Greek in the pleasure she takes from full public expression of her sorrow. Cf. 285–86 below. The directness and candor of Greek self-pity, acceptable and expected by ancient audiences, may prove less congenial to modern audiences. The chorus will urge moderation, in good part because they see she is harming herself (213–20), to which Electra will plead compulsion (221).

98 Who shared her bed: like Electra, the chorus believes that Clytemnestra's motives were erotic (see 196, 492–94). **Aegisthus** is a seducer (see 562 and 586), and this is Electra's charge even before the debate with her mother (see 114 and 272–74). While the condemnation seems to stick, we cannot fail to notice a certain sexual obsession in Electra that gives vehemence to her hatred but at the same time dissipates the ethical and religious focus of her arguments. In Aeschylus, a father, head of the house, and king has been murdered, and that motivates revenge; in Sophocles, more personal motives, such as Clytemnestra's lust and her sorry treatment of her children, broaden and lower theme and tone. Jones (pp. 149–53) has some remarks on sexuality in the two dramatists; he is wrong, however, to claim that "the Sophoclean Furies are preoccupied with sexual wrongdoing to the point of reacting against marital infidelity as the sharpest of provocations" (pp. 152–53). Up to now Clytemnestra has not been bothered by these demons, and Electra's invocation (Jones cites 110–14 and the lyric at 488–94) does not make it so.

99 For the death of Agamemnon see *Agamemnon* 1382–86.

102 Cruel also suggests shameful (as at 217) and base (as at 487). They not only murdered but also mutilated Agamemnon (447).

107 For the **nightingale** see 149.

110–12 Hades (**Death God**) and Persephone are invoked because they house the spirit of Agamemnon; **Hermes** leads the spirits of the dead to Hades (cf. *Aj* 832). The **Curse** is on the house from earlier generations (see the note to 10) and is also felt to belong more specifically to the unavenged spirit of Agamemnon. Curse(s) and **Furies** are sometimes identified (see on *Eumenides* 417 and OC 1375–76). References to the Furies will be found at 276, 491, 1079b, and 1389. Winnington-Ingram's chapter on the *Electra* sees Electra as "a Fury, a wrathful agent of infernal powers; she is a willing matricide" (p. 246).

117–20 Orestes is present, and that dramatic irony qualifies Electra's despair and bitterness (e.g., 164–72). She is not **alone.** Grief (also "pain/vexation") is so balanced against her that she is near madness (136) and cannot control herself (221–25).

121 Wretchedest is the superlative of "unhappy" (95) and occurs at 77 in the cry from within (Electra of herself). **Ceaseless lament** (cf. "insatiate woe," *Persians* 549a) is natural, but a Greek will see anything excessive as dangerous.

127–29 The switch to Aegisthus (**him**) is surprising after the weight on **mother,** more so in that **lawfully** (*themis*) would be the expected qualification for wishing her dead, whereas Aegisthus is beyond the pale.

129a Girls: the comparison at 234 and the address at 372 suggest the chorus is composed of mature women.

136 Madness is a common theme: Athena drives Ajax mad (*Aj* 52), and his recovery is the focus of the first half of that play; Heracles goes mad from pain and kills Lichas (*Tr* 778–80; cf. 999); Philoctetes' pain is such that he calls it madness (see *Phil* 1194–95); the chorus sees Oedipus' self-blinding as a manic act (*OK* 1300). Whether physical or psychological, madness characterizes both the excess of the protagonist and his power to endure great suffering. Cf. below 140–41, 156–57. Although Ruth Padel's "Madness in Fifth-Century Athenian Tragedy" does not extend its range to include characters like Electra, it is a good place to begin the study of this theme.

138 The **lake of Death** is Acheron (182); see on *Ant* 805–14.

148–49b The nightingale's complaining notes have their origin in the story of Procne and Tereus. Procne, mother of Itys, killed her son and fed him in a stew to her husband Tereus after he had raped her sister Philomela. When Tereus discovered her revenge, he pursued her, and during their flight she was transformed into the nightingale, he into hoopoe. The cry **Itys** is the mother's lament for her dead son. The usual messenger of Zeus is the eagle; here the scholiast suggests that the nightingale's return to Attica in the spring makes her Zeus' messenger. More germane to the context, and more allusive, is Kaibel's view that Zeus has sent her the bird in order to prompt her to lament.

150–51 For the suffering of **Niobe** see on *Ant* 824–31. She is called "God's child and god she was" by the chorus at *Ant* 832 (with reference to her descent from Tantalus). Here, too, Kaibel offers a deeper meaning:

Niobe's eternal lament is, for Electra, a kind of happiness that is divine. The ironic inversion of what is normally thought happy is underlined by **suffered all.**

154 Not alone to you is familiar consolation, as at *Medea* 1017.

158–59 Homer knows three daughters, **Chrysothemis,** Laodike, and Iphianassa, sometimes identified with Iphigeneia, whose sacrifice Homer does not mention. Hesiod and Xanthus, an early lyric poet, both know Electra, and she may have figured in Stesichorus' *Oresteia.*

160–63 Prince = "prosperous"; they do not actually know his condition any more than Electra does, and they try to pick up her spirits. For this reason, **if God will bless** can be translated more positively: "with his coming blessed by Zeus." **Noble** belongs to Orestes; cf. 858–59 and 1080.

166–67 Electra's age cannot be determined. **Till I'm past childbearing** translates the privative "childless," and **past marriage** is simply "unmarried"; both of these motifs are commonplaces of self-pity (cf. 186–87 and *Ant* 813–14, 865).

169d–72 She will mention these secret **messages** again when she laments his supposed death (1154–56).

174 Zeus protects houses, fathers, and exiles and therefore may be expected to guide Orestes. See her prayer at 209–10.

176–77 Overbitter . . . overmuch: the excess of grief and complaint is also marked at 156, 213, 219, 236 (acknowledged by Electra), and 255. When she is reunited with Orestes, "superfluity of speech" (1288) remains a problem.

179 Time: cf. 781 and

> Time is the author both of truth and right
> and time will bring this treachery to light.
>   (*Spanish Tragedy* 2.5.58–59)

and

> For just men Time is the best savior.
>   (Pindar frag. 132)

For the Greek the gods appear in life as those effective forces shaping decision and event. If the passage of time reveals what is hidden or unsuspected, then time becomes an agency revealing the truth about the world, that is, about an immortal and immutable aspect of life only evident to the divine. Zeus is all-seeing because he knows the truth that time alone will reveal to man.

180 Crisa, the home of Strophius, is below Delphi toward the Corinthian gulf.

182 For **Acheron** see 138.

188 With **dishonored** cf. 71, 242, 446–47. Electra cannot and will not have honor from those who have murdered her father (239a and 355–56; cf. 363). Revenge brings honor (983) and fame (985), just as the present abuse dishonors her and the house.

190 **Ugly** is not literal ("shameful," as at 217, is more the idea), but her appearance should suit her complaint. For costume see also 360–61. Cf. Euripides *Electra* 304.

192–95 In the *Agamemnon,* Clytemnestra kills her husband while he is bathing (see 1540 and the discussion at 1372ff.). Sophocles seems to have had in mind the Homeric version (*Odyssey* 11.405–26), where Agamemnon and his men are killed at a banquet (cf. 204) given by Aegisthus, "with the help of his sluttish wife," as Agamemnon says (410–11). **Couch,** then, refers to the lounge at table. Jebb also calls attention to Agamemnon's report:

> and the most pitiful was the voice I heard of Priam's
> daughter Kassandra, killed by treacherous Klytaimestra
> over me; but I lifted my hands and with them beat on
> the ground as I died upon the sword.
>
> (*Odyssey* 11.421–24)

Pitiful . . . cry may imitate this passage or the anguish of the Aeschylean Cassandra. The manuscripts contain a pronoun that indicates the cry is Electra's; most modern editors emend it away. Despite the apparent Homeric allusion, the natural referent for the cry is either Agamemnon himself or, more generalized, his followers.

196 For **craft** see on 38; for this motif in the *Oresteia* see the note to *Agamemnon* 886. Homer's account implies that Aegisthus seduced Clytemnestra, a view our chorus and Electra (562) prefer to any thought of Iphigeneia (see Electra's argument at 570–80).

197–200 The **Shape** has been identified as what Clytemnestra calls the "old stark avenger" (*Agamemnon* 1501; Greek *alastôr*) and as the Fury, which comes to much the same thing. Clytemnestra claims that not she but the avenging *daimôn* killed Agamemnon, and that kind of thinking is behind **divine or human** here.

213–17 As the context shows, **speak too far** refers not so much to the preceding prayer's content as to their concern that public denunciation will only win her still more degrading abuse. **Shamefully** echoes "shameful" (205). **Self-inflicted** puns on "belonging to the house" and "proper to you."

219a–220 There are two aspects to her misfortune: she herself is disturbed and she risks further offense to the **princes.**

221–25 **Terrors** (*deina*) = "dreadfully . . . dreadful" (197–98); the word may have an objective cast, as "hard conditions" at 26, but more often it denotes the subjectively "strange" (it occurs in Clytemnestra's ruminations at 767 and 770). With **compelled** cf. 256, 309a–b, 620, and 1193 (all the *anagkê* stem). What is strange and terrible is the unnatural mothering of Clytemnestra (see 260ff.); Electra may yield or resist. Yielding would be impious and resisting is self-destructive. **Mad cries of misery** (the phrase translates *atê*) responds to "destruction" (216). Since the chorus returns to this language at 235 (in the repeated "sorrow"), we should probably try for the same referent in English in all three passages; Campbell's "this fatal course," though hardly literal, suits the sense.

226 **Right** is also "fitting" (see the note on *kairos*, 21–22).

230 **Cureless** = "cannot be loosened." It is a matter of deliverance (143), of freedom (339–40, 970–71), rather than of a remedy.

239 **Instinctive** is a biological metaphor ("be born/grow") and thus answers "breed" (235); cf. "breeding" 219a.

240 **If I dwell with any good thing** = "if my lot is better."

242 **The wings of shrill lament** remind us of the nightingale (149). Pindar knows the wings of song:

> May he be lifted on the shining wings of the Muses,
> the melodious.
>
> (*First Isthmian* 64)

243–50 Electra's argument, traditional in its language and thought, has two connected conditional clauses and a compound conclusion. The first clause, if the dead are nothing (i.e., have no power from the other world), and the second clause, if murderers never pay for their crimes in kind, are implicitly linked by the idea that the dead somehow effect justice. One function of lament keeps the dead conscious of the dishonor they have suffered. Electra's tendance of her father's memory, then, is a kind of **piety** (*eusebeia*) that would be pointless if her father's spirit does not respond and the killers do not pay. **Shame** (*aidôs*) inhibits, but if the dead are nothing and powerless, why should anyone fear justice? Thus the failure to obtain justice implies that the dead are powerless to help themselves and their friends, and the conclusion must be that neither positive values (piety) nor negative (shame) have any practical foundation in experience. Cf. the arguments at 499–501 and at *OK* 883–96.

262 With **all hatred** she marks the unnatural situation in which a mother becomes an enemy and the house, the natural locus of friends (*philoi*), is torn apart by the feeling appropriate to war.

270 The **hearth** is the most sacred place in the house, where offerings (**libations**) are poured out by the head of the house.

271 **Insult** is *hybris;* cf. 293. That the ultimate affront is sexual,

rather than, say, political or social, tells a good deal about Sophocles' conception of her character. In the *Libation Bearers* Orestes' first words with his mother charge her with sexual perfidy (894–907), but after he has killed her (972ff.), it is more the murder of Agamemnon than her infidelity that weighs in his indictment.

275–76 Daring is "most brazen" at 440. **Paramours** is elsewhere, (e.g., 359), simply "lives with," but there is no want of punch in **polluted**. Cf. 449, 494, and 605. If Clytemnestra **fears no Fury**, she is not without anxiety (see 417–28); Electra naturally exaggerates.

277–80 Electra repeatedly charges Clytemnestra with **laughing** at her (cf. 808 and 1153), and Orestes also characterizes the enemy in this generic fashion (1295), even as he waits his turn (1300). Not generic, however, is the **festival** of thanks: like many Greek heroes, Agamemnon had a cult, and with ironic inversion Sophocles has made Electra attribute the historical founding to the hero's murderer.

285–86 As my heart would have me: Jebb's translation brings out the idea of pleasure in grief (see the note to 89): "as much as my inclination makes it pleasant (to weep)."

287 Mazon notes that such irony (**all nobility in words**) is rare from Electra. Cf. "distinguished bridegroom" at 300.

291 My curse upon you! = "May you perish miserably!"

299a She **howls** like a dog.

301 Dastard is right, but **mischief complete** is idiomatic in Greek tragic diction (it is "utter devil" at *Phil* 623).

306–7 A latent irony derives from the commonplace that "exiles feed on hope" (*Agamemnon* 1668; cf. 1460 below). For her **hope** see also 184, 810, 833, 858, and 953. It is not only despair but resentment (321) that motivates her. **Possible and impossible** (= "present and absent") may be one of those popular but occasionally illogical polar expressions or the equivalent of "hopes present and those absent/fled."

308–9b Cf. the last lines of Electra's prayer in the *Libation Bearers:*

And for myself, grant that I be more temperate
of heart than my mother; that I act with purer hand.

(140–41)

The contrast is more telling, and probably a conscious recollection, for the fact that the Sophoclean **be moderate and restrained** translates the same stem (*sôphron-*) as the Aeschylean "more temperate of heart," and **pious** renders the same stem as the Aeschylean "purer." Of course she means she cannot, if she reveres the memory of her father, be pious toward her mother. **Evil** (*kaka*) means that in such harshly demeaning circumstances she must respond by trying to hurt her enemies. This Electra owes more to Medea:

> I am overcome by evil.
> I know indeed what evil I intend to do,
> But stronger than all my afterthoughts is my fury,
> Fury that brings upon mortals the greatest evils.
>
> (Euripides *Medea* 1077–80)

All the evil here is *kaka;* Medea has been hurt and will give it back in kind. This is the old heroic ethic reduced to psychological and meaner social dimensions.

312–14 She is prisoner in her own house and can expect worse yet (see 380–83); see also 514–16.

323 Gentleman (*esthlos*) implies both honesty (*OK* 611) and valor (*Aj* 1345).

325–28 The coryphaeus announces the entrance of Chrysothemis and identifies her burden, which the audience could not be expected to recognize. Neither Aeschylus nor Euripides brings on a sister or a comparable confidant. Of Sophoclean characters Ismene is the nearest in ethos and dramatic function.

330 Learning naturally figures in a play of recognition and reversal, and in the *Electra* this theme is much elaborated, from the paedagogus's topographical instruction (110) and Orestes' request for correction (30–32) to Electra's "instruction" of Aegisthus (1450–54; cf. 1480). Before she learns the truth, Electra will believe the messenger's false report and persuade Chrysothemis of its truth. Meanwhile a strong didactic tone pervades the argument between mother and daughter (e.g., 535, 559, 585, 621). See also 343–44 and 395–96.

331 Empty means "vain/futile." **Give way to** implies gratification and self-indulgence.

334 If I had strength: cf. Ismene's argument at *Ant* 61–68. **Under pain of punishment** = "Evil is all around me" (309a, with note).

338 References to **justice** at 70, 474, 561, 583, 610, 1440, 1508. Naturally enough, Electra, Orestes, and their friends claim to act in justice, and there is little doubt that retribution would seem justified to the old Greek way of thinking. Yet many critics are troubled by the malice of Electra (e.g., 1417: "If you have strength—again!"; cf. 1487–90) and the lack of compunction in Orestes. Meanness and amoral pragmatism lower the tone of the play, which critics like Kitto and Woodard try to save by seeing a higher, cosmic law illustrated in the action. Sophocles "is demonstrating a law in things, that violence must produce its recoil; and the fact that the *dikê* here is so grim and unrelieved is a measure of the hideousness of the original offence" (*Greek Tragedy*, p. 141). Reacting to Kitto's "hideousness," Woodard argues that "judged by the standards of probability, normal psychology, and moral immediacy, perhaps the play affects us as implausible, inhuman, or "ugly." But responding to its cosmic drama we shall witness in the *Electra* a new definition of good and evil, when a more than human reality, active through humans, achieves justice. An idealized hero and heroine punish a pair of stylized villains; the revenge story does not preach vendetta but symbolizes harsh, beneficent forces in the nature of things" (Woodard, part 2, pp. 216–17).

339–40 There is more paradox in her conclusion if **and not as a prisoner** is translated "free."

345–47 Since the whole speech abuses Chrysothemis—she will turn to softer persuasion at 431 when she learns the purpose of the burial offerings—the **choice** is probably specious; thus **to be a fool** means "to think imprudently" (as Electra does), and **to be sensible** means to think pragmatically (as Chrysothemis does in neglecting her kin and natural friends). The division, if this is the correct view, comes down to "be me or be yourself," a sarcastic dismissal. It is also possible, however, to take the Greek to mean "think basely (as you do now) or sensibly (as I do) and forget these false friends (Clytemnestra and Aegisthus)."

349–50 There is no indication in the text of when she tried to **take vengeance** or if her vengeance was ever anything more than the vehement mourning.

355 **And I hurt them:** cf. 552–54, 558–59, and 655, in all of which "pain" echoes hurt. **And so give honor** denotes result rather than purpose, a nuance that makes her antagonism more personal.

357 **Pleasure** (*charis*) also implies "gratitude."

358–59 Just as Orestes, she supposes, is all promises and no rescue (319–21), so now she is the real hater (**in fact**), while Chrysothemis merely talks (**in word**) hate.

360 **Feel pride** = "revel/delight." The sneer will have more point if Chrysothemis is wearing her party dress. She anticipates the commonplace **yield** to authority (396, 1013–14).

362 The Greek phrase behind **quiet of my conscience** has often been emended. It is, more literally, "For me, let it be food enough that I do not pain myself" (Jebb, whose interpretation the translation follows). **Food** is obviously metaphorical, in contrast to the rich banquets Chrysothemis enjoys—so "consolation/sustenance." But "not to pain myself" seems weak and vague, and because the verb is the same as "hurt" in 356, some editors favor emending to "it is enough for me to pain/hurt them." That way is more in keeping with her aggressive tone. Although Greek of this period has no specific word for **conscience**, the idea of adhering to princi-

ple for its own sake is not altogether absent. But is Electra that sort of person? In fact, her principle (308–9b) dictates an eye for an eye.

364 Sound of mind translates the same stem (*sôphron-*) as "be moderate and restrained" (308); see also 464–65. Since she implicitly asks her sister to be what she has said she herself cannot be, she would seem to contradict herself. As at 345–47, arguing for "good sense" may be a little ambiguous when values are not explicitly defined, and values become muddy and confusing when one feels compelled to hate kin and to urge a sister to hate her mother and abandon all self-interest as well.

367 Antigone also charges Ismene with being a **traitor** (*Ant* 45–46). The motif of betrayal finds a place in all the plays and often becomes a central dramatic theme, as in the *Philoctetes*. Some lines highlighting betrayal will be found at *OK* 331, *OC* 649, *Aj* 589 (see note to 1266–67) and *Phil* 923.

368–71 Anger = "spirit" (223). **Value** = "profit" (61). **Follow her advice** = "learn from what she has said." Kamerbeek compares the similarly vain mediation at *Ant* 724–26.

376 Your terror (*deinon;* see 221–25): she cannot imagine a greater misfortune (374) and speaks in mock disbelief. Cf. *Ant* 95–96 ("this terror").

378–86 Antigone is imprisoned in a **cave**, where Creon expects her to die of starvation (*Ant* 773–80). Here the only point—the threat is not mentioned again—is to show the hostility of Clytemnestra and Aegisthus and the resolution of Electra. **Take thought** = "show some sense"; this is the language (*phronein*) of the disjunction at 346–47. Cf. 394.

388 The absence of Aegisthus is mentioned at least four times (310–14, 388, 514–16, and 1369). In Aeschylus' *Libation Bearers* he is also away, but neither Orestes nor Electra knows that. Sophocles' conception insists on the virtual slavery of Electra in her father's house; Aegisthus' absence explains how she is able to complain so bitterly, and so publicly, without repraisal such as Chrysothemis has just reported.

389a My poor darling (*talaina*) does not carry special intimacy or sympathy; it is "wretched" at 273, 450 (Electra of herself), and 883. Cf. *Ant* 82 ("my poor sister") and see on 674 below.

390 Ismene's response (*Ant* 42) to Antigone's call for aid in burying Polyneices is virtually the same:

What will you risk? And where is your intent?

Are you crazy = "what are you thinking of?"

392 Care is also Jebb's rendering of a word whose primary meaning is "memory," which makes Chrysothemis a bit more obtuse.

395 Falseness to those I love = "to be base toward my friends."

398 **Fall through stupidity** is repeated at 429a.

400 Ismene (*Ant* 65–66) also hopes the dead will **pardon** her.

401 The intellectual cast of a moral argument is typical; cf. frag. 925: "Stupidity is the very sister of Vice."

405–6 **Burnt offering** is proleptic for "offerings to be burnt." In her reply Chrysothemis uses the word proper for libations at the grave (cf. 435 and 442). The conversation now returns to her original mission (327–28).

410 Sophocles borrows this nightmare from Aeschylus (*Libation Bearers* 523–39). Clytemnestra wants to appease the ghost that sends the dream (cf. 459a–60). Both Electra and Orestes take heart from this news, since it implies that the spirit of the dead may yet help them win revenge (see 453–55).

417–24 In the *Libation Bearers*, her dream—she gives birth to a snake that draws her blood with milk when she nurses it—is more threatening because more sexual and violent. The burgeoning **scepter** may have been suggested by Achilles' oath on the scepter at *Iliad* 1.234–37, while **foliage . . . shaded all the land** may be indebted to the dream of Astyages (Herodotus 1.108).

425 Apart from the dramatic usefulness of a character speaking to the sun and sky, which here explains how Chrysothemis knows the dream, the scholiast offers the following explanation: "it was the custom for the ancients, whenever they saw a fearful dream during sleep, as soon as dawn came to tell the dream to the sun, that, since the sun is opposed to night, it would turn away the dream"; cf. Clytemnestra's prayer at 637–40, and

> I dreamed last night a deathly dream. Perhaps
> The morning will dispel it if I speak it.
> (*Iphigenia in Tauris* 42–43)

In Euripides' *Hecuba* the prologue is delivered by a ghost, who reports the appearance of the dead Achilles demanding human sacrifice; then Hecuba enters and sings of her terrible dreams (*Hecuba* 1–98).

428–30 The final three lines of the Greek text (from **And, by the Gods . . .**) do not cohere, are redundant and weak, and may be an actor's interpolation.

431–35 If such sacrifice to a dead enemy were against **God's law** (not *themis*) and impious according to any objective or generally held standard, then Clytemnestra, from fear of the gods, would not send the sacrifice. In fact, the murderer thinks she can appease or ward off the dead spirit, and Electra's urgency makes sense only if she too believes in its possible efficacy. In the *Libation Bearers*, when Electra asks the chorus what to do with her mother's offerings (84a–105), it counsels her to "Say words of grace for those of good will, as you pour" (109) and thus to deflect the purpose of Clytemnestra. See the prayer below at 634–59a, which can only be sincere, however vain it will prove.

435 Lustral is the literal translation and naturally refers to the bath for the dead, a regular feature of mourning. Thus at 448 it is "purification": Clytemnestra perversely bathed her murdered husband in his own blood, thereby denying him proper rites and asserting that his death was on his own head. Here the word is metaphorical for the libations of water offered the dead (honey, oil, wine, and barley broth are also regularly offered).

442 Enemy is transferred from the person to the thing she does ("hostile libations").

447 Mutilated refers to cutting off the extremities of the victim and tying them under his armpits; it is a bit of magic designed to render the dead spirit powerless.

> Know then, they hobbled him beneath the armpits,
> with his own hands. She wrought so, in his burial
> to make his death a burden
> beyond your strength to carry.
> The mutilation of your father. Hear it.
>   *(Libation Bearers 439–43)*

448–49a See the note to 435. It is Clytemnestra who is stained (see the note to OC 1132–37), and normally the murderer would attempt to expiate the guilt (**quittance offering**) by sacrificing a pig whose blood then washes away the stain on the culprit. Clytemnestra perverted this ritual by making the victim she killed the victim she would use for expiation. Sophocles has fused two distinct rituals, i.e., bathing the dead and expiating blood guilt, into a single bizarre inversion.

449b–52c For the **lock of hair** see 53. There is no reason for it to be **lustrous**, nor for her to refer to it as such. In fact the text is corrupt, and a suitable reading has not been found. The **girdle** is not a corset but a belt or sash worn around the lower part of the body.

453–55 The chorus calls to the dead Agamemnon:

> Hear
> us, hear. Come back into the light.
> Be with us against those we hate.
>   *(Libations Bearers 459–60)*

464–65 Speaks well and **wise** bring together the same two ideas discussed at 309. She has spoken piously and Chrysothemis will be prudent and discreet if she follows her advice. Cf. "piety" at 969a and 1096. This is the virtue of Antigone as well (*Ant* 872).

466–71 The verbal inflection (**will do . . . to do**) is followed by the signature word for "deeds" (*ergon:* **this**). Contrast the use of silence at *Ant* 84–87.

Exit Chrysothemis. Electra remains on stage.

472–513 The first stasimon is triadic (strophe, antistrophe, epode). The Aeschylean tone of the lyric may be seen in the theme and personification of Justice (474; cf. the personification of the ax at 484), the retribution of the Fury (491), and the reflections on the ruined house (502–13).

472–77 With **prophet** (of the chorus, beginning a lyric stanza) cf. *OK* 1087 and *Agamemnon* 104–6. **Foreshadowing** echoes prophet ("prophet . . . prophesying"). For **Justice** as a theme in the *Oresteia* see the note to *Agamemnon* 250. **Justice . . . just** are sequential in the Greek. **In vengeance** is interpretative but the obvious implication of **victory**. Because to give *dikê* (justice) in Greek legal idiom means "to pay a penalty" (as at 298 and 539), it falls naturally into both the language of revenge and forensic argument; so it is translated "revenge" at 34. See Clytemnestra's claim at 528–29.

481 Of sweet savor = "breathing sweetly," as if the dream comes on a breeze; the connotation is "happy inspiration."

482–87 That the dead and revenging spirits remember is a tenet of Greek religious thought: "the secret anger remembers the child" (*Agamemnon* 155), and the Furies "hold memory of evil" (*Eumenides* 387–88; cf. *Aj* 1390). For the motif in this play see 238, 342, 347, and 1287. **Nor** (has) **the ax of old** (forgotten)": Long (p. 113) compares similar personifications at *El* 242 ("wings of shrill lament"), *Aj* 907–8 ("This blade . . . declares it"), *OC* 698 ("the olive tree . . . the terror of our enemies"), *OC* 714 (the rein is the "healer" for the horse). Such personifications are rare in Sophocles, fairly common in Aeschylus. Jebb notes another side to the trope: "Such a personification recalls that practice of Athenian law by which inanimate objects which had caused death were brought to formal trial in the court called (the Prytaneion), and, after sentencing, cast beyond the boundaries, in the presence of the Archon Basileus and the sacrifical officers of the tribes." **Bronze-shod** (cf. on 491) and **double-toothed** are compound adjectives derived from Aeschylus and Homer; cf. "bronze-sided urn" (55).

488–91 From personified Justice to the victim demanding it to the spirit (**Fury**) that will exact it. For descriptions of the Furies see on *OK* 418–19, 1389 below, and the ambush at *Ant* 1075–76. Since **many-footed** and polypus (octopus) are homonyms, and the polypus is proverbial for waiting in **ambush,** we think of the swarming tentacles grappling the unsuspecting victim. **Bronze-shod** is more literally translated than the compound above (485), which means "striking with (or "forged from") bronze." Homer applies the adjective to horses.

492–94 Another version of two compressed lines: "Murderous hurrying passions for a marriage which ignores the bonds of wedlock and the nuptial couch, entered into those unlawfully" (Long, p. 136). With **stained** cf. "polluted" at 276.

499–501 Soothsaying = "oracles/divine prophecies." **Fulfillment:** Jebb sees a nautical metaphor for coming safely into port (literally at *Phil* 220–21). The argument is similar to that at 243–50; cf. *OK* 892–96 for a more adventurous argument in the same vein.

502–13 Oenomaus, king of Pisa, had a daughter Hippodamia whom he did not wish to give in marriage; nonetheless, he offered her to any suitor who could beat him in a chariot race. After several suitors tried and failed, forfeiting their heads for the defeat, **Pelops**, the son of Tantalus, won the race when **Myrtilus**, the charioteer of Oenomaus, did not insert the linchpins in the wheels of his master's chariot. After Myrtilus had tried to rape Hippodamia on the way home, Pelops threw the charioteer into the sea, not, naturally, before the dying Myrtilus cursed Pelops. Aeschylus is content to trace the troubles of the house to the crimes of Atreus; Sophocles takes them back to the sexual crimes of Pelops. With the present version cf. Electra's lament in Euripides' *Orestes* 985–95. **Loaded with disaster** is repeated in 512 (in "destruction"); it is another *polu-* compound, as in "many-footed" (488). **Deadly** = "persistent." **Wreck** and **ruin** translate the same noun, which is "baseness" at 487; the word suggests humiliating physical and social degradation.

514 The queen is accompanied by at least one servant, who carries offerings (634). She should be dressed in her finery. She detests her daughter and also fears her a little. There is no scene for mother and daughter in the *Libation Bearers*. Cf. Euripides *Electra* 988–1141, where a pair of speeches is also followed by stichomythia (but Aegisthus is already killed and Clytemnestra exits to be murdered). **Loose again, wandering** may suggest an animal freed from bonds.

521–23 Brutally: the idea is "boldness/daring," which, depending on context, may be "audacity" (*Aj* 46) or "confidence" (*El* 994). Brutal treatment may, however, be included under *hybris* (= **insulting**), which is repeated in **insolence.**

524–25 The reciprocal nature of **abuse** has already been asserted by Electra at 309a-b; cf. 609–9b.

528–29 For the plea of **Justice** see *Agamemnon* 1432, and for the claim **not I alone** see *Agamemnon* 1497–1504.

531 Had the brutality = "dared," with the connotation of becoming hardened for some rashness or suffering. The same verb occurs as "endured" in what looks like the Aeschylean source:

> He endured then
> to sacrifice his daughter
> (*Agamemnon* 223–24)

532–34 Your sister is Iphigeneia, who was sacrificed by Agamemnon at Aulis; see 564–77 and the notes there. Aeschylus' Clytemnestra also alludes to the mother's pain in childbearing (**toiled for her**):

> he slaughtered like a victim his own child, my pain
> grown into love, to charm away the winds of Thrace.
> (*Agamemnon* 1417–18)

535–36 The first lyric of the *Agamemnon* represents the king as torn between his obligation to the army and natural reluctance to kill his daughter. Finally he acts **for the sake of the Greeks.**

538–41 The war was "waged for a woman," Helen, wife of Menelaus, but Agamemnon leads the expedition. As Electra will argue (570–77), the children of Menelaus are not to the point because Artemis demanded Agamemnon's daughter, not just any child. Like the rest of her speech, the argument is rationalistic and legalistic rather than mythic: it dismisses the dilemma Aeschylus contrives from Agamemnon's divinely appointed mission (Zeus sends the Greeks against Troy: *Agamemnon* 55–59) and from Artemis' refusal to permit sailing without sacrifice (*Agamemnon* 133–37). The **ought** (*eikos*, a favorite topic in Sophistic rhetoric) argues for probable and logical causality against the, for her, specious claims of divine demands.

546–47 Thoughtless or with bad thoughts = "callous and perverse" (Jebb). As at 562, "bad" (*kakos*) is something like "vile."

548–49 Would bear me out = "would agree." Oedipus also argues the dead would assent to his argument (*OC* 999–99a). And in a more mundane sphere the orator Lycurgus, while calling witnesses to a contract, says, "If Amyntas had been alive, I should have produced him in person" (Lycurgus 23).

550 Wicked is possible, but the whole passage is so argumentative that I would prefer "if you think that I can't think" (the opposite of "learn common sense," 394). **Judgment** is translated "act" at 546 and is untranslated in 547: the emphasis is on "judgment/purpose." **Keep your . . . and** = "when you have gotten . . . then." **Righteous** echoes "justice" (528); next in Electra's rebuttal (560).

555 The formality of the request for speaking time emphasizes the forensic character of such scenes; for the request cf. Euripides *Electra* 1055–57, where the *agôn* ("debate contest") is less artificially integrated than often is the case in Euripides.

559a–60 She begins and ends (609–9a) on **shameful**, as if it were a more serious charge than injustice.

562 **Seduction** = "persuasion" at *Tr* 662 (note). Aegisthus' motives were not exclusively erotic: in the tradition he avenges the murder of his brothers whom Atreus, Agamemnon's father and his uncle, had fed in a stew to his father Thyestes (see *Agamemnon* 1577–1611 for his version). In the *Agamemnon,* Clytemnestra clearly kills to retaliate for the death of her daughter and not because she has been seduced, though her children are bound to bring that charge against her (*Libation Bearers* 894ff.).

564–66 With a dual role typical of Greek divinities, **Artemis** protects both the hunter and the hunted, i.e., she rules everything pertaining to the hunt. **Aulis** is on the coast of Boeotia opposite Euboea and was the mustering camp for the expedition against Troy. **You dare not learn** is, rather, "it is not right (*themis*) to learn from her."

567–73 Electra swims upstream against Aeschylus' version as Sophocles gives her an argument found in the *Cypria* but not in the *Agamemnon* (see the note 131–38). According to the ancient summary of the poem, the **boast** was that not even Artemis (the **daughter of Leto**) could shoot so well. The proper thing to do was pray to the goddess for her help in the hunt.

574–75 In the Aeschylean version Agamemnon apparently has the option of disbanding the army and giving up the expedition. On Electra's version her father had no choice but to sacrifice her sister, whereas in the *Oresteia* the children must more or less ignore Iphigeneia's fate (see *Libation Bearers* 242 and 246–63).

579a–83 **By what law?**: this sort of question does not arise in Aeschylus, or certainly not in such a rational, skeptical form because the *Oresteia* presumes the validity of "an eye for an eye." Secondly, Orestes is threatened by the disfavor of Apollo and the pursuit of his father's Furies if he does not kill his mother. Neither Orestes nor Electra questions the propriety of retribution as such, though the son hesitates at the killing of his mother.

585 **Please tell me**: cf. 535. **Ugliest** = "most shameful"; cf. 559a. "Scandalous" (594) continues the idea.

589 We hear of two **children**, Erigone and Aletes, and a Sophoclean title *Erigone* may refer to the sister's story.

599a **A mistress** refers to her domination of the house, not to sexual liaisons. **Bedfellow** is in itself not a sexual term but simply means "partner."

602 Sad (*tlêmôn*) is the same word translated "daring" at 275; she can use it of both Clytemnestra and Orestes because, from an underlying meaning of "suffering" it developed two significations: (1) hardened to suffering and so "bold" and (2) given to suffering and so "patient/ enduring."

605 Murderer (*miastôr*) = "foul, polluted creature" at 276, which is the primary meaning (cf. *OK* 353). Rather than take it as a synonym for avenger, we may see Electra's boldness reaching to affirm Clytemnestra's worst recrimination: "even if he must be foul and polluted, as you say, yet would I nurture him for vengeance if I could."

609–9b She concludes with a perverse version of the "like from like" motif (cf. *Ant* 471–72 and *Libation Bearers* 421–22). Once again the Greek stresses "deeds" (*erga*) while **naturally** and **nature** add a bitter, sardonic genesis to the motif of reciprocity (cf. 309a–b). Some manuscripts have "evil" (*kaka*) rather than "deeds" (*erga*), a reading that makes sense and ties in more closely still with 309a–b; "deeds" appears explicitly in the Greek of 614, 619, 622, and 625.

610–12 It surprises us to hear the sympathetic chorus questioning the justice of Electra's attack, and some editors take **she is angry** of Clytemnestra, which seems unlikely. Electra's tirade carries her beyond justice. Dawe translates an emended and differently punctuated text: "I can see that she is furious, but whether she is on the same side as Justice, this is a further point that I cannot make out" (from his note to *OK* 115). As often, a chorus between antagonists straddles the fence. Clytemnestra's **thought** responds to the same word in 611 ("is her thought/concern just?"), and I take the meaning to be "what should be my attitude toward her, who. . . ."

618 Wrongly, so unlike myself = "intemperately, so unseemly."

620 Against my will translates a pleonastic "forcibly."

625 Deeds invent the words = "deeds find their (matching) words.

627 For results of your behavior (= "audacity") see on 521–23.

630–33 Clytemnestra's purpose was to **sacrifice** and now, in a small triumph for Electra, she asks leave to continue. If Electra continues to vilify her mother, efficacious sacrifice is impossible; in "real life" she would want to ruin the prayers, as she has urged Chrysothemis to void the intended offerings at the grave, but dramatically the prayer, with its apparent answer in the messenger (660), manages both a kind of closure for the first part of this scene and a bridge to the next. Cf. Jocasta's prayer and the arrival of the messenger at *OK* 911–25.

634–36 As often in tragedy, statues and altars to one or more gods grace the stage near the palace door (cf. the opening to the *Oedipus the King*). This King here is Phoebus Protector (Apollo: see on *Tr* 205–15).

639–40 Unfold is a metaphor from opening a scroll or book. For to the light see 425.

642 Bad means "rash" and so "in vain," i.e., as she would like to imagine the reports.

644 Double meaning: the dream (417–24) may be ambiguous in that it does not directly or violently threaten her.

645 For Lycaean see on line 6. In the present context, however, its connection with light argues for the sense at *OK* 919a (note).

649–53 Some: naturally she is euphemistic, and for this reason with those I love (653) may be better rendered as "with my friends."

659a The son of Zeus shares in his father's powers; for "all-seeing Zeus" cf. 174–75 and *Ant* 184.

660 Pat he comes like the catastrophe in an old comedy. She has not prayed for Orestes' death, but in her heart she knows that they cannot both live (see 766–69 for her feelings). Her prayer seems answered, as we see—the paedagogus is not in disguise—the second step of the intrigue put in place.

Foreign ladies is standard address to a stranger and particularly to one who is an actual or potential friend. The coryphaeus and Clytemnestra address him with the same word ("sir") in the masculine singular. He comes in from the parodos, speaks to the coryphaeus, then approaches (666) the queen.

667 And your friends should read "from your friend."

670 For Phanoteus see the note to 44–45.

674–77 Standing nearby, Electra cries out. As at 788, 808, and 1108 O God and God help me translate self-pitying exclamations; the first is *talaina* (see the note to 389a), the second *dustênos* (discussed on 121). I am dead: cf. *Phil* 742. I cannot live now = "I am nothing" (see on *Ant* 1321).

678 Leave her to herself translates an imperative addressed to Electra: "take care of your own business!"

680 Brevity (673) finds the longest speech in Sophocles on its heels, a set speech to delight messengers, if not the actors playing Clytemnestra and Electra. In terms of dramatic function in an intrigue, the trader in *Philoctetes* has a similar role, with a partner already on stage. The messenger's report at the end of the *Colonus* (1586–1667) is comparable in length and circumstantial detail, incomparably more significant for the action. For a chariot wreck cf. the messenger's report at *Hippolytus* 1173–1254. Nestor's advice to his son Antilochus and the subsequent chariot

race in *Iliad* 23 are the ultimate inspiration for this topic (*Iliad* 23.306–48 and 362–513, with much dramatic business).

682 The **Delphic Games** are the Pythian games (48).

697–98 The paedagogus takes the part of a sententious messenger; cf. *Ant* 1152–70 for great length of this sort and *Ant* 614–23 for the thought here.

701–2 Since **Libyans** (Greeks settled in Libya) do not belong to the heroic age, **Achaea** may be the district on the Corinthian gulf rather than the Homeric Achaea of Achilles.

704 **Thessalian** horses are the best.

705–7 **Aetolia** is in the northwest, **Magnesia** is the southeastern peninsula of Thessaly, and the **Aeneans** live in the mountains south of Thessaly and north of the Sperchius River.

708 The Homeric **God-built** is adopted by the dramatists for more patriotic purposes.

723–26 **Hard-mouthed** means that the bit does not pain them enough to make them respond. **Sixth lap:** markers (742, 748) were set at either end of a course and the chariots doubled around them to begin a new lap. Apparently the Aenean's chariot failed to straighten out and so went on around the post and **head-on** into one of the Libyan chariots trailing him. **Barca** is a town in Libya.

728–30 For the **plain of Crisa** see 180. The hippodrome was below Delphi on this plain.

749 Hippolytus, tangled in his reins and beaten against the rocks, shouts in vain to his team (*Hippolytus* 1234–43).

765 **Root and branch:** for the imagery cf. *Ant* 600 and *Aj* 1179–79a.

766–69a Terrible (*deina:* see on 221–25) **but for the best** (*kerdos* = "profit" at 61) suggests a mixed bag out of which she can find something profitable despite the pain (the second **terrible:** "it is painful for me if . . ."). Electra will deny her mother's sincerity (804–8), though the only reason Clytemnestra could have for feigning grief would be one of social propriety, and if her feeling is feigned, why admit to *mixed* feeling? Again, the mask, but not her gesture, keeps the audience from seeing her reaction; so the paedagogus's **dejected** interprets what we should also hear in her tone.

Despite the address to **Zeus,** the lines are not strictly a prayer; they are more to herself than to the other characters or chorus (so Bain, *Actors and Audiences,* p. 78; Schadewaldt, *Monolog,* p. 30).

776 **From my soul** (*psychê*) may be better "from my life" (as at 786) since the following lines dwell on physical as well as spiritual alienation.

779a–82 **Charged** is legal for "accused" (*OK* 703); **terrors** is the third use of *deina* (767, 770) in this passage. Her anxiety clearly goes deeper than the recent dream, deeper than the harassment of Electra. **Solace** hides a metaphor from roofing/covering/sheltering: "neither day nor night did sweet sleep cover me." **Supervisor** is "the one who stands before (her)," hence her guide and lord. **To inevitable death** = "as one constantly expecting death."

783 **With this one day:** see the note to *OK* 438 and cf. 1149.

785–86 **Draining** likens Electra to a Fury drinking the blood of its victim:

> Our Fury who is never starved for blood shall drink
> for the third time a cupful of unwatered blood.
> *(Libation Bearers* 577–78)

See also the note to *Ant* 531–33.

787 **The light of day** is less emphatic than it appears in translation, being no more than implicit in **I'll have peace.**

790–94 The natural ambiguity of **be right** also yields: *El.* "Are you content?" *Cl.* "Not with you. But he is content as he is." Cf. her question at 817, where the bitter rejection might be phrased "Can I live with this?" **Nemesis** embodies the indignation and retribution of the gods; Electra no doubt thinks of the Nemesis who exacts justice for the dead, (Aeschylus frag. 266). Clytemnestra, however, thinks "God's vengeance" (*Orestes* 1361) has struck the would-be avenger. See 1469.

795 **Will you not stop this:** I would interpret this question to mean "Well, will you and Orestes stop this (my luck)?" Note the fourth **stop** at 798.

808–9 The losers always claim the winners are **laughing** (cf. *Aj* 368), and we need not assume actual laughter. **Your death is my death:** cf. *Ant* 871.

813 **Where should I turn?** Sometimes this question is dramatic and directed to others (*Tr* 385, *Ant* 1098); elsewhere it marks, as here, despair (*Aj* 458).

815 **Slave:** see the note to "mistress" at 599a.

817 On **right** see the note to 790–94.

818–21 With **waste away** cf. "I shall shrivel to death alone" (*Phil* 955). **Unloved** = "without a friend." **Agony** is the same language discussed at 355 ("hurt/pain"); she admits defeat.

823–70 A lyric dialogue takes the place of the second stasimon. Electra has just announced her refusal to return to the house; now she and the chorus lament her fate and Orestes'. Such dialogues are more frequent in later tragedy. With the broken, interrupted way of this dialogue compare *Phil* 1081–1218, where the continuous lyric stanzas give way at 1170 to shorter elements (as here, exclamation, imperatives, questions are the chief elements), and OC 510–48.

823–26 If they see this may refer to the death and unfulfilled vengeance of Orestes; the more immediate injustice is the suffering of Electra. The **sun** is invoked as universal witness, **Zeus's thunderbolts** as the instruments of punishment.

827–31 The scholiast suggests that the chorus fears that Electra, who accompanies her cry with a gesture of defiance, is about to utter some irreverent rebuke of the gods (**great word**). If that is the correct view, **You will destroy me** is not so much a response to 830 as an anticipation of an implicit hope (833; cf. 810) in their call for restraint.

837–45 Amphiaraus' wife Eriphyle took a golden necklace as a bribe to persuade her husband to join the expedition against Thebes (see OC 1313). When his chariot fled in the rout from Thebes, the earth opened and he vanished. Apollodorus (3.6.8) says Zeus made him immortal, and that is one sense offered for **reigns over all the spirits there,** for which I would prefer "reigns in full vitality." For such rule in the underworld see *Libation Bearers* 354–62. Alcmaeon, Amphiaraus' son, killed his mother in revenge for her treachery and, also like Orestes, was driven into exile. Between **earth** and **reigns** Electra utters an exclamation, apparently thinking of Clytemnestra's deceitful murder of Agamemnon, whereas the chorus aims to offer some consolation. The want of communication between chorus and Electra is further stressed by **pitiably,** which translates a feminine adjective apparently intended to modify Eriphyle (perhaps "she cruelly killed him" is their thought). Given this feminine form, **he died** must be "she died" (the pronoun is not expressed): Electra thinks of the **deliverer** (Alcmaeon) who, unlike Orestes, lived to take revenge. Although sympathetic, the chorus's thinking does not harmonize with Electra's.

848–52 For the inflection translated by **unhappy . . . unhappiness** cf. "dreadfully . . . dreadful" (197–98), "sorrow from sorrow" (235) and "hate . . . hate" (358). The Greek often juxtaposes these inflections, and the next line (850), for example, offers a pair of words, the second of which is a compound from the first ("witness, fully-witnessing"), while line 851 in the Greek begins with consecutive words prefixed with *pan-* ("all"). **Surging:** the metaphor suggests the detritus swept up and accumulated from a torrent.

854 We know what you mean is hopelessly prosaic. Diggle's emendation yields something like "you cry out to one who understands."

858–59 Hope: see 810, 833. **Kinsfolk** and **nobles** both look to the lost Orestes: "no help from the hope that a noble brother would bring."

861–64 On the one hand, the generic "wretched" (**poor darling** is *dustênos:* see on 121); on the other, a unique compound in **wild competing hoofs,** while **leather reins** translates an allusive metaphor in which the noun suggests both a winch and the furrows made by ropes or lines. Only its adjective ("cut"), used of the reins at 749a, leads from "traces" to **reins.**

866–70 These lines are interrupted, after **hand of mine,** by a choral exclamation.

871 Chrysothemis returns from the tomb, bringing good hope, which Electra's despair casts aside. This scene is no more necessary to intrigue and revenge than was Clytemnestra's scene.

876–77 **And who are you to find it** interprets the tone and rests on contrasting pronouns: "you, help for *my* troubles. . . ." Since Electra couples their "troubles" at 879a–80, we should probably not find snide rejection here.

887 **Proof:** Chrysothemis' evidence is from inference (909a), on which she confidently takes an oath (881), whereas Electra thinks she has a firsthand witness (926). The scholiast equates **afire** with hope; cf. *Aj* 478. **Incurably** also suggests that "afire" may be used of a fever.

895 **Milk,** water, and wine were all offered at the grave; see *Persians* 610–20. **Coffin** = "tomb."

898 The verb in **who would be near me** suggests the danger of assault.

901–2 For **pyre** understand "tomb," in this case probably a mound heaped over the original pyre. The **lock of hair** is taken from *Libation Bearers* 167, where Electra herself discovers it and infers, from its resemblance to her own (176), that it has been sent as an offering by Orestes. In the Euripidean recognition the old man who saved Orestes reports that he has found a lock of hair and sacrificial offerings on the tomb, from which he infers the presence of Orestes (*Electra* 508–23). Euripides' heroine dismisses such flimsy evidence (524–31). **Jumped within me** may reflect a metaphor from embossing: "the familiar sight pressed itself on my spirit."

905–6 Had she seen the lock of hair, thought of a resemblance, and cried out in grief for the absent Orestes, such a cry would have been **ill-omened.**

909a–15 Such arguments from probability, almost too carefully worked out, testify to the influence of contemporary rhetoric.

917 **Genius** is also the translation of *daimôn* at 998, 1156, and 1306; the stem appears in "action divine" at 1270. Here the primary meaning seems to be "luck."

920 **Liking** = "pleasure" at 891, as well as twice in Chrysothemis' opening lines (871–75). The context sets up an antithesis between good

sense and pleasure, with the obvious irony that Electra quickly convinces her sister that her happiness and relief (874) are illusory.

921 The idiom in **where your thoughts are** is more boldly translated at 390 ("are you crazy?"). The metaphor from travel comes to something like "where you are or where you're going"; cf. *OK* 1310.

930 Alas again repeats the exclamation of 925.

943 This line is the first hint of her new plan (947–89).

944 Long (p. 105) says that the choice of diction indicates Chrysothemis' "unrestricted willingness to help." On the contrary, the stipulation is cut from the same timidity as that of 946; it is the guarded assent of one who will never brave the doorman, much less men (996).

947–89 From despair to resolution: although Chrysothemis will certainly not aid in any revenge and Orestes is in the wings, Electra attempts to persuade the one to do the work of the other. Looking ahead, we may note that at the end of this scene Chrysothemis and Electra seem completely alienated and that the aggressive resolution evident here comes into full play in the final scene when she acts as partner to Orestes in the killing. The speech is neatly organized and well marked in its transitions: (1) she has a plan (947); (2) their present lack of friends offers no hope of revenge (948–54); (3) consequently, the two of them must avenge Agamemnon and kill Aegisthus (955–59); (4) they have no hope for personal prosperity so long as Aegisthus rules (959a–66); (5) but the rewards of revenge are freedom and praise (967–85); (6) Chrysothemis, to avoid shame, must act for father, brother, and self (986–89). She skillfully omits direct reference to Clytemnestra and emphasizes that Chrysothemis' expectations are no better than her own (960–66), and in the longest section, describing their successful lot, she reveals how bitter her sense of social deprivation actually is.

947 Have laid: a variant reading puts weight on her confidence that she will accomplish what she has planned.

954 To avenge translates a metaphor that makes Orestes a public official in charge of exacting payment for fees and penalties. Aeschylus uses it of the Furies at *Eumenides* 320.

957–58 Your true-born sister does not insist so emphatically on the bond as the first line of the *Antigone*. **Aegisthus** is postponed for the final hiss; note the plural at 979. Unlike the Aeschylean Orestes, who has some filial reservations about killing his mother, Electra has none, but a speech about matricide will not sell to the feeble sister any more than it will win the audience's sympathy for Electra.

959a What are you waiting for . . . hesitant?: the translation's phrasing might be taken to indicate that Chrystothemis has shrunk away or otherwise indicated by gesture her unwillingness. Kaibel suggests that Chrysothemis' silence sponsors the more materialistic argument that follows. But the sentence may also mean "For how long will you wait, indifferent (either to their crimes or to the hopelessness of her situation)." Taken this way, the sense begins a vigorous second stage in her argument.

963 Without a marriage: cf. 166–67.

969a One striking difference between Electra and Antigone is that the latter tends to see **piety** in light of divine obligation, and of course burial of the dead is more a concern of the gods than revenge, while Electra's piety is rooted almost exclusively in familial values. See also 309 and 464–65.

974 Reputation will be echoed by "fame" (985) at the end of this section. For the motivation see *Ant* 502–3.

975 By doing this = "if you listen to me," as at 986.

978–83 For the use of imagined future opinions see *Aj* 494 and *OK* 1497–1500. **Revere** is the same Greek stem as "piety."

989 Base means shamefully self-degrading. Noble by birth and free-born, they live as slaves. For the thought cf. *Aj* 472–73.

990–91 The vapid comment is their way of not agreeing; cf. 1015–16.

994–95 For **confidence** see on 521–23. **To what can you look** = "What are you (waiting) for" (959a). Perhaps "ally" (990) suggested the metaphor in **arm yourself. Help** is a metaphor from rowing a ship and so of menial service generally.

996 For **a woman—no man** see *Ant* 61–62 (Ismene's argument).

997–98 Strength: cf. her stipulation at 946 as well as her concluding "weaker" (1013). **Genius:** see on 917. *daimôn* and luck are joined at *OK* 1478–79.

1006–9 No gain = "it doesn't free (loosen) us." **Dishonorable** has the same stem as Electra's "reputation" (974) and "fame" (985). The form of the sentence concedes that they might win a noble reputation (by attacking him) but assumes the failure of their effort with its consequent inglorious death. The next two lines (**For death . . . death**) are an obvious non sequitur; they should be deleted.

1011 Temper is the old demon (see on *OK* 338); cf. Ismene's "hot mind over chilly things" (*Ant* 88). For **unspoken** cf. Ismene's promise at *Ant* 84–85.

1014 The last word is **give in** ("yield"); see 360.

1017 Nothing unexpected comments on Chrysothemis' character, which is little more than a foil to Electra's resolution.

1021–24 Felt so seems to indicate purpose, to which Electra replies that her natural inclination was the same, but she lacked the mature judgment (*nous*); Chrysothemis has already used this word at 1013 ("Be sensible") and returns to it in 1024, apparently taunting Electra with "you have your judgment (from experience) but could really use some common sense." "Sensible mind" (1016), "advice" (1025), and "judgment" (1027) all play on the *nous* stem.

1032 No learning: "at long last" (1013) and "a long future" (1030) have anticipated the motif of late learning, which is also the issue in the dispute over "judgment" (1023 ff.).

1042–43 For Chrysothemis on justice and pragmatism see 338–40. Cf. *Ant* 451–52.

1052–54 There is something to be said for giving 1053–54 to Chrysothemis: the charge of **folly** has been throughout this scene the cry of the weaker sister. **To make so hopeless an attempt** (= "pursuing/chasing futility"), which as the text stands must refer to Electra's effort to win her sister's help, has a nice parallel in Ismene's

> Wrong from the start, to chase what cannot be.
>
> (*Antigone* 92)

And this suits Chrysothemis, if the lines are hers and refer to Electra's proposed revenge. Dawe assumes a line has been lost after 1052 and assigns 1053–54 to Chrysothemis.

1057 Chrysothemis exits into the palace. Electra remains on stage through the choral lyric.

1058–97 The lyric recapitulates and comments on the preceding scene. Though it has urged caution and prudence, the chorus now has only praise for Electra, and the second pair of stanzas (1082–97) addresses her with praise and prayer for a fate commensurate with her piety (the last word in this lyric).

1058–69a The song actually begins with the question here deferred to 1062 ("Seeing **the birds . . . why do we not**). **True in their wisdom** denotes understanding, which is defined by **caring for the livelihood** (reciprocating the nuture; cf. 777, 1144–48). Honoring parents was one of the three great unwritten laws. Both the stork (Aristophanes *Birds* 1353–57) and the lark (*Birds* 471–75) are types of piety, and for a people who constantly turned to divination from the cries and flight of birds, to call birds wise was little short of understatement. The implicit point here is that Electra has been dutiful in remembering her duty to family, Chrysothemis has not. **Lightning Bolt:** see 823. This appears to be the only place in Sophocles where **Themis**, bride of Zeus and upholder of law, is personified; see Aeschylus *Suppliants* 359–64. The personified **Voice** is vague and apparently stands for whatever carries word to the dead; the commentators cite Pindar's personification of "Message, daughter of Hermes" (*Olympian* 8.22). **Atridae** is strictly Agamemnon and Menelaus; cf. "them" in 1070. **Tell of wrongs . . . dance:** three words in the Greek leave a concise ambiguity. **Wrongs** = "reproach/disgrace" and may refer either to dishonor on him (as at *Libation Bearers* 495) or on the house (the former would be implied censure for not coming to the house's aid). **Untouched by joy of the dance** is the privative ("danceless") and denotes both the present lack of any ritual observance at his grave as well as the spirit's fate if he does not rise to their aid. But this is not a prayer to evoke the dead, and the most obvious sense will emphasize the disgrace that consists of choirless ritual, i.e., no ritual.

1070–81 **Waves of sorrow** is the same metaphor found at *OK* 24. For the **nightingale** see 149. **No thought** is a variant on "forethought" (990). **Furies** are spirits of vengeance. So any person whose action causes vengeance may be called a Fury (cause for effect), as an Aeschylean chorus calls Helen a Fury on Troy (*Agamemnon* 749); cf. on 785–86 and *Tr* 895. **Noble:** see on 160–63.

1082–88 The lyric echoes the sentiments of Electra; for **basely** see 989, for **renown** see 974 ("reputation"): "no one who is noble is willing to shame his good reputation by living ignobly." **Wise and best:** it is worth note how far this view is from that implied by their approval of Chrysothemis' last speech (1015–16); they are friendly but weak, and not an untypical chorus in that respect.

1094–97 For **nature's greatest laws** see Antigone's defense at *Ant* 450–57. **Piety:** see the collection at 464–65. It is **toward Zeus** in that the high god protects father and house. Talk of piety will quietly drop out of the play now, for it is the ambiguous nature of their piety that it must impiously kill their mother. "This dilemma is Aeschylean. It is the primary point of controversy in the interpretation of this play whether it is Sophoclean also, whether in obeying the law of Zeus they are not inevitably breaching it" (Winnington-Ingram, p. 245). In this regard the great difference between the *Libation Bearers* and the *Electra* rests on the fact that in Aeschylus, Orestes is conscious of his guilt and is punished for it. The dilemma is faced and only resolved in the *Eumenides,* where the hero, who has suffered banishment and been ritually cleansed, is exculpated by god and man.

1098 Pylades accompanies Orestes; one or more servants are also present (1123).

1103–4 Of some untranslatable bombast here, apparently alluding to the presence of Pylades, Long (p. 112) observes: "The phrase is highly pompous and its formality is characteristic of the way in which messengers announce themselves." Long means the messengers of drama, not of life.

1108 O God, O God: Cf. "Alas" (1115, 1144, 1179, 1210). All these passages are exclamations using the same word (*talaina:* see on 674–77).

1110 For **Strophius** see the note to 11–17.

1121–22 Note that the lament is **for myself,** a self-centered expression characteristic of Greek lament.

1123–25 Some readers have supposed that Orestes recognizes Electra immediately, others that it is not until the coryphaeus speaks her name (1171) that he knows her. The present lines, and especially 1125, suggest at least a premonition, but it is hard to believe that his reaction to her lament (1126–70) is feigned. Her lament lays the emotional ground for recognition, without actually revealing for certain who she is.

1126–30 The contrast of past and present is frequent in ancient lament and is here marked by **from what I hoped** and **now;** cf. the sequence of tense at 1131–37 and the climactic "now" at 1149 and 1167. "After the introductory address, which frequently contained questions, the mourner turned to reflect on what the dead was in his lifetime, and what he has come to now; the hopes cherished then, the despair he has now caused; the journey he is now making to Hades, and the desolation of those left behind" (Alexiou, p. 165). With **nothingness** cf. *Ant* 1321. **Brilliant:** light and shining hope (cf. 68, 1226, 1354).

1131 Would that you should be "Would that I." Her death would have entailed his (1134). Here a common form of prayer ("Would that X had died before": see *OK* 1348–55 and the note to *Libation Bearers* 345–53) is elaborated into a double death. See Alexiou, p. 178. The motif is Homeric: it is better to die gloriously, e.g., on the battlefield, and win an honorable funeral that to live longer only to find an anonymous or ignoble death in exile (1137).

1139 Wash you refers to bathing the dead in preparation for the funeral rites.

1141 For **to the fierce blaze** read "from the fierce blaze," i.e., she did not take his ashes from the pyre for internment.

1144–48 Nursing and **nurse** carry the motif of nurture that is **all for nothing,** i.e., without the subsequent support that sisters and a mother expect from the son (a variant on failed hopes: 1129–29a). For this motif see Alexiou, p. 193–95.

1149 You called me "sister" avoids identifying her as his sister and makes it possible for Orestes to understand "sister" as merely affectionate address.

1151–53 Our father lacks the possessive in the Greek; Orestes will understand "your father." The same holds for **our enemies.** Exactly what she means by **I am dead in you** is not clear, and given her condition, it may be wrong to look for more than intense despair. Her life has been one of suffering and hope; with hope gone, she is as good as dead. Cf. 809.

1154 On **mother no mother** see the note to *Phil* 534–35. **Promised me in secret messages:** see 171–72. Such allusion must prick him to recognition. Cf. "O brother" in 1163.

1159a Idle is the same stem as "all for nothing" (1145): his ashes and shade cannot play the avenger.

1160–62 Three lines of exclamation and apostrophe interrupt the iambic speech. Death is commonly depicted as a **journey** to the under-world, but Jebb and others take it more literally of Crisa to Mycenae.

1164 Habitation = "this house," i.e., the urn.

1170 One hopes this commonplace is an interpolation. The chorus replies in kind, but one word (**Electra**) has more than enough dramatic pulse.

1174–76 Orestes' lines will be an aside if he has known all along that he is speaking to Electra. More likely, the coryphaeus's "Electra" clinches the natural inference from her speech; he is genuinely shocked and sur-prised at the sight (1177) of her miserable condition. His words are more to himself than to her or the chorus; she sees his confusion but cannot know the cause. See Bain, *Actors and Audiences*, pp. 79–80, who com-pares *Phil* 895–97.

1182 We have single line stichomythia from 1176 to 1209. Electra does not understand the effusive and personal remarks of this stranger (= **sir**) and so calls them **ill-omened,** which here may mean "to speak disparagingly of."

1190–92 The compound translated **live with** suggests a foster child. **Him** is not expressed, and there is some merit in West's suggestion ("Trag-ica III," p. 105) to put a row of dots at the end of 1190 to indicate that Electra's sentence is unfinished. Of course he knows who the murderers are, but it is the excitement of this prolonged recognition that leads to the question, not any continuing pretense of a role. **Guilt** (*kakon*) has been "suffering" and "sorrows" in recent lines; here "harm/evil." **Slave:** cf. 815 and 599a; this theme, the dishonor that takes the form of the degrad-ing status of slave, does not occur in Aeschylus, where the status of the exiled, dispossessed brother is more the focus.

1201 For **your pain** the manuscripts also offer "the same/equal pain," which forces the recognition less rapidly.

1202 The implication of **in some way** is he may be a remote kinsman unknown to the immediate family. The dialogue has now brought her to an intuitive recognition.

1205–10 Dawe thinks that a line has dropped out after 1208 (1208a); it belonged to Orestes. Dawe would arrange the section as follows:

Orestes: Give up this urn then, and you shall know all.
Electra: By your beard! Do not rob me of what I love most!
Orestes: (1208a)
Electra: Don't take it from me, stranger—by the Gods!
Orestes: Do what I bid you. You will not be wrong.
Electra: I will not let you have it. O Orestes!
Alas, if I may not even give you burial!

With this change all of line 1209 is attributed to Electra (no antilabe until 1220), and we should accept his recognition of a lost line even if the stylistic arguments for the rearrangement are, as Dawe sees, speculative.

1208 In formulas of supplication the suppliant may extend the hand to the **beard** or to the knees, or both. The gesture is as old as Homer and originally recognized the helplessness of the suppliant as he touched from an inferior position places of physical power on the person supplicated.

1211 **Ill omen:** you have no right to speak of burying the living.

1213 **Call him by that name,** i.e., speak of him as dead: "it is not right for you to speak thus (of him)."

1217 With **fiction** (*logos*) cf. "our tale of lies" (58). Appearance and reality, word and deed, reach their climax and resolution in this scene, which in many respects is more truly the goal of the play's action than the revenge to follow. Orestes' metaphor is drawn from the decorative arts, so the "body" is "dressed/decked out" for the tale.

1219a–20 Antilabe, the first in this stichomythia if Dawe's change at 1209 is accepted. Except for Orestes' line and a half (**Look at this signet**), half-line dialogue continues until **Dearest of women.**

1226 For **O happiest light** cf. *Phil* 868 and the note there. "Happiest day" may be more natural in English.

1228 With **voice** Jebb compares Philoctetes' "Friendliest of tongues" (*Phil* 236). Cf. 1282.

1229a They embrace.

1231–87 In this lyric Electra sings while most of Orestes' verses are spoken iambics, which suits the restraint and caution his lines urge. Such duets have their origin in the old epirrhematic forms of Aeschylus and his precedessors (see on *Agamemnon* 1072) and may be seen in early Sophocles at *Aj* 349a–428. Earlier forms are laments or, more generally, intended to evoke pathos, while the present passage celebrates the reunion of brother and sister. Similar "reunion duets" are found only in Euripides (*Helen* 625–97, *Ion* 1437–1509, *Iphigenia in Tauris* 826–98), whose examples are astrophic, while the present passage is triadic (strophe: 1232–52; antistrophe: 1253–72; epode: 1273–87). It is a shame that we don't have the music and some notion of the singing and recitative style. Electra's first lines begin with two dochmiac rhythms, the freest and most excited of lyric meters, only to change in midsentence (**you have come**) to a final line in iambic trimeter, the meter of speech and the one used by Orestes in the next line. It is hard to believe that she switches from song to speech so suddenly, so abruptly, but if her iambics are sung, why not his?

1237 Silence is the leitmotif of his speech: 1239, 1251, 1259, 1288–92, 1322. His caution continues the intrigue; her ecstasy marks the end of the play.

1240 Women is a true plural (Clytemnestra and Aegisthus).

1244–50 Cf. the simpler version of Jebb: "Alas, ah me! Thou hast reminded me of my sorrow [*kakon*], one which, from its nature, cannot be veiled, cannot be done away with, cannot forget!" Note the personification of **sorrow** (better "evil") in "cannot forget"; Aeschylus would have used Folly (*atê*) or Curse in this figure. **Expiation** and Jebb's "done away with" hide a stem referring to "loosening" (see on 230): "not to be dissolved" (cf. on 1006). **No measure can fit** is a misreading (= Jebb's "my").

1251–52 Perhaps the lines mean "Whenever an opportunity shows the way, then it will be time to recall their deeds." The Greek is not clear. Cf. "occasion" at 1258.

1255 Hardly now = "only just now/with difficulty."

1260–62 With a feigned protest she agrees: "since you have appeared, who would trade (the license of) speech for silence (which you and your presence require)."

1281–84 Electra refers, apparently, to the report of Orestes' death, after which she could not hope (expect) to hear his voice. Two or three syllables have dropped from the Greek text; if we had them, the contradictions in **speechless** and **did not cry out** might be resolved.

1290–92 Drains metaphorically speaks of drawing the water out of the hold of a ship, then of exhausting something by draining it dry. **Luxury** and **waste** translate verbs signifying to pour out and to scatter rashly. For **opportunity** (*kairos*) see the note to 21–22.

1295 Mocking foes: see on 277–80 and cf. 1300. There is not a trace of moral scruple in this speech. Cf. Orestes' final instructions to Electra and the chorus at *Libation Bearers* 554–84.

1297 We two: Orestes and Pylades.

1300 Laugh = "mocking" (1295). **Freely** must be taken with it as well as with **show your joy**.

1301 The **pleasure** of reunion (1272) gives way to the pleasure of revenge.

1304 Good = "profit" (Orestes at 61).

1306 For **Genius** see on 917.

1308 Aegisthus is not at home when the false messenger arrives in the *Libation Bearers,* but in that play he is summoned by a nurse, returns, and is killed before Clytemnestra. Our audience does not know how Sophocles will manage the sequence, which naturally provides some suspense.

1311 Of **steeped in it** Long (p. 141) observes that the metaphor describes "hatred hardened within Electra like a metal which has solidified inside a mold."

1315 The **miracle,** with no religious overtones, is "unforeseen," so strangely unexpected that it works on her as the dead returned to life might.

1321 The sentiment and disjunctive form are virtually the same as Ajax' "Let a man nobly live or nobly die" (*Aj* 479). As at *Ant* 72 and 97, the idea in **good** denotes more an aristocratic and aesthetic ideal than a moral one; for the connection with fame/glory see Euripides, *Orestes* 1151–52.

1322 What does he hear? Perhaps the door: see *Ion* 515–16.

1323–25 Electra immediately assumes her role, though she cannot refrain from speaking ambiguously. The translation's punctuation, with a dash before **nor be glad, once he has got it,** might be taken to represent an aside, which is not required here, or even pointed. Some editors give these lines to Orestes, or to the chorus (not so likely).

1326 The audience will have expected Orestes to go in. The paedagogus, urging opportunity all the while (e.g., 1337–38, 1368), stays for another reunion and thus prolongs the scene by sixty lines.

1330–33 From lines such as these we understand that the house within, though never revealed on the Greek stage in an interior scene, is imagined by the playwright and his actors as a real extension of the actual scene before the audience. We may assume the audience accepted this premise and consequently felt that Orestes' admonitions to silence were practical and not hopeless protests at Electra's effusions. **Your plans:** the old man riddles a little, with "your business (*ta drômen*') would be in the house before your bodies (*ta sômata*)." There is similar internal rhyme and assonance at 1330, where the Greek postpones "deadliest danger" so that what is "near" is not revealed until after "in."

1334–38 For these motifs in a different tone cf. the coryphaeus's admonition and exhortation:

None can find fault with the length of this discourse you drew
out, to show honor to a grave and fate unwept
before. The rest is action. Since your heart is set
that way, now you must strike and prove your destiny.
(*Libation Bearers* 510–13)

High time: cf. 22. **With our task** is not expressed in the Greek; since **have done with** is repeated (from 1334), we may prefer to supply "talk" (after "speeches" of 1335).

1344 Cf. his response to Electra at 1364–67. He will not tell her, or us, at the end of the play, and the vagueness of this phrase teases us not only in itself but in its refusal—the poet's refusal—to report that "Clytemnestra danced for joy," i.e., to corroborate Electra's judgment at 804–8.

1354 O light most loved = "O happiest light" (1226).

1355 In what a shape takes the Greek question as expressing her astonishment; it is literally "how/in what way did you come?" He will put her questions aside, but the excitement is obvious (1359–59a is a similar question in the Greek).

1358 Service of feet most kind: the point of this grandiloquence is obvious enough, but whereas she can take his hands, she won't take his feet in the second half of the line. Though idiomatic in tragic style, this phrase may miss the mark, even in the Greek.

1359b–60 Words and deeds (**reality:** *erga*), her compulsive speech against their will to action (1368, 1372). **Bless you** is the standard greeting ("Greetings" at 666).

1362 Within the selfsame day: for the crisis of a single day see the note to *OK* 435–40.

1368 Chance (*kairos*) is "opportunity" (1292).

1374–75 Statues of Apollo, Hermes, and other divinities were often placed by the main door; in many cases they were aniconic, i.e., simply small stone pillars. There was also an altar, probably distinct from the statues, for sacrifice. The **forecourt** was a porch over the front door. Whether the stage building actually had such an architectural feature is not certain.

Exit Orestes, Pylades, and Paedagogus.

1383–84 Wickedness is impiety. Tragedy often demonstrates the power of the gods, and it is natural for its characters to see that power in a moral light. Theseus summons the broken body of his son:

> He [Hippolytus] swore that he had never wronged my wife.
> I will refute him with God's punishing stroke.
>
> (*Hippolytus* 1266–67)

Cf. *Aj* 118.

Exit Electra, who returns immediately after the following song (1385–97).

1385–97 Two responsive stanzas give the revengers time to take up their business and Electra opportunity to return with a report of their progress.

1385–86 The **War God** is Ares; cf. 1422. He is, literally, "breathing blood"; cf. 1395. **Vengeance, invincible** translates a single compound (= "hard to contend with"); **bloody** stands for their desire for blood, a desire the victim cannot resist.

1387–89 The Furies are described as **hounds** (cf. *Libation Bearers* 924) pursuing their victims within the house. Euripides (*Electra* 1342) concludes his play with the announcement that "the hounds are here" to track Orestes.

1390–91 **That hung** should read "that hangs"; the verb suggests suspense and anxiety.

1392 **Stealthy, stealthy** translates a compound ("with guileful foot") that identifies Orestes with the Fury (cf. "bronze-shod Fury" at 491).

1395 **With his hands . . . new-whetted:** "having in his hands blood newly whetted." The blood he will draw is substituted for the weapon. It is hard to accept textual suspicions of a figure so vivid and succinct.

1396–97 Literally, "Hermes conducts *him,* disguising the crafty deed" (*dolos,* which also occurs in "stealthy"). For the god of tricks see *Phil* 133.

1398 Electra returns. In his *Agamemnon,* Aeschylus lets Cassandra describe the murder within the house; more realistically, Sophocles sends Electra off briefly, so she can return to paint the scene. From here to 1441 the chorus (coryphaeus) has lyrics, Electric iambics.

1398–99 With **work** and **silence** (cf. Orestes at 1237–39) she adopts a role fitted to the business at hand, taking part as guard (1403) and at the same time taking the role usually given to a servant/messenger belonging to the house.

1404 Clytemnestra's cry from within is derived from *Agamemnon* 1343 and 1345, where the dying king is given two trimeters from offstage. Clytemnestra also speaks in iambics, but she is given more time to die, with half-lines which Electra picks up in response. Cf. Euripides *Electra* 1165–67.

1406 **Someone cries out, inside:** Kamerbeek calls this "derisive and jeering" and compares Euripides *Heracles* 747–48, where a brutal tyrant, not a mother, is being killed within. By contrast the chorus, though sympathetic to the revenge, cannot refrain from calling the cry "unbearable" (= **terror to the ear**).

1409 **Oh! Oh!:** this is the same cry that Electra uttered at 1108 (note).

1414–15 **Miserable** is sympathetic ("pitiful/suffering"); **generation** = "family." **Fate** (moira) can die because of its common meaning "lot/portion."

1416 Oh! I am struck is taken verbatim from *Agamemnon* 1343; **Once more! Oh!** is verbatim from *Agamemnon* 1345.

1419a Courses is a misprint for "curses"; see the note 110–12. The plural (**men long dead**) includes the ancient evils (502–13) as well as the more immediate Agamemnon. **Fulfilled:** this stem (*tel-*) occurs frequently in the exodos, e.g., 1344 ("at the end"), 1399 ("finishing"), 1435 and 1464 ("do" and "have done").

1421–22 With the beginning of the antistrophe they announce the appearance of Orestes and Pylades. **Blame** is an emendation; it is generally accepted and seems necessary.

1424–25 The repeated **well** recalls 1345, where the same word frames the line, 1321 ("good"), and the jeering at 790–93 ("right"); cf. 1494–95, where this stem appears as "fair" (*kalon*). The form of the condition is open and so does not itself cast doubt on the prophecy. If there is any ambiguity in his attitude, then, it depends on his tone.

1426–27 Proud mother: again (see on 1424–25), only his tone can make this mean proud: more literally, "your mother's will/purpose."

It appears that some lines following Orestes' response have dropped from our manuscripts, if Sophocles used responsive trimeters as well as responsive lyric meters. The sense runs on well enough, and filling the lacunae, if they exist, is guesswork.

1431 Perhaps He is in our power should be punctuated as a question, or a double question: "Do you see him? Do we have him?"

1432–33 Full of joy is Jebb's phrase, and true enough to the sense, though a modern audience may want something more brisk ("elated" or "overjoyed"?). The word for **vestibule** is rare and the meaning uncertain; it seems to mean an area opposite the door, inside or outside.

1437 The stage direction (**hiding himself**) leaves them outside the palace, but unless she is lying to Aegisthus at 1451, they have gone in. If they are not offstage, we must hide them but keep them handy for an unobtrusive reappearance at 1464. It is easier and more in the way of Greek practice to take them off and bring them back with the body of Clytemnestra.

1440 If Justice is not personified, then Aegisthus rushes to a contest in the matter of what is right (*dikê:* at 1508 it is "judgment/penalty").

1442 Aegisthus appears at the end of the *Agamemnon* (1577) and is on stage briefly (838–54) in the *Libation Bearers,* where he is killed before Clytemnestra. Sophocles not only reverses the order of their deaths but also brings Aegisthus face to face with Orestes. Aeschylus brings Clytemnestra out, after the death of Aegisthus, to face her son on stage. The change in order obviously plays down the significance of Clytemnestra's death and gives Aegisthus unexpected dramatic status.

1444 The repeated **you** and **bold** imply that Electra has adopted a sulky, beaten posture.

1450 Clearly, the **strangers** are not in sight. They will bring the body out, and Aegisthus will not wonder that it is a body and unlikely to have been conveyed so far.

1451 The ambiguities are of two sorts: the verb (have found) means "have come to" and its object ("the house" or "the murder") is omitted; **kind** (*philos* is the stem) also means friendly, with a play on the fact that the hostess is related to the strangers.

1460–62 Exiles are proverbial for feeding on **empty hope.** Aegisthus thinks some locals have pinned their hopes on Orestes and that, when they see his body, they will be readier to accept the bit (**bitting**) of his rule; for this imagery see *Tr* 1261 and cf. Clytemnestra's metaphor from an unchecked animal at 514. He is exultant.

1465 Her meaning is more pregnant if we translate "everything is being accomplished on my side."

1467 As the doors are opened (1458) the trolley (eccyclema) is pushed out, with Orestes and Pylades on either side. They are present as Electra speaks 1465–66.

1467–69b The **envy of Gods** would be, in his view, their just punishment of Orestes. **Nemesis** is the goddess personifying righteous indignation and retribution, and he checks himself from further speculation, as Lloyd-Jones suggests (*Classical Review* 28, p. 220), "out of hypocritical politeness." So, despite his threats and triumph, he will give it the **due mourning.**

1470 Orestes' costume identifies him as a traveler and Aegisthus assumes that he is one of the Phocians.

1478 The *Oresteia* takes **the net** as one of its major motifs and images; see the note to *Agamemnon* 358. Sophocles uses it infrequently; cf. *OC* 763–64. Aegisthus himself is the **victim;** the word (*tlêmôn*) belongs to the "poor wretch" category (see on 602): "into whose net have I helplessly fallen?"

1479–79b The translation follows Jebb, who with most modern editors emends the text and thus gets an allusion to the ambiguity of *Libation Bearers* 886. Change is unnecessary: "haven't you noticed that the living (you) are talking with the dead?"

1485–86 **Time** certainly matters to Aegisthus. These verses, an "all too apparently gnomic phrase" (Dawe, *Studies,* vol. 1, p. 202), look like a marginal gloss.

1487–88 She actually says: "Kill him as quickly as you can, and having killed him throw him out to the buriers, such as suit him." The obvious meaning, though often rejected (e.g., see Bowra, pp. 254–55), is that his body is to be thrown out to the birds and dogs. The Homeric version, reported by Nestor to Telemachus, takes this line; had Menelaus come home in time, he would have avenged Agamemnon:

> Even after his [Aegisthus'] death none would have heaped any
> earth upon him,
> but he would have lain in the field outside the city, and the dogs
> and birds would have feasted on him, nor would any Achaian
> woman
> have wailed over him.
> (*Odyssey* 3.258–61)

It is also the plan of Euripides' Orestes (*Electra* 896–98; cf. 1276–77 for the divine mandate). There would be no occasion to mention the burial if the only point were to get him out of sight. Such hatred is known from Achilles' response to Hector's plea for decent burial (*Iliad* 22.338–54).

1489a Redemption is "release/freedom" (636), "quittance" at 449a, where Electra puns on the similar sounding "purification" (448). Since a sacrificial animal can be described as releasing one from the guilt of murder, she may think of his body on the dung heap as an atoning sacrifice.

1493–95 Aegisthus is almost too self-conscious of his role. No one is murdered on the Greek stage; so he must go **to the house.** This secondary meaning in his taunt will be followed by the bravado of 1500–1504.

1498–99 Evils to come would seem to allude to a retribution to fall on Orestes, but it is very odd, if we are to see a covert reference to Furies, that it comes from him. Kirkwood (see his note 22, pp. 241–42) is not alone in seeing "an atmosphere of shadow and questioning" at the end of the play, but it is hard to find any shadows in Orestes' manner.

1502 Go now . . . go first is a single line in the Greek, a rare double change of person. Jebb cites as the only other instances OC 832 (–34), *Phil* 810 (–12), 814 (819–19b), 816 (819e–g). This is no place for comedy, yet Aegisthus' "after you" treats the issue as one of manners, not matter.

1506 As you choose = "according to your own pleasure." This noun for "pleasure" occurs ten times in the *Electra,* more than a third of its total appearances in Sophocles. Cf. 286, 872, 874, 891, 920 ("liking"), 1153, 1272, 1279b ("joy"), and 1301.

1508–9a These lines, together with the final choral comment, have been condemned by several editors. Though typical of closings, the generality has little point and the sense is not altogether apt. More literally: "It would be better if justice (judgment) fell directly (immediately) on all, on whoever is willing to act above the laws, (justice) by killing. So there would not be much wickedness." We can get the future (**shall be taken**) only by inference from the actual condition. **Act above the law**(s) must refer to laws of homicide, unless Orestes advocates executing whoever violates any law. His conclusion (fewer **villains**, less crime) is too impoverished for comment. Alteration by actors was particularly easy at the beginning and end of the plays, and these are also just those places where a manuscript is likely to be damaged or a page lost.

    1509b–10 Freedom has been a primary theme; see on 230, 339–40, 1190–92. **Perfected** is the frequent *tel-* stem (see on 1419a); its sense here is not very clear, nor is it made easier by the Greek behind **deed**, which usually means "impulse" (subjective) or "onset" (objective).

Philoctetes

PHILOCTETES' story is old and familiar. In his catalogue of ships Homer tells how Philoctetes had been left on the island of Lemnos because he had been bitten by a "wicked water snake" (*Iliad* 2.723). Yet soon, the poet goes on to say, the Greeks were to remember Lord Philoctetes. With this thought the poet apparently alludes to the tradition, used by Sophocles, that the Greeks had learned from the Trojan seer Helenus that Troy would not fall until Philoctetes and Neoptolemus, son of Achilles, joined the army before Troy. Both Aeschylus and Euripides had previously dramatized versions of how the Greeks managed to win Philoctetes' return (for accounts of their versions see Jebb's introduction).

Philoctetes is valuable because he possesses the magical bow of Heracles. When Heracles was dying he commanded his son Hyllus to carry him to a pyre on Mt. Oeta. Hyllus, however, was reluctant to set fire to the pyre, and when Philoctetes, or his father Poeas, performed this service for the hero, Heracles in thanks gave him his bow, whose arrows were invariably accurate. Philoctetes later joined the expedition to Troy. When the ships put into the island of Chryse and offered sacrifice to the local divinity, Philoctetes was bitten by a snake. The wound would not heal, and his cries of pain interfered with the ritual. Taking this wound as a sign of divine displeasure, the Greeks abandoned Philoctetes on the nearby island of Lemnos, which in Sophocles' version is uninhabited. There Philoctetes was to manage a bare survival for ten years, until the army's need drove it to send an embassy that sought to bring him to Troy. With so much time to reflect on the wrong done him, and in constant pain from his wound, Philoctetes was less than eager to oblige his former comrades. Thus a central dramatic problem for all three of the dramatists was to depict how the embassy achieved the return of the reluctant invalid. That problem was heightened by the fact that the tradition made Odysseus, one of the chieftains responsible for abandoning him, the head of the embassy.

As given to Sophocles, the story is one of intrigue: how will the hated Odysseus manage to force or persuade Philoctetes to help the Greeks, who have been altogether indifferent to his plight until they require his services? Sophocles complicates the plot by making Neoptolemus the lieutenant of Odysseus and the primary agent in securing the man and his bow. In Sophocles' play Neoptolemus is a young man, honest and straight, much in the mold of his father Achilles. As we see in the prologue, he is not by nature given to deceit. Yet, Odysseus assures him, Philoctetes can only be tricked into coming to Troy, for he will never willingly give aid and comfort to those who betrayed his trust. For a time Neoptolemus enters into the plot, but his good character and the pitiful condition of the wounded hero struggle against the dishonest stratagem. Finally, though he has already secured the bow, his conscience leads him to return it to Philoctetes and to reveal the Greek plot.

Thus Sophocles has welded into the intrigue against Philoctetes a kind of dramatic Bildungsroman in which ethical themes come to be at least as dramatically significant as the course of the action. He has highlighted the ethical element still further by imagining Odysseus as a pragmatic, self-serving captain whose great concern is success at any price. Their prize, Philoctetes, is long-suffering, betrayed, vengeful, and a man of very strong character. As much as he suffers, he cannot bring himself to help his enemies, who now promise medical assistance if he will return to their camp. Even when Neoptolemus gives up deceit, returns the bow (thus proving his true friendship), and urges him to win the glory and cure promised at Troy, Philoctetes cannot relent in his hatred. Sophocles has created an impasse, for all verions of the story that we know reported that Philoctetes did in fact go to Troy. Only an epiphany of the deified Heracles, who announces that Philoctetes must accept his fate, succeeds in turning their sails toward Troy.

Three rather different problems face the reader. The first has to do with staging and the scene. How Sophocles represented the cave of Philoctetes is uncertain. Was it built along the stage so that both openings were visible, or was the main stage door the single visible entrance? Secondly, there is the question of exactly what Odysseus and Neoptolemus are after: is it the man, the bow, or the man and the bow? Sophocles may have teased us with some intentional ambiguities on this score, in part out of interest in suspense, in part because getting the bow and persuading the man are radically different projects. Finally, there is the volte-face for Philoctetes occasioned by Heracles. Sophocles has given us two endings, one growing organically out the character and personality of his agents, particularly Philoctetes, the other answering to the "demands" of received myth. Some critics have been able to find dramatic necessity, or at least plausibility, in the second ending. If the endings are contradictory, and surely to some extent they obviously are, it seems clear that Sophocles saw how to avoid the contradiction and preferred to bring on Heracles.

Neoptolemus comes too close to persuading his new friend to go to Troy for us to believe that Sophocles did not see that "happy ending" as he proceeded to add a puzzling, questioning closure.

1–6 For Sophocles the island is uninhabited; Aeschylus used a chorus of Lemnians, and Euripides had his chorus of Lemnians apologize for not having come round to visit Philoctetes sooner. Odysseus' tone is more matter of fact than **desolate** and **marooned** may suggest ("uninhabited"; "I put him off"). Philoctetes' father's name (**Poias**) is often Latinized to Poeas; his native district is Malis in southern Thessaly, not the island of Melos. With **eaten away** cf. Tr 1082–84 (Heracles' wound).

7–9a He does not address the young man in order to excuse himself (**had orders**): "I, posted to this work by the princes, put the son of Poias out here."

9b–10 His howls of pain prevented the rites of sacrifice (**festivals . . . touch the wine and meat**). The Greeks would normally keep silence during a sacrifice, so Philoctetes' **terrible cries** were ill-omened. **Haunted:** "filled the army with his ill-omened cries."

14 The stem (*soph-*) translated in **plans** connects Odysseus with Sophistic reasoning and ethics and occurs in several thematically significant contexts: with "sharpen your wits" (79) Odysseus recommends that Neoptolemus become a thief to further this project; "a wise man" (119) is what Neoptolemus will be if he manages this trick; at 431–32 Neoptolemus uses the adjective twice ("cunning") to characterize Odysseus; Philoctetes assents ("clever" at 440) and later says Neoptolemus has learned "to be clever in mischief against his nature and will" (1014). Cf. 1245f.

15–20 It is not clear from the text whether both entrances to the cave are visible. Robinson ("Topics," pp. 36–37) believes that Sophocles may have made a cave extending along the back of the stage so that Neoptolemus could approach one end, examine an entrance, and come out at the other end. Other commentators suppose that only one is visible, the second being imagined behind the scenic building. See the next note. Painted panels may have depicted the scenery. Robinson (p. 37) calls lines 16–20 "a characteristically self-excusing detail for Odysseus to mention." Friendless Odysseus.

26–30 They enter together, and reach the area between the stage and center of the orchestra by line 25, when, looking around, Neoptolemus spots the cave before Odysseus. The cave, if it is at the central door of the stage building, as seems most reasonable, cannot be very elevated, despite the apparent implication of **above or below**. For **cannot** (line 28) read "do not." Neoptolemus moves on ahead of him, but we cannot have the kind of realism implied by Jebb's "Neoptolemus . . . is climbing the rocks. Odysseus is on the sea-shore." If with Jebb we compare 1000–1004, we shall find that, since there is no conceivable way a realistic cliff could be represented, we ought not to expect "on the rocks" here. Neoptolemus has reached the stage level and finds **no trace of a footpath;** the manuscripts also offer "no sound of a foot-fall." As Jebb says, Odysseus' answer (30) coheres better with "sound" than with "path."

31–39 The **hut** may suggest a dwelling separate from the cave, but the Greek means "place to live" or "dwelling"; cf. the note on 147. The following description, evoking the misery of Philoctetes' existence does not presuppose that Neoptolemus is moving into the cave, or through it, to come out the other end, as Robinson (p. 37) suggests. If he is on an elevation, he can look in, then report, step out, and then note the **rags.**

45–47 Odysseus expects Philoctetes from the country (i.e., from the theater's parodos, stage right; they have entered from the harbor, parodos stage left), not from the cave (some commentators have argued he appears from the cave). For Philoctetes' hatred see 262–78.

50–54 Neoptolemus has not been told the details of their mission. The repeated **serve** (cf. 15, 93–94, and 143) emphasizes his subordination to Odysseus. **Loyal** = "noble" (as in "nobility" at 476; see on 796). True nobility is a major topic of the play. Lines 52–53 mean simply "something new and previously unmentioned in my plans."

55 Although Philoctetes is the object of a hunt (see 116), here **ensnare** means "deceive" (the verb appears again in 969a as "crafty victory"). It is repeated in "lie" (58) and echoed in "a thief" (79).

60–66 See 343–90 for Neoptolemus' elaboration of Odysseus' instructions. Odysseus knows his man. Philoctetes' hatred is such that he is completely taken in by the story (323–24 and 402–8). Ajax, son of Telamon, has previously died because of **Achilles' arms** (*Aj* 41; *Tr* 410–13).

69–69a The epic tradition made both Philoctetes and Neoptolemus requisite to the capture of Troy; their mutual dependence is crucial to Odysseus' argument. Here and below (113, 115) he speaks as if the bow alone is required, but at 101–3 he implies that they must have the man as well. He does not raise the issue of taking one without the other, and at this point in the play the implication of his casual change of reference would seem to be that bow and archer are considered inseparable. Later in the action the question of whether the bow alone suffices for Troy's fall becomes paramount (see the note to 839–42).

72–75 As comrades in arms all the princes had taken an oath to restore Helen to Menelaus. They had thus bound themselves by mutual oaths of friendship, such as we hear of at *Seven against Thebes* 43–49a.

79b–85 Those critics who see the play primarily as a Bildungsroman whose central figure is Neoptolemus call attention to themes highlighting conflicts between natural bent and instruction. Odysseus candidly faces the conflict, confident that only deceit will work. The language of this passage echoes throughout the play, most immediately in the responsion of "natural antipathy" (88) to **natural bent;** "tricks and stratagems" (89) to **contrive** (the *technê* stem, translated "cunning" at 139) and "win by cheating" (97) to **prize of victory.** For the theme of education versus heredity in this play see 874–75, 902, 950, 971, 1310.

For similar arguments in a more traditional context see the note to *Aj* 472. An open appeal to act shamelessly for the sake of personal advantage would be unthinkable in the Homeric poems, where people do in fact act shamelessly if they see likely gain (the suitors in the *Odyssey* are the obvious case). "Vile . . . lying" (108) and "shame" (120) reflect the language and values of traditional, aristocratic culture. See the next note.

86–97 Like father, like son (see *Aj* 471–72 and *Aj* 547–49). The old nobility acts so that there will be no disparity between words and deeds (cf. Odysseus' response, 98–100). **Treachery** (*dolos*) = "craft" (101, 102, 107, 133, 949b). This kind of language (cf. 123–35) sets us up for a play of intrigue. The conflict between acting with honor and acting ignobly, on the other hand, gives the plot an ethical focus (see on 1228). With the antithesis and sense of lines 96–97 cf. *Aj* 479–80, *Tr* 721–22.

98–99d Cf. the exchange between them at 1245–48 and between Philoctetes and Neoptolemus at 1290–93. For this commonplace ("words and deeds") see the note on *El* 21–22.

102 For **persuasion** cf. 563–64, 595, and 612. Ultimately, after he has secured the bow and then returned it, Neoptolemus will try to persuade Philoctetes to come voluntarily (1314–48).

105 Heracles' **arrows** were tipped with poison; Philoctetes never misses the mark. No doubt this paradox of power and debility made Philoctetes particularly attractive to the dramatists.

111 **Gain** (*kerdos*) is often associated with mean motives; see the notes to *Tr* 191 and *El* 59a–60.

113 After his arrival before Troy Philoctetes killed Paris, but it was the stratagem (*dolos*) of Odysseus' wooden horse that finally took the city.

114–15 From these lines we gather that Neoptolemus was told only "you are necessary for the fall of Troy," while the equal need for Philoctetes passed unmentioned. Because he is already cast as Odysseus' lieutenant, we are ready to accept his ignorance of what seems a crucial reservation. Cf. his authority and new information at 839–42. Pohlenz

(*Erlaüterungen* 2, pp. 134–35) points out that the original premise of the myth did not require both heroes.

116 Since Philoctetes must himself hunt for food (165), metaphors from hunting have more dramatic vividness here than in some plays. Other examples at 839, 955–60 (Philoctetes sees the tables turned), 1004–7.

119 The pairing of **wise** and **good** would have shaken the oldtimers in the audience, for whom wise ("clever") and good ("honest/noble") make uneasy company.

122 **Understood** = "agreed to what you have said."

123–31 The disguised sailor—why should Philoctetes be expected to recognize such a nobody?—will appear at 542. The conditions of his return (**too slow**) are vague, but no more so than the **clever story,** from which the novice Neoptolemus is to improvise. This proposal adds, apparently, an intrigue of plot to the deceit, but in the event there isn't much substance to it. And if we look back to the instructions to which Neoptolemus has assented (56–67), we find that Odysseus has recommended nothing more than securing Philoctetes' favor via some slanderous inventions. If we have time to think about what is actually planned—and we probably aren't meant to have such time—we may guess that they hope to get Philoctetes on a ship and then take him off to Troy, or perhaps Odysseus thinks only of stealing the bow after the wary cripple has been taken in. At any rate, we aren't given much specific detail about their plot, save that it depends on winning Philoctetes' trust.

133 Pausanias (7.27.1) saw on the road to Pellene "a statue of Hermes called Crafty Hermes, always ready to grant human prayers." This is **Hermes** *dolios* (see on "treachery" at 86–97); cf. Orestes' prayers and the note at *Libation Bearers* 1 and 726. At *El* 1396–97 the chorus sings that "Hermes . . . conducts the crafty deed to its end."

134–35 The personified **Victory** was only one of many concepts given a temple and cult by the Greeks (the small temple of Athene Victory still stands on the western bastion of the acropolis). **Athena** is Odysseus' special patron in both the *Iliad* and *Odyssey,* so naturally he calls on her for success; less to the point is the **City Goddess,** since the audience will think of their own patronness (Athene Polias, as here).

136–219 It is not certain the chorus has already entered. But as Webster says, "suspicious" (137) and in fact the entire first strophe imply they have overheard some of the conversation; others, like Campbell, feel their presence would mar the privacy of the prologue. They begin the lyrics directly; Neoptolemus responds in recitative anapests. There is a single line (161) in iambics, spoken by the coryphaeus. At 202, and responsively at 211 in the antistrophe, Neoptolemus has a brief phrase at the beginning of each stanza.

136–43 Since **suspicious man, cunning** (see on 79b–85), **serve you** (see on 50–54), and the emphasis on his youth (**young lord:** cf. 79b and 98) and descent (140–42) echo motifs in the prologue, the lines imply they have overheard at least some of the conversation. As Odysseus has instructed their master, so they would be instructed by him (cf. 1072). The **scepter** symbolizes the prince's power; Nestor says to Agamemnon:

Zeus has given into your hand
the sceptre and rights of judgement, to be king over
the people.

(Iliad 9.98–99)

144–48 The **you** is singular; only the coryphaeus will move to the cave, for the stage will certainly not accommodate the entire chorus. **On his crag** is the translator's interpretation, probably based on 1000–1004 (see the note there). **At the edge** is vague; both "on the shore" and "in a remote part of the island" have been understood. Because **from the hut** (= "dwelling") may also be taken with **returns**, Webster and others consider this passage evidence that Philoctetes will enter from the cave (see the note to 15–20). The text has also been emended to read "the man from this dwelling." Our version is plausible. **Terrible** *(deinos)* means "strange": at 104 it is used of the strength and confidence of Philoctetes; it describes his disease (759 and 759a) but also fits, as something out of the ordinary, Odysseus (it is "dexterous" at 440).

150–58 Safety means "opportunity" or "advantage" *(kairos)* and is repeated in the compound Greek adjective translated **amiss. Attack** may also be "come upon" (as in line 46).

159–60 Two-fronted is another reference to the two entrances to the cave (see note on 15–20). It is the place where he **sleeps,** but the lines do not need to mean that he is now at home.

161 Like **unhappy,** several generic terms for sympathy ("miserable," "I pity him," "god pity him," and "his wretchedness": 165, 168, 175, and 186) imply a moral bias on Philoctetes' behalf. Neither Neoptolemus nor the chorus has reason to be insincere, so we must infer some ambivalence. Their deceit is based on practical need while their later decision to help him is founded on a humane pity they feel even now.

164 Dragging along suggests "making a furrow" (Jebb) and looks forward to our first view of the lame Philoctetes. Read "this path" and see line 29.

171 For the motif in **savagery** see also 226, 265 (in "cruel"), and 1321.

176–77 Lachmann's conjecture in line 176 gives a contrast between the divine and human:

Ah, the devices of the gods!
Ah, the unhappy generations of mortals!

These are exclamations, and **woe to** and my "ah" are best taken as indications of tone.

180 Jebb says that **perhaps** does not imply a doubt about Philoctetes' noble birth—they know that well enough—but "merely gives a certain vagueness to the surmise that no one was nobler." The chorus is composed of old soldiers who had accompanied Achilles to Troy ten years before.

187 Blabbering seems an unlikely word for a lyric; "babbling" (Jebb) or "irrepressible" (Campbell) for a compound adjective that means "(having) a mouth without a door."

191–200 In the prologue Neoptolemus appears, a little surprisingly, ignorant of their mission. Now he speaks of Chryse and evidently knows more of the circumstances of the wound than we might have expected from his conversation with Odysseus. As we see from 1327–33, his present speculations are held with some conviction and not merely vaguely joined to the chorus's sympathy. **Chryse** is the name both of a neighboring island and of a *daimôn* worshipped there. Later tradition tells us that Heracles and Jason sacrificed to Chryse, and it may be that Philoctetes, whose father Poeas accompanied Jason, led the Greeks to this divinity to whom they were required to sacrifice for a safe journey. Sophocles leaves the ultimate reasons, if there was a **God's plan,** in mystery. Like many pious Greeks, Neoptolemus reasons back from the inexplicable to the gods, but in this case no more evidence is given.

201–20 The question is whether Philoctetes enters from his cave or from the parodos (stage right: the island). They hear his footfall before his voice and lines 207–9a imply the labored groaning of a man dragging a bad foot over the rocks. If he enters from the cave, he will not be seen until he speaks, and it would seem the full visual and dramatic force of his crippled walk would be more strikingly represented by an entry via the parodos (Robinson's view). But Winnington-Ingram asks (*Sophocles,* p. 285, n. 16) "How often does a chorus *see* a character approaching and not *say* so?" Neoptolemus' description at 163–65 anticipates the scene we have here.

213–14 Robinson (p. 39) suggests this comparison to a shepherd has its point in the dress of Philoctetes.

216–19 Moaning (*ioe*) points to Philoctetes' first word (*io:* not translated) and indicates he is calling to them; cf. 395 and 736–37 where it is used in calling on the gods. Of course his tone may be one of pain (has he stumbled?) or surprise, especially if we prefer Campbell's version of 218: "Or eyeing the inhospitable moorage of our ship." But we should understand that he calls out to them (the chorus may "hear" this cry before the audience). The verbs are present tense (so "stumbles," "looks at," and "is").

220 On first appearance Philoctetes is in rags, looking wild, and carrying his bow, which is not explicitly noticed until 655.

222 **Without offense** exaggerates his deference.

224 **Dear to me** is the first of seven occurrences on this page (lines 224–43) of the *phil-* stem, which as a substantive may mean "friend" (228 and 229a) and as an adjective "dear," "one's own," "beloved." He is effusively free with superlatives here, and the theme is strongly marked throughout the play (see, e.g., 531–33, 587–88), not merely verbally but especially in the tug of war for the friendship of Neoptolemus.

226–28 He confirms their conjectures (cf. 168–73).

230 Philoctetes may be a sight to make the eyes sore. Can we go so far as Webster? "Neoptolemus hesitates at the thought of deceiving such a pitiable figure." Steidle (p. 177), too, detects early signs of inhibition and aversion to his task, for example, in "Now you know everything" (241), with which he compares "This is the whole tale" (389). In these colorless phrases Steidle senses Neoptolemus' relief.

237–38 **In such a place** is interpretative and probably overstresses the possible irony in **such a man,** the most obvious meaning of which is that he is Greek.

239c In the hope that he might not go to Troy, Thetis sent her son Achilles to the island of **Scyrus** and disguised him as a girl in the court of Lycomedes. But he was a man and seduced a daughter of the king while he waited for Odysseus to discover his identity.

249c **Boy** translates the same word as "young lord" at 141. No disparagement is meant in either case.

251 **Rumor** is also the usual Greek for "fame": Philoctetes is supposed to believe that he has not even gained so much inglorious fame as such suffering might normally bring. **Wrongs** (*kaka*) may have both a moral and physical sense ("hardship").

254 **God:** here, as elsewhere, the Greek commonly gives a plural. A pious Greek will call himself blessed by the gods when he is fortunate, hateful to the gods when he is unfortunate (cf. the wish at 462–63). He often does not think of a particular divinity; he is simply willing to see what he might call good and bad luck as somehow the business of the gods (see the note to 448–52). The translation emphasizes divine presence and action. For example, "outraged God" (257) translates an adverb which Jebb renders "wickedly" ("unrighteously" or "impiously" would also be fair translations). Several wishes have been cast into English as though they contained reference to divinity (e.g., at 278 and 509), others

(e.g., at 528) change the Greek plural to a singular, and in some cases (339a) there is no warrant at all or a rather tenuous one (as when "unlucky" is translated "God pity him" at 175). All Greek tragedy is religious drama to some degree, but it seems to me that Grene has stressed too much that aspect of this play; see his introduction to the play for a fuller exposition of his views on divine purpose in the *Philoctetes*.

258 For the motif in **laugh** see the note to *Aj* 67. Cf. 1023 below.

259 **Increases** is a common botanical metaphor (so "blooms," as at OC 683, or "is in its glory," as *Phil* 420).

263–64 The **two generals** are Menelaus and Agamemnon. At *Iliad* 2.631–36 the **Cephallenians** are said to inhabit seven islands, including Odysseus' native Ithaca, and to be led by him.

265 **To their shame**, i.e., as he sees it; see the note on 79b–85.

269–77 Apparently they left him on Lemnos before going to Troy. Despite the detail in this passage, we cannot be sure whether they put him ashore asleep or whether, as the translation takes it, they left him after he had fallen asleep.

278 More simply: "may they find the same!" The wish is typical: cf. 316–17, *Tr* 819–20, *Ant* 928–29.

279 In the verbal play of **awakening ... awoke** the translation achieves the effect of the Greek. These words are not in the same line in the Greek, and such jingles grate less on the Greek ear. So in 285 "time" is repeated as the object of a preposition (Jebb tries for this with "season by season"). More naturally "stone on stone" at 295.

286 The motif "alone and abandoned" is stressed repeatedly, and particularly in the later speeches of Philoctetes (117, 265, 269, 471, 489, 955, 1018, and 1071).

302 In Sophocles' time Lemnos was not the deserted island Philoctetes makes it out; it had its towns and anchorage. Even in myth it was a port of call for Jason, with whom Philoctetes' father sailed (Apollodorus 1.9.17). Both Aeschylus and Euripides in their versions of the story had choruses composed of Lemnians.

312 The omens at Aulis prior to sailing predicted Troy would fall in the tenth year of the siege (*Iliad* 2.295–329).

313–14 For the metaphor of **feeding** the **disease** cf. 695, 747, 1165 and *Tr* 1084 and 1088. Popular thinking connected disease with daimonic possession (cf. note to 759c); so the body may be said to nourish a resident alien. This is the idea at 1164–67.

315 **Atridae** means "sons of Atreus," i.e., Menelaus and Agamemnon.

316 **Gods that live in heaven** = "Olympian gods."

319 At 307–11 Philoctetes contrasts sympathetic words with pragmatic help. The chorus—the coryphaeus actually speaks these iambics (see on *Tr* 291–92)—has already expressed its pity even before seeing him (168 and 186). For other occurrences of pity see 229, 501, 507, 966, and 969. Because Neoptolemus and the chorus sympathize with his misfortune even before he arrives but are now beginning a deception, the extent and quality of their sympathy remains ambiguous until they abandon the deception.

319a–24 Witness and **grounds** (= "charge") are legal terms. The Greek phrasing in 319a–20 is a little odd, and Campbell suggests that the legal metaphor expresses "that Neoptolemus enters into the cause of Philoctetes and is not merely an auditor of his case."

327 Agamemnon is king of **Mycenae**; Menelaus is king of **Sparta**.

332–36 Fatefully may allude to the fact that Achilles was fated to die soon after he killed Hector (thus Thetis at *Iliad* 18.96), or it may be used more loosely in the sense "when it was his time." The tradition made Achilles the victim of Paris and Apollo, which is to say Paris is credited with divine aid. Later in the *Iliad*, Achilles says Thetis told him:

I should be destroyed by the flying shafts of Apollo.

(*Iliad* 21.278)

It reflects more glory on Achilles to say a god killed him.

339a God help you apparently translates a vocative which Jebb renders "unhappy man," and that is the translation at 1196, where the chorus speaks to Philoctetes. Otherwise, this word (*talas*) occurs twelve times in this play (it occurs frequently in all the plays) and is always spoken by Philoctetes of himself or, in a single case, of his cave (1084 of the passageway in his cave). So far as I can tell, it is translated only once ("miserably" at 293), probably because these appositional self-descriptions and exclamations (for the pair at 957 and 959a Jebb offers "wretched one" and "alas") are both self-pitying and trite, qualities we do not associate with tragic heroes.

343–51 Sophocles' lost play *Scyrians* seems to have dramatized the trip of Odysseus and Phoenix (**my father's tutor:** see on 561) to fetch Neoptolemus. The ship was probably **decked with ribbons** to celebrate the summoning of the young hero to take his father's place at Troy. **God's decree** (*themis*) may also be translated "it was right," i.e., according to custom, as the phrase is interpreted at *Tr* 809, *El* 129, etc. For their story cf. 113–15.

This clever speech is nicely calculated to wheedle sympathy from Philoctetes. By identifying himself with his father (an old comrade of Philoctetes), making himself the victim of Philoctetes' worst enemies, and working up a heavy lather of indignation, Neoptolemus fashions a lie worthy of Odysseus. Note the effective details: **great Odysseus** (the epithet is borrowed from Homer), said with a sneer; his suspicion of their story (346–47); his pious wish to see his dead father (353–54); his popular acclaim (357–58). See Philoctetes' reaction at 402–8.

354 Lines 352–53 of the Oxford text have not been translated:

Then there was the added attraction for me in their report
that, if I went, I would sack the bastion of Troy.

356 Sigeion is a promontory near Troy, here described by an untranslated "bitter," which proleptically alludes either to the fact that Achilles was buried there or to the bitterness Neoptolemus was to feel at his treatment there; or both.

362 He will be betrayed by **friends**, just as Philoctetes was.

367 According to the tradition, which Sophocles made the background to his *Ajax*, the Greeks decided to award the armor of Achilles to the next greatest warrior. Odysseus is **Laertes' son** (cf. 407).

374 Ajax and Odysseus saved the body, the former carrying it out of battle while Odysseus fought off the Trojans.

378 **No way given to quarreling** is another touch of verisimilitude: Odysseus had a reputation for self-control; he would not be expected to become involved in a public row. I cannot see why Webster says "Sophocles wants us to see Neoptolemus' embarrassment in abusing Odysseus." See the note to 385–88.

385–88 Kamerbeek approves Webster's notion that these lines are a self-defense, i.e., calculated to extenuate his own conduct in deceiving Philoctetes as well as Odysseus' in taking the arms. The question is, how much ambivalence concerning the deception does he reveal? That is, does the audience sense that he is struggling with his conscience, even though Philoctetes apparently does not?

391–401 This lyric strophe has its responsive stanza at 507–14. They invoke the Phrygian goddess Cybele, identifying her with **Earth** and Rhea (**Mother of Zeus**). She rules over (= **Dweller in**) the river **Pactolus**, which washes gold down from Mt. Tmolus and flows past the Lydian city Sardis. Though the text is not explicit, they apparently invoke her as a great local goddess who would witness and condemn the *hybris* of the Atridae. In art she is frequently associated with bulls, lions, and other wild animals, often in procession; **rides** means she sits in a chariot drawn by lions. Webster prefers to see her "sitting on a throne decorated with lions slaying bulls," and we know the sculptor Pheidias made such a statue for her sanctuary in the Athenian agora (Pausanias 1.3.5). Achilles' arms are called **that wonder of the world** because of their beauty; the work of Hephaestus, they are described in the eighteenth book of the *Iliad*.

402–4 **Half . . . matches** is the translator's gloss on **tally.** The Greeks used broken dice and other halved objects as identifying markers; Neoptolemus' suffering, says Philoctetes, is the counterpart to his own. "Clue" at *OK* 222 is the same word. *OK* 1112 ("consonant") offers a musical metaphor similar to **rings in harmony.**

407 Note the irony of **tale** after the same word at 389.

410–15 Epic poetry knows two men by the name of **Ajax.** This one (cf. notes to 367 and 374) is the son of Telamon, known as the "greater" (= **the Elder**) to distinguish him from Ajax the son of Oileus ("the lesser"). For Homer's distinction see *Iliad* 2.527–30. The son of Telamon committed suicide when the Greeks awarded Achilles' armor to Odysseus.

416–18 The **son of Tydeus** is Diomedes, who, although he is voluntarily associated with Odysseus in a night raid (the tenth book of the *Iliad*), has an exemplary reputation in epic. They had other business together, e.g., in some versions Odysseus and Diomedes went to Scyros to fetch Neoptolemus, and Euripides in his *Philoctetes* had sent them to Lemnos for Philoctetes; see 570–75. The slander that Odysseus is the bastard son of the trickster **Sisyphus** had become a joke before Sophocles' time. **Sold** implies that Laertes paid Autolycus, Odysseus' grandfather, for tainted goods (a pregnant bride).

422–25 The catalogue continues with **Nestor,** the oldest active warrior in the *Iliad,* who is the senior counselor to Agamemnon (see his mediation at *Iliad* 1.247ff.). His son **Antilochus** is a minor character in the *Iliad* and is later killed by the Trojan ally Memnon. Since Antilochus is killed when he diverts Memnon from his father, we have another notable example of filial piety.

426–28 **Ah! . . . Alas:** Philoctetes is stout-hearted but, like all tragic protagonists, he is vocal and demonstrative in expressing his feeling.

433 The Trojan prince Hector kills **Patroclus,** Achilles' closest comrade, during the fighting of *Iliad* 16.

435–38 In the present context this sentiment is cynical, but since the **bad man** is the coward who flies, and the **good man,** like Patroclus and Antilochus, always faces the enemy, the proverbial thought may also praise.

442 **Thersites** has a brief day in the sun in the *Iliad* when he publicly mocks Agamemnon (2.211–43), for which Odysseus gives him a good beating. In Arctinus' *Aethiopis,* a lost epic from the Trojan cycle, he was killed by Achilles.

448–52 With the idea of line 448 cf. 435–38. One may blame the gods (for the topic see on *Tr* 1264–74; cf. Philoctetes at 1020 and 1038 and contrast his implicit assumption at 1040) or endure the fortune they give (see 1316–20). The allusion in **turning back from Death** apparently glances at Sisyphus (see on 416–18 and 624–26) who tricked Hades into releasing him from the underworld, so that **find their pleasure** is a bitter inversion of the usual tale. As Kamerbeek points out, **praising** may mean "wanting to praise"; the paradox is that the pious man wants to praise divinity but can find only harmful and malignant gods. For a similar distinction cf. frag. 919 (Pearson): "For you would not understand things divine if the gods hide them, not if you go to every length in your scrutiny."

457–59 Philoctetes' example of Sisyphus escaping death implies a world that is morally upside down. Now Neoptolemus responds with a similar moral and social paradox: **the worse** are superior to **the better.**

461–65 His decision to leave surprises us, and Philoctetes, by its suddenness. **God's blessing** is simply "farewell." With a signal to the chorus he starts to leave.

469–72 Philoctetes goes to his knees (see the note to 487) in the traditional attitude of a suppliant, which he explicitly recognizes by saying "a suppliant **I beg**" and in the later appeal to "Zeus, God of the Suppliants" (485). The suppliant knows he is a helpless victim and puts himself at the mercy of the person supplicated. This a frequent and fundamental motif in Greek tragedy.

475–80 His arguments echo several earlier motifs and themes: **Put up with it:** cf. Odysseus' "bear up" (82; both characters recognize the strain they are putting on Neoptolemus; cf. "endure" at 481); **nobility:** cf. 337 and the note to 50–54; **shameful:** cf. 83, 108, and 120 (next at 524); **honorable, ugly story,** and **say their best** all bear on the motif of reputation ("fame"; cf. 81–85 and 94–97). **One day,** like "endure," marks both crisis and stress (cf. Odysseus' "one . . . day" at 83).

485 Zeus protects guest and **Suppliants;** Philoctetes is the one and would be the other.

487 Since the suppliant posture commonly entails extending the opened hands to either the knees or chin of the person petitioned, some commentators interpret this line: "I fall at your knees."

489b–92 **Chalcedon** is the father of the leader of the Euboeans (*Iliad* 2.540–41) and a contemporary of Poias, father of Philoctetes. If he rules in the north of Euboea, he can provide easy transport across the gulf of Malis. Mt. **Oeta,** the town of **Trachis,** and the river **Spercheius** are all in the district of Malis over which Poias rules.

507–14 This is a lyric, the antistrophe to 391–401. **Pity** responds to the appeal of 501.

511 I would prefer to understand their meaning to be to **set their ill treatment** of you [Neoptolemus] **to his gain.** They cleverly suggest Neoptolemus can serve himself by helping Philoctetes.

514 Offense is *nemesis,* the indignation of the gods that anyone risks who turns away a suppliant; the word appears at 601–2 in "the Gods who punish evil doings." See on *El* 792.

524–29 Ashamed: see on 475–80. In **render . . . service** we have a certain ambiguity: "to act opportunely for (in the case of) a stranger." In a similar way **where we choose to go** vaguely covers his intent to carry Philoctetes to Troy, not home.

534–35 After the elation of 530–33, we naturally assume **Let us go** responds to "Let us sail" (526). But **earth** is a doubtful emendation that Kamerbeek rightly thinks incompatible with "let us go to the ship." Lines 536–39a are concerned with the cave and by extension the manner of life he has had, so they also tempt us to interpret "Let us go into the cave (that you may know how I have lived)." Because the trader forestalls whichever movement is intended, we cannot get much help immediately beyond 539b. Later, however, after this false start, they once again think to leave, and this time (645–55) they talk of fetching things from the cave. On balance, then, the gesture here is probably toward the cave, but if we don't accept **earth** we can take the cave as a transition to departure:

> Let us go then, first having saluted my homeless
> home within, that you may know
> from what I've had my living.

This translation involves a healthy pleonasm (Campbell neatly compares our own "interior of a cave") and assumes the transmitted text is sound.

Homeless home, like "a sleep unsleeping" (848) translates the common alpha privative prefix that corresponds to the English *un-*. The meaning of the Greek *a-* makes the English suffix *-less* a natural equivalent. The Greek poets often find paradox and contradiciton in such pairs, e.g., in "mother, no mother" at *El* 1154 and Aeschylus' favorite, "graceless grace" (*Ag* 1545). Shakespeare has examples such as

> Here's such ado to make no stain a stain
> (*Winter's Tale* 2.2.19)

and

> All form is formless, order orderless.
> (*King John* 3.1.253)

In the present passage, Long (p. 34) describes the second noun, which is more abstract than our "home," as an "ironical extension" of the usual abstract formation; perhaps "homeless habitat" catches something of his interpretation.

536–39a He may be ironic about his rough bench, but he is also attached to this place (see 936–39, 1081–92, 1451–66); a certain ambivalence, a sentimental feeling for the barren rocks that have been home, may be seen in the varied emotions swirling through this brief speech.

Necessity means, as often, "force of circumstance"; in the negative is "unforced" at 72.

542 Why does Sophocles introduce the trader? Apart from Odysseus' previous promise of help, why bring him on when Neoptolemus has virtually got Philoctetes on the ship? Further deceit is not required for that, and how self-conscious this false departure is can be seen from 645, where entering the cave, now forestalled by the trader's entrance, is reintroduced. Information, rather than action, must be the point of the following scene: as the plot has been defined, Neoptolemus cannot, without rousing Philoctetes' suspicion, bring news of the prophecy of Helenus (605–13) and of Odysseus' pursuit (614–18). The pursuit of Philoctetes is linked by significant verbal emphasis to the theme of persuasion (e.g., 563, 595, 612, 622, 629–30); persuasion is tied to the threat of violence (564, 595) so that the ambiguities of the prologue are kept alive and even compounded, particularly through the report at 612–17. To anticipate the ultimate problem, note that the more the truth concerning Philoctetes' fate is revealed, the more he resists his own lot. Whether we call it divine will (1413–15), the audience's knowledge of the story, or both, he is going to Troy. That dramatic knot, i.e., his resistance to a known fate, is further complicated by this scene. How will they manage to persuade (or force) a man so firmly set against them? How will Sophocles accomplish what his character rejects?

548 Peparethus is a small island southwest of Lemnos, about halfway to the northeast end of Euboea.

552 His anticipation of a reward is of a piece with his commercial calling, a realistic touch that will encourage Philoctetes to credit the news; this man does not belong to the class of heroic traitors who have abandoned Philoctetes. His (feigned) caution at 573–77, his concern not to be caught out (582–83), and his interest in the dollar (584–85) are aspects of his game.

559 Prove unworthy echoes "natural bent . . . mischief" (79b–80) and "natural antipathy . . . tricks" (88–89) and thus for the audience ironically (and self-consciously?) underlines the deceit; a natural ambiguity allows the meaning "unworthy to be your accomplice," i.e., "poor at the game."

560 Jebb suggests new also connotes "strange" or "startling," senses which imply a lively sensitivity.

561 Phoenix, family retainer and surrogate father for Achilles, plays a leading role in book 9 of the *Iliad*. Acamas and Demophon, the two sons of Theseus, do not have a role in the Homeric poems. As far as we

know, neither Phoenix nor the sons of Theseus have any particular relation to Philoctetes in the tradition.

570 **Tydeus' son** is Diomedes (see on 416–17).

573–81 It is obvious from Philoctetes' **What does he say, boy?** that he does not clearly hear 573–74 and 576–77, which the trader speaks in an undertone as an aside to Neoptolemus. But as Kamerbeek notes, line 575 (**famous Philoctetes**) preys on the outcast's vanity; Neoptolemus speaks openly and flatters. Poor Philoctetes is completely taken in, even as he sees the trader is doing business at his expense (**bargain**).

586–89 Neoptolemus adopts the principles and language (**friend**) of Philoctetes in order to snare his new "friend."

589a **Sir** translates the same word translated "boy" at 578, and "boy/child" is the primary meaning. Everyone addresses Neoptolemus as if he is obviously young (see the note to 249c). That "son" is also a proper translation appears from its use in line 592.

601–3 See the note to 514. He seems to mean that the gods may have decided to punish the Greeks for their injustice to Philoctetes—at least his new friend can take it that way.

605–6 Homer calls **Helenus** "Priam's son, best by far of the augurs" (*Iliad* 6.75); the tradition of his capture by Odysseus and his prophecy concerning the prerequisites to Troy's fall goes back to the (lost) *Little Iliad*. Aeschylus and Euripides had both used this story as the context for their Philoctetes plays.

609 **All base and shameful things** does not refer to any particular outrage against Helenus; the trader wants to lay as much dirt on Odysseus as Philoctetes can enjoy.

610–17 **Persuaded** and **against his will** are apparently contradictory: it may be that we should take the persuasion to include the sort of deceit they now practice (but note the antithesis of "craft" and "persuasion" at 102); or **willing** may = "conscious of the facts" while **against his will** = "unconscious of the facts" (see the note to *OK* 1214 for this meaning); or the trader may wish to advertise the bravado of the ambitious Odysseus, who would bring them back alive, whether or not there is any profit in it.

There is no mention of Helenus' prophecy in the prologue, where Odysseus' exposition assumes Neoptolemus' ignorance of much past and present circumstance (that apparent ignorance may be, at least in part, a convenience for exposition). Later in the play, however, Neoptolemus elaborates Helenus' prophecy with such authority that we feel sure he has known it all along (see the speech at 1314–48). Finally, Heracles (1409g–44) reaffirms the prophecy and adds incidental details. As to the actual content of the prophecy, the present passage dwells on the man rather than the bow (the focus of Odysseus' argument in the prologue: see 112–16). Thus a question about what is really required, the man or the bow or both, is implicitly raised, and, once again, it appears from later passages (839–42, 1327–43) that Neoptolemus knows more than he appears to know in the earlier scenes.

We run some risk of misconstruing the course of the action when we look, as I have just now, to later events to confirm earlier obscurities and ambiguities. The trader is a tool of Odysseus and certainly lying in part; Kitto (*Form and Meaning*, p. 119) argues that we don't believe any of his story. The response to this argument seems to me of two kinds: there is a general truth in the trader's report, namely that the Greeks want Philoctetes (that "truth" is established both by the tradition prior to Sophocles' play and by various lines in the play [14, 112, 126, 196–200] that point to the man rather than the weapon); secondly, the audience did know of Helenus' prophecy from the literary tradition and, when the trader introduces it, the audience will immediately ascribe to it the kind of truth that the tragedians constantly rely upon.

617–18 Jebb points out that this vow belongs to the Homeric Odysseus:

> If once more I find you playing the fool, as you are now,
> nevermore let the head of Odysseus sit at his shoulders.
>
> (*Iliad* 2.258–59)

Similarly at *Odyssey* 16.102.

622 Odysseus knew he would not be persuaded (see 102–3), and that is the note that touches the nerve. For the motif see on 542.

624–26 Persuasion cannot bring the dead back to life, but when he puts himself in the category of those who cannot **be persuaded** to try another round of life, he becomes a unique Greek. Even the example he offers (Sisyphus is Odysseus' **own father**) reminds us of everyman's eager desire to cheat death. In such stories as we have on the journey to Hades, it is always the burden of the hero to escape death either by force or persuasion. Philoctetes' hyperbole seems based on a cliché (the dead are deaf), but his example demonstrates how upside down his world is: other men try to persuade Hades to free them, but he would rather remain dead, i.e., be Death itself, than listen to soft talk (629a) from these best friends who have become his worst enemies. Cf. 631–32.

629a With **words soft** cf. Oedipus' "A cruel thing, for all your soothing words" (OC 774a); the messenger's "soft . . . tales" at *Ant* 1194; Tecmessa's "soften!" (*Aj* 597).

629b–30 Blaydes notes that **Exhibit me** echoes "brought . . . before the Greeks" (609a–9b); cf. 615 (Odysseus' boast) and 945 for this typical fear of public humiliation. Athena displays the mad Ajax to Odysseus so that he can "publish it to all the Greeks" (*Aj* 65–67).

637–38 At 524–29 Neoptolemus was eager to depart **in due season** (*kairos*); now the tables are turned. **Rest** means "sleep," an unconscious foreshadowing of the sleep that will overtake him in the next scene. Philoctetes seems excited, perhaps a bit afraid, and it seems psychologically natural that he should be tired.

639–40 Why does Neoptolemus stall? Webster says his "hesitation after his haste in 464 is nonsense in the fictitious situation made by the Emporos [trader]; it must belong to the real situation, his dislike of tricking Philoctetes." Webster sees sympathy for Philoctetes as early as line 575 (in the "famous"!). Other allusions and references to **the wind** (464–65, 855, 1450) imply that we must take its direction as an objective fact and not merely the invention of Neoptolemus, but I doubt we can go so far as Campbell, who attributes this wind favorable for Troy as "a providential circumstance." That Philoctetes' reply is proverbial and not a querulous "what are you talking about?" also argues we are to take the "ill wind" as a matter of fact. Neoptolemus yields to Philoctetes' persistence (643–44) and reminds him to collect his gear (645–46). Kamerbeek may be right to say "he is playing his role all too well," but the path of true ambiguity, somewhere between Webster and Kamerbeek but skirting Campbell's providence, offers the most suspense and dramatic tension.

649–50 An alternative translation: "A herb I have, the chief means to put the wound to sleep so as to tame the beast." This reflects the order of the Greek words, with its mild hysteron proteron ("last first"), since taming the beast (see the note on 313–14) would seem naturally prior to soothing ("putting to sleep") the **wound.**

657–58 Because the bow is magical (it never misses) and the gift of the deified Heracles (cf. 943–44), it is sacred and worthy of worship (**like a god**). There is also, however, an old motif from Greek myth that involves the god-defying hero who swears by his weapon (rather than by a divinity). So the Arcadian hero Parthenopaeus:

> By this lance he swears—and with sure confidence
> he holds it more in reverence than god
> (Aeschylus *Seven against Thebes* 529a–30)

Something of that reverence for the favorite weapon may, indirectly, influence this passage, where we need not doubt Neoptolemus' sincerity, even if he is still fully committed to returning man and bow to Troy.

661–62 **Lawful** translates *themis* ("right"; cf. *Tr* 809). A familiar form of assent in Greek simply repeats a significant word.

664–68 The anaphora found here in **the sight** and the repeated **you**

reflects the occurrence of five relative pronouns in three lines: "who have given me the light of day, who (have given) friends, who have raised. . . ."

669b–70 **Good deed** is the Greek *aretê* ("merit"), which he defines by **friendly help** (a motif introduced at 50–54 in "serve"). Philoctetes set fire to the funeral pyre of Heracles, and thereby won this gift (see *Tr* 1193– 1215).

671–74 The Greek puts this sentence negatively and perhaps looks obliquely at the awful appearance of Philoctetes: "I am not troubled by looking at you and taking you as a friend."

Perhaps Neoptolemus has touched the bow, but he certainly has not taken it from Philoctetes (contra Taplin, "Significant Actions," p. 36). After the veneration of the bow and another overture to friendship, the invitation to **Go in** comes a little abruptly, all the more so in the Greek where it is a part-line finished by Philoctetes.

675 They enter the cave.

676–727 This is the first stasimon and the only choral lyric in the play which is not shared with an individual actor. Philoctetes is off-stage while the chorus sings with great sympathy for his past suffering. Commentators have had a little nervous stomach from squaring sincere sympathy with the chorus's part in the deception of Philoctetes (the "hunt" is still on: see 833–42), and a special problem arises at 721–22 where the chorus says "our prince . . . will carry him . . . home" (see the note there). As Kamerbeek puts it, "The song remains within the framework of the fraud but insists on the hero's pitiful and undeserved fate" (p. 104). Modern critics worry about the chorus's hypocrisy, and of course Neoptolemus runs along the same shoals. On this point their sympathy for Philoctetes expressed in the entrance song, before they have even seen him, is worth remembering. From the start both the chorus and Neoptolemus have been well disposed toward the man, but self-interest, which is emphasized, and duty, which is not, require actions contrary to their natural humanity. What makes this play particularly problematic is that this obvious tension between feeling and self-interest is often suppressed. For example, this ode would be a perfect opportunity for the chorus, which might be viewed as a reflection of Neoptolemus' own feeling, to pose explicitly the moral dilemma facing them. What we have, however, is a song that, if it were not for the larger dramatic context, would reveal absolutely no moral ambiguity at all; in short, it reads like the resolution of a problem rather than a reflection of one.

676–80 Ixion killed his father-in-law, and when no one else would purify him, Zeus himself accepted the suppliant. Ixion then attempted to rape Hera (the euphemistic **him that once would have drawn near** represents a single abstract noun and its article). For this offense he was **bound**

... **on a running wheel** of fire. **Wheel** means "headband," then "headband for a horse," and, from this second sense, "a horse's bridle." Robinson (pp. 42–43) ingeniously connects this third sense with the metaphor of a bridle (or bit) for insolence: "in a horse's bridle only the headband is circular, but in Ixion's *ampux* the fiery circle *is* the bridle" (Robinson, p. 43).

680–85 Kamerbeek, noticing the similar comparison at *Ant* 953–63, calls this comparison of Ixion and Philoctetes antithetical, which means that the differences in the two examples are far more striking than the similarities. In the present passage, unlike that in the *Antigone*, the differences are strongly marked by **wronged no one** (perhaps "cheated" no one) and **nor killed**. There is full justice in Ixion's punishment, but no equity at all in the **destiny** (*moira:* his "lot") of Philoctetes. This may be a case where the Greek and Sophoclean love of antithesis has strained too much the limits of relevance. The parallelism in **by hearsay** and **by sight** with the first line of the strophe (676) underscores the comparison.

693–95 These three lines in English translate seven words in the Greek: "with whom he could lament the groan antiphonal, devouring, bloody." In the Greek the word for **plague** is suppressed in favor of the "groan" it causes; then the adjective "antiphonal," which would naturally modify the speech of the person responding, modifies "groan," while "devouring" (**ate him up**) and **bloody**, which naturally modify plague, are added as two more attributes of the "groan."

698 To quiet = "to put to sleep."

700 Maggot-rotten translates a more general Greek adjective which Headlam (note to *Agamemnon* 566f.) translates "verminous" (Lattimore has "lice" in his version at *Ag* 561). Webster translates "inhabited by a wild beast, the snake of the disease," and the first of his two phrases seems the literal meaning, while the scholiast seems to have thought this adjective alludes to the bite of the snake. **Maggot** is not the sort of word we find in Sophocles, and after **ate** (695) an allusion to the devouring *daimôn*/ disease (see the note to 313–14) seems right. See also the note to 759c.

701–4 The point of the simile likening him to a **child** is not **suffering** but the erratic, crippled walk of the man and infant (cf. 288–89, where Philoctetes uses similar language of himself).

706 Heart-devouring (= "biting the spirit"), a common type of compound adjective, occurs only here in Sophocles. **Suffering** is *atê*.

717–22 The clear meaning of these lines is that Neoptolemus is going to take Philoctetes home to Malis, not Troy. Since lines 833–38 unambiguously indicate that they still subscribe to the plot against Philoctetes, we must resolve the apparent contradiction. Kamerbeek suggests the chorus "can be supposed to think of what will happen after

Troy's fall," but this view entails a very abrupt ellipsis and transition (if we had something like "when he has triumphed and been healed, then he will end fortunate," this theory would have its support). With Philoctetes offstage, Greek dramatic convention would not let the chorus assume that it is overheard, unless some explicit statement of that danger is made. Since nothing is said of Philoctetes' overhearing them, Jebb and others have assumed that he and Neoptolemus reenter at 717, thus precipitating a reassuring final stanza (the second antistrophe begins at 717) on his imminent good fortune. With this interpretation we would have a visual explanation for the new topic, which otherwise too unexpectedly and unnecessarily returns to the deception. Webster's objection to this explanation—namely that the chorus should use the second person if Philoctetes is present—ignores the common use of the third person verb and demonstrative pronoun for a character present on the stage and also denies Sophocles the subtle interaction of song and staging. (Webster's own explanation is that "they simply accept the situation as Neoptolemus has put it," i.e., they believe Neoptolemus has abandoned the deceit.)

723–27 The **Malian nymphs** are the familiar native spirits of the district of Malis, whose primary river is the **Spercheius. The hero of the bronze shield** is Heracles as a hoplite warrior, a common mode of depicting him on contemporary vase paintings but strange in a play that revolves around his bow, which hoplites did not carry for arms. Here we have the clear reference to the deified Heracles that we lack in the *Women of Trachis* (see notes to *Tr* 821–30). His mortal remains were consumed on a pyre set on **the ridges of** (Mt.) **Oeta** and lit by Philoctetes.

730–31 Neoptolemus and Philoctetes have no sooner stepped out of the cave than a paralyzing (**transfixed**) attack signals yet another unexpected turn in the plot. Within fifty lines Neoptolemus has the bow, given to him freely by its owner who realizes that he will fall into a deep sleep when the attack passes.

732–36 The dialogue continues in iambic trimeters, but here (**Oh! Oh!**) and at 737 ("O Gods!"), 744, and 750 ("Quick, boy, quick"), extra metrical phrases break the even pace of the rhythm. Shared lines at 733–34, 753–56, 757–58, and 759b–c also lend an excited, irregular rhythm. Philoctetes attempts to repress the attack and reassures Neoptolemus (**I feel better**), who does not at first understand what is happening.

741 **Pain** translates the word of all duty *kakon*, which is repeated in the "it" of 743. This word is "the attack" at 766, "pain" at 806.

742–47 Cf. the repetition (**I am lost**) at 747. It translates the same verb in Greek as Electra's "I am dead" (*El* 677). The language belongs to the standard diction of pain and lament; cf. "I am lost" at 978 and "I am destroyed" at 1187. In the same way, the repeated verb translated **through**

me is much in the style of tragic pain, and **miserable** . . . **eaten up** is virtually the same phrase as that used by the dying Heracles at *Tr* 986–87.

748–49 Cf. Heracles' call for someone to put him out of his misery (*Tr* 1013–17).

750 For the stage direction (**silence**) see the note to 802–4. The text does not indicate that Neoptolemus touches or otherwise helps Philoctetes before he takes the bow (777). Neoptolemus' response (751–52) remains neutral, as if he still does not comprehend the cause of Philoctetes' agony.

753–59 These lines translate three trimeters. Note the quadruple **know**. The editors are divided on the punctuation of 753 and 755, which need not be made questions: "You know, boy." "What is it?" "You know, son (that my foot is killing me)." Webster keeps the interrogation and suggests that we are to understand either "do you know (what you promised) . . . do not desert me" or "do you know the bow . . . keep it for me." Since Neoptolemus seems reluctant, I would punctuate with periods (as above) and assume that Philoctetes is trying to force the innocent young prince to face the horror of his affliction. The **Oh! Oh!** translates a half-line cry of pain which at 747 (a single Oh!) is extended through an entire line of the Greek text. The emotional breakthrough comes at 759 (**terrible**), with which Neoptolemus admits the evidence of his eyes and ears.

759b **What shall I do** is addressed to Philoctetes, of course, not to the chorus. Cf. 761, and see the note to 895.

759c **Leave** also means "betray." **She** refers to the disease, which is like a vagrant *daimôn* that from time to time comes home to tear his flesh. Cf. 806–7 and note on *Tr* 1025–30.

759f **Most unhappy** represents a repeated adjective (*dustênos*) in the vocative, the same word Philoctetes uses of himself at 746 ("miserable"). That is to say, Neoptolemus has taken up the language (and attitude?) of the victim.

762 The pain is already easing, but another attack is indicated by the exclamations at 785–90. The temporary respite gives him a chance to tell Neoptolemus of what will follow and to remind him of his obligations.

770–73 **Beg** might be translated "bid" or even "command." He suffers but he does not grovel. **Willingly or unwillingly** looks back to the merchant's report of Odysseus' boast (616–17). **Trick** (*technê*) also shows that he has Odysseus' cunning in mind (see on 79b–85). **Kneeled** refers to his (successful) supplication (see 469ff. and 487).

775–76 Although it seems to me we have now seen genuine sympathy on the part of Neoptolemus, these lines remain thoroughly ambiguous (**good luck** for whom?).

777–79 He gives Neoptolemus the bow. **Bow in prayer** = "adore" at 658 (see note to 657–58) and "kiss . . . reverently" at 534–35. It connotes both reverence and submission and would naturally be followed by an object denoting the thing revered, i.e., a god or image. Here, however, the **envy** (*phthonos*) that prompts divine retribution is substituted for the deity. By implying that his **sorrow** ("trouble," "pain") as well as Heracles' came from possession of the bow, Philoctetes continues to treat Neoptolemus with sensible reserve and caution. The dramatic context hardly gives us time to speculate on precisely how the bow might have been responsible for their troubles.

779a–81 Grant us both this: Philoctetes has not prayed. As Jebb says, "the vague phrase covers his secret prayer,—that, sharing the possession of the bow with Philoctetes, he may also share the victory over Troy." Likewise **Where God sends us** is ambiguous, but we should also remember the young man's pious certainty that Philoctetes' suffering is the gods' doing (191–200).

784–85 A line has been omitted from the translation. After two exclamations of pain he says "O foot, what pain will you make for me?" Cf. 1188, where he also apostrophizes his foot, though the English deflects the vocative.

788 The **man of Cephallenia** is Odysseus (see on 263–64).

791–93 This wish should be in the present tense: "would that your bodies might feed . . ."

794 Death: cf. the call to Hades at *Tr* 1085 (in Heracles' agony).

796 Good boy means "noble" or "loyal" (as at 51).

800 Lemnos was volcanic in antiquity; Philoctetes can ask Neoptolemus to perform a service for him similar to that he performed for **the son of Zeus** (Heracles: the frequent references, most recently at 725–27 and 779, are natural and very subtly anticipate the *deus ex machina* of the final scene).

802–4 Here the text clearly calls for some pause between questions as Neoptolemus hesitates to answer. The actors are wearing masks that preclude significant facial response; it is body gesture that counts. We may suppose Neoptolemus turns away briefly, or perhaps looks down or away, as he contemplates the desperate request. **Where are you?** means "what are you thinking of?"

805–6 See the note to 907. Much is left to the audience's imagination here: what exactly is going on in Neoptolemus' mind? Philoctetes fears, mistakenly, that he will yet be deserted.

807–9 She: see the note on 759c. Since some critics are inclined to see Neoptolemus as completely won over by Philoctetes' pain, it may be worth noting that Philoctetes' own perception, which is certainly colored by the anxiety, is that the young man may lack the courage to stand by him.

813–16 Even though he has the security of an accepted supplication, he has been disappointed too often not to think of an oath, which he is a little embarrassed to mention. **May** is italicized because Neoptolemus says "it is not *themis*" (see on 347). **Your hand** is a pledge, and, practically speaking, as good as an oath.

817–20 Five lines of antilabe (810, 813, 814, 816, 817 in the Greek text) account for the length of our translation between 810 and 820. Neoptolemus extends his hand as a pledge, and Philoctetes continues to hold on for support. **Take me away from here:** the Greek lacks a verb and repeats a word meaning "(to) there" a second time (the stylistic indication of a seizure: see 742–50, 785–90). Philoctetes looks or gestures **up, up:** does he point to a rock from which he hopes to jump (see 1000–1004), or does he simply look wildly toward the sky? He is certainly suffering another attack (**madness**), but Robinson (p. 41) thinks the passage may be a "ruse to get loose" to throw himself from the cliff. Apparently his need for support quickly passes to wild pain at the **touch** of Neoptolemus, who (afraid that Philoctetes will harm himself?) refuses to release him until he is calmer. The apostrophe to **Earth** marks the end of the attack and Philoctetes' last words as he faints to the ground.

827–65 With Philoctetes fast asleep, the chorus sings an interlude: a single strophe, a mesode (Neoptolemus' four hexameters), the antistrophe, and an epode (855–65).

827–32 This brief hymn to **Sleep** begins with an address to the god (both Sleep and **Lord** are vocatives in the Greek), speaks of his attributes and powers (that he **knows not pain nor suffering** means that sleep brings freedom from pain and suffering), and asks for his blessing (**kindly**) and presence (**come**). The exact meaning of **radiance** is much discussed (and the word emended), but the translation is well chosen to suggest a glowing mantle or cloak over the eyes. Webster: "Paion, healer, is an epithet of Asclepius [god of healing], and Aigla [radiance] is his daughter, the gleam of serenity which the god of healing brings." **Upon us** refers to the usefulness of sleep for their enterprise (another and untranslated "for us" precedes **Lord Healer**).

833–38 Look to your standing: rather, "consider where you stand," i.e., what your situation is. **He sleeps** is Herwerden's emendation for the manuscripts' "you see now (that he sleeps)." **Ripeness** (*kairos*) means "opportunity" and should be read as a personification. With this idea that "occasion decides everything" Kamerbeek compares *El* 75–76 and Pindar *Ninth Pythian* 78:

Season in all things
keeps the utter heights.

Cf. the same stem (in "seasonable") at 862–63.

839–42 To the chorus's suggestion that they take the bow and run, Neoptolemus replies that both man and weapon are required. Although the focus has shifted somewhat ambiguously from bow (Odysseus' emphasis) to the man (Helenus' prophecy), it is probable that the audience has thought all along of the archer and his bow as a single unit; the literary tradition did not make the subtle distinction between the powers of man and bow that have teased so much speculation from modern critics. Sophocles has introduced doubt and ambiguity, both about what will happen and about Neoptolemus' motives. The chorus clearly thinks they can steal the bow and leave the man. It is not the sense of these lines but the motive(s) of Neoptolemus that have sponsored modern debate: Has a new sympathy for Philoctetes led him to modify Odysseus' expressed emphasis on the bow? Has he believed the prophecy of Helenus, even though he has been told the story is bogus? Has he been after man and bow all along (in which case we must suppose the chorus has misread their mission), or does he realize (and only now?) that the bow without the man is a shameful, because empty, boast? A variety of permutations on these questions are possible. For example, Kamerbeek approves Knox's view (*Heroic Temper,* p. 131) that Neoptolemus "understands the real meaning of the prophecy of Helenus even though he has heard it only in the carefully calculated version of Odysseus' spokesman. It was not a promise of victory for the Greeks, with Philoctetes the instrument of their triumph; it was the recompense offered Philoctetes by the gods for all that he had suffered." This view, apart from other difficulties, ignores both an ambiguity in **His is the crown of victory** and the plain sense of line 842. In fact, lines 1314–48 make it clear—if he is sincere!—that he knows of the prophecy before the trader's report. Others make much of the so-called "oracular hexameters" (oracles are customarily delivered in hexameters), but Webster reminds us that hexameters are present, without oracles, in the epirrhematic structure at *Tr* 1004–42.

The four lines need to be taken together. Like many critics, this translation places much emphasis on the first two lines, and does this by repetitions (**in vain** and **vainly; have hunted** and **have captured our quarry**) that are not found in the Greek. Jebb translates: "I see that in vain have we made this bow our prize, if we sail without him." ("Prize": see 609b). How do the next two lines cohere with the first two? **His is the crown of victory** means that the crowning success of taking Troy is reserved for

Philoctetes; but the phrase may also be translated "in him is the prize," which would continue the metaphor of Philoctetes "as the prize for which Neoptolemus is now striving" (Winnington-Ingram, *Sophocles*, p. 287, note 26). We cannot suppose, in this context, that Neoptolemus is purposefully ambiguous, and this second version makes more sense as a link with line 842, which can only refer to the **shame** Neoptolemus will get if he returns with a hollow boast belied by **victory unwon**, i.e., the partial "victory" of the bow without the man.

This reading, more cynical than pious, squares with the fact that all along Neoptolemus has been trying to get Philoctetes, not just his bow, on the ship (Hinds, p. 174, emphasizes this). That is to say, it has been implicit in the entire preceding episode that because Neoptolemus is trying to get Philoctetes on the ship, the man himself is required at Troy. The trader's story supports this, and later Odysseus will threaten to take Philoctetes even against his will (982–88). In a sense we are disregarding Neoptolemus' motives and the subtle shift in his sympathy as we look at what the plot says, and yet it would be foolish to deny that much of this play is ethical and distinctly shaped to reveal character in crisis. In stressing either plot or character most interpretations shortchange one or another significant aspect of the whole play. In my view, Neoptolemus has already experienced profound pity for Philoctetes, and in some sense he may be fooling himself with these lines, just as—if we want to continue the psychology lesson—he may at some level need to assert his authority and intellectual superiority to the chorus. But the simple fact is the play would be over if they only needed the bow: as soon as Philoctetes hands it to Neoptolemus, everyone in the theater knows something more (the man? willing or unwilling? deceived or persuaded?) will be required. The audience may also sense Neoptolemus' frustration and embarrassment with this deceit, and in that direction lies the return of Odysseus. Yet another complication, and one quite impossible to factor into the equation with any certainty, derives from the audience's knowledge that Philoctetes did go to Troy, whether we call their source literary history, myth, or divine necessity alluded to in the familiar prophecy of Helenus, which Sophocles cannot introduce and then dismiss unexplained.

843   The chorus does not seem to find Neoptolemus' lines very problematic. **The God** is the usual "a god," i.e., any god who takes an interest in this business will sort it out as he likes.

847–48   The oxymoron here is not so much in **sleep unsleeping** as in "keen-eyed sleep."

849–54   **To the limits of what you can** probably means no more than "so far as you are able." **This** (850) seems to refer to stealing the bow but possibly also to Neoptolemus' stipulation that they must take the archer.

Webster thinks **of whom** and **this man** refer to Odysseus, but this seems terribly allusive even for the chorus, which is more bent on not disturbing Philoctetes than on being specific. For **of whom** I would prefer "You know what I am talking about" (reading a neuter pronoun with Dawe). **This man** is Philoctetes. **Trouble,** though vague, may look to the obvious difficulty of persuading Philoctetes to go with them. Metaphorically, in its meaning "no way," trouble leads to "fair wind" (855); cf. note at *OK* 689–96. The ambiguities here stem from vague allusion more than from the syntax or diction.

855–65 **Fair wind** may be literal (cf. 639–42), but it is also clearly figurative: cf. **seasonable** at 863, which itself echoes "ripeness" (837). They are back on the line they took at 833–38, not much troubled over the difference between man and bow. **Blanket** is not literal but seems the right metaphor (cf. 830). **Asleep in the sun is good** may be a gloss. Kamerbeek notes that **causes the least fear** means "which is not attended with danger."

The chorus's attitude toward Philoctetes, opportunistic and even brutal, if we think of the consequences of leaving him without his bow, is, to say the least, unexpected after their previous sympathy, even if we were to grant that all the sympathy expressed while he is onstage is feigned. It is hard to see them "as an instrument with which to guide the mind and emotions of his audience in any direction required by the immediate dramatic context" (Burton, p. 238), unless we are to believe they play the foil to Neoptolemus, whose repentance we are soon to witness (895 ff.). Their pragmatism is thoroughly Greek (Odysseus himself is far more typically Greek in this respect than much modern criticism would have us believe), and in a rough manner this pragmatism guides their argument and remonstrance with Philoctetes in their next major involvement (1080–1221). Perhaps we should define their "character" as one parallel to Neoptolemus' but with a predominance of interest over justice (925–26), whereas the son of Achilles will finally come down for justice. Such an attitude suits their social (military) standing and gives them a more subtle dramatic role.

870–72 **Pity** and **support** (= "put up with") point to his continuing anxiety that his disgusting wound will yet cause them to abandon him; cf. 876, 891, 900 for more signs of this concern. **The Atridae** are introduced by way of contrast and antithesis ("you endured, but they did not endure").

874–75 **Noble nature . . . noble . . . parents** is compressed into a single line (ABA structure: "noble the nature from noble [parents]"). For the motif "like from like" see the note to *Phil* 86–97, and cf. 384. For the theme of "noble nature" see the note to 79b–85 and Neoptolemus at 902–

3. Philoctetes is unconsciously raising the issue that touches Neoptolemus most deeply.

879–95 Raise me up initiates an important dramatic gesture: Neoptolemus' reluctance to help Philoctetes (884–85) reflects his final effort to suppress pity in favor of self-interest and honor. Philoctetes, however, will put all the burden on the boy (**lift me up yourself,** 887), and Neoptolemus then extends his hand to raise the sick man (**take hold yourself** at 893 should be read to mean "take hold of me"). Touching and supporting the old soldier, Neoptolemus gives a cry of anguish (**Now is the moment** at 895 translates the same cry rendered "Ah!" at 785 and 787) that equates his guilt with Philoctetes' physical pain.

887 As you thought of it means "just as you intend to."

895 What shall I do?: No play of Sophocles seems to pose this question more often. This one marks the crisis of self-doubt and is addressed to himself, though of course Philoctetes overhears. Cf. the appeal to Zeus at 909; similar questions at 949d, 969b, 974, and 1350, but each one has a nuance of contextual distinction. Taken together, this questioning is related to the themes of learning and education. Dramatically, the questions give the play an openness in its ethical texture unique among the extant plays.

897–98 At a loss = "trouble" at 854 (note). The repeated word or stem in consecutive verses of stichomythia is very common in Sophocles. In the following dialogue, for example, "disgust" (902) picks up the same word in 900; "father" (904) translates a participle from the same stem (*phu-*) as "nature" (902); "wrong" (910) is the same word as "base" (909); cf. "leave" in 911 and 912; "learn" in 918 and 919. See the note on 907.

902–4 The paradigm of the noble father (among other passages: 356–60, 720, 874–75) now becomes useful for argument. Cf. the appeals at 940–41, 950, and 998.

906 Dishonorable = "vile" at 108 and "most foul" at 909a; see also on "shamelessly" at 79b–85.

907 I am afraid of that translates a clause that appears again at 913 (= "and I dread this"). This emphasis is all the greater for the presence of an untranslated temporal adverb meaning "for some time." This is evidently a marked word for Sophocles. It has already appeared at 805–6 in "I have been (for some time) in sorrow for your pain" and will appear again at 968 (note). See Kirkwood, pp. 159f.

909–9a Cf. 895. Neoptolemus' share of the dialogue is as much "to himself" as to Philoctetes, who is both afraid and bewildered (see 914).

915–16 Of course he hides, or passes over, a great deal, but by now his frustration with the deception has driven him to the point that we can hardly expect a reasoned explanation. So he begins at the end, astounding Philoctetes with a fiat that drives him into just the kind of rage and panic we might expect.

922 **Necessity** could refer to the will of the gods (see the note to 1316–20) or to the constraint of duty (see 925–26). Such vagueness is obviously not the best way to win Philoctetes' assent.

923 **Stranger** (*xenos*) is the word that marks a special attachment between host and guest or, as here, between strangers who have accepted claims on one another which would otherwise exist only between friends. The acceptance of the suppliant is the key fact in this case, while the entrusting of the bow was the reciprocal gesture. The same word is "friends" at 869.

925–26 **Justice** and personal **interest** are more often antithetical. Although Philoctetes does not understand, Neoptolemus alludes to the will of the gods and his own share in the glory of conquest. Kirkwood (p. 148), however, thinks that his sense of duty keeps him from returning the bow.

927–30 Long (pp. 114–16) points out that even Homer uses abstract language (**horror, engine, mischief**) for abuse and that such usage is common in the comic poet Aristophanes. Consequently, we should find here vigorous denunciation, despite the fact that the translator's faithfulness to Greek idiom may fall on the English ear with more affectation than energy. Perhaps we should not even look too closely for the reasons behind **fire** (like fire, says Jebb, Neoptolemus is a "ruthless destroyer") and **horror** (what stealing the bow inspires). More to the point, thematically, is **engine,** which is formed from the *technê* stem and so recalls Odysseus' "to contrive such mischief" (80) and Neoptolemus' antipathy to "tricks and stratagems" (89). Abstract for concrete, especially where abstraction modifies abstraction is a species of periphrasis, but the Greek habit of using these abstract nouns abusively in the colloquial idiom of comedy probably lent them a less artificial ring than they have for us. Philoctetes, of course, is unconscious of his irony in referring to Neoptolemus as the "product of *technê,*" nor does he know the depths of the **treachery** (= "deceived" at 949c), nor is he aware that Neoptolemus felt shame even at the prospect of this deceit.

931–33 The Greek word for **livelihood,** which is commonly translated "life," is spelled the same as one word for bow; lines 931, 933, and 1282 ("stolen my life") pun on these two words (both spelled *bios* but with different accents). In the Greek line 931, the words for "life" and "bow" (*toxa,* the more common word always used until now in this play) are adjacent, and, especially in light of the repetitions, there is little doubt that Sophocles intended a pun. Modern commentators deny the pun largely because they fear any humor in this passage, but a more serious objection would seem to be the rather obvious, and therefore flat, character of a play on "bow = life" in this play. Robinson (pp. 43–44) compares the pun of Heraclitus, "the bow's name is life and its work is death" (frag. 48), but the Heraclitean aphorism plays on a vital paradox while, as Robinson sees, in line 931 the literal meaning and the pun come to much the same meaning.

I beg you is the suppliant's language (cf. 469) and may indicate that he has gone down on his knees in appeal (cf. 485–87).

934–35 This aside, spoken to himself but within the hearing of Neoptolemus, is preceded by an untranslated exclamation of grief. Cf. Euripides Hecuba 813–15.

936 The numerous apostrophes to the island and his natural surroundings (cf. 988, 1081, 1144, and, finally, 1451–68) lend a "romantic" color to his melancholy existence.

940–50 Although he does not speak or argue directly to Neoptolemus, this passage is full of ad hominem argument: Achilles' son, his right hand (see 816–17), sacred bow (see 657–58), and arguments from pathos that reach a climax in Be your true self again. To show it to the Argives: see the note to 629b–30. For vaporous shadow . . . wraith see the note to Aj 126. For craft (dolos) see on 86–97.

950–51 The distinction between true self and a temporary aberration from character is drawn by Odysseus at 79b–85; cf. Aj 636–40 and Tr 721–22 for similar contrasts.

955–60 The metaphors from hunting become, in this imagined future condition (see on Aj 495–507), the literal fact. In another variation on the "world-upside-down" the hunter becomes the hunted. In life for the life . . . repay there is a legal metaphor denoting the security put up or claimed in compensation for injury. The oddity is that he pays reprisal to the birds and wild beasts because a party quite indifferent to his "quarrel" with them has seized his bow. See also the note to 339a.

961–63 The structure of these three lines (two lines in the Greek) reflects both his bitterness and faint hope. The first word utters the curse, which he immediately retracts (Jebb translates: "Perish! no, not yet, till . . ."), and the last two words (Jebb: "die accursed") repeat the curse, now modified by the temporal stipulation.

964 Here, as often, the coryphaeus is the first to respond to a long speech, but the questions give this response more dramatic point than we usually find.

966–68 All the time is interpretative. Cf. the version of Winnington-Ingram (Sophocles, p. 284), "In me a terrible pity has come to lodge and has long been there." Like the translator, Winnington-Ingram seems inclined to think that Neoptolemus' sympathy began with the first sight of Philoctetes, but Sophocles' language is not as precise as the translation implies. For this same temporal expression (*palai*) see on 907. **Compassion** = "pity" (1074). Philoctetes has repeatedly appealed for pity (501, 759a, 870).

969–69a Blame echoes "ugly story" (478), "reproach" (523), "shame . . . our boast" (842), and perhaps Odysseus' argument at 83, if we read "blame" there (for "shameless"). Odysseus argues that success brings the fame the young hero desires; Philoctetes argues that even successful deceit will bring social censure.

969b–70 An exclamation of grief and frustration precedes this question, the same cry (untranslated) that precedes Philoctetes' "He does not say a word" (934). The rocky island of **Scyrus** seems to have had the reputation of being a place anyone would be happy to leave. The wish is a familiar type that would annul the present by revoking the past; cf. *OK* 1157, *Tr* 997–99.

971 Teaching: cf. 1013 and the language of Neoptolemus at 918–20.

973–75 Despite his question, Neoptolemus is apparently about to hand over the bow when Odysseus appears, interrupting with his own question, which takes the second half of the Greek line (antilabe). Philoctetes does not immediately see him.

978 With **sold** compare the commercial figure in "bargain" at 578–79. Note the silence of Neoptolemus, who does not speak until line 1073.

984–86 Just as Neoptolemus has said that Philoctetes, as well as the bow, must come to Troy (915–16, 919a–20), so Odysseus insists that the man must accompany them; cf. 999–99b: "*you* must take Troy." **Against my will** (= "with violence" 989a) echoes a similar (untranslated) adverbial phrase in 984: "**or these will bring you** by force." This motif was first introduced at 103 ("force"); cf. 563 and 595.

988–89a The **all mastering brightness** belongs to the local volcano (see on 800), which is thought of as the forge of Hephaestus, the god of fire.

989b–90 It is Zeus apparently alludes to the prophecy of Helenus (note that the prophecy at 610–21 makes no reference to Zeus), but his manner of offering this authority is both peremptory and unexplained, and we are hardly surprised that Philoctetes will have none of it (991–93). Although he proves right (see Heracles' "the plans of Zeus" at 1414), the audience—fully sympathetic with Philoctetes, yet aware he must go to Troy—will likely share Philoctetes' suspicions, if only because they are listening to a self-professed liar. The dogmatic and coercive Odysseus plays a role designed to frighten and isolate Philoctetes, not to persuade him. **Servant** echoes the motif of 50–54 (note); cf. 669b–70 and 1024.

995–96 The pace and excitement of this scene are indicated in part by five lines in antilabe (974–75; 981–82; 986–87; 995–96; 1001–2).

997–98 Fathers should be singular. **We** is the plural for singular, as often. **Free** appears at 1007 as "noble."

999–99b It is destined = "you must" at 984 (i.e., there is no overt reference to a prophesied fate). **Dig her down:** cf. the metaphor of the spade of Zeus at *Agamemnon* 525.

1000–1004 Here translates a demonstrative (*this* **rugged precipice**), and even if he only gestures toward it, Odysseus' prompt action seems good evidence that the audience must imagine a cliff nearby from which Philoctetes might throw himself (see the discussion at 817–20). Webster thinks "the additional height of the eccyclema, as well as the steps leading from the *orchestra* to the stage, make the cliff." There is a danger, in the name of illusion and realism, of creating a pitiful little cliff from which no one could sprain an ankle. Did Shakespeare build a cliff for Gloucester's fall?

They do **hold him** (see 1015–16). **Hands of mine:** cf. Heracles' apostrophe at *Tr* 1089. Assonance leads to punning on **hands** and **lack** (*cheires* and *chreia* are in the same line in the Greek).

1008–14 Sophocles makes Philoctetes intuitively grasp the truth about Neoptolemus' role, but this exculpation of the young man may also be seen as a desperate argument: Neoptolemus still has the bow and a humane instinct and may yet save him. **Shield** is also a "screen." **You see** may imply that something in the manner or attitude of Neoptolemus suggests remorse. **Slit-eyed:** the metaphor suggests psychological prying into the depths of Neoptolemus' soul. **Clever** (*sophos*): see on 14. **Against his nature** translates a single word that occurs only here in Sophocles (*aphuês*, a privative from the same stem as *phusis:* see on 79b–85 and cf. the thought at 950.)

1018 Without friends or comrades or city is redundant, and a much stressed motif (see on 286; next at 1071 in "alone"). Few Greeks of the classical era would have voluntarily become hermits; Philoctetes has been completely denied the normal civic life. The phrase may also reflect Sophocles' fondness for triads: cf. 72–73 for a functional triad and the three questions at 1031–33, all of which are introduced by "how" in the Greek. See on 1029a.

1019 For the **curse** cf. 961; the same verb, also in the imperative, occurs again, at 1035.

1020 If the gods had given him anything **sweet,** Odysseus would be dead from the curse ("may you perish!").

1025–26 An untranslated verb makes this "yoked" **by constraint,** a phrase that apparently alludes to Odysseus' attempt to evade service in the expedition by feigning madness. When the ambassadors of Agamemnon came to Ithaca to fetch him, he yoked an ox and began to plough the sandy beach. Palamedes, suspecting a trick, put the baby Telemachus in his path, and of course Odysseus swerved to avoid hitting his only son, thereby giving his game away. The commentators see an allusion to this incident at *Agamemnon* 841–42, where the king says of Odysseus that "once yoked to me he carried his harness." For the common metaphor see also *Aj* 123. It is typical of Sophoclean irony that **trickery** echoes the language used by Odysseus in the prologue ("ensnare" at 55, "lie" at 58; Philoctetes has previously condemned the word at 644 and 969a ["crafty"]).

1029a This line actually has three questions, but the second is virtually the same as the first. Some commentators have been tempted to emend, but in an agitated speech, with so many imperatives, exclamations, and questions, we cannot be sure of Philoctetes' control.

1035 In ugly form is the omnipresent *kakos,* this time as adverb: "may you die vilely!" The verb is in the plural.

1036–39a He shrewdly sees that only desperation would bring them to Lemnos. **My happiness** and **a need** are the translator's (correct) interpretative additions, but Sophocles' Greek is bolder since "a divine goad for me" entails the suppressed equation "goad consists of a need." For the image see Aeschylus *Suppliant Maidens* 101 ff. and the note there.

1040 For the **Gods that look on men's deeds** see the note to *Agamemnon* 1270. It is natural for a Greek to look to the gods for vengeance. Oedipus, when he curses his son, invokes "Justice that sits with the ancient laws of Zeus" (*OC* 1382) and calls on the powers of the underworld and on Ares (*OC* 1389–93) to fulfill his curses.

1045–46 On the theme **no yielding to suffering** see the notes to *Ant* 471–72 and *OC* 1179.

1047–61 Odysseus dismisses Philoctetes' rage, orders the attendants to release him, and announces that they will take the bow and leave the archer. Critics continue to debate whether Odysseus is bluffing, but that is not the point for the scene at hand. Philoctetes believes him (1062–63), Neoptolemus acts as if he believes him (1073–80), and the entire lyric that follows (1081–1217) takes as the premise of its argument that Odysseus and Neoptolemus will leave without Philoctetes, unless he changes his mind (T. von Wilamowitz-Moellendorff, p. 307, sees this clearly). Apart from Philoctetes' dismay, the audience will be completely surprised by this new turn, even if it doesn't recall the trader's report that Odysseus vowed to take Philoctetes, even "against his will" (617).

1057 Teucer is an archer and half-brother of Ajax (*Aj* 342, 1120; cf. *Iliad* 23.859–69). Odysseus did not take his bow to Troy, but it is the prime engine of his revenge on the suitors (*Odyssey* 21 and 22).

1060–61 The speech is wonderful for its arrogant sarcasm: "have a good day taking your stroll on Lemnos!" **Your prize** is of course the bow. A tacit assumption is that anyone who has the bow can make proper use of it; otherwise Philoctetes would mock his empty threats.

1062 The question (cf. 949d) is preceded by a gasp (*oimoi:* the same cry mentioned in the note to 969b–70, where the question is exactly the same). As often, Philoctetes also characterizes himself with (untranslated) "wretched" (a synonym of the word discussed at 339a; cf. another at 1090), as at 949c ("am lost") and then again at 951 (untranslated). The translator's problem is that what is idiomatic to Greek tragic diction is completely alien to modern tragic diction—unless the translator takes a free line (see on *Ant* 919)—and equally alien to the modern sensibility that wants irony and not self-advertisement, which is not what the Greek audience would have found in these exclamations. They expected their heroes to weep and cry out. See Homer's description of the grief of Achilles, *Iliad* 18.22–35, and of Odysseus crying on the beach and longing for home, *Odyssey* 5.150–58.

1065–68 Odysseus' response recognizes both the power of his pitiful appearance and the danger of Neoptolemus' noble nature (**generosity** = "loyal" at 51). **Our future** (*tychê*) may also be translated "our luck."

1074 For his **pity** see the note to 966–68. Those who would have Neoptolemus quivering with pity from the first sight of Philoctetes must reckon with the fact that now, in what must seem to Philoctetes a crucial moment, he has more regard for Odysseus' opinion than for his admitted sympathy for the cripple.

1078 Better thoughts are, practically, second thoughts.

1081–1217 This shared lyric passage stands in place of the usual stasimon. Both Philoctetes and the chorus sing these lyrics which, until 1170, are divided into strophic responsion. The difference between this passage and the standard epirrhematic form is that the parts given to the chorus, rather than being metrically distinct, simply continue the responsive strophes and antistrophes that in each case are begun by Philoctetes. Consequently, there is a metrical and rhythmic continuity through the passage, whereas the sense of each utterance by the chorus is one of argument against the intransigence of Philoctetes. The lamenting hero hardly takes notice of their arguments until 1170, after which a lively lyric dialogue replaces the alternating lament and unanswered argument.

1081–84 This apostrophe to his cave and its passageway will be followed at 1144 by an apostrophe to the birds and wild creatures of Lemnos (cf. 936–39 and 952).

1091–92 The translation seems to follow Pearson's text, which does supply a verb ("will pass by") with **birds**. The text, however, is unsatisfactory; among the many suggestions, I like best that which is approved by Kamerbeek and printed by Dawe: "Come, you who once cowered aloft; come through the shrilling breeze; I can no longer bring you low" (Kamerbeek's translation). Cf. 1144–52.

1093–1100 Philoctetes, says the chorus, has only himself to blame. His **mischance** is his "luck" (*tychê*), which he made for himself by not being sensible (= **wisdom**), i.e., by not accepting the opportunity of going to Troy. For **opportunity** the Greek offers, typically, "preferring the worse to the better *daimôn*." Cf. the similar practical criticism of the chorus at *Ant* 852–55 and 875.

1101 Sorrow, sorrow is mine represents one way of handling the stylistic problem discussed in the note to 1062. In the Greek a repeated adjective (*tlamôn*) modifies "I."

1110 Unmarked = "unnoticed." It is generally assumed that he refers to Odysseus rather than Neoptolemus (cf. 1008–12).

1111–13 In this wish he says explicitly "my" pain; see 278, 316–17, and the note to *Tr* 1036–40 for similar wishes for an enemy.

1114–23 Will = "fate" or "lot"; of course it was **craft** (101), as they very well know, and have practiced, while singing of their pity and friendship (676–727) and then urging Neoptolemus to take the bow during Philoctetes' sleep (833–38; 854–65). If we are to take the chorus seriously as a character, we must probably admit that now, caught out by the facts, they resort to vague talk of the will of the gods (cf. 1316), deny their own complicity, which would be manifest if Philoctetes cared to examine it, and call their solution (his journey to Troy) friendship on the grounds that it is best for all concerned! We can see their friendship is more or less totally self-interested; Philoctetes is, to this point, too involved in his own suffering to listen.

1126–31 Forged is a misprint for "forced," i.e., "taken violently from." **That I loved** and **that loved you** translate forms of *philos,* which is here used in the common sense of "my own"; there may be subtle echoes of the "friendship" theme, but the word is so frequent in this thematically less significant sense that we run some risk of overreading the text. **Successor** is an emendation, but the reference to Heracles is secure.

1140–43 For 1140 some versions offer, less ambiguously, "it is the part of a man to call the expedient just," which would naturally be taken of Odysseus. The sense of the passage is that it is fair enough for Philoctetes (**a man**) to speak his case, but when he has spoken he should forgo **rancor**; Odysseus, he should remember, is doing the work assigned to him by others.

1159 Who can live on air: by contrast Ajax says "feed on light breezes" (*Aj* 559a), and in general ancient writers seem to have preferred to represent the winds and breezes as benign and nurturing.

1164–67 Doom (*kêr:* see on *OK* 473) is usually taken in this sense, but **to feed** and **cannot learn** are both so strongly personifying that we may also translate "demon" and think of the wound as inhabited by a daimonic power (*kêr* also occurs at 42, where it is the untranslated cause of his disease; see 1187 and the notes to 313–14 and 759c): "It is in your power to flee this *daimôn;* it is pitiable to feed it, a thing that cannot learn. . . ."

1178–81 Their readiness to leave, like Odysseus' departure, takes him aback. Zeus **listens to curses** because he protects suppliants, and **beseech** reminds them of his earlier appeal.

1187–90 These four lines should begin with two cries of pain. He is suffering another attack. **It is the God, the God** is simply *daimôn, daimôn* (as in Heracles' cry at *Tr* 1025; cf. on 1164–67), which I take to be his notice that the beast is biting his foot again. **My foot** is actually an address to his foot: "what shall I do with you?"

1193–95 Storms carries a common image; cf. 1460 and the extended simile at *OC* 1240–48. Once he seems to relent, the chorus renews its appeal.

1197 One dramatic point of this scene is to demonstrate Philoctetes' refusal to relent. Just as their appeals fall on a deaf ear, even a third attack, so severe that he once again wants to kill himself (1204–17), cannot persuade him to follow his old enemies. **The Lord of the Lightning** is Zeus, who on provocation has actually blasted men with **flame and glare** (see *Ant* 123–33). Ironically, the son of Zeus will be sufficient to change his mind.

1204 Cf. the similar request at 748–50.

1207–9 Cf. Heracles' appeal at *Tr* 1015–17 ("cut off my head!") and to Hyllus at *Tr* 1035–40. Some editors change **head** to "flesh." **On death, on death:** cf. the iteration at 1187.

1215–16 City is Malis; **holy streams** = the river Spercheius.

1218 Now am nothing echoes similar phrases at 951 and 1030. He must exit with this line, rather than after 1221, since the next lines announce Odysseus and Neoptolemus, whom he is surprised to see at 1263–66.

1219–21 These lines return to iambic trimeter and are spoken by the coryphaeus. Their function is clearly transitional. Taplin ("Significant Actions," pp. 39–44) wants a "full stop" at this juncture, "thus exploring a pessimistic ending which is then rejected" (p. 39), and for this and stylistic reasons he condemns these lines as an interpolation, perhaps from a later production. The style of the lines is certainly redundant and pedestrian, but Taplin's arguments on this score seem to me tendentious. It should be noted, moreover, that the lines contain a personal pronoun referring to Philoctetes ("you would already have seen me on my way . . ."), which makes them look back as well as forward. Without them we have an unannounced entry of a rare type in which the characters enter speaking in dialogue (cf. *Phil* 730ff.).

1222–62 Neoptolemus left (1074–80), apparently resigned to obeying Odysseus and hoping that Philoctetes might change his mind. Now he returns, having resolved to give back the bow. While the young man's change of mind is not a change of heart, this abrupt and decisive gesture is yet another surprise in a plot characterized by surprising turns. Offstage decisions of this order are rare. They must enter from the parodos, and they come toward the cave. Although the lines are in stichomythia, we hear the beginning of their talk, as Odysseus tries to discover Neoptolemus' reason for returning.

1222–23 After this opening in which Odysseus has two lines in the Greek, we have strict stichomythia (each character taking a single complete line in iambic trimeter) until 1249a ("How can it be just . . ."), where each has a line and a half.

1224–25 **Wrong** is *hamartia* and its cognate verb. Often these words are morally neutral (= "error/mistake"), but here the context (especially 1228) gives it a definite moral sense. See the note to 1249c–d.

1228 An alternative version: "I took the man by shameful craft and treachery." His shame, until now, has been determined by what Odysseus and the army think is worthy; now it is defined by what he feels is just (1234). **Craft** (*dolos*) is "treachery" at 1283 and "trick" at 1288.

1230–33 Occasionally in stichomythia the sense of a line is only completed by the same speaker's next line:

Neoptolemus: Nothing rash, but to the son of Poias
Odysseus: What? I am afraid to hear what you will say.
Neoptolemus: from whom I took this bow, back again.

He does not finish his sentence because with **give it** Odysseus supplies the verb.

1235–36 Or:

Odysseus: By the gods, do you say this to mock me?
Neoptolemus: If it is mockery to speak the truth.

The difference is a matter of tone, or perhaps I should say that Odysseus' suggestion of mockery in 1235 prompts Neoptolemus to real mockery at 1238. This sparring, with gestures (1256–57, where they play with their weapons) as well as taunts, continues with the snide indirection of 1241 and the batting about of "clever" (1245–49).

1245 Clever (four times in three lines of the Greek) is *sophos* (see on 14). Just as at 431, the Greek adjective frames the line, with one at the beginning and the other in the final position:

> "Clever by nature, Odysseus, yet you say nothing clever!"

To cap this Odysseus ends the next line of his response with "clever." This interest in language and the form of the line may strike us as detracting somehow from the seriousness of the argument, but the Greek poets did not find verbal artifice inappropriate to dramatic and thematic crisis.

1249c–d The alliteration and assonance reflect the Greek. **Sin** = "wrong" at 1224–25. This is the same verb that we find in "to fail" at 96–97: "I would prefer even to fail with honor than win by cheating." So Neoptolemus is returning, after a voyage into shame, to his native standards of conduct.

1250 As in Thucydides, honor, fear, and advantage are the three most common factors in personal motivation. In the prologue Odysseus tempted Neoptolemus with "the prize of victory" (81) and "gain" (111), with the implicit suggestion that the glory of taking Troy is a kind of material acquisition that can be had by buying and selling without regard for honesty (82). Having failed to convince Neoptolemus that honor and advantage are much the same thing, or that honor can be bought at the price of honor, he turns to fear. We might compare his dealings with Philoctetes. Odysseus knows that Philoctetes cannot be persuaded since neither the honor of taking Troy nor the personal advantage of being healed can sway the hatred Philoctetes has nurtured; so he resorts to force and fear (he will leave Philoctetes alone and without his bow), and he throws in the final taunt that other men will have the honor that was rightly Philoctetes' (1060–61).

1251–52 At least one line (for Odysseus) has dropped out of the manuscripts. In light of Neoptolemus' reply to it (**nor shall I yield to force**), we may suppose that it contained a threat to use force.

1259c–60 Prudent introduces a very sarcastic goodbye to his would-be mentor (cf. "learn moderation" at *Aj* 1259). The summons of Philoctetes prompts Odysseus to beat a retreat quickly, but he doesn't go far (see 1293–94).

1264 Friends is addressed to the chorus; he doesn't recognize Neoptolemus' voice. The first two lines of this speech may be spoken as he comes from the cave; it is only with a bad thing that he sees Neoptolemus.

1267–69 The diction from 1267 to 1280 is studded with words referring to "speech," "saying," and "words," all of which point to the antithesis at 1290–93 between words and deeds. Handing over the bow is the "plain fact" (1292) that repudiates the lies that have won it from Philoctetes. How deliberate this thematic use of diction is can be seen from the offrhyme it creates at end-line position. Here Neoptolemus says (1267) "listen to the speech (*logous:* "words") I bring; Philoctetes responds with two Greek lines ending *logôn* ("from words") and *logois* ("with words"); at 1276–79a three successive lines in the Greek end with *legô* ("I say"), *logois* ("with words"), and *legôn* ("saying"). *Legô* and *logos* are cognates, like English "speak" and "speech." Philoctetes, with little reason to trust Neoptolemus, taunts him with wasting words.

1270 Repentance has an intellectual cast in the Greek (= "changing my mind"). Neoptolemus is the only major character in extant Sophoclean drama who seeks to redress a wrong and manages to do so in time. Creon in the *Antigone* acts too late, and the other protagonists either can or will do nothing. Deianira can do nothing; Ajax, Antigone, Oedipus, and Electra will do nothing.

1273–75 Neoptolemus has not given up hope of getting Philoctetes to go to Troy. Cf. 1305, where "neither yours nor mine" indicates, even before his speech at 1314–48, that he has come back not only to return the bow but also in the hope that he may yet convince Philoctetes to travel to Troy.

1282 For the possible word play in **stolen my life** see the note to 931–33. A certain redundancy of expression in the Greek, like "by taking you deprived," seems to me to make a pun of bow/life likely.

1284 Bad = "most shameful" (cf. 1234 and 1249d for his shame). Cf. the implicit use of **father** as paradigm at 1065, and see the note to 902–4. **Odysseus** translates "the son of Laertes." Cf. 1310–13.

1290–93 For the contrast of **words** and deeds (**fact**) see 1248 and 99–99d.

1294 Philoctetes has the bow. Odysseus' abrupt intervention raises the question of how near he is. Apparently he enters from the parodos, but the timing of his entrance would seem better served if he were nearer. We do not know whether the conventions of Greek staging permitted him, after his last "exit," to take a place that was within the spectators' view but understood to be outside the other characters' range of vision. His brief time on the stage may be compared to Orestes' quick visit at *El* 1421–37. Note that Philoctetes does not immediately see him (1296).

1296 Boy: cf. "dear boy" at 1301. Philoctetes is convinced and reverts to the familiar address.

1299 In your despite means "by force" (see the note on 984–86). After his last intervention (975–1061), when he was able to stop Neoptolemus from handing over the bow and then departed triumphantly, this is a particularly inept performance, a fact underscored by his double-time retreat, head down and running in fear of the cripple's arrows.

1310–13 Nature and true breeding brings together a pair of motifs that go back to the prologue. The obvious irony is that this praise of Neoptolemus becomes a preface to a speech that, among other things, condemns Philoctetes for obstinate rejection of a friend's advice.

1314–48 Neoptolemus tries persuasion without deceit. The structure and argument are clear and well chosen: (1) I'm glad you appreciate my friendship (1314–15). (2) Suffering is everyone's lot but man must help himself when he can (1316–20: the general principle governing the human condition). (3) You, however, are obstinate in your refusal to listen to a friend (1321–24: the principle applied to the individual). (4) Yet I am a friend and sincere (1325–26: the oath). (5) You are sick and can be healed if you are willing; you may also conquer Troy (1327–35: statement of fact, analysis, and prognosis). (6) I have authority and evidence of these views (1336–41). (7) So it is up to you—if you would be healed and win glory—to relent and to go to Troy (1342–47: with more emphasis on **renown** than previously).

Although Neoptolemus appeals to his newly proven friendship, the tone of this speech is didactic. Beginning with a commonplace of Greek thought, he proceeds to argue that Philoctetes' behavior is so exceptional that he has only himself to blame if he remains alone and ill. Until the last five lines, his emphasis is much more on the sick man's power to heal himself than on the conquest of Troy. Recurrent motifs (the work of the gods, willfulness, and healing) add to the cogency of his argument, which profoundly moves Philoctetes.

1316–20 There are numerous parallels in prose and poetry for the idea that man must endure the **fortunes** (*tychê*) given by the gods (see Aeschylus *Persians* 291–92 and the note to *Seven against Thebes* 719). A fragment from Sophocles' *Phaedra* (Pearson 680) is typical:

> No mortal, women, against whom Zeus
> sends trouble, may escape shame.
> It is necessary to endure godsent ill.

See, too, OC 1694a-b. **Wilfully:** see the notes to 610–17 (the trader's "willing") and 770–73; echoes follow in 1332 and 1342 ("yield and be gracious"). Cf. Philoctetes' response at 1392.

1321 For the motif in **savage** see the note to 171.

1325–26 The oath in the name of **Zeus** (cf. *OC* 1766–67), freely given this time, makes an emphatic transition and prologue to his argument for the divine origin of Philoctetes' wound.

1327–35 **God's sending** repeats "fortune" (*tychê*) of 1316. No particular deity is intended; as above, the meaning is that "this bad luck is the gods' work." **To keep it from violation** is a natural interpretation but the phrase is the translator's and not in the Greek. We are never told what, if anything, Philoctetes personally did to merit this unnatural suffering (e.g., was he the first man to "violate" the shrine? did he somehow desecrate the sacred place?). Philoctetes never has thought of himself as the victim of some peculiar divine anger, nor will the pronouncement of Heracles name any specific guilt or other cause of his sickness. Neoptolemus will say (1336–41) that he has this on the authority of Helenus, but Sophocles never gives that prophecy verbatim, and, as such things go, we cannot suppose Helenus to have been as discursive as Neoptolemus' account. **Your own will:** everything in this speech implies that the man, and not just his bow, is all important. The **Asclepiadae** are the "sons of Asclepius," the divine healer and father of medicine (see 1437). In the *Iliad* they are Podaleirios and Machaon (2.729–32; for the healing art of Machaon see 4.193–219). **By my side** echoes the notion that the two will share the glory (cf. 1305 and in the prologue 69–69a and 115); by contrast, and more persuasively, the final lines focus on the unique renown of Philoctetes.

1336–41 We would have never gathered from the prologue that Neoptolemus knew of **Helenus** or the conditions he set for Troy's fall. But unless he is fabricating this argument from the cloth of Odysseus and the trader, he must have been more knowledgeable than he was represented.

This "contradiction" seems a clear case of immediate dramatic purpose (representing the young man as innocent and inexperienced) taking precedence over total dramatic consistency. In the *Iliad* Helenus is, as in Sophocles, a prophet, the Trojan equivalent to the Greek seer Calchas. He is "best by far of the augurs" (6.75) and gives acceptable tactical and religious advice to his brother Hector (6.77–101). In tragedy such pronouncements have a peculiar authorial sanction that the audience accepts as necessarily true and binding, unless an equally valid claim opposes them.

1342–47 We might also translate the Greek for **be gracious** as "willingly." The last four lines of the speech define **glorious heightening of gain,** and the stress falls on **judged pre-eminent** among the Greeks. **Renown** (*kleos*): for the motivation cf. *El* 974–85.

1348–72 Moved by the sincerity of Neoptolemus' appeal (**friendship**

in 1351 echoes "in pure goodheartedness" in 1323), Philoctetes once more hesitates (**What shall I do?**: cf. 1062) and thinks the unthinkable (**yield?**: cf. Creon's "To yield is dreadful," *Ant* 1095). It is worth noting that he does not question that "the sickness is of god's sending" (1327), nor does he even allude to the prophecy of Helenus; he cannot forget or forgive past wrong.

1350 Distrust does not imply any suspicion of the truth or sincerity of Neoptolemus: "how can I not follow the advice of one who plainly wishes me well?"

1352–53 Philoctetes, not the men, is **so miserable** (see on 339a): "how can I, in this miserable condition, face them?" **Come before the eyes of men** also means "come (back) to the light," i.e., from the dead; his initial question (1348–49) implies he would be better off dead.

1358–61 Dawe (*Studies,* vol. 3, p. 134) doubts the authenticity of these lines because it seems out of character for this man to weigh more heavily **wrongs to come** than **wrongs past.** "Sententious but inapposite" they may be, but they do lead to his argument (1362–66) that Neoptolemus himself ought to remember past wrong and so stay away from these proven enemies.

1362–66 Philoctetes does not see that **robbed you of your father's arms** is all a lie. Tangled in his own deceit, Neoptolemus cannot reveal explicitly how self-serving his part has been: "by my side" (1335), "with me as friend" (1375), and "best for you and for me" (1381) have very different shading for the audience and for Philoctetes.

1368–72 Bad and **wicked** translate forms of *kakos,* which appears four times in the Greek. This didactic tone colors the following stichomythia (cf. especially 1387, 1389, 1393–96).

1376–79 Sons should be singular (it refers to Agamemnon). I take it that **this suffering foot** signifies both the symbol of grievance and the source of potential mockery. In response Neoptolemus refers to the physicians (**those**); one argues from future good, the other from past wrong.

1382 Blush is echoed by **ashamed.** Webster takes **do you not blush before God?** as indicating that "Philoctetes still believes that the whole Helenus story is a fiction." But how can he trust Neoptolemus if he thinks his argument is a fiction? He must, on Webster's view, think that Neoptolemus is still the dupe of the trader's story, but if that is his view, why does he not say as much? Better to take the line with Jebb: doesn't the mere thought of the gods make you ashamed to call this my good? **To do good to another** translates an emended text (emendation seems necessary): "Why should a man be ashamed of benefiting his friends?" (Jebb). **Good for the Atridae** might be sarcastic, and certainly Philoctetes resists the pragmatism that puts self-help before honor (Neoptolemus has taken on the role of Odysseus in the prologue!), but he does not mistrust Neoptolemus' motives, as we see from his request at 1397–99. They are at loggerheads over the nature of honor and advantage (the good), but as lines 1402–9 show, their mutual trust is stronger than their differences. Each would teach the other, but the intractable Philoctetes has his way.

1392 Of my will: see note to 1316–20.

1394–96 As often, the Greek takes an antithetical form: "it is easiest for me to give up talking, but for you to live. . . ."

1398 Promised and touched my hand refer to 813–17, where Neoptolemus' assistance was interrupted by an attack; there is no explicit promise.

1402–9f The meter changes (to trochaic tetrameter) as, in the Greek, all but the last line of this false exit utilize antilabe. Taplin ("Significant Action," p. 30) compares the dialogue and action at 893–96, where, about to leave, Neoptolemus interrupts their progress by confessing his real intentions. Noble: see on 874–75. Brace yourself (against me); now Neoptolemus freely offers the physical aid Philoctetes sought at 877–93. They start to leave, supporting one another, and Neoptolemus thinks of Greek reprisal. Help echoes "good" at 1383–84. Bow of Heracles foreshadows the imminent appearance of the god (see note to 800). Kiss this ground farewell resumes another earlier gesture (see the Philoctetes' "let us first kiss the earth" at 534) that is also aborted by the arrival of a new character (the trader).

1409g Heracles, *deus ex machina* (in the strict sense, which I am not using here, the "machine" was a crane that lowered the divinity to the level of the stage), appears on the top of the scenic building, which is here represented as the cliff backing the cave. Although this is the only extant play in which Sophocles uses the *deus ex machina*, we know he had brought on Heracles at the end of one of his versions of the Athamas story. In that play, produced fifteen years or more before the *Philoctetes*, Heracles saved Athamas from being sacrificed, and this is a common function of the *deus ex machina* in Greek tragedy, i.e., to avert a threatened course of action. In Sophocles' *Syndeipnoi*, for example, the goddess Thetis appeared to resolve a quarrel between Achilles and Agamemnon (one of whom might otherwise have killed the other). The frequency of this device in Euripides also warns us against being too surprised at Heracles' epiphany here; plays within a few years of the *Philoctetes* that use it include the *Helen, Orestes,* and *Bacchae.* The Greek audience familiar with late fifth-century drama had come to expect such epiphanies.

We naturally look, nonetheless, for the dramatic logic of this second finale. Yet organic, Aristotelian coherence is elusive. In the preceding scene, and particularly in lines 1402ff., Sophocles has done everything but pull the curtain on a plot that his audience knows cannot end as the characters would have it end. Philoctetes did go to Troy. Homer and legend had it so, and the playwright—whatever freedom he may take—cannot repudiate that "fate," anymore than in the *Orestes,* produced a year after the *Philoctetes,* Orestes can murder Hermione and burn down the palace of Agamemnon. In these late plays the dramatists explore alternative actions based on psychological probing of character and situation. While the concepts of fate and divine mandate are not abandoned, their necessity relents to the extent that man may exercise his freewill and ethical self-determination to the very barrier of received legend, which, even for Greeks of the Sophistic era, still had the status of historical fact. We may find an analogy among the recent films featuring a president of the United States. As long as the president is purely fictional, his fate is undetermined; but when the film uses the name Kennedy or Johnson, the reality of history makes certain dramatic events, e.g., election to a second term, impossible. Within these external limitations, however, the personalities of Kennedy and Johnson can be represented with great freedom. Since literary and theatrical convention inclined, if not compelled, the Greek dramatist toward familiar stories, toward what was, in effect, history, he has locked into their ultimate conclusions, no matter what new logic he found in character and situation. In the recurrent references to the bow of Heracles (used to conquer Troy in the preceding generation), in the vague but insistent assertions that Philoctetes' wound is of divine origin, and in the repeated claims for the authority of Helenus' prophecy, Sophocles carefully reminds the audience that the play knows well enough what must happen. For the Greek audience such references probably contributed to the exciting tension of the plot: how will he get the stubborn Philoctetes and the honorable Neoptolemus to go along with the machinations of Odysseus, who, whether we call him vile or pragmatic, is certainly working "on the side of the gods"? (One modern interpretation argues that Heracles is in fact the disguised Odysseus!—the same actor would have played both parts.) In reality, Sophocles has no good answer, unless we are willing to believe the gods know better than Philoctetes himself what choice he should make. Because Heracles does not bring new facts that might have influenced Philoctetes' thinking, we cannot say Philoctetes would have acted otherwise had he but known; in fact, he never disputes Neoptolemus' claim that he is called by divine destiny to sack Troy. Philoctetes simply refuses, until Heracles appears, to accept that authority. So Heracles may say he comes to serve (1412) Philoctetes, and he may draw a vague analogy between his own career and Philoctetes' (1417–24), but neither of these claims nor his subsequent prophecy (1425–40) offers a new fact or a perspective not previously available to the wounded hero.

Needless to say, other modern commentators have found the epiphany a more natural and logical finale than my analysis suggests. Alt sees Philoctetes as a victim of delusion whose willful refusal to follow the destiny of his bow must be set right; whose offer to protect Neoptolemus from the Greeks with the sacred bow borders on hybris; who, because he does not understand the fate entailed by the bow, must be told—not commanded—by the god. Alt (p. 173) says, "Such obedience is no contradiction to willingness; even Achilles, to whom Athena appears (see *Iliad* 1.194ff.), is not compelled to sheath his sword." For me the poverty of this comparison lies simply in the fact that in the Homeric example Athena asks Achilles "if he will listen" (*Iliad* 1.207) and promises "gifts three times over" if he will obey and follow her advice. To this Achilles answers:

> If any man obeys the gods, they listen to him also.
> (*Iliad* 1.218)

In the *Iliad*, Athena bargains with Achilles and thus persuades; in the *Philoctetes*, Heracles tells characters (and audience) how things must be, and almost without comment the characters accept this pronouncement. The trouble, then, with Linforth's formulation (p. 156, cited by Alt: "He must consent to go, but he cannot go willingly") lies simply in the fact that, after Heracles' prediction, Philoctetes does go willingly, or at least there is absolutely none of the truculence and bargaining we find in the Homeric Achilles. The reversal is clean, absolute, sudden, as if a completely new Philoctetes leaves for Troy, a man so transformed we recognize only the rags, not the soul.

1409g–16 The first lines are anapests and may imply that Heracles advances from the back of the building to the front edge. **Not yet** interrupts. Lacking an introduction, he announces who he is. **My home among the dead** may suggest Hades, which it should not: "from my home above." When Odysseus claimed to speak for the plans of Zeus (see 989b–90), Philoctetes dismissed his claim as an outrageous pretext. Heracles' purpose is **to turn you back from the road to Malis.**

1417–21 Story is "fortune" (*tychê*). **Merit** is *aretê:* the word refers both to the excellence that permits achievement in any sphere (so it = "best warrior" in 1426) and the recognition ("glory": cf. 1423) that crowns achievement (at 669b *aretê* is translated "the good deed you did."). It is this **deathless** (immortal) **merit** that Philoctetes **can see in me now** (Jebb suggests that Heracles wears a laurel wreath as a sign of the apotheosis).

1422–23 The exact relation between the **suffering** and the **glory** is not precisely defined, and several commentators take **out of this suffering** to mean simply "after this suffering," even though a causal relation is possible. The first **suffering** suggests experience rather than pain; so Campbell translates: "This fate is destined." In Heracles' own case the later tradition often reports that he was promised immortality if he could finish the labors, while the earlier stories imply that his immortality was a divine gift, the bounty rather than the promise of the gods.

1424–32 The translation has changed the participles and future indicatives to imperatives. So **Go with this man** is more strictly "when you have gone with this man, you will find. . . ." **You shall kill** does not represent a future imperative but rather a simple future indicative: "you will kill"; so, too, "Troy you *will* take," "You *will* win the prize," and "*will* send the spoils." It is not until **you must dedicate** that Heracles uses an imperative.

Paris is the cause of the trouble (**evil**) besetting Troy but only remotely the cause of Philoctetes' trials. The **prize of valor** would be some token from the spoils that signified the army's esteem. In the *Iliad*, Briseis is such a prize, but she is also a part of the spoils, and Heracles may refer simply to the general acclaim of the army. It was customary to dedicate, usually in a temple or sacred precinct, spoils from a successful campaign. The site of the pyre on Mt. **Oeta** would be such a precinct.

1436 The comparison of the warrior to a lion occurs frequently in the *Iliad;* Orsilochos and Krethon are compared to twin lions at 5.554.

1437 Neoptolemus said the sons of **Asclepius** would heal Philoctetes; now Heracles affirms that the god of healing himself, Asclepius the son of Apollo and Coronis (or Arsinoe), will heal him.

1438–40 Heracles rescued Hesione, the daughter of Laomedon from a sea-monster, having set as his fee the horses Zeus gave Laomedon in compensation for Ganymede. When Laomedon cheated him of this pay, Heracles returned to Troy and sacked the city. So Troy (**Ilium**) will fall **twice** to his bow. See *Iliad* 5.638–42, 647–51.

1440–44 According to the epic tradition, the Greeks committed various acts of sacrilege, not the least of which was the killing of King Priam by Neoptolemus after the old king had taken refuge at the altar of Zeus, god of the household. Nothing in this passage or the play alludes specifically to this other, violent Neoptolemus. See Euripides *Trojan Women* 15–17 and *Hecuba* 481–84 for the death of Priam. This sort of foreshadowing, which takes advantage of stories known for truth by the audience, is a frequent device in the tragedians. See, e.g., *Agamemnon* 320–47, where Clytemnestra foresees outrages during the sack of Troy.

1451 The end of the play is signaled not only by the preceding anapests (1445–50) but also by an untranslated "as I depart" in line 1451. Appropriately for a man who has so often in this play called on nature, Philoctetes begins with a final apostrophe to his familiar haunts.

1453 For the **nymphs** cf. 1470, and see the note to 723 and *Tr* 215.

1454 The pounding of the sea on the headland is **male** because of its low, deep roar.

1460 **Hermes mountain** is the "Hermaen horn" (*Agamemnon* 283), a promontory on Lemnos.

1461 The **Lycian well,** otherwise unknown, is apparently connected with Apollo Lykios (see note to *El* 6).

1463 There is a metaphor from embarking on a ship here, as well as some ambiguity in **hope:** "though we never embarked upon this thought" (Campbell, who comments: "He refers partly to his steady refusal to go to Troy, and partly to his abnegation of all hope.")

1465 **Blame me not** translates a Greek adverb ("blamelessly") and may imply, as the translation takes it, violating his trust with the island that has become his native place. More commonly it is understood in the proleptic sense: "so that I shall not have reason to blame (i.e., reason to complain)."

1466–68 Note the triad (see note to 1018): his **destiny** (*moira*) has been announced by the **all-conquering spirit** (the *daimôn* Heracles) and previously advised by his **friends** (Neoptolemus).

1470 The **nymphs of the sea** are the Nereids, daughters of Nereus who can ensure a safe voyage.

Bibliography
Subject Index
Index of Proper Names
Index of Greek Words

Bibliography

THIS bibliography of writers cited in this commentary is divided into four parts: (1) translations of Greek writers other than Sophocles; (2) texts and translations of the fragments of Sophocles and other writers; (3) Greek texts, commentaries, and translations of one or more plays of Sophocles; and (4) articles, monographs, commentaries, and other texts cited in the notes.

Translations of Works by Greek Authors Other Than Sophocles

Aeschines. *The Speeches of Aeschines.* Edited and translated by Charles Darwin Adams. Loeb Classical Library. London: William Heinemann; New York: G.P. Putnam's Sons, 1919.

Apollodorus. *The Library.* Greek text with English translation by James G. Frazer. 2 vols. Loeb Classical Library. Cambridge, Mass.: Harvard University Press; London: William Heinemann, 1921. Reprinted 1963.

Aristophanes. *Plays.* Translated by Patric Dickinson. 2 vols. London: Oxford University Press, 1970.

Aristotle. *Rhetoric.* Translated by W. Rhys Roberts. In *The Basic Works of Aristotle,* edited with an introduction by Richard McKeon, 1317–1451. New York: Random House, 1941.

———. *Aristotle's "Poetics."* Translated with an introduction and notes by James Hutton. New York: Norton, 1982.

Heraclitus. See Translations of Fragments.

Herodotus. *The Histories.* Translated by Aubrey de Selincourt. Revised with introduction and notes by A. R. Burn. Harmondsworth, Eng.: Penguin Books, 1972.

Hesiod. *Hesiod, the Homeric Hymns, and Homerica.* Edited and translated by Hugh G. Evelyn-White. Loeb Classical Library. Cambridge, Mass.: Harvard University Press; London: William Heinemann, 1936. Reprinted 1954.

———. *The Works and Days, Theogony, The Shield of Heracles.* Translated by Richmond Lattimore. Ann Arbor: University of Michigan Press, 1959.

Homer. *The Iliad.* Translated by Richmond Lattimore. Chicago: University of Chicago Press, 1951.

———. *The Odyssey.* Translated by Richmond Lattimore. New York: Harper and Row, 1967.

Homeric Hymns. See Hesiod.

Pausanias. *Guide to Greece.* Translated by Peter Levi. 2 vols. Harmondsworth, Eng.: Penguin Books, 1971.

Pindar. *The Odes of Pindar.* Translated by Richmond Lattimore. Chicago: University of Chicago Press, 1947.

Plato. *The Laws.* Translated by Desmond Lee. 2d ed. Harmondsworth, Eng.: Penguin Books, 1974.

Sappho. *Greek Lyrics.* Translated by Richmond Lattimore, Chicago: University of Chicago Press, 1955.

Solon. *Greek Lyrics.* Translated by Richmond Lattimore. Chicago: University of Chicago Press, 1955.

Theognis. *Elegy and Iambus: Greek Elegiac and Iambic Poets from Callinus to Crates.* Edited and translated by J. M. Edmonds. 2 vols. Loeb Classical Library. London: William Heinemann; New York: G. P. Putnam's Sons, 1931.

Thucydides. *The Peloponnesian War.* Translated by Rex Warner, with an introduction and notes by M. I. Finley. Harmondsworth, Eng.: Penguin Books, 1952. Reprinted 1978.

Texts and Translations of the Fragments

Gorgias. *Ancilla to the Pre-Socratic Philosophers: A Complete Translation of the Fragments in Diels, Fragmente der Vorsokratiker,* by Kathleen Freeman. Cambridge, Mass.: Harvard University Press, 1948.

Heraclitus. *The Presocratic Philosophers.* G. S. Kirk and J. E. Raven. Cambridge, Eng.: Cambridge University Press, 1957.

Kannicht, Richard, and Bruno Snell. *Tragicorum Graecorum Fragmenta II: Fragmenta Adespota.* Göttingen: Vandenhoeck and Ruprecht, 1981.

Pearson, A. C. *The Fragments of Sophocles.* 3 vols. Cambridge, Eng.: The University Press, 1917.

Radt, Stefan. *Tragicorum Graecorum Fragmenta IV: Sophocles.* Göttingen: Vandenhoeck and Ruprecht, 1980.

Solon. *Anthologia Lyrica Graeca.* Edited by Ernestus Diehl. Fasc. 1, 3d ed. Leipzig: Teubner, 1949.

Greek Texts, Commentaries, and Translations of the Plays of Sophocles

Editions of the Plays in Greek

Dain, Alphonse, and Paul Mazon. *Sophocle.* Edited by Alphonse Dain and translated (French) by Paul Mazon. 3 vols. 2d ed. Paris: Les Belles Lettres, 1981.

Dawe, R. D. *Sophoclis Tragoediae.* 2 vols. Teubner: Leipzig, 1975 and 1979.

Pearson, A. C. *Sophoclis Fabulae.* Oxford: Clarendon Press, 1967.

Commentaries and Translation

All Seven Plays

Blaydes, Frederick H. M. *Spicilegium Sophocleum.* Halis Saxonum: in Orphanotrophei libraria, 1903.

Campbell, Lewis. *Sophocles.* Edited with English notes and introduction. 2 vols. 2d ed. Oxford: Clarendon Press, 1879–81.

————. *Paralipomena Sophoclea.* Supplementary Notes on the Text and Interpretation of Sophocles. London: Rivingtons, 1907.

Jebb, R. C. *The Plays of Sophocles.* Edited with commentary. 7 vols. 2d ed. Cambridge, Eng.: Cambridge University Press, 1892–1900.

Kamerbeek, J. C. *The Plays of Sophocles.* 7 vols. Leiden: E. J. Brill, 1963–1984.

Schneidewin, F. W. *Sophokles.* Edited with commentary by F. W. Schneidewin and A. Nauck, revised by E. Bruhn and L. Radermacher. 7 vols. Berlin: Weidmann, 1910–14.

Ajax

Lobeck, C. A. *Ajax.* Greek text edited with commentary. Leipzig: Weidmann, 1809.

Stanford, W. B. *Ajax.* Edited with introduction, revised text, commentary, appendixes, indexes, and bibliography. London: MacMillan, 1963.

Antigone

Müller, Gerhard. *Antigone.* Edited with an introduction. Heidelberg: Carl Winter, 1967.

Electra

Kaibel, Georg. *Elektra.* Edited with introduction and commentary. Leipzig: Teubner, 1896.

Kells, J. H. *Electra.* Edited with introduction and commentary. Cambridge, Eng.: Cambridge University Press, 1973.

Oedipus the King

Dawe, R. D. *Oedipus Rex*. Edited with introduction and commentary. Cambridge, Eng.: Cambridge University Press, 1982.
Gould, Thomas. *Oedipus the King*. A translation with introduction and commentary. Englewood Cliffs, N.J.: Prentice-Hall, 1970.
Sheppard, J. T. *The Oedipus Tyrannus of Sophocles*. Introduction, translation, and commentary. Cambridge, Eng.: Cambridge University Press, 1920.

Philoctetes

Webster, T. B. L. *Philoctetes*. Edited with introduction and commentary. Cambridge, Eng.: Cambridge University Press, 1970.

The Women of Trachis

Easterling, P. E. *Trachiniae*. Edited with introduction and commentary. Cambridge, Eng.: Cambridge University Press, 1982.

General Bibliography

Alexiou, Margaret. *The Ritual Lament in Greek Tradition*. Cambridge, Eng.: The University Press, 1974.
Alt, Karin. "Schicksal und ΦΥΣΙΣ im *Philoktet* des Sophokles." *Hermes* 89 (1961): 141–74.
Arnott, Peter. *Greek Scenic Conventions in the Fifth Century* B.C. Oxford: Clarendon Press, 1962.
Auerback, Erich. *Mimesis*. Translated by Willard Trask. Garden City: Doubleday & Co., 1957. (Reprint of the Princeton University Press edition of 1953.)
Ax, Wilhelm. "Die Parodos des *Oidipus Tyrannus*." *Hermes* 67 (1932): 413–37.
Bain, David. "Audience Address in Greek Tragedy." *Classical Quarterly* 25 (1975): 13–25.
———. *Actors and Audiences*. Oxford: Oxford University Press, 1977.
Barrett, W. S., ed. *"Hippolytus" by Euripides*. Oxford: Clarendon Press, 1964.
Bond, Godfrey W., ed. *"Heracles" by Euripides*. Oxford: Clarendon Press, 1981.
Bowra, C. M. *Sophoclean Tragedy*. Oxford: Clarendon Press, 1944.
Boyes, John Frederick. *Tragedies of Sophocles: Illustrations of the Tragedies from the Greek, Latin, and English Poets*. Oxford: Vincent, 1844.

Bradshaw, A. T. von S. "The Watchman Scenes in the *Antigone*." *Classical Quarterly* 12 (1962): 200–211.

Burkert, Walter. *Greek Religion*. Translated by John Raffan. Cambridge, Mass.: Harvard University Press, 1985.

Burton, R. W. B. *The Chorus in Sophocles' Tragedies*. Oxford: Clarendon Press; New York: Oxford University Press, 1980.

Carrière, Jean. "Ambiguïté et Vraisemblance dans *Oedipe-Roi*." *Pallas* 4 (1956): 5–14.

Cary, C. "The Second Stasimon of Sophocles' *Oedipus Tyrannus*." *Journal of Hellenic Studies* 106 (1986): 175–79.

Chantraine, Pierre, and Olivier Masson. "Sur quelques termes du vocabulaire religieux des Grecs: La valeur du mot ἄγος et de ses dérivés." In *Sprachgeschichte und Wortbedeutung: Festschrift Albert Debrunner*, 85–107. Bern: Franke, 1954.

Curtius, Ernst Robert. *European Literature and the Latin Middle Ages*. New York: Pantheon Books, 1953; New York: Harper Torchbooks, 1963.

Davidson, J. F. "Sophoclean Dramaturgy and the *Ajax* Burial Debates." *Ramus* 14 (1985): 16–25.

Davies, Malcolm. "The End of Sophocles' *Oedipus Tyrannus*." *Hermes* 110 (1982): 268–77.

Dawe, R. D. "Some Reflections on Ate and Hamartia." *Harvard Studies in Classical Philology* 72 (1967): 89–123.

———. "Sophocles, 'Electra' 1205–10." *Proceedings of the Cambridge Philological Society* 19 (1973): 45–46.

———. *Studies on the Text of Sophocles*. 3 vols. Leiden: Brill, 1973 and 1978.

Dingel, Joachim. "Requisit und szenisches Bild in der griechischen Tragödie." In *Die Bauformen der Griechischen Tragödie*, edited by Walter Jens, 347–68. Munich: Wilhelm Fink, 1971.

Dodds, E. R., ed. *"Bacchae" by Euripides*. Oxford: Clarendon Press, 1960.

———. "On Misunderstanding the *Oedipus Rex*." *Greece and Rome* 13 (1966): 37–49.

Dover, K. J. *Greek Popular Morality in the Time of Plato and Aristotle*. Berkeley and Los Angeles: University of California Press, 1974.

Drexler, H. "Die Teiresias-Szene des 'Konig Oedipus.' " *Maia* 8 (1956): 3–26.

Duchemin, Jacqueline. *L' Ἀγων Dans la Tragédie Grecque*. 2d ed. Paris: Société D'Edition "Belles Lettres," 1968.

Easterling, P. E. "Oedipus and Polyneices." *Proceedings of the Cambridge Philological Society* 13 (1967): 1–13.

———. "Philoctetes and modern criticism." *Illinois Classical Studies* 3 (1978): 27–39.

Edmunds, Lowell. *Oedipus: The Ancient Legend and Its Later Analogues.* Baltimore and London: The Johns Hopkins University Press, 1985.

Ehrenberg, Victor. *Sophocles and Pericles.* Oxford: Basil Blackwell, 1954.

Ellendt, Friedrich Theodor. *Lexicon Sophocleum.* 2d ed. Emended by Hermann Genthe. Hildesheim: Georg Olms, 1965.

Else, Gerald F. *The Madness of Antigone.* Abhandlungen der Heidelberger Akademie der Wissenschaften 1976/1. Heidelberg: 1976.

Erbse, Harmut. "Neoptolemus und Philoketes bei Sophokles." *Hermes* 94 (1966): 177–201.

Finley, John H., Jr. *Three Essays on Thucydides.* Cambridge, Mass.: Harvard University Press, 1967.

Flickinger, Roy D. *The Greek Theater and Its Drama.* 4th ed. Chicago: University of Chicago Press, 1968.

Frazer, James G. *Pausanias's Description of Greece.* 6 vols. London and New York: MacMillan and Co., 1898.

Friis Johansen, Holger. *General Reflection in Tragic Rhesis: A Study of Form.* Copenhagen: Munksgaard, 1959.

———. "Sophocles 1939–59." *Lustrum* 7 (1962): 92–288.

———. "Heracles in Sophocles' *Trachiniae.*" *Classica et Mediaevalia* 37 (1986): 47–61.

Fritz, Kurt von. "Haimons Liebe zu Antigone." In *Antike und Moderne Tragödie,* 227–40. Berlin: Walter De Gruyter & Co., 1962.

Fuqua, Charles. "Heroism, Heracles, and the '*Trachiniae.*' " *Traditio* 36 (1980): 1–81.

Furley, David. "Euripides on the Sanity of Herakles." In *Studies in Honour of T. B. L. Webster,* edited by J. H. Betts, J. T. Hooker, and J. R. Green, vol. 1, 102–13. Bristol: Bristol Classical Press, 1986.

Garner, Richard. *Law and Society in Classical Athens.* New York: St. Martin's Press, 1987.

Garvie, A. F. "Deceit, Violence and Persuasion in the *Philoctetes.*" In *Studi Classici in Onore di Quintino Cataudella,* vol 1, 213–26. Catania: Universita di Catania, 1972.

Gellie, G. H. *Sophocles: A Reading.* Melbourne: The University Press, 1972.

Goheen, Robert F. *The Imagery of Sophocles' Antigone.* Princeton: Princeton University Press, 1951.

Goldhill, Simon. *Reading Greek Tragedy.* Cambridge, Eng.: Cambridge University Press, 1986.

Greiffenhagen, Gottfried. "Der Prozess des Ödipus." *Hermes* 94 (1966): 147–74.

Groningen, G. A. van, ed. *Theognis: Le premier livre*. Amsterdam: N. V. Noord Hollandsche Uitgevers Maatschappij, 1966.

Guthrie, W. K. C. *The Greeks and Their Gods*. Boston: Beacon Press, 1951.

——. *A History of Greek Philosophy*. 6 vols. London and New York: Cambridge University Press, 1962–81.

——. *The Sophists*. London and New York: Cambridge University Press, 1985.

Harrison, A. R. W. *The Law of Athens*. 2 vols. Oxford: Clarendon Press, 1968–71.

Harrison, E. L. "Three Notes on Sophocles." *Classical Review* 12 (1962): 13–15.

Haslam, Michael W. "The Authenticity of Euripides, *Phoenissae* 1–2 and Sophocles, *Electra* 1." *Greek, Roman and Byzantine Studies* 5 (1975): 145–74.

Hegel, G. F. *Hegel on Tragedy*. Edited by Anne and Henry Paolucci. Garden City: Doubleday/Anchor, 1962.

Heinimann, Felix. *Nomos und Physis*. Basel: Friedrich Reinhardt Verlags, 1945.

Henrichs, Albert. "The 'Sobriety' of Oedipus: Sophocles OC 100 Misunderstood." *Harvard Studies in Classical Philology* 87 (1983): 87–100.

Hester, D. A. "Sophocles the Unphilosophical: A Study in the *Antigone*." *Mnemosyne* 24 (1971): 11–59.

——. "Very Much the Safest Plan or, Last Words in Sophocles." *Antichthon* 7 (1973): 8–13.

——. "To Help One's Friends and Harm One's Enemies: A Study in the *Oedipus at Colonus*." *Antichthon* 11 (1977): 22–41.

——. "Oedipus and Jonah." *Proceedings of the Cambridge Philological Society* 23 (1977): 32–61.

——. "The Banishment of Oedipus." *Antichthon* 18 (1984): 13–23.

Hinds, A. E. "The Prophecy of Helenus in Sophocles' *Philoctetes*." *Classical Quarterly* 17 (1967): 169–80.

Hoey, Thomas F. "The *Trachiniae* and Unity of Hero." *Arethusa* 3 (1970): 1–22.

——. "Ambiguity in the Exodos of Sophocles' *Trachiniae*." *Arethusa* 10 (1977): 269–94.

Hogan, James C. "The Protagonists of the *Antigone*." *Arethusa* 5 (1972): 93–100.

——. *A Commentary on the Complete Greek Tragedies: Aeschylus*. Chicago and London: University of Chicago Press, 1984.

Hölscher, Uvo. "Wie soll ich noch tanzen? Über ein Wort des sophokleischen Chors." In *Sprachen der Lyrik: Festschrift für Hugo*

Friedrich, edited by Erich Kohler, 376–93. Frankfurt: Vittorio Klostermann, 1975.

Howe, Thalia Phillies. "Taboo in the Oedipus Theme." *Transactions of the American Philological Association* 93 (1962): 124–43.

Hug, Arnold. "Der doppelsinn in Sophokles *Oedipus König*." *Philologus* 31 (1871): 66–84.

Jens, Walter, ed. *Die Bauformen der griechischen Tragödie*. Munich: Wilhelm Fink, 1971.

Jones, John. *On Aristotle and Greek Tragedy*. New York: Oxford University Press, 1962.

Jordan, Borimir. *Servants of the Gods*. Hypomnemata 55. Göttingen: Vandenhoeck and Ruprecht, 1979.

Kells, J. H. "Problems of Interpretation in the *Antigone*." *Bulletin of the Institute of Classical Studies, The University of London* 10 (1963): 47–64.

———. "Sophocles' *Electra* Revisited." In *Studies in Honour of T. B. L. Webster*, edited by J. H. Betts, J. T. Hooker, and J. R. Green, vol. 1, 153–60. Bristol: Bristol Classical Press, 1986.

Kirkwood, Gordon MacDonald. *A Study of Sophoclean Drama*. Ithaca, N.Y.: Cornell University Press, 1958.

———. "Homer and Sophocles' *Ajax*." In *Classical Drama and its Influence: Essays Presented to H. D. F. Kitto*, edited by M. J. Anderson, 53–70. London: Methuen, 1965.

Kitto, H. D. F. *Greek Tragedy*. London: Methuen, 1939; New York: Anchor Press, 1954.

———. *Form and Meaning in Drama: A Study of Six Greek Plays and of "Hamlet."* New York: Barnes and Noble, 1960.

Knapp, Charles. "A Point in the Interpretation of *Antigone* of Sophocles." *American Journal of Philology* 37 (1916): 300–316.

Knox, Bernard M. W. *Oedipus at Thebes*. New Haven: Yale University Press, 1957.

———. *The Heroic Temper*. Sather Classical Lectures 35. Berkeley: University of California Press, 1964.

———. "Sophocles, *Oedipus Tyrannos* 446: Exit Oedipus?" *Greek Roman and Byzantine Studies* 21 (1980): 321–32.

de Kock, E. L. "The Sophoklean Oidipus and its Antecedents." *Acta Classica* 4 (1961): 7–28.

Kranz, Walther. *Stasimon*. Berlin: Weidmann, 1933.

Lacey, W. K. *The Family in Classical Greece*. Ithaca, N.Y.: Cornell University Press, 1968.

Latte, Kurt. "Schuld und Sünde in der Griechischen Religion." In *Kleine*

Schriften, edited by Olof Gigon, Wolfgang Buchwald, and Wolfgang Kunkel, 3–35. Munich: C. H. Beck, 1968.

Lattimore, Richmond. *The Poetry of Greek Tragedy.* Baltimore: Johns Hopkins University Press, 1958.

———. *Themes in Greek and Latin Epitaphs.* Urbana, Illinois: University of Illinois Press, 1962.

Lesky, Albin. *A History of Greek Literature.* Translated by James Willis and Cornelis de Heer. London: Methuen; New York: Crowell, 1966.

———. *Greek Tragic Poetry.* Translated by Matthew Dillon. New Haven and London: Yale University Press, 1983.

Liddell, Henry George, and Robert Scott. *A Greek-English Lexicon.* 9th ed. Revised and augmented by Henry Stuart Jones and Roderick McKenzie. Oxford: Clarendon Press, 1940.

Linforth, Ivan M. "Religion and Drama in *Oedipus at Colonus.*" *University of California Publications in Classical Philology* 14(4) (1951): 75–191.

———. "The Pyre on Mount Oeta in Sophocles' *Trachiniae.*" *University of California Publications in Classical Philology* 14(7) (1952): 255–67.

———. "Notes on *Oedipus at Colonus.*" In *Studies in Honour of Gilbert Norwood,* 68–75. Toronto: The University of Toronto Press, 1952.

———. "Philoctetes: The Play and the Man." *University of California Publications in Classical Philology* 15(3) (1956): 95–156.

———. "Antigone and Creon." *University of California Publications in Classical Philology* 15(5) (1961): 183–259.

Lloyd-Jones, Hugh. "Notes on Sophocles' *Antigone.*" *Classical Quarterly* 7 (1957): 12–17.

———. *The Justice of Zeus.* Sather Classical Lectures no. 41. Berkeley and Los Angeles: University of California Press, 1971.

———. "Notes on Sophocles' *Trachiniae.*" *Yale Classical Studies* 22 (1972): 263–70.

———. "The Text of Sophocles." Review of *Sophoclis Tragoediae I,* edited by R. D. Dawe. *Classical Review* 28 (1978): 214–21.

Long, A. A. "Poisonous 'Growth' in the *Trachiniae.*" *Greek, Roman and Byzantine Studies* 8 (1967): 275–78.

———. *Language and Thought in Sophocles.* London: Athlone Press, 1968.

Maas, Paul. *Greek Metre.* Translated by Hugh Lloyd-Jones. Oxford: Clarendon Press, 1962.

McCall, Marsh. "Divine and Human Action in Sophocles: The Two Burials of the *Antigone.*" *Yale Classical Studies* 22 (1972): 103–17.

MacDowell, Douglas M. *The Law in Classical Athens.* Ithaca, N.Y.: Cornell University Press, 1978.

Mikalson, Jon D. "Zeus the Father and Heracles the Son in Tragedy." *Transactions of the American Philological Association* 116 (1986): 89–98.

Müller, Gerhard. "Das zweite Stasimon des *König Ödipus*." *Hermes* 95 (1967): 269–91.

Nestle, Walter. *Die Struktur des Eingangs in der attischen Tragödie.* Hildesheim: Georg Olms, 1967.

Nilsson, Martin Persson. "The Men in Their Own Power." In *Opuscula Selecta,* vol 3, 26–31. Lund: C. W. K. Gleerup, 1960.

Padel, Ruth. "Madness in Fifth-Century (B.C.) Athenian Tragedy." In *Indigenous Psychologies: The Anthropology of the Self,* edited by Paul Heelias and Andrew Lock, 105–21. London and New York: Academic Press, 1981.

Parker, Robert. *Miasma.* Oxford: Clarendon Press, 1983.

Parry, Hugh. *The Lyric Poems of Greek Tragedy.* Toronto and Sarasota: Samuel Stevens, 1978.

Pohlenz, Max. *Die Griechische Tragödie.* 2d ed. Göttingen: Vandenhoeck and Ruprecht, 1954.

Reinhardt, Karl. *Sophocles.* Translated by Hazel and David Harvey. New York: Barnes and Noble, 1978.

Robinson, David B. "Topics in Sophocles' *Philoctetes.*" *Classical Quarterly* 19 (1969): 34–56.

de Romilly, Jacqueline. "L' excuse de invincible amour dans la tragédie grecque." In *Miscellanea Tragica Festschrift J. C. Kamerbeek,* edited by J. M. Bremer et al., 309–21. Amsterdam: Hakkert, 1976.

Sandbach, F. H. "Sophocles, *Electra* 77–85." *Proceedings of the Cambridge Philological Society* 23 (1977): 7–73.

Schadewaldt, Wolfgang. *Monolog und Selbstgesprach.* Berlin: Weidmann, 1926.

Schwinge, E. R. *Die Stellung der Trachinierinnen im Werk des Sophokles.* Hypomnemata 1. Göttingen: Vandenhoeck and Ruprecht, 1962.

Seale, David. *Vision and Stagecraft in Sophocles.* Chicago: University of Chicago Press, 1982.

Segal, Charles. *Tragedy and Civilization: An Interpretation of Sophocles.* Martin Classical Lectures 26. Cambridge, Mass.: Harvard University Press, 1981.

Sheppard, J. T. "*Electra:* A Defence of Sophocles." *Classical Review* 41 (1927): 2–9.

Sicherl, M. "The Tragic Issue in Sophocles' *Ajax.*" *Yale Classical Studies* 25 (1977): 67–98.

Simon, Erika. *Festivals of Attica*. Madison, Wisconsin: University of Wisconsin Press, 1983.

Simpson, Michael. "Sophocles' Ajax: His Madness and Transformation." *Arethusa* 2 (1969): 88–103.

Steidle, W. *Studien zum antiken Drama*. Munich: Fink, 1968.

Stinton, T. C. W. "Hamartia in Greek Tragedy." *Classical Quarterly* 25 (1975): 221–54.

———. "Notes on Greek Tragedy, I." *Journal of Hellenic Studies* 96 (1976): 121–45.

Taplin, Oliver. "Significant Actions in Sophocles' *Philoctetes*." *Greek, Roman and Byzantine Studies* 12 (1971): 25–44.

———. "Did Greek Dramatists Write Stage Instructions?" *Proceedings of the Cambridge Philological Society* 23 (1977): 121–32.

———. *Greek Tragedy in Action*. Berkeley and Los Angeles: University of California Press, 1978.

———. "Sophocles in His Theatre." In *Sophocle*. Foundation Hardt pour L' Étude de l'Antiquite Classique Entretiens 29, 155–74. Geneva: Vandoeuvres, 1983.

Vickers, Brian. *Towards Greek Tragedy*. London: Longman, 1973.

West, M. L. "Tragica III." *Bulletin of the Institute of Classical Studies, The University of London* 26 (1979): 104–17.

Whitman, Cedric Hubbell. *Sophocles: A Study of Heroic Humanism*. Cambridge, Mass.: Harvard University Press, 1951.

Wilamowitz-Moellendorff, Tycho von. *Die Dramatische Technik des Sophokles. Philologische Untersuchungen*, vol. 22. Berlin: Weidmann, 1917. (Reprint: Zurich, 1969.)

Winnington-Ingram, R. P. "Tragedy and Greek Archaic Thought." In *Classical Drama and Its Influence: Essays Presented to H. D. F. Kitto*, edited by M. J. Anderson, 29–50. London: Methuen, 1965.

———. *Sophocles: An Intrepretation*. Cambridge and New York: Cambridge University Press, 1980.

Woodard, Thomas M. "*Electra* by Sophocles: The Dialectical Design." *Harvard Studies in Classical Philology* 68 and 70 (1964 and 1965): 163–205 and 195–233.

Subject Index

This index is selective rather than complete. It is keyed to notes in the commentary where definitions, examples, problems, further references, and longer discussions will be found. Separate indexes, also selective, are provided for common proper names and for the Greek words discussed.

Index of Proper Names

Index of Greek Words

This index is also selective. The passages cited offer definitions, discussions of semantic problems and thematic clusters, and cross references.

James C. Hogan is Frank T. McClure Professor of Classics and chairman of the Department of Classics at Allegheny College. He is the author of *A Guide to the Iliad* and *A Commentary on the Complete Greek Tragedies: Aeschylus*. His current interests are the French language and literature, the drama of Euripides, and strategies for survival in the late twentieth century.